THE
LAST PRIESTS
IN AMERICA

THE
LAST PRIESTS
IN AMERICA

Conversations with Remarkable Men

TIM UNSWORTH

CROSSROAD · NEW YORK

1991
The Crossroad Publishing Company
370 Lexington Avenue, New York, NY 10017
Copyright © 1991 by Tim Unsworth

Printed in the United States of America

Library of Congress Cataloging-in-Publication Data

Unsworth, Tim.
    The last priests in America : conversations with remarkable men /
Tim Unsworth.
        p. cm.
    ISBN 0-8245-1139-5 (hard)
        1. Catholic Church—United States—Clergy—Interviews.
    2. Catholic church—United States—History—20th century.
    I. Title.
    BX1407.C6U57   1991
    282'.092'273—dc20   91-22374
                                                              CIP

Benedictus qui venit in nomine Domini

In gratitude and affection
to the 34,230 diocesan priests
in America

and for Jean,
the instrument of my peace

But we're like madmen stretching our hands to clasp the moon reflected in water.

George Bernanos:
Diary of a Country Priest

Do not depend on the hope of results. When you are doing the sort of work you have taken on . . . you may have to face the fact that your work will be apparently worthless and even achieve no result at all, if not perhaps results opposite to what you expect. As you get used to this idea, you start more and more to concentrate not on the results, but on the value, the rightness, the truth of the work itself. And there, too, a great deal has to be gone through, as gradually you struggle less and less for an idea and more and more for specific people. The range tends to narrow down, but it gets more real. In the end, it is the reality of personal relationships that saves everything.

Thomas Merton: *Letter to a Young Activist*

Contents

Acknowledgements ix
Preface x

INTERLUDE I I

1 · John R. Aurelio: Pastor, Storyteller, Dreamer 2
2 · Blaine G. Barr: Charts, Circles, and Diagrams 8
3 · Joseph L. Bernardin: Cardinal 13
4 · R. Peter Bowman: Mega-Pastor, Delegator 24
5 · Patrick J. Brennan: Evangelizer 29
6 · Thomas P. Cahalane: FBI (Foreign-Born Irish) 34
7 · Daniel M. Cantwell: Priest for the Laity 42
8 · John C. Cusick: Minister to Young Adults 48

INTERLUDE II 53

9 · Michael L. Donovan: Heartland Priest 55
10 · Leonard A. Dubi: Recovering Alcoholic 60
11 · Harvey F. Egan: Skilled Infuriator 68
12 · John J. Egan: Pastoral and Social Ministry 74
13 · John Tracy Ellis: Church Historian 81
14 · John Everyman: Every Priest 88
15 · Thomas R. Franzman: Blue Collar, White Collar 92
16 · Joseph Gallagher: A Sweet Mystery of Empty Hands 96

INTERLUDE III 104

17 · Dennis J. Geaney, O.S.A.: Clerical Prophet 106
18 · Dominic J. Grassi: Urban Parish Rejuvenated 112

19 · Andrew M. Greeley: Sociologist, Author, Novelist   116

20 · Edward J. Griswold: Vocation Director   124

21 · Martin J. Hegarty: A Resigned Priest's Apostolate   129

22 · J. Bryan Hehir: Scholar, Professor   138

23 · Eugene Hemrick: Pulse Taker   142

INTERLUDE IV   149

24 · Terence M. Keehan: Young Priest, Old Church   151

25 · William G. Kenneally: Valuing the Things
That Really Matter   156

26 · Joseph E. Kerns: To Live Is to Be Loved   161

27 · Patrick R. Lagges: Canon Lawyer   166

28 · Rollins E. Lambert: Black Priest, White Church   173

29 · Raymond A. Lucker: Rural Bishop   182

30 · John R. Lynch: Seminary Prof, Psychologist   190

31 · Richard P. McBrien: Theologian *sans* Ivory Tower   195

INTERLUDE V   202

32 · William E. McManus: Retired Bishop   204

33 · Peter B. McQuinn: Seminarian   213

34 · Jose Luis Menendez: Latino Dreamer   220

35 · Thomas J. O'Gorman: Creative Survival   225

36 · J. Timothy Power: The All-American Parish   233

37 · Gary Reller: More Than Just a Union   240

38 · Peter Simon*: HIV Positive   246

39 · Daedalus Stephens*: Disillusioned Idealist   255

40 · Theodore C. Stone: The Faith of the People   261

41 · Mel Swift*: Sex Offender   269

42 · James E. Wilbur: Once a Priest   276

*Pseudonymous

Acknowledgements

My thanks to the forty-two priests who gave so generously of their time. If they were not friends already, they became so during these interviews. They revealed themselves with honesty and faith. Only a fraction of their hours of reflection survived, but much of what they said will remain with me for years to come. They told wonderful stories, provided food and drink, friendship and prayer. I shall never be the same.

My friend, Marty Hegarty, one of the priests interviewed, deserves a special place in this work. He suggested many of the priests interviewed. He listened to endless reflections from me with insight and patience.

My wife, Jean, traveled with me, waited patiently, listened while others spoke, proofed each chapter and made many suggestions that enriched the text.

Michael Leach, president of Crossroad, welcomed my outline, encouraged the work, made numerous suggestions, was patient with the inevitable tardiness, and stayed with the project from start to finish. Frank Oveis shepherded the manuscript to completion. Bruce Cassiday, who edited the copy, removed all the lumps.

There were many other priests whose names do not appear in this book, although they are a vital part of it. They listened to what the others said and made many useful comments. Like good confessors, their contribution is a silent one.

Preface

Along Chicago's Michigan Avenue, the city's elite private clubs nestle next to the buildings that house the offices of Chicago's movers and shakers. Inside, behind the collegiate gothic facades, the elegantly tacky decor echoes another age, another set of values. The clubs feel remarkably like old churches; one even has a bronze statue of a discus thrower whose toe, to hold with club tradition, must be touched.

The clubs are sturdy, reassuring, safe. Uniformed attendants greet the members by their surname while the members address the staff by their first name. A civilized caste system is observed. A bulletin board and passout material quietly announce coming events.

The club members can afford the hefty initiation fee and monthly charges. They know how to make a buck. Yet, the clubs are in trouble, partly because the membership has been slow to respond to the changing times. Some still do not accept women. No club will admit it, but many offer membership only to a few token Jews, some Catholics, and an exceptionally rare Afro-American. In some instances, even bringing "undesirables", i.e. women, Afro-Americans, Jews, to the oak dining rooms is frowned upon.

The clubs have become the objects of ridicule. They are synonyms for irrelevancy. They are conceptually akin to Yale's notoriously selective and secretive Skull and Bones Society, a male bastion which now sounds more like a heavy metal band than a group of serious students. Companies are now reluctant to pay membership dues for their executives while denying the same privileges to other executives. Meanwhile, elite eating clubs have opened on the upper floors of the new skyscrapers. They offer a superior table and generally have only one criterion for membership: an ability to pay.

Members of the old-guard clubs are good people. Many serve on committees that work for social change. Some edit newspapers that ferret out injustice and report it to the wider community. They are sometimes embarrassed by the narrow traditions of their club. Some protest that they are working for change, although the ultraelite clubs make no such apology. Ironically, some clubs still extend clergy memberships to high-level clergy only. Incredibily, some clergy still accept it.

It's changing. Unless the clubs keep pace with the complex chemistry of an evolving society, they will soon become mere footnotes to this country's history.

This rather lengthy analogy applies with frightening reality to the Catholic priesthood. Unable to change because a stubborn administration clings to customs it now considers sacred, its numbers are dropping rapidly. Its bishops still speak of the pendulum effect, suggesting that the decline will reverse itself or bottom out. But exhaustive research sponsored by the bishops' own U.S. Catholic Conference contradicts that view. The most recent study, a 163-page report titled *The Catholic Priest in the United States*, confirms earlier studies that showed a 20 percent drop in the number of diocesan priests between 1966 and 1984, and it projects an additional 20 percent drop from 1985 to 2005. The study, funded partially by the Lilly Foundation, was conducted at the University of Wisconsin by Richard Schoenherr and Lawrence Young. They collected data from 86 dioceses. Among its conclusions, the study stated that "at average current replacement rates if the bishop ordains three men in any given year, two of the five positions vacated that same year by resignations, retirements and deaths go unfilled."

Schoenherr, who directed the research team, said the findings are sobering. A resigned priest himself, he is cited in an article in *National Catholic Reporter* by Robert J. McClory saying, "If, for example, the U.S. Medical Profession were losing 40 percent of its doctors at a time when the number of patients were growing steadily, we would have nothing short of a national crisis."

While most church publications carried objective reports of the study, they also carried sidebars that quoted church officials as suggesting that Schoenherr's research was skewed by the fact that he was a resigned priest or that, in the words of one bishop, "No one was taking into account the influence of the Holy Spirit." Commenting on the crisis, a Catholic University professor, Dean Hoge, author of *Future of Catholic Leadership: Responses to the Priest Shortage*, said that "the shortage of priests is an institutional problem, not a spiritual problem." Hoge estimates that, given the increased number of Catholics, the U.S. Church will need 72,000 priests simply to maintain the current ratio of priest to parishioners. Instead, it will have about one-third that number.

Worldwide, the situation is far worse. According to London's reliable independent *Tablet*, Latin America has 52,452 priests, approximately 13 percent of all the priests in the world, for some 378 million Catholics, 42 percent of all the Catholics in the world. In Europe and North America, which has 38 percent of all the Catholics in the world, there are 293,933 priests, or 73 percent of the world total. Cuba has one priest for every 20,037 Catholics; Honduras one for every 16,272 and, in the diocese of Ilheus, Brazil, one for every 44,140. These figures are included as a partial response to those who would say that the Vatican will surely respond to a crisis such as the present priest shortage in the U.S.

Informal observers suggest that the Schoenherr study's findings were conservative. *The Catholic Priest in the United States* states that there will be a 40 percent loss of priests between the years 1966 and 2005. However, close observers believe that the loss will be closer to 50 percent. Further, the study states that by 2005 almost 46 percent of the clergy will be fifty-five or older and that only 12 percent will be thirty-four or younger. However, other observers believe that the present average age is already fifty-five and that there will be less than 12 percent of priests thirty-four or younger. (The average age at ordination is rising. In 1966 it was twenty-seven; it's now thirty-one, and still rising.)

"We are losing them through deaths, retirements and resignations," one close observer in a large diocese said. "And, most important, even fewer are entering the system. And, for the third year in a row, the number ordained in this diocese didn't even cover the number who resigned." The study does confirm that those dioceses with the highest number of ordinations also have the highest rate of resignations.

The NCCB/USCC funded study is a mass of charts and statistics. There are disturbing figures showing that 37 percent of a typical ordination class will resign before the class's twenty-fifth anniversary. Again the figure may be higher for some classes. When the Chicago class of 1966 gathered for their twenty-fifth anniversary, only nineteen of the original forty-three remained. In 1966 only 3.4 percent of clergy were retired while 20.1 percent will be retired, sick, or on leave by 2005; that for every ten priests lost only six are ordained. Finally, because of the growth of the Catholic population, even those dioceses that report an increase in ordinations will actually be losing clergy.

"That's fine," one priest in this collection of interviews said, "Maybe we need to break the structure down completely before we can build a new church." But the majority don't see it that way. They want increased involvement by the laity, but they feel strongly that the priesthood has an irremovable place in the Catholic tradition. They recognize that the priest may no longer be needed as a social worker, job finder, psychiatrist, marriage, or addictions counselor, or that he can no longer go to the local pub on paydays and clear it out. But they contend that he is still needed as a celebrator of the Eucharist and an announcer of the Scriptures. The vast majority are willing to see married men and/or women ordained in order to maintain the priesthood. A common response was: "We can have Eucharist or a celibate priesthood. We cannot have both."

The interviews were as filled with surprises as they were insights. The selection of the forty-three was completely unscientific. In fact, seventy names were gathered and the ones not interviewed could readily supply equally good insights. Only four asked to be excused, two for personal reasons, one because he "doesn't give interviews anymore," and a fourth because he felt that the chosen format would not permit him to explain his priesthood or "the richness of the theology of *Opus Dei*," of which he was a member.

I found virtually no institutional paranoia. While some were more cautious than others, no one seemed intimidated by what the bishop or others would say. As a free-lance writer, I have had the experience of being engaged to do an article or a speech and, during the interview process, I have found the very person who engaged me being extraordinarily cautious. I had no such experience with these priests. I was flattered by their trust and impressed by their openness.

The priests interviewed freely discussed the morale problem. They were familiar with the 1988 document issued by the Committee on Priestly Life of the National Conference of Catholic Bishops. "Although there are present today powerful individual examples of priestly ministry shared in creative and energizing ways which continue the ministry and mission of the church," the document opens, "it is also clear to us that there exists today a serious and substantial morale problem among priests in general." They agreed, but their own morale sounded resolutely strong. Among the issues the document and the priests listed were the perception that they have little control of their lives, issues of loneliness and isolation, polarization within presbyterates, celibacy and sexuality, retirement, lack of vocations, conflict with administrative policies, a sense that lay involvement is diminishing their ministry, conflict with conservative groups, restrictions placed on women's roles, increasing administrative and diminishing pastoral duties, distancing from their own chancery offices, undue expectations both from the hierarchy and the parishioners, insufficient areas for advancement, fewer rewards and promotions, and suppression of thought. Many felt that they have worked hard to implement Vatican II but they sense that the effort is now being blunted by the Vatican and the local chancery. The slow pace of renewal has left them weary; they must deal with the well-organized orthodox Catholics who appear to have the ear of the chancery. When they open a new child-care center in their parish, they receive no call from the chancery, but when a member of CUF (Catholic United for the Faith, an ultraconservative group) reports an infraction to the chancery, they receive a worried call or formal letter.

The list seems endless. Few priests would disagree with it. Yet, what I found were priests willing to set aside their frustrations in order to get their work done. In fact, they seemed more anxious to talk about their work than about their working conditions. They love their ministry and, with rare exceptions, would do nothing else with their lives.

Priests are changing their lives and life-styles. In their parishes they are making pastoral decisions that meet the needs of their people, everything from permitting altar girls (they simply call them "servers") to quietly granting annulments without recourse to the marriage tribunal. They are experimenting with different life-styles such as living in community with other pastors, other religious, or laity. They maintain a certain loyalty to their ordination classmates but, increasingly, they are forming prayer and social groups with other priests, laity, even ministers of other faiths.

Female staffers predominate in virtually every parish. If a parish has a full-time staff of five, three will be women. In some parishes the proportion is much higher. The women are having an enormous impact on the clergy. The long-term effect of the presence of women in offices once dominated by men remains to be seen, but priests report that the insights they have gained from years of working with women have colored both their ministry and their personal lives.

Although educated at a level equivalent to lawyers and physicians, priests tend to think like cops. The quasi-military structure of the priesthood seems to fuel some of this. The fact that many police officers are former seminarians is no coincidence. The administrative chemistry is much the same. Like the police officers who see themselves as the thin blue line between the upper and lower classes in society, the priest tends to see himself as a thin black line between the cathedral church and the pilgrim church. The chancery church is perceived as one that issues edicts and wags its finger, while the parish church must meet the parishioner where the tire meets the street. It is the parish that provides the Alcoholics Anonymous groups, addiction counseling, post abortion healing, and that attempts to help the nearly one-third of their parishioners who are involved in irregular marriages.

The priests interviewed rarely pointed to the gap between the upper and lower Church. Indeed, one suggested that such comparisons smacked of knocking on open doors. But they did admit to some tension. They described their bishops as decent men but they expressed a wish that the bishops would stop facing Rome and start facing their people. Privately, they expressed the opinion that the bishops themselves would be more respected by the Vatican if they stood up to the curial bureaucracy. Describing the hierarchy, the expression "office managers" occurred occasionally. Like police officers, the priests understand internal politics but are impatient with it. They regret what they perceive as the growing secrecy of their bishops, their loss of credibility on moral issues, and the bishops' fear of the country's more powerful bishops. But they applaud their bishops for trying, for courageous pastorals on peace and the economy, and for at least attempting to publish one on women's issues.

Although the subject of scandal rarely came up, when it did the priests expressed great anger. The sins of a few have tarred them all, they felt, making them objects of suspicion and ridicule. "We ought to fire about 10 percent of the guys," one man said. "The morale would zoom up." However, they see their bishops locked in a codependent relationship with the flawed priests. The sexual deviate or the womanizer knows that he has a license; the bishop will never publicly bring him to task. The prudent ordinary will continue to treat deviant behavior as a legal matter, calling the diocesan attorneys and arranging out-of-court settlements.

(One lawyer who had handled a number of cases involving priests who have jilted women said that he has found a key to settlements. "I charge the diocese with negligence rather than malpractice," he said. "They're glad to pay." A psychologist who has treated victims of sexual misconduct by priests said: "I just send my bill each month. They pay immediately, no questions asked." One of the priests interviewed told of his still searing pain over a call from a former parishioner who told him of her son's terribly flawed life. The son had been sexually abused by another priest in the parish. "You knew it and you did nothing, Father," she continues to tell him two decades later. In fact, he had reported the offender and was assured by the chancery that the matter was "being handled." The offender remains an active priest.)

Such failure of accountability angers most priests. Although a boy has a greater statistical chance of being sexually assaulted by his father than by his parish priest, the manner in which most dioceses deal with such cases only brings shame on all the clergy. They are disgusted; they want the offenders fired. (One chancery official, not in this book, protested that his office is doing something about it. "It's not that easy to fire them," he said. "It takes time." But nearly two years after he made the statement, there was no evidence that anyone had been fired or even disciplined.)

But the picture is getting distorted again. These priests talked about prayer and parishes, not the spoiled fruit in the vineyard. The priests interviewed, even the more critical ones, were more positive than negative. While these priests see the proportion of priest to parishioners lessening (Los Angeles went from one priest for every 2,557 Catholics in 1970 to one priest for every 3,958 Catholics in 1980), they still believe that the parishes can meet the needs of the people if the laity are permitted to take roles within the structure. One Irish monsignor called the laity "our greatest resource." He boasted that his parish has between 700 and 800 parishioners involved in the 2,500 unit parish and that "the more the laity are involved, the stronger I feel as pastor."

Few priests had words for it, but three models emerged from the conversations. The careerist priest views his vocation as a profession. If he considers his parishioners at all, it is in a competitive position. For the careerist, personal advancement is primary. Careerists have limited interaction with their parishioners; they are authoritarian, miserly with their emotions, and poor listeners. They preach love but place themselves beyond love's reach. Contact with their fellow priests is limited; relationships are superficial. Although only approximately one out of ninety diocesan priests becomes a bishop, the careerist spends a great deal of time thinking about his clerical career. His numbers appear to be on the wane but there is some small evidence that he is emerging among the recent batch of seminarians.

The guild priest forms the heart of the current priesthood. The guild priest views priesthood as a privilege, but his obligations derive from his membership in the priesthood rather that his obligations to his parishioners. For all his years of priestly training ("training" is almost always used instead of "education"), he has been far removed from the very people he is supposed to serve. He is repeatedly cautioned that he "has an obligation to do this or that or to refrain from doing this or that because you are a priest." There is little to say about his parishioners except that the parishioners' needs provide a reason for the existence of his profession. The guild priest was taught to stick with his own kind; to retreat and vacation with them; to take part in an endless series of anniversary masses recited in empty seminary chapels; to be laid to rest in the priests' plot at the local seminary. For years, the Catholic in the pew was regarded as passive, uninformed, and spiritually needy. True, the priest had powerful obligations toward them, but they remained "lay people" to be served by the self-standing entity called the priesthood. The guild priest remains very dedicated to his people, but his name remains the only name on the signature cards at the parish's bank.

The guild priests are undergoing the greatest change. In some convoluted way, they reminded me of crops: picked and cultivated for genetic uniformity in order to increase their yield, but, like genetically created plants, identically vulnerable to disaster. When changes came, it affected them all.

The guild model is breaking down. Even the rectories that priests lived in have been turned into parish centers. It is the guild priests who are forging the interactive model that views participation with the laity as a partnership of equals. Guild priests are now sharing power with their parishioners, turning administrative tasks over to them, concentrating on sacramental and scriptural ministries, explaining the wider church to their people. Presently, most priests are functioning somewhere between the guild model and the interactive model. If the American church is to survive, the interactive model, which creates a relationship between equals, will have to emerge as the operative model. The careerist and guild models, with their heavy layers of clericalism, will simply not survive. The priests may be trying harder than their parishioners to introduce this model.

Pastoral styles differed widely. There were what Father Phil Murnion of the Pastoral Life Center in New York described as the ring masters, pastors who announced the acts with great enthusiasm and kept the show going. There were the party throwers who said to their parishioners: "Great idea, let's have a dinner and get people together." There were the organizers who love charts, circles, and graphs. There were those who ran their parish, as Gregory Augustine Pierce describes it, "as if they were campaign headquarters, giving service, getting out the vote."

In the small talk at which most clergy are very good, the priests readily accepted some of the comparisons offered. Thus, they agreed that they often thought, or at least responded, as police officers, although they resisted the negative implications of some of that comparison. They accepted comparisons with all-male, fraternal organizations such as the Knights of Columbus, Elks, Moose, etc., all of whom are trying to cope with a dwindling, aging membership.

One priest had worked for the retailing giant, Sears, before World War II. He was very comfortable with the analogy of Sears and the American church. "The people loved the company," he said. "The company had the same aspirations as they did." He recalled the encouragement he received to be both innovative and responsible. The local manager, like the local pastor, had considerable leeway in ordering for his stores. The store had floorwalkers who were simply there to guide people. Clerks were given incentives to know and sell their products. Then, however, the giant marketing firm centralized. They developed their own brands, closing out others. Their quality remained good but it often didn't have much to do with customer needs. They began moving into other areas such as insurance, that did well for them but weakened their central focus. When Sears built its gigantic 102-story Sears Tower in Chicago, it seemed to change its entire personality. Now they were centralized; individual initiative was discouraged. Corporate bean counters made decisions for stores they had never visited. Merchandising groups had power and incentive pulled from them. Now, while Sears remains the nation's largest retailer, it continues to slip rapidly against its competitors, which have only a fraction of its resources but have remained in touch with the people they serve. "Now," the elderly priest said, "someone will buy Sears and call it something else."

The comparison lags a little when one considers the Church, but the comparisons found a home in most priests' minds. They continue, however, to resist more creatively. They make pastoral decisions in the face of differing central office policies. As a consequence, as American Church leadership continues to grow more cautious and shy of innovation, many of its parishes are flourishing. Thus, while I read carefully crafted, innocuous statements about ecumenism released from bishops' offices, ecumenical activity at the parish level is alive and well. Writing in the *New York Times*, Peter Steinfels observes that: "At the parish level, where statements by bishops or even popes may have only a faint impact, observers insist there is tremendous resilience and vitality." Father Andrew Greeley puts it another way: "As an institution the Catholic Church is in terrible condition but the Catholic community prospers."

The priests interviewed seldom initiated discussions of personal problems. Although I had charts listing base pay and fringe benefits for every diocese, figures that showed clearly that they received only modest salaries and even more modest pensions, none complained of money. Virtually all called for a change in the celibacy discipline, and the majority found loneliness and isolation their greatest burden.

Priests read. Most are undisciplined readers. Perhaps that is why they remain interesting. They read both secular and religious material. All seem well-informed on the world and church events. Most had good-sized libraries of old and new books. Virtually every library had books by Andrew Greeley. Some term him their hero; others found him contentious; but virtually all agreed with his vision of the parish and the parish priest. They read *America* and *National Catholic Reporter* and a variety of scripture-related publications to fuel their homilies. They read their local papers and, where available, the *New York Times*. I didn't glean the faintest idea what their politics were. They sound like Democrats; their bishops sound like Republicans.

They are men of prayer. Virtually all belong to some form of prayer group, composed largely of fellow priests. The groups appear to be therapeutic, a chance not only to pray but to unburden.

Enough. The rest is in the interviews. Joe Gallagher is among them. I found the priests to be just as he did in his over thirty-five years of priesthood. Joe says that "in no group of human beings have I found a greater proportion of loving, caring, admirable, Christ-like, even heroic men."

One final point. I have already said that these interviews occupied hours. Some of the priests interviewed have been friends for years. Although formally interviewed, some of their observations were derived from conversations over a period of years. In other cases, some thoughts were expressed over dinner during which no notes were taken, or while walking through a park or museum. While some interviews were taped and three were returned to their subjects for additions and corrections, these interviews are woven from threads of long and unorganized conversations. I had no prepared questions; I wanted the priests to say what was on their minds. In order to have some continuity, I frequently condensed or rephrased what they said. I think I got the music but I may have missed some notes. My apologies for any errors.

Tim Unsworth
May, 1991

❧ INTERLUDE I ❧

I was ordained in 1945 after seven years of study under a very strict rector. The class went home for a week for First Masses at our parishes and what seemed like an endless stream of parties.

We returned to the seminary for a weeklong "reheat" before going to our first parishes. But the week of celebrations had unwound my biological clock and I couldn't sleep.

I put on my cassock and biretta and took a late-night walk on the seminary grounds. It was an idyllic evening, full moon, cool, peaceful.

Outside the philosophy building, I met Mike, the night watchman. Mike must have had the most boring job in the world, walking from building to building during the night, just to ensure that the seminarians were safe from all harm. Some of our fathers had jobs like that. They lived in bungalow houses with our mothers, sisters, and brothers, sharing one bathroom and eating red meat only once a week. We young priests had our own small room and bathroom. We ate well. It left us feeling a little guilty.

Mike and I chatted about the lovely weather and some other small talk that I have long since forgotten. Of course, he had a brogue. That's how it was in 1945.

After a few minutes of soft talk, I told Mike that I thought I'd go back to my room and try to sleep. Mike tipped his hat and said: "Well, good night, Father."

For nearly fifty years, I've been trying to live up to that tip of the hat.

Chicago pastor, now retired.

· 1 ·

John R. Aurelio:
Pastor, Storyteller, Dreamer

If John Aurelio's hands were tied to his side, he would not be able to talk. He has the intensity of a high-school coach during a half-time talk. A small bearded man, his voice is growing more gravelly, but it is rich gravel, the kind some famous actors have. He has the blood of Southern Italy in his veins. It boils at room temperature.

We went to Piccolo Mondo, a trendy Italian restaurant with passable pasta. Aurelio was a little disappointed with his dish. He knows Italian food. But he wasn't upset. He'd rather talk than eat.

His most recent book, *Skipping Stones*, is a series of brief reflections on Old Testament themes. Aurelio detests brief reflections. "Sermonettes produce Christianettes," he says. But the insightful skipping stones are for people caught in an eternal rush hour. "We schedule religious services by the clock, not on the spiritual needs of people," he writes. His skipping stones are an accommodation. Aurelio hopes his readers will go deeper.

He is wonderfully naive about the politics of priesthood, just as he is about showing affection. "Oh, dear Jesus!" he says when he hears clerical gossip. "That can't be!" And he is saddened by the paranoid mentality that tracks priestly conduct. "When I was a chaplain for retarded children, I could hug them and cry with them. Now, we're not supposed to touch anybody. It's inhuman!"

We talked all afternoon.

I'm from Buffalo. I want to stay there. It's where my family and friends are. It's home. When I was ten years old my father packed up our family and moved us lock, stock, and barrel to his little backwater hometown in Sicily, a place called Ficarazzi. It was supposed to be a marvelous adventure but the novelty wore off after a few months. I learned to speak the local language. It's more like Greek than Italian. It's spoken, not written. My brothers and I were terribly lonesome. My father asked me what he could get me that I missed the most. I said: "A milk shake!" In 1948 in Sicily no one had ever heard of milk shakes. Ficarazzi was a wonderful place, but home was where the milk shakes were! We came back to Buffalo.

I was ordained after two tries in the seminary. I hated the seminary but I loved the priesthood! Between periods in the seminary, my studies in psychology only confirmed how much I was opposed to the seminary.

For seventeen years, I was chaplain in a New York State institution for the mentally retarded. Then I spent time as a pastor. I'm on sabbatical now, going home soon, but I don't want to be a pastor. Pastors have to deal with money and I hate the stuff. I'm just no good at managing money, not even my own. When I was a chaplain, I would go into the payroll office when I needed money and ask them when I was going to be paid. Then, I'd discover that I had three checks waiting there! I'm awful with money. I hate the stuff! My priest friend, Corky, suggested that we could run a parish together. He'd look after the finances and I'd look after the pastoral stuff. But Corky and I are just too close. If we worked together, I'd drive him nuts!

During my first period in the seminary, I was sent to Rome to study. I was there prior to Vatican II and had an opportunity to attend the first synod of priests. It was a forerunner to Vatican II and I remember saying to myself that, if this was going to be what Vatican II was going to be like, they shouldn't even bother! It was awful! Everything had been worked out ahead of time. Some Vatican monsignor read to us in perfect Ciceronian Latin. The cardinals up front slept through the whole thing. Everyone was terribly intimidated. No one dared asked a question. Finally, after three days, someone got up to make an objection. We all froze. The guy was objecting to the use of the ablative instead of the dative in one of the monsignor's sentences. Can you believe it? I went home and quit the seminary.

That was 1960. The Olympics were in Rome that year. The synod was nothing more than a legislative gathering for the priests of Rome. They were being told that priests were not to attend spectacles. Yeah, that's what they called them. Spectacles! They were told that they couldn't take part in organized hunts or even go to the opera. Can you believe it?

Of course, the Italian priests went to the Olympics and the opera. That's the way it is in the Church. The Italians make the rules; the Germans refine them, and the Americans keep them.

Later, at Vatican II, some bishops did object. They didn't rubber-stamp the documents. They tossed out some of the drafts. That was a sign of hope! John XXIII could never have dreamed it would come out the way it did. He was a great guy but he just wanted a nice time, a quiet Council. He would not have gone for the pulling of beards that went on. But John did his part. The

Vatican attitude toward the Church is that it's *cosa nostra*, our thing, just like the Mafia.

When I came home, I went to Fordham University and got a masters degree in social work. During my time in New York City, I was in group psychiatric work and work with teenage gangs. I learned a great deal. I also learned that I'm not very good dealing with bureaucracies and institutional thinking.

I remember getting my first job after I got my M.S.W. It was with Catholic Charities and I earned $4,800 a year. Well, state social workers were getting $5,400 with an M.S.W., so we asked for more. So, they raised the starting salary to $5,200 but the boss, a layman, put a memo on the bulletin board that said the new rate would only be for new hires. Then he went off to Florida on vacation. Can you imagine that? The man justified the nutty decision by quoting the parable of the laborers in the vineyard. That's not even what that parable is all about!

I'm afraid that we're treating our older priests that way now. Men my age are just too old to look for a new profession. So, we are neglected while the young priests are given anything they want. A lot of older men would quit, but it's too late.

But God has been so good to me. I wanted to be a priest so much. So, although I hated the seminary, I returned to Buffalo in 1962 and reentered. I was ordained in 1966.

I was ordained with twenty-one others. About half are still around. They are good guys. During all my years working with the mentally retarded, they were always good to me, always supportive when I was trying to raise money to get things for the retarded. I wasn't in their work; I was speaking and traveling and writing. They didn't always understand what I was doing, but they never objected, at least openly.

Before becoming a state chaplain, I was assigned to teach high-school English. Now, that was crazy! I never wanted to teach in a classroom. But that's the way things were done in those days. You were just assigned. I had no training in teaching. But you were supposed to obey. I had a degree in social work and they sent me to teach English. They even wanted me to teach French. I barely know a word! All they wanted in the classroom was a warm body!

Anyway, during my years as a chaplain, I got very involved in the politics of institutions. We had 1,700 children at the facility and right next door the state was building an olympic-sized swimming pool for another institution with one hundred disturbed people. Our people had one of those backyard portable pools. 1,700 kids and one portable pool!

Things like that really get to me. I started to complain and ran into a lot of opposition. Finally, I started to raise money for the pool. I figured that our portable pool cost about $2,500 so I could get one ten times bigger for only $25,000. Do you see how I am about money? Not very good! The pool cost $250,000 or something like that. But, eventually, we were able to get one, thank God.

I did a lot of speaking on behalf of the retarded. I became an advocate. In those years, too, I got involved in the Cursillo retreat movement and another one called Mission, an eight-day renewal. I got very involved in Mission. I was also writing. I've done eight books. Some are for young people. They were inspired by the wonderful retarded people I work with. The last two are on biblical spirituality. During fifteen of the years I was a chaplain, I did help-out work in a suburban parish. And finally, I was pastor of St. John the Evangelist in Buffalo for the past four years. Those were hard years. I was an Italian priest in a German-Irish parish. After ninety days, I had a bleeding ulcer. I don't work well with parish councils. I tried to listen and to go along with their wishes, but it was killing me. After my sabbatical, I'm not going back to that parish. I've resigned.

I'm fifty-three now. I know where my gifts are. I don't want another parish. I'd like to give retreats and workshops and to help out in parishes. The bishop will want me to take a parish. We'll see.

The vocation problem is a big one. It touches on married and celibate clergy and on the role of the laity. In the current structure, there is no hope for increased vocations. The biggest problem is that the priests are unhappy and, if they're not happy, how are others going to be attracted? Who wants to go into a profession of frowners?

I keep hearing that sexuality is a problem. I guess it is. But as the age level of the priests goes up, it will most likely decrease. Maybe it will cease to be a problem!

And then there's the present pope. I spent three weeks in Poland some time ago. I learned something about the status of priesthood there with people running to kiss the priest's hand. And that's what he's brought to the papacy. It isn't gonna change!

We have a program in Buffalo. It's titled "Called by Name." Priests and others are supposed to identify good people and send in their names. Then, they get invitations to learn more about the priesthood. It's pure Madison Avenue. It's asinine! I sent in a few names. I tried to be loyal, but I had an instinctive negative feeling. The system relies on numbers, not on the Holy Spirit. We need to have happy priests and I don't see them. Called by Name seduces children. It has nothing to do with God!

The priests in the vineyard are tired. The ones who want to work are overworked. They see the young ones coming in and getting preferential treatment. The older men get their toes stepped on. And the system still refuses to change. It's incestuous and incest leads to retardation.

In Buffalo, we're using a reward system that isn't beneficial to the priesthood. We're making monsignors. Monsignors are nothing more than a format for emulating the bishop. You're rewarded by being told that you can dress up to look like a bishop. It's crazy! Did you ever notice that there are three ranks of monsignors, and the higher you go, the more you can dress like the bishop? Dressing up like daddy! It's a terribly unhealthy system. And it's passed out in an unfair way. A man can be made a monsignor for just paying off the parish debt and another guy, in a poor parish, can be doing great work and will be ignored. I'm not against rewards, but there should be a system for any guy who wants to work for a promotion. There should be standards. Then, let a guy work for them. Right now, rewards are distributed terribly unevenly. It's at the whim of the bishop.

What does the priesthood have to offer today? I'm not sure. I recall giving scripture classes to the players with the Buffalo Sabres, a National Hockey League team, and their families. We used to meet in different players' homes. I loved it. It was a blessing. I recall listening to Mary, one of the players' wives, telling me about bringing a group of teenagers to see the work being done by sisters. She found a nun working in a shelter for battered women. Next to her desk the nun had a baseball bat and, when she was asked what it was for, she told them that this was a dangerous place and that battered women and the nuns sometimes had to defend themselves. These kids were terrified! The kind of kids we're after to enter the seminary or religious life just don't come from situations like that. I mean that nun was doing good work but, if she thought she was going to inspire these kids, her ass was in Egypt! It's like bringing them to a cloister. Who the hell would want to do that today? And all the priests got a letter some time ago, asking us to volunteer for films or posters or something. They asked for good looking guys. Pure Madison Avenue. What does that say to the priests?

As for the Catholic Church in the United States, I see difficult days ahead. Christianity doesn't do well in an affluent society. The rich don't need a Messiah. The wealthier we become, the more watered down the practice of the faith will be. The "haves" will become more tight-fisted in order to ensure that they can keep what they have. And they will continue to bend religion to their purposes. They'll do this through over intellectualization of their faith. I don't see a frontal assault. That probably would be better. We'd be healthier for it. No, it will be a gradual erosion.

It's in progress already. Consider the average Catholic's attitude toward marriage and divorce, birth control, abortion, euthanasia, the elderly, and all that. I realize that each of these issues should be argued on its own merits. My point is that there's a general malaise that is simply willing to go along with the expedient.

Among the general populace, I fear that Christianity will be reduced to a "feel-good" religion. It will also take on strong elements of "magic" as a condition for survival, especially with regard to death and resurrection.

I think that the downward trend will continue and reduce Jesus to a mere man, especially among the clergy and religious. Many of them will either fall away and become atheists or agnostics, while others will just remain on the job. Many, too, will come to our seminaries and convents because they will see religious life as "a nice job."

We'll need to look carefully and prayerfully at our future shepherds. The issue is no longer celibacy. It's beyond that. It's like arguing about who should be made headwaiter on the Titanic. The fact that we believe that the Church is eternal is no excuse for planning for the year 3000 when we can't meet the needs of the year 2000 with the disciplines of the year 1000! We are already paying the price for that kind of intellectual and religious pride.

The Western World is fast becoming effete. Our obsession with youth is symptomatic. Cases of child seduction and abuse will only increase as our fear of growing old and dying gets worse. The affluent don't want to die to enter the kingdom when they already supposedly have it. The only kingdom their wealth cannot hold on to is youth, so they will further continue to seduce or resent it. They will also continue to look the other way when it comes to the aged. These are the "now" issues. The Church has got to address itself to these with all the force and inspiration at its disposal.

That all sounds bad, but I'm not without hope. There's still a way out of this morass. To say "Jesus" sounds too magical. But let's say "generosity." Strong, heavy doses of generosity, the way people take vitamin C when they feel a cold coming on. I see big trouble ahead. Now's the time to apply this overdose of generosity, not just with money, although that can break down our selfishness. At the same time, we might even give less to our churches. I believe that a lean church is a healthier church. But we also have to be generous with the talents God gave us. We have to give soon, and in large doses, as individuals, families, and as a nation. We have to give the way Scrooge did after he saw the light.

Oh, I've wondered and prayed about it. The Holy Spirit is winnowing through. I think that things will get more difficult. Maybe the old system with all its trappings has got to go and a whole new spirit has got to come in.

All I ever wanted to do is to love God and be a good priest. I'm giving my life to the Church. I know it will survive. The Holy Spirit will see to that. God's gonna take care of me.

N.B. Not long after the interview, John Aurelio was appointed to the faculty of Christ the King Seminary for the diocese of Buffalo.

Blaine G. Barr:
Charts, Circles, and Diagrams

The Parish Community of St. Joseph in New Hope, Minnesota, may be better organized than a German track meet. Typically, when I arrived at his rectory, Blaine Barr, the pastor, had a stack of information about the parish ready for the interview. The materials amounted to a veritable parish almanac. Each apostolate within the parish had submitted a report so detailed that I felt like a spiritual auditor. The data informed, for example, that there were thirty-nine lectors, fifty-two musicians, 110 care givers, fifty hospitality ministers, etc. I received attendance figures for virtually every meeting and learned that volunteers had logged 725 telephone hours. One learns that the neighborhood social service representatives contributed 1,105½ hours last year. In a church where a significant number of parishes still do not publish annual budgets, and do not have a parish council, St. Joseph's tells its people what is happening everywhere but the Reconciliation Room.

It would be easy to caricature the parish and its pastor. Both have had their share of critics already. But such criticism would be as unfair at it is inaccurate. Blaine Barr believes in structure. He clearly has problems with the cult of the personality in a pastor. When he leaves the St. Joseph community, a viable structure will be in place. It won't collapse in the vacuum caused by the loss of a cult figure. The new pastor won't have to look for the keys.

St. Joseph's has two churches. One is a Christmas card, a charming white church on top of a hill that now overlooks a sylvan setting on one side and a shopping center on another. "The old pastor could have bought that property for next to nothing years ago," Barr said. Father Barr, a man already planning for the year 2000, is still miffed at the lack of foresight. It meant that the new, vastly larger church is some two miles away. Now, shopping-center cars encroach on church property. "Thou shalt not park," the signs in the driveway read.

Father Barr's rectory is on the site of the old church. It is a comfortable, well-kept place that Barr had enlarged with the help of the parish. (My wife, Jean, weary from an eight-hour drive and an earlier interview, curled up on the couch as if at home. She was.) Father Barr still reads, perhaps more than most priests. There are books in the rectory and at his office in the main church. While criticizing aspects of his Roman education, he remains something of an intellectual. He prefers pastoring, but books are a great resource for him. Barr is a prism of priesthood, reflecting anger, hope, loneliness, pastoral concerns, weariness, and vision. His concerns are many, but he loves his priesthood.

When I came here in 1967, I wanted to model St. Joseph's on Vatican II from top to bottom. I'm never satisfied; I'm always impatient; I feel we should be doing more.

I've been pastor here for twenty-three years. I was ordained in 1951 for the Class of 1952. There were thirteen local men in an ordination class of twenty-seven. We were in Rome, studying at the North American College.

I was the youngest priest in my class to be named pastor. That's something of a surprise, since I'm known for asking a lot of questions. Back in my brasher days, I sent a twenty-seven page letter to the bishop. I always keep asking why? I'm persistent, determined, strong-willed.

I've been alone here for the last five years. I do get some Sunday help-out. We have six Masses on weekends; I say four of them. Then, I do a repeat Mass on Tuesday evening for those who couldn't make it on Sunday. We never have more than one daily Mass during the week.

We're still growing. Last year we had 1,573 households with 4,720 parishioners and a budget of $855,000. There were seventy-nine First Communions, fifty-four Confirmed, fourteen marriages, and eleven funerals. We baptize every two months; had about ninety last year.

We don't have a lot of weddings like some parishes this size. I have very strong feelings about weddings. I want the couple to really understand their relationship with each other and with God. I insist that they be part of the worshiping community. If I find that a couple is already living together, I ask them to separate or to practice celibacy. You know, 90 percent of them agree. They tell me that no one has ever talked about marriage to them. When I ask them: "Does this make sense?" they agree. I stress communication with them. I guess the word has gotten out. So, we don't have a lot of weddings. I'm not trying to punish them; I just want them to have a relationship. Their families say nothing to them; they've been programmed to accept our decisions. We can't blame the parents for not educating their children for marriage. After all, we told them in our Catholic schools that we priests were the only teachers.

In my homily at weddings, I tell the couple that my homily is my gift to them. I tell them what a good marriage means. I get good feedback from most people; the Protestants in the congregation, even the wedding photographers, tell me that they like what they hear.

Many parishes today are attracting people who have left the Church. They're coming back, asking questions, and bringing their families. They want to be actively involved. I think St. Joseph's allows them to be. At least a thousand of our parishioners are active in one or more parish activities.

Two things came from Vatican II: first, the Church is the people of God, and, second, that means the community, not the institution, is central.

I believe that the hope of the Church is in the small group. The whole purpose of the organization of this parish is to break it down into something people can handle. Our parish is divided into fifteen neighborhoods. By 1989, we had formed twenty-one small communities; by 1994, I'd like to see fifty to seventy-five small communities; by the year 2000, we hope to have 100 to 150 communities in the parish. Did you read about that minister in Korea? He's filling his church six times each Sunday with around 18,000 people at each service. He has 12,000 small groups in his parish. They build the larger community.

Before Vatican II, the priest did all the ministering. He was the professional. Now, we have lay staffs doing most of the ministry. At St. Joseph's, there is one priest with a lay staff of thirteen full-time people and anywhere from seventeen to twenty-seven part-time people. We have five to eight people who work eight to twelve hours per week. They're paid $6 to $8 per hour, and out of them we have drawn our part-time people. Most of the staff are women. They're not angry women; I think most of the truly angry women have left the Church.

Now, we can buy a great deal of professional material, including curriculum for our programs. But we're wary of professional liturgists. They want to redo everything and they just don't know our people. So we do a lot of our own liturgy planning. I see the parish as a small diocese. We're divided into five deaneries or regions and fifteen neighborhoods. We use secular names for the groups to give them a sense of neighborhood.

At St. Joseph's, we want parents to be responsible for their children. At Baptism, the ritual says that the parents bring them up in the practice of the faith. When I studied in Italy, I found that children learned early that they went to church only when they were hatched, matched, and dispatched. Our people like our Baptisms. We stress parental responsibility. My job as pastor is to lead the community in prayer and to help them with the sacraments. But it's the parents who must bring their children up in the faith.

I'm close to about a dozen priests. There are six in our prayer group. We have lunch together or do an overnight retreat. We started it when Vince Dwyer came through town, telling us about small prayer groups. It's worked here. We even vacation together. We're closer than a family.

One of the hardest things I have found about priesthood is being the priest in my family, especially being the oldest and a priest. Too much is expected.

I've been a rebel, I guess. I was active in Young Christian Students. In the seminary, I read *Orate Fratres, Integrity, Commonweal, America*. I was reading about the Baroness de Hueck, the founder of those Friendship Houses. I read her book, *Dear Bishop*, a kind of open letter to the bishops. I read all the revolutionary books, at least they seemed so at the time. It wasn't easy to do that in the seminary in those days. After lights out, you had to read in the john. They had a master switch that turned every other light off. You had to leave the book in the john if you wanted another guy to read it. Liberal magazines were all read in the john.

In Rome, I never got one of the coveted house jobs. They went to the docile guys. I was always asking "why" instead of jumping. I was the dreamer and the visionary, I guess. And stubborn. Contrary to what people think, only a few of the guys made bishop, maybe four in my class. I'm surprised how some have changed. There was George Grotius (pseudonym), for example. He was a very nice fellow. You could go to his room with a question and he'd go out of his way to give you an answer, and it was always a good one. Now, look at him. He's so conservative! I don't know when he went over the wall.

In Rome, I was elected to the Missionary Society. That's not a group to ransom babies. I raised money for the society by selling books. I was really turned on by Danielou and de Lubac and pressed them with the other guys. I traveled throughout Europe. I witnessed the priest-worker movement in France. I attended Masses where the priest was facing the people, an un-heard-of thing at the time.

After ordination, however, I left my unfinished doctorate in Rome. I found all the Latin hard. I just wanted to be a parish priest.

I think that priests take on celibacy without sufficient reflection. Ten of the guys who worked for me in this parish are now married. I think that if we used annulment as a criteria instead of the laicization process, all of the guys would have their ordination annulled. I think that at least 85 percent of priests don't have the charism of celibacy. Before Vatican II, celibacy was relatively easy. You never left the rectory. You never took off your black suit. You had to be home by 10:30. You only saw the shitty side of marriage. You only heard about alcohol abuse. But after Vatican II, I found that I could look around. I discovered healthy people in healthy relationships, people who would say "good bye" to you and then walk away, arm in arm. I knew that they were going to bed together. I began to feel the difference. Now, it's much harder to deal with it. At least now we're talking about it, but the more lonely priests become, the more we are going to be alone.

The worst pain in the priesthood, however, is caused by our superiors. They have a different agenda. We love what we're doing. Yet, our hours are not good. There's too much pressure; we're alone; we have to deal with every age group from infants to the elderly; we're expected to be teachers and leaders; no time for other interests; there's the lack of other priests in the rectory and the terrible loneliness that comes with it.

I think we ought to change the preparation structure. I'm in favor of adopting the medical model, you know, seminarian as intern, then as resident, working with and learning from other people, not competing with other people. Then ordain him.

I think I could accept a parish administrator who could run the parish. That's not a pastoral administrator. That's the role of the priest. Those roles must be clear, otherwise the staff would get a mixed message.

Look at the charts I gave you. Oh, I know I'm known around here as the director of CCD—charts, circles, and diagrams. I like them. I try to design a chart that looks back and then forward. I don't forecast the future, but I dream about the future. I ask "what if?" I think more and more about a stewardship program, about a retreat program for everyone in the parish. I tithe myself and the parish tithes. We gave $166,000-plus last year to outside causes, including our diocesan assessment.

We've done some new programs at St. Joseph's that have drawn criticism from the diocese. But then, five years later, they adopt the same program. Lately, we've been writing our own program, kind of reformating the old Young Christian Students model of observe, judge, act. We've inserted "reflect" after observe. Chardin said that the only real road was to build a future. We must do the same.

We do our Renew program only once a year, during Lent. Otherwise, it's like having two Lents a year. We got about 700 the first year; now, we get a steady 450.

I think it was George Bernard Shaw who first said "I dream of things that never were and say 'Why not?'" And all I can add is: "Why not here at St. Joseph's?"

· 3 ·

Joseph L. Bernardin: Cardinal

The cardinal's mansion on Chicago's North State Parkway is a monument to Church triumphalism. It symbolizes an era that saw an immigrant church come out from under the hatred of the Know-Nothings and the American Protective Association to become a major power. Built in 1885 by Archbishop Patrick A. Feehan (1880–1902), it represented a church that was flexing its muscles in a city that was growing as fast as it could find immigrant bricklayers. (During his twenty-two years as archbishop, Feehan opened 119 parishes. It's entirely possible that Joseph L. Bernardin will also be archbishop for twenty-two years, during which time, he might be forced to close 119 parishes. Like the church elsewhere, the Archdiocese of Chicago is in recession.)

The mansion has at least a dozen chimneys and some thirty-three rooms. Once a symbol of power, it is now viewed as an ecclesiastical white elephant and a source of criticism by some observers who feel that it doesn't represent a pilgrim church. The archdiocese claims that the sale of the gingerbread house would not relieve its strained financial situation, since zoning laws would not make the property attractive to developers. They are stuck with it.

But the old house symbolizes much more. It once housed a throne room in which the archbishop greeted invited guests. Once each year, pastors arrived to pay their respects to princes of the Church such as George Mundelein and Samuel Stritch. They introduced their curates, some had a half-dozen, and, by prearrangement, dropped their envelope into the hands of a chancery official. Then, the pastors feigned surprise and breathed a "Lord, I am not worthy" when the cardinal named them monsignors. The system, with its equal measures of dedication and corruption, worked. The tribute monies built the largest diocesan structure in the U.S. Earlier cardinals were seldom without a model of a proposed church or school in the trunk of their car. At one time, the archdiocesan school system was the third largest in the country, public or private. (Although Los Angeles has nearly a million more Catholics, it has fewer parishes, schools, priests, etc.)

Chicago was the birthplace, or at least the growthplace, of many social movements—the Catholic Interracial Conference, Young Christian Students, Young Christian Workers, Christian Family Movement, etc. It was clearly the most influential diocese in the American church.

Chicago's first cardinal, George Mundelein, preferred to live in another mansion, located on the grounds of St. Mary of the Lake Seminary in Mundelein, Illinois, a rural community, once called Area, and named after him not long after he donated a new fire engine to the town. Stritch and his successor, Albert Meyer, divided their time between both mansions. Cardinal John Cody spent most of his time in growing seclusion at the State Parkway mansion, living alone, rarely even welcoming visiting bishops, including one named Cardinal Karol Wojtyla, who would become John Paul II. (Cody would later make it up to him by allegedly promoting Wojtyla's candidacy at the consistory and arranging an elaborate welcome for him when he visited Chicago not long after his election as pope.)

The mansion's use reflects the differing styles of the bishops. Cardinal Joseph L. Bernardin uses it as a home and part time office. He lives there with two priests, using a small second-floor office and private suite as his living and working space. The remainder of the house is used for occasional clerical gatherings and fund-raising efforts. The throne room is now a parlor. The "drop" parties and the awarding of the purple piping are long gone. Bernardin doesn't miss them, but he could use the money.

Bernardin is one of twelve American cardinals, six of whom presently head U.S. sees. Bernard F. Law is in Boston; John J. O'Connor heads New York; James A. Hickey is in Washington, D.C. In June, 1991, John Paul II named Anthony J. Bevilacqua, archbishop of Philadelphia, and Roger M. Mahony, archbishop of Los Angeles, to the College of Cardinals. In Rome, William W. Baum, former archbishop in the nation's capital, is now prefect of the Congregation for Catholic Education, and Edmund C. Szoka, former archbishop of Detroit, is president of the Prefecture for Economic Affairs of the Holy See. Two cardinals, John J. Krol of Philadelphia and John J. Carberry of St. Louis are retired. (The remaining two are not part of the American hierarchy. One is Myroslav Lubachivsky, a naturalized American, archbishop of Lwow in the Ukraines, recently returned to his diocese after a banishment of fifty years, during which he lived in Rome. The second is Luis Aponte Martinez, archbishop of San Juan, Puerto Rico, a U.S. territory.) Baltimore, St. Louis, and Detroit are all considered cardinalate sees, but, in the words of one bishop, their ordinaries "slipped through the cracks." With a Latino population that may account for forty percent of the American Church by the turn of the century, there have been rumors of a Latino-American cardinal. There are still only a handful of Latino-American bishops, however, and none are in the power structure or are heads of large dioceses.

Cardinal Bernardin is considered the only progressive moderate in the group. Law may be the most conservative, but Hickey and O'Connor, as well as Baum and Szoka in Rome, are viewed as conservatives, and growing more so. Bevilacqua describes himself as "orthodox" and Mahoney, once outspoken on social justice issues, has retreated, although he did make an effort to decry the U.S. war in Iraq before Bernard Law, a close friend of George Bush, urged the bishops to hold discussions behind closed doors. The cardinals head dioceses with largest numbers of Catholics but with among the lowest percentage of practicing Catholics. They tend to view the clergy, particularly the bishops, as the custodians of the faith, and the laity as citizens of the worldly community. Although their primary role is that of pastors and teachers, they hold tight to temporal power. They speak of some limited democracy within the Church, but they remain closer to the monarchial model of church. There is little evidence that they have distributed power or money decisions among the faithful.

They still prefer telling language such as "extraordinary minister" when permitting their fellow baptized Christians to distribute the Eucharist. At the functional level, Holy Orders remains the primary sacrament; the Vatican gets their primary loyalties. Presently, if changes are occurring, the shift is toward even more conservative thinking and practice.

As archbishop of the nation's second largest diocese with 2.35 million members, Bernardin is called constantly for his views on everything from Middle Eastern conflicts to the use of girls as Mass servers. He is a favorite target of the far-right, who may have done some substantial political damage to him during his Chicago years. Once considered the most influential bishop in America, he appears to have been shunted to the side by New York's O'Connor. Although O'Connor's statements are predictable, he manages to make them sound outrageous and thus garners more headlines. More important, from an ecclesiastical point of view, O'Connor sits on the Vatican congregation that presents the pope with recommendations for bishops. He takes his role seriously, attending as many meetings as he can and getting reports on others. He can be called "the bishop maker" although the Pro-Nuncio and the Vatican itself have a great deal to say. Like most bishops, Bernardin now has little say even in the appointment of bishops in his ecclesiastical province. Presently, he has been waiting over a year for a new auxiliary, a courtesy once extended virtually automatically to megabishops.

In Chicago, his diocese continues to wrestle with the politics of cutbacks. In 1990, the archdiocese announced the closing of thirty-eight parishes while only one new parish was opened. Chicago has lost one priest every eighteen days since 1984 through death, retirement, and resignations. In 1990, five priests were ordained for the archdiocese, the lowest number in history. By 2005, it is expected that there will be approximately four hundred active diocesan priests and that only 12 percent of these will be under forty. This represents a 55 percent drop since 1965. Presently, there are just over sixty seminarians for Chicago in the major seminary. Bernardin's goal is a hundred. A recent visitor to the major seminary was impressed by the sincerity and faith of the seminarians; only the low numbers were discouraging. Bernardin's observation: "I must be a man of hope. Without hope, I might as well resign."

In a city where, as he observed, "everything is political," he has managed to be a voice of reason among many factions. He is asked to comment on virtually every issue from abortion to the building of a new public library. He generally responds by citing Church teaching on the moral issues and appealing for reasonableness on the political ones. His liberal critics fault him for not being more outspoken on local issues, especially race, housing, and the loss of jobs within the city. A diocese once closely associated with labor now rarely sends clerical collars to labor gatherings. Once famous for its many clerical voices on pressing issues, it now has few who speak out, although the cardinal maintains that he is not muffling them. Whatever the case, the climate isn't the same. Surely Bernardin would never ride down Michigan Avenue in an open limousine with the president of the United States as George Mundelein once did with Franklin Roosevelt. Far too much has changed.

Bernardin likes to write and to speak. He is still invited to elite forums to deliver addresses and he has contributed extensively to the major pastorals, especially the one on peace.

Although liberals are sometimes impatient with Bernardin's adherence to the Church's often mysterious and always plodding ways, he remains their only hope among the major bishops. "He is an incredibly patient and prudent man," another bishop said of him. "That's not just his style; it's the way he is." He appears to be well-liked by his fellow bishops who have been known to wince at the excesses of the other major bishops, e.g., Bernard Law's support of George Bush during Desert Storm; O'Connor's veiled threat to excommunicate New York's Governor Mario Cuomo because of his refusal to take a pro-life stand; James Hickey's firing of theologian Charles Curran from the faculty at Catholic University.

Joseph L. Bernardin is a career bishop. Born in Columbia, South Carolina, in 1928, he is the son of an Italian stonecutter and a seamstress. Ordained in 1952 for the diocese of Charleston, he caught the attention of his bishop, Paul J. Hallinan, who would later bring him to Atlanta in 1966 as his auxiliary at the age of only thirty-eight, making him the youngest bishop in the country. In 1968, he was named General Secretary to the National Conference of Catholic Bishops, where he came under the tutelege of Detroit's archbishop, Cardinal John Dearden, his second mentor, then president of the NCCB/USCC, and served until being appointed archbishop of Cincinnati in 1972. He served as president of the NCCB/USCC from 1974 to 1977, a position that brought him national attention. He was named archbishop of Chicago in 1982 and a cardinal in 1983.

Here, you've seen this before. It's my pastoral letter on the Church [*The Family Gathered Here before You*, 1989]. It represents where I am in terms of the Church.

It didn't get much play because it was published just before we announced the closings and consolidations of the parishes, and so the attention shifted. Nonetheless, it's beginning to come to light again. It's being used in various places for discussion groups.

I thought I'd ask you to take a look at it. It puts the priesthood, as I see it, within the context of the larger Church. I worked on it for two years.

I've written a number of pastorals. I've done one on lay ministry and, in that context, also talked about priestly ministry. My first pastoral was on liturgy, particularly the Sunday Eucharist. I agree that bishops should write their own pastorals, but there is also a place for collective pastorals like the ones being published by the bishops' conference. I think that the one on war and peace was excellent and did a lot of good. The one on the economy was also very good. But I also think that bishops themselves should write their own pastorals. They have more freedom than we do when we write a collective pastoral. The collective ones get quite long, but, sometimes, that is because you need support. At times you have to shape them in a way you may not have originally planned in order to get broader support.

Yes, I've heard all the talk about Archbishop Weakland's pastoral in which he raises questions about the possibility of ordaining married men as priests. I was asked by the *Tribune* and the *Sun-Times* to make a statement, and I did. I praised his commitment to the Church and his candor. I stated that both have been forged over a long period of service to the Church. Archbishop Weakland deeply loves the Church; he appreciates its theological and historical tradition. I see no defiance and disregard of that tradition. Even his current proposal regarding the ordination of married men, while certainly raising a challenge, was made with the acknowledgement that it would require the approval of the Holy Father.

Now, personally, I hold a different view. I maintain that we have not adequately explored the possibilities of attracting men to the priesthood. People who share my view believe that, if the priesthood were presented in a more positive and persuasive way, and if it were supported by the entire Catholic community, many more candidates would come forward. So, my approach would be different from Archbishop Weakland's, but I acknowledge the value of discussion that would force us to probe more deeply and to articulate more clearly our convictions in the matter. I respect his position, but, of course, in the final analysis, we are obligated to work within the parameters set by the official Church. I share Archbishop Weakland's concern about the effect of the shortage of priests in a Church that is so deeply rooted in Eucharist. The 1971 and 1990 Synods of Bishops, as well as other authoritative documents, have reaffirmed the value of celibacy and its normative status for priests of the Latin rite. I stand with the Church; I've taken an oath to uphold the Church's teaching and discipline. In my own ministry, I work within the parameters that have been set by the Church. I don't want to give a double signal. One of the difficulties we encountered in the 1960s and 1970s is that, in training priests, many were saying that the requirement of celibacy would change. There were a number of men who went through the seminary thinking that eventually it would change, and it didn't. This created a certain disillusionment for some. I don't want to do that. Secondly, I do see the value of celibacy. I support it. If at the level of the Church's magisterium a change is ever considered, I would be part of that process. But the difficulty even there is that you have to be careful in the way you go about it. If you say, for example, that you're open to a discussion of the matter, then immediately some would say: "He's pushing for optional celibacy or married men as priests," or, "He's not supportive of the church's position." It creates a dilemma. Again, I sincerely support the Church. At the same time, it is rather hazardous to say that a change will never be considered.

I've read some of Gene Hemrick's data [Reverend Eugene Hemrick, director of research for NCCB/USCC]. He's sent some of it to me. You've seen it, too. Contrary to what some people are saying, there's a great commitment by priests to priesthood. I feel strongly that we have to make that known. One of the difficulties is that more attention is focused on some of the conflicts and problems than on the real commitment that I see. Sometimes the impression is given that we have a totally demoralized corps of priests. That is not true. It has also been said that I personally have glossed over the morale problem among the priests of this diocese, that I have said there is no morale problem among our priests. I have never said that. What I have said is that some priests surely have a morale problem but, on the basis of my contacts with priests generally, I maintain that there are many who are happy, very committed. They are certainly aware of the difficulties we face and they are concerned about them. But overall they cope quite well. So when speaking about priestly morale, I avoid generalizing.

Let me come at it another way: There is no doubt that priests today face a number of problems, such as loneliness, difficulty with some Church teachings or chancery policies, the direction in which they perceive the Church to be going, the unfair criticism they receive at times from parishioners and others, the stress caused by financial concerns, anxiety about the future because of the decreased number of priests, etc.

Some of these issues become a very serious problem for many priests, undermining their morale, causing them to be quite negative, less productive and creative. At times this results in some leaving the active ministry.

There are those who speak or write very publicly and candidly about the difficulties, giving the impression that they are very discouraged and unhappy, ready to throw in the towel. But when you get to know them, you find that they are basically very happy in their ministry. They are innovative, pastoral, effective. They have no intention of giving up.

Then there are those, the majority, I think, who are certainly concerned about particular issues or problems, but they don't go out and speak negatively about the Church or priesthood. They are committed, happy, trying to serve their people as best they can. Difficulties? Yes, but probably no more than in any other walk of life, they would say.

To sum up, there are problems we face as priests, but it is better not to generalize because they do not affect all priests in the same way. That having been said, however, we must address the issues that are of concern. Not to do that will indeed create a more general morale problem. I am committed to addressing them, but I can't do it alone.

I instinctively believe that it's healthier to let people say what they want and not clamp down. Let them get whatever it is out of their system. The only time I have a real problem with that is when a really serious church issue is involved and someone, in his capacity as a priest, says, "Well, the Church says this, but I'm saying you can do the opposite." Then I have to clarify the matter. But, if a priest is simply expressing his personal opinions and is respectful of the Church's position, I don't get too excited about it. If I did, I would have to have some kind of clerical CIA to monitor all that is being said! (Laughs.)

Generally speaking, I'm rather tolerant. This is a large and diverse archdiocese. I would never attempt to control everything that is said. I do have people both on the "left" and the "right" who at times say to me: "Why did you let that person say that? You should do something about that!" This comes from both sides. But I think that, in the long run, you accomplish more by letting people get things out of their system.

It's true. I seem to be a focal point when the press and others want reactions. And when I speak, even if I make it clear that I am speaking personally or am expressing an opinion, it is usually viewed as the authoritative statement of a bishop and a cardinal; people interpret everything I say in the light of who I am. But let's step aside from that. I personally think that we are on the verge of breaking out into a more positive, more persuasive mode of Church. Despite all the conflicts, I sense that the faith is very much alive. Why do I say that? I base it primarily on my own experience. If I sit at my desk and look only at the problems that come to my attention, I could become very negative and start asking myself "What in the world is this all about?" But I go out every week to visit the parishes and I spend time with priests and people. I see a totally different mentality, a church that is quite different from the one portrayed in the problem situations. Somehow, we've got to capture that positive mentality, that vitality and dynamism; we've got to build on it. And I think it's going to take not just one person, I can't do it alone, but many people with vision, imagination, creativity. Looking at it from my perspective, I think it can and should be done within the parameters of our teaching and tradition. I am convinced that we *can* do it within the ecclesial structure as outlined in Vatican II.

One of my themes in the past year has been the significance of the twenty-fifth anniversary of the Council [Vatican II]. I'm very much aware of the fact that there are some people who wish that the Council had never existed and, if they had their way, they would turn back the clock. Then there are others who think that the Church and the times have moved beyond the council. They say that the council did a good job, did what it had to do, but that now we're in a postcounciliar period that requires something quite different. I'm not in agreement with that. I don't think that we have totally understood the significance of the council; I don't think that generally we understand the full implications of the council, nor have we adequately implemented its teachings. It takes more than one generation to *fully* understand and *fully* implement something as broad and significant as the council.

Now, I realize that there are some issues that are controverted and, in due time, they will undoubtedly be clarified; but if I spent all of my time just focusing on those, I would be missing a great deal in the meantime. This is why I am quite sanguine about the possibilities of moving forward. It is going to take leaders who can persuasively articulate the positive dimensions of the Church, who are not cowed by people who disagree with them.

The issue of the isolation or loneliness of the priests is a very real one. It has to be addressed. But if the only solution proposed is the possibility of marriage, I don't think we will address it adequately. Marriage may be one way to go, but, within the context of the celibate priesthood, there are many ways to address the issue of loneliness. We have not been creative enough; we simply have not explored the potential that exists, and I'm committed to doing that.

As for episcopal authority, are people saying that there should be no episcopal authority? That somehow we should do away with the hierarchial structure of the Church? If that's what they're saying then, obviously, I don't agree. I believe that this is the way that the Church is constituted. If I didn't, I would not have accepted the position I have.

However, how should that authority be exercised? That's the real question. We're struggling with that now. One of the realities we face is that authority in the Church is being exercised in different ways; this causes tension and controversy. All I can do is exercise my authority in the best way I know how. I believe in consultation; I try to include as many people as possible in my exercise of authority. I'm not afraid to stand up and take a position, but I find that, if I include more people in the actual decision-making process, the outcome is accepted much better. Now, the flip side, as you well know, is that when you do consult, you are accused by some people of being indecisive, of lacking courage, of trying to hide behind a consultative process because you're not willing to make a decision. However, some of the very people who emphasize the importance of consultation will hold it against you if you don't produce quickly enough for *them*.

The third issue for priests is disagreement on moral issues and that is a very real problem. I've been dealing with that since the very beginning of my priesthood, well, not so much my priesthood as my years as a bishop. I was ordained in 1952, well before the council; I was named a bishop in 1966, three months after the close of the council, so my whole episcopacy is post Vatican II. I've had to face those many moral issues as a bishop for the past twenty-five years. It's a real problem. One of those issues is abortion. It would be tragic if the right to life of the unborn is totally disregarded in our society. Such a position or attitude negatively impacts other rights. I've spent more than seven years developing a rationale for a "consistent ethic of life" and, incidentally, I think I've made a contribution. "Consistent ethic" is now part of today's moral or ethical vocabulary, especially as it refers to the broad spectrum of life issues. I feel very strongly about the abortion issue. This doesn't mean, however, that I agree with some of the strategies used by some pro-life groups. But, I have not criticized them openly the way they have criticized me. I haven't criticized them because I don't want to give the impression that we are divided on the basic issue. If we start arguing with each other or condemning each other publicly in regard to strategy, we will accomplish little.

Yes, I'm aware that some pastors are impatient with the need to go to

Rome for permissions. I know that a million dollars is not much money when you consider the size of the Archdiocese and its overall budget, but the canons still require that I ask permission when properties or other assets totaling that amount are sold or otherwise alienated. I'm obligated to do that. I think that the formula used for this purpose will be changed. And, may I say this? Some of the pastors who are impatient with rules, such as those governing money, have rules of their own in their parishes that they insist must be obeyed!

As Americans, we like instant results. We don't always appreciate the mysterious ways of the Church. I don't want to give the impression that I'm just sitting here, wringing my hands, operating in a vacuum. I'm involved in many things within the Church. I truly believe that God is working through me and I must do what is expected of me. However, I don't want to give the impression that God has somehow given me a personal message or mission. Nonetheless, I'm here in Chicago. Remember, I started off in South Carolina and came here by way of Atlanta, Washington, and Cincinnati. So, I feel that I'm here for a purpose and I do have a vision of the direction in which the Church should be going.

I have another twelve years before retirement. I'll be sixty-three in April and, if God gives me life for that long, I'll be the diocesan bishop until 2003. How much will be accomplished during that twelve years? I hope to spend the remaining time pursuing the vision that I articulated in the pastoral on the Church I gave you.

Yes, I believe there will be a crowd at my retirement dinner in 2003. The Church is not going out of existence; it will still be strong. And the crowd will include newly ordained priests. If I didn't believe that, do you think I would be building up the seminaries and saying again and again that the priesthood is still a good thing and exciting?

Incidentally, I'll be celebrating my twenty-fifth year as a bishop in April. We're planning a very modest celebration. I realize that, years ago, Cardinal Spellman in New York could collect enough money in connection with such an anniversary to build a new school. But these are different times. A celebration that was used as a fund raiser would simply backfire. We'll have a Mass at the cathedral and each parish will be invited to send representatives. Later, in June, we'll have an afternoon of reflection and celebration at the seminary for the priests of the diocese.

Yes, new bishops ordained today are older than a generation ago. Very few men under forty are ordained bishops today. Whether that's good or bad I don't know, but it does seem to have shifted to a higher age. It's changed.

The future? This is a decisive moment in the Church's history. What happens during the next decade will have great impact on the third millenium of Christianity. The renewal begun by the Second Vatican Council, I submit, will continue.

I hope that we will find a way in the future, both in structures and in attitudes, to keep our focus on essentials. I hope that the Church of Chicago can be a source of unity and reconciliation and that it will continue its search for Christian unity. I hope that we will be a community that reaches out to others. In practice, this means such things as effective RCIA programs, support groups for those who are searching for faith, and a warm and welcoming attitude in the entire community. I hope that we will be successful in welcoming our most recently arrived immigrants and that, within the context of our Catholic faith and the Church's living tradition, we will come to a better awareness of the gifts of women in the Church. I know that it won't be realized without pain. The dialogue with women in the Church requires wisdom, courage, and perseverance, so that there will be no winners, no losers, but only people confirmed in their shared discipleship to Jesus Christ.

I hope that we will continue to speak out clearly and persuasively on life issues, whether it be an unborn child whose life may be terminated by abortion, an aged person threatened by euthanasia, or noncombatants in war at serious risk because of indiscriminate bombing. I hope that the quality of our worship, especially the Sunday Eucharist, will grow greatly and that we will find more effective ways of handing on the faith to our young people. I hope that the Church will be home to rigorous intellectual inquiry and to creative explorations of imagination. And, finally, I hope that in the future, we will teach one another to pray better.

This is my deepest experience of the Church: people gathered together with a rich heritage of the past, with present struggles and celebration, with future hope.

· 4 ·

R. Peter Bowman: Mega-Pastor, Delegator

St. James Church, Arlington Heights, Illinois, is not the biggest parish in the U.S. There are parishes in New York, Brooklyn, and Los Angeles with over 5,000 households. According to Francis K. Scheets, O.S.C., a Catholic priest and church planning and management specialist, the average Catholic parish with two or more clergy has 1,719 households with 5,349 members. Officially, St. James has three full-time priests, although one has been on a six-month sabbatical. The core staff includes a full-time religious sister who preaches every Sunday and "hears" confessions. She is considered by the vast majority of parishioners as an associate pastor. The parish community would readily call her to orders. There is one part time "in residence" priest, and the pastor emeritus, who retired in 1978.

St. James has 3,800 families, over 14,000 people, and is still growing. The average parish with two-plus priests in the U.S. has one priest for 692 households or 2,149 parishioners. The core clerical staff at St. James, including Sister Kathleen, average 950 households or 3,500 parishioners per cleric. (In 1948, when the parish reached 400 families, the pastor requested and got a curate. Dioceses are now closing or merging parishes under 500 units. Most parishes under 200 units or 550 people no longer have a full time priest. The average Episcopalian, Lutheran, or Methodist parish with two or more clergy are all measurably smaller than the Catholic parishes now being merged. In the 1940s, some Chicago megaparishes had as many as twelve priests. As recently as 1980, the ratio of clergy to laity in the Chicago church was 1 to 943. The national average is now one priest to every 1,954, six times the ratio of Lutheran minister to parishioners.

By 1992, the parish expects to lose one full-time priest and, by the turn of the century, the most optimistic prediction is that there will be only two full-time priests. The pastor will be seventy years old (retirement age) and the associate will be fifty-five.

The archdiocese of Chicago listed 866 active priests and 423 parishes in 1989. Since 1984, it has been losing a priest every eighteen days through death, retirement, or resignation. In 1990, it ordained five, the smallest number in the history of the diocese. In the same year, it announced the closing of thirty-eight churches. More closings will follow. By 2005, there will be only 400 active priests to minister to over 2.5 million Catholics. While the decline of priests across the nation is expected to be 34 percent by the year 2005, the decline in the Chicago Church could reach 55 percent. Further, by 2005 only 12 percent of the clergy will be under thirty-five. The majority of active clergy will be over fifty-five.

Peter Bowman has been pastor since 1978. After two six-year terms, archdiocesan guidelines called for his resignation. However, the cardinal, Joseph L. Bernardin, has been extending virtually all twelve-year pastors. Bowman also serves as area dean to twenty-six parishes, a position that requires increasing amounts of his time.

In spite of the clerical shortage, Bowman pastors very effectively. He is a master delegator to a large and efficient staff. St. James has a $2,000,000-plus budget, eight permanent deacons, over eighty organizations, a 700-student elementary school, and a large Religious Education program. Its parish bulletin is rarely less than sixteen pages and has reached thirty-two pages, including syndicated columns, wedding announcements (two hundred per year), baptisms, deaths, job opportunities, and a medley of services for the addicted, divorced, post abortion counseling, and a host of educational activities.

Peter Bowman may be among the last priests in America, but he is getting enormous mileage out of his priesthood.

I didn't become a diocesan priest for very noble reasons. I was the ninth of ten children. Then, there were my parents and a maiden aunt who lived with us in Oak Park. Thirteen of us and only two bathrooms! I graduated from Loyola Academy and spent two years at Loyola University, all with the Jesuits. My brother, David, entered the Jesuits, so I thought about them a great deal. But I was still dating while I was at the academy and, at the university, I came to the conclusion that I was more attracted to parish work than to teaching. Besides, the thought of sharing bathrooms with 150 guys was more than I could stand! At the archdiocesan seminary, each seminarian had his own bathroom. That was terribly attractive!

Seriously, there were lots of good influences that brought me to the priesthood. I was never an altar boy, but we went to weekly confession. Our parents had lots of clergy friends. My mother was very active in the parish.

My father worked at the old Stevens Hotel (now the Chicago Hilton and Towers). He brought a sense of service and an orientation to people. There were good priests at Ascension and I recall a mission speaker from Savannah who came to the parish and spoke of the need for diocesan priests. In a matter of six weeks, I told my parents and visited Packy Ryan at Mundelein [the University of St. Mary of the Lake, the seminary operated by the archdiocese of Chicago].

I can still recall my mother saying: "I think you ought to stay at least a month." Another one of my brothers had left the Jesuits after only one week. He's got eleven kids now. It serves him right! (Laughs.)

I've never had any serious doubts since, at least none that would give me ulcers. Sure, celibacy isn't easy, but my widowed sister once told me that you can't even know loneliness until you've lost your spouse. She's leading a celibate life now. You can't have it all.

I was ordained in 1955. There were forty of us. Four or five are dead and we lost a few along the way, but there are still thirty of us. I think one of the things that kept us in was our closeness. We met every Wednesday and still do. But when I was at Victory [Our Lady of Victory], the other associate was a classmate and Zock [Monsignor Raymond F.] wouldn't let both of us go out on the same night. I was already taking some time with the CCD office, so I told my classmate to go. I kind of fell away from the Wednesday get togethers. I guess I could have done better at it, but I've found community in the rectory. Life in the rectory has been a problem for some priests, never for me.

When we were ordained, celibacy and priesthood were not separate questions. They are now and rightly so. The older I get, some of the pain of priesthood is knowing that I will leave no children behind. I quote my father a lot. He was a celebrator. Mom was the supreme organizer, and celebration and organization are what parish life is all about. When people called me "Father," I used to give a wiseguy answer. "I'm not your father," I used to say. Now I don't deny the reality of that title.

I've learned that a priest only has to be a supreme listener. I know that you have to be careful here. People will take advantage. But that's what the priesthood is for. I must first be a priest, not an administrator.

The years before St. James have prepared me. At St. Denis, I was just breaking in, but the people there taught me how to be a priest. At Lawrence O'Toole, I got interested in Vatican II. At Victory, I wasted a lot of time with the kids in the teen club. It was good. At Timothy's, I spent nine years doing parish work, working in the CCD [Confraternity of Christian Doctrine] office and getting a Masters at the Pastoral Institute at Loyola. It all prepared me for this parish.

Jim Doyle [Chicago priest] taught a lot of us that good pastoring was being there for your people on Sunday morning, going to wakes and visiting the hospitals. That's 80 percent of it. Sure, it can get tiring. Last Saturday, I buried a parishioner and then said three wedding Masses. On Sunday, I had my two Sunday Masses and a third Mass for the Theology on Tap (a young adult) group. That's seven Masses on a weekend and that's not too uncommon. But I don't feel burned out. I take my day off. And I took my vacation with my sister and brother up in Lake Geneva, Wisconsin. I sleep well. I don't have any relaxing hobbies, just some occasional light reading. But I'm not tired. I love what I'm doing.

What would I like to do soon? I'd like to go back to school for some study and I want very much to make a thirty-day retreat. I've got to get to that. I like being a dean, but I'd never want the dean's job to become full- time. I'd much rather be pastor.

I guess you could say that we're the new version of the old St. Mel's. When Doc Purcell was pastor there, they had a dozen priests. We've got only two here most of the time, along with a resident and the former pastor and eight permanent deacons.

I don't know if I'd want to spend less time with marriage preparation. Sure, they sometimes come here with some very thin links to the parish. Sometimes, they just say "I like your church." But I have found that they are good people. I know that there is evil in the world but I find little of it with the people who come to us. Perhaps I'm naive but if you say "no" to them, it dictates what's going to happen after that.

You know, as Dick Westley [a Loyola University philosopher] says, the Church is a gift. It's not necessary for salvation. I'm not a policeman and I don't want to be one. Priests are supposed to help people reconnect. The goal of the Church is to help people live well.

John Cusick [a Chicago priest] likes to say that when he was growing up he didn't know what it meant to be Catholic, but that it felt good. I suppose that the modern jargon is "bonding." I believe that parish life only begins to make sense when someone puts down roots—kids or a mortage. I'm attracted to what Andy Greeley [priest, sociologist, author] writes about parish life. I haven't read his novels but his other writings have influenced me. Andy believes in the parish school. So do I. There is great trust in us from the parents. We've got over seven hundred in the school. There are a lot in CCD classes, but the bonding isn't the same.

Money does make a difference here. We're not rich. We're still paying off a $250,000 debt, but we can afford the things that make a difference. Our music budget may be larger than any parish in the diocese except Holy Name [Cathedral], but it's worth it. Our Sunday liturgies are first class.

Talking about the priesthood is like talking about falling in love. It's a marriage between the people and the priest. And I can't exaggerate the myth role of priest as father and pastor. I just love Sunday mornings. Celebrating the Eucharist is like a ritual of lovemaking.

You know, Bill McCready [sociologist] says that a pastor is a myth builder, a guarantor, a grandfather. Some of the kids here actually call me "gramps." I don't mind. I've learned never to sweat the small stuff and, over the years, I've come to realize that it's all small stuff.

Criticism bothers me. So I try to anticipate it. I try to think ahead. Just now, for example, we're trying to open a shelter for the homeless. There are suburban homeless. They sleep in their cars or at the train station. The police often send them here and I'm glad that they do. The police look to the parish. We had a voucher system but we've got to do more. Anyway, we announced the shelter in our bulletin at least three times. I wrote about it in my pastor's notes, too. Then, we told the people again from the pulpit. We visited all the homes that border on the parish property and informed the people. We headed off complaints by communicating. We got a lot of support.

As pastor, I'll speak to anybody. I'll deal with anybody, but I won't leap frog. We have people here whom I trust. They're not yes people. They'll challenge the pastor. They provide a context out of which we all work. We've got office hours and, at night, a phone answering service. I hate those recordings. They're too depersonalizing. We use them only on Saturday nights because most of the calls then are about Mass times. And I've got a beeper that can reach me anywhere. I return my phone calls. It's important.

In some ways, I'm the wandering gossip here. I talk about things before they happen and that gets things going. Our ninetieth anniversary is coming soon. I think we ought to do something, and, somehow, we've got to do something about the bigness of this place.

The future for the priesthood? I'm an optimist, I guess. I believe that the Lord will take care of his church. I think that we could survive with only one priest here. We must delegate even more. Somehow, things will work out.

· 5 ·

Patrick J. Brennan: Evangelizer

One of Pat Brennan's friends describes him as "beyond burnout." Sometimes forgetful, always late, always weary-looking, he overschedules and overcommits. He would like to be a pastor but is drawn to the work of his office, the workshops, writing, travel, and people he meets. He is constantly reimagining parish life, striving in his own words to be more of a "magician" than a "warrior." He is president and founder of the National Center for Evangelization and Renewal and director of the Office for Evangelization for the archdiocese of Chicago. He is the author of four books, the most recent titled *Re-Imagining the Parish* (Crossroad, New York). When not traveling to give workshops, he lives at St. Michael's Parish, Orland Park, Illinois.

I just got a nice letter from the archbishop of Los Angeles [Roger M. Mahony]. He told me that he spent nearly two days of his vacation reading my last book. That's nice to hear. He said he didn't agree with all of it, but it feels good to know that you've had an impact. I sent the letter up to the cardinal [Joseph L. Bernardin] and learned that he's reading the book, too.

We've lost only three or four of our ordination class. There were forty of us. I think it's because we had some really strong modeling about what good priests looked like. We were sort of a bridge class that began in the old seminary and emerged in the new. We were rooted in the old ways but formed in the new. We were ethnic and Catholic to the very fiber of our being. We were at the older end of the baby boom population, ordained in 1973 after eight to twelve years of seminary training. In the last seventeen years, I've come up to the wire a number of times, but I didn't bolt. I acquired something of the Gorman style [John R. Gorman is the former rector of Chicago's major seminary, now vicar general and auxiliary bishop of the archdiocese]. We've had a hyphenated priesthood, that is, we were encouraged to do other things as well as our priesthood.

The Church has been a discouraging organization to live with. The bishops' image is turning from that of shepherd to one of corporate raider. We learned to be selfstarters, to have some motivation from within. But that has changed to a centralized mode. Now, after ten years in this office, I don't know if I can turn it around. I thought I was doing things right. I've brought some of the best people in the world to speak here, but little has changed. They're doing an organizational study in this pastoral center now. They've brought in Price Waterhouse. I don't feel that I've been listened to. Perhaps what I have reported intuitively, the Price Waterhouse study will say officially.

My ministry was born in pain. When I was in my early twenties, still in the seminary, I had a breakdown. Perhaps it was rooted in some genetic problems. Whatever the case, I was suffering from anxiety and agoraphobia (a fear of open spaces). I was stable but unpredictable. I started to choke on it all. So, I went to Jack Gorman [seminary rector and a clinical psychologist] and told him that I should leave. Instead he invited me into therapy.

The therapy experience helped me to break through the Southside of Chicago God to the God of the Scriptures, the God of Luke 23:46 ("Father, into your hands I commend my spirit") and of I John 23:18 ("There is no fear in love, but perfect love drives out fear, and so one who fears is not yet perfect in love").

I think I left the priesthood twice. I left the clerical priesthood during my first assignment at St. Hubert's. The people there were all young. Families all seemed to be about thirty-three years old. "Get out of the ontological priesthood," they seemed to be saying to me. "Get into priesthood." I got into small group work and became the Director of Religious Education. I found a therapeutic approach to spirituality. The toxicity of rectory life there allowed me to get the clerical priesthood out of my system, but it hurt to leave that kind of priesthood. It meant that I was dropped by a number of my clerical friends.

The experience taught me something. I came to see the superficiality of seminary friendships. We were barely out of the seminary and guys were buying vacation homes where they could live together, apart from lay people. I asked why I wasn't being included in these vacation home deals and was told: "No, Pat, you'll bring parents and kids and turn the place into a retreat house."

In the years that followed, I was greatly influenced by Jack Shea [Chicago priest, seminary prof, author, and speaker]. He gave me the words and the vision for the things that I was doing intuitively and taught me how lay people could assume control of the parish. The new seminary is the parish, you know. Phil Murnion [National Pastoral Life Center] says that, too.

I didn't even interview for my second parish. I just took an assignment to St. Albert the Great in Burbank. The parish was living in the ecclesial Middle

Ages. There were no women in the sanctuary. The pastor had at least twelve people giving Communion at the altar rail. I was still a mixture of timidity and assertiveness, but the situation there caused me to reach what my coworker, Dawn Mayer, calls "tipping point" anger.

Partly because of the demands of the place, I got into psychological training at the Adler Institute. The profs there are predominantly Jewish, but they have an understanding of things Catholic.

Cardinal Cody asked me to come to the Pastoral Center in 1979. I really wanted to stay in the parish, but I naively said "yes." I thought that I could really do something.

The next two years were awful. The cardinal was growing more and more paranoid. One always had to get his personal permission even to do a mailing and one could only use his approved mailing list. But after a little while, I had compiled a list of my own. I would use my mailing list first. They were people who were really interested.

We planned our first "Jesus Day." The cardinal made me change the name because he felt that "Jesus Day" sounded too Protestant. In that same year, he moved our office right into this chancery. He wanted more control. It was then that I realized that the Evangelization Office was simply window dressing. He didn't really want anything done. He just wanted an office he could point to.

We used his mailing list but we counted on the one we had developed. Before we used his lists, we already had 1,100 people registered. Cody was furious. He called me "headstrong." We had to do everything on the sly. There were just no support systems.

One day I was called to his mansion. He wanted to chide me for something or other. At the time, the federal government was virtually on his doorstep, ready to indict. I telephoned and suggested that the cardinal might want to defer our meeting in view of his own, more pressing problems. But I was told that the cardinal insisted that I be at the mansion. The place was crawling with lawyers. He was having trouble with his legs at the time and had people nursing him. But he brought me in; wagged his finger at me and told me that I was an incorrigible priest. It was unreal.

I left the institutional Church at that point. The paradox is that I'm still here in the central office and that Cardinal Bernardin has asked me to stay on.

In those years, a different kind of priesthood emerged. I began to use the term "ordained ministry" for the priesthood. Anyone trying to be above or below other forms of ministry is neurotic. There is something very neurotic about any organization that sends someone away for twelve years to convince him that he is special. This is institutional neurosis. I made that statement to a group of bishops some time ago. They laughed. Sadly, we still have that Tridentine view of church.

During this time, celibacy became a great crisis. I became very, very lonely. I needed a close relationship with a woman. I got into more therapy. I fell in love.

It was the most painful period in my life. What it revealed was not so much the need for genital sex as for companionship. The relationship was, and has remained, chaste and celibate. I felt the void of having no kids. I have a strong ascetical streak and cultural roots. I can make a decision that is painful. But this wasn't an academic issue. I made a decision, but the pain of that decision has gotten worse. It was a process of letting go. It still scares me. But the love is still there.

The demons come up when I go on vacation. I am a host on vacation, inviting friends and relatives. There are couples there with children and sometimes the woman I love. She's married now. We are still friends. I'm a real crier. When they leave, I cry. When my young nieces leave, I cry. Forty-three to forty-five is a tough age. I've spent a lot of time in recent years taking care of my folks. Now, I'm wondering who will be there for me.

I valued that struggle. It showed me that I had the capacity for intimacy. I think I learned a lot about sacrificial love. I love someone so much and realize it's better if she go. It's been better for the person but not for me.

I think I have a charism for preaching. Certainly, a deep part of me would be lost if I couldn't preach. I think that I can help people experience God in their lives. It has come largely through suffering. This role has allowed me to grow into what Church could be.

This office is a perch from which I can do some writing and speaking. The church is crumbling. The present structure is unfixable. A new structure is needed. While still the place where the action is, when it comes to spirituality and faith, the parish is experiencing difficulties. There's a shortage of priests and religious; a significant number of so-called believers who no longer worship or relate to a faith community; others who are only minimally involved in the parish community by way of Mass attendance; a misguided young adult population often motivated more by wallet than conscience; a great unevenness among congregations and celebrants in the quality of liturgy; and school and CCD programs that seem to fail in achieving their mission.

The parish many of us knew and loved as we grew up is inadequate to meet the evangelical needs of believers in the future. We hear lots of Vatican II language and we've had an explosion of lay ministries, but the paradigm for parish remains pretty much the same as it was for our grandparents: child-centered, school, and CCD programs and organizations. That structure was institutionalized almost a century ago. With all the social changes that our age has witnessed, that structure simply isn't as effective as it once was.

I've got three lenses to offer for future parish life. I've been advocating small intentional communities, an emphasis on adult faith formation, and an expanded family consciousness in parish ministries.

Being a Chicago-born Irish Catholic, I hold the parish to be one of the loves of my life. Even if I were not an ordained minister, I think that my personal spirituality would motivate me to be highly invested in the parish in which I would reside. I think that the parish can change. I believe that it has to change. The small communities, adult faith formation, and family involvement in parish ministries are already happening.

The creative burden is on our imagination. We need to adapt models, to create new models, ones that fit the local situation. Imagination is the prophetic artist of the future. What we imagine will eventually become reality and others will institutionalize it. Then it will lose passion again and we will have to reimagine all over again.

Imagination is a great gift. It's a holy gift. There is not so much failure in this life as there is learning from evaluating, then reshaping and trying again.

· 6 ·

Thomas P. Cahalane: FBI (Foreign-Born Irish)

When Barry Fitzgerald won the Best Supporting Actor Academy Award for his portrayal of the eldery Irish pastor in *Going My Way* in 1944 (Bing Crosby was named Best Actor, Leo McCarey Best Director, and the movie itself Best Film), he capsulized the role of the immigrant Irish priest in the extraordinary growth of the American Catholic Church. Fitzgerald's character had built a parish and established an elementary school. Inferentially, he was a political force in the neighborhood, capable of nudging City Hall or the cop on the beat who shared his faith and his brogue. He understood the political axiom that one hand washes the other and his Irish conscience wasn't terribly troubled if he dipped into the Altar and Rosary Society's funds for a dollar to treat his curates to a game of golf. Such benign infractions were what made the parish work. Crude stereotypes perhaps, but the nearly fifty-year old movie still warms cockles.

From the earliest French and Spanish missionaries to the present diminished numbers of Polish, Indian, and Asian priests, the immigrant priest has had a profound impact on the American Church. The foreign-born Irish clergy, affectionately nicknamed the FBI, have had the greatest influence. Although there are more Latino-Americans and German-Americans in the U.S. Catholic Church, it is the Irish who put their stamp on the American Church, particularly on its clergy.

When great numbers of their people did not follow them to the New World, the Spanish and French clergy withdrew. They were replaced by German and Irish priests, brothers and sisters, whose people were arriving in great numbers, particularly after the Great Irish Famine of the 1840s and between the years 1880–1920 (cf. John Tracy Ellis chapter).

For a great many complex reasons, the Irish quickly gained the advantage. First, there was their deep faith, one that resonated with the Vatican's, although the Irish have traditionally had a disdain for the

Vatican bureaucracy. (Rome has reciprocated. The Irish are vastly un-
derrepresented at the Vatican; even the number of officially canonized
Irish-born saints would not form enough to hold a game of bridge.)
Irish priests spoke English; they followed their people to the big cities
where they quickly climbed the episcopal ladder. They came "across the
pond," as Monsignor Cahalane describes his crossing, with little
thought of returning. Most fell in love with their new country, becoming more American than the Americans themselves. (The famous Archbishop John Ireland of St. Paul often rebuked his non-Irish clergy for
their isolationism and the suspicion of American ways they communicated to their people. Ireland was recruiting Irish people by the
boatload.) Unlike other sending countries, there was little for the Irish
priest to return to; the country was devastated by famine; it had a
surplus of priests. At "home," as the romantic Irish clergy term their
native land, there were many incentives for entering the seminary: it was
a step up the economic ladder and many steps up the educational ladder;
priests enjoyed almost universal respect; the village priest was the acknowledged authority on many topics beyond his theology; a son in the
priesthood eased the financial burden of a farm family and raised its
social status; the English-imposed laws required that property be passed
to the oldest son, thus sending other sons abroad or to the cloth; the
Irish faithful supported the seminaries that sent men to the foreign
missions. So it went.

After a time, the system began to feed on itself. Irish clergy who had
become bishops, chancery officials, or prominent pastors, returned to
Ireland to recruit others. Even non-Irish bishops such as the famous
Juan Bautista Lamay of Santa Fe, a Frenchman, missionary, and prime
civilizer of the frontier Southwest, recruited priests from Ireland. At one
time, less than fifty years ago, 80 percent of the clergy in the Archdiocese
of Los Angeles were Irish-born. The Spanish-founded and still predominantly Latino diocese is presently led by Roger M. Mahony, who
succeeded Timothy Manning (FBI), who followed James McIntyre and
John J. Cantwell (FBI).

The American clergy also benefited from immigrant Irishmen who
entered American seminaries, sometimes after an aborted seminary experience back home. The huge numbers in the Irish seminary system
produced a certain arrogance among the seminary faculties. A candidate
could be expelled for flunking Latin or failing to understand Aquinas's
strangulating sentences. Rigid seminary rules often grated on independent personalities and caused them to leave, emmigrate, and enter
American seminaries where the climate was less controlling. This author
has interviewed FBI priests who were dismissed from Irish seminaries

for smoking (disobedience) or for consistently beating their rectors in handball (lacking in humility.) One was "sent away" for having a thin cushion on the seat of the desk chair in his room (a luxury); another for knowing how many windows were in the chapel (failure to guard one's eyes); a third for joking about the fact that, on Sundays, the roosters were separated from the hens in the seminary's coop ("talking filth"); a fourth for neglecting to don the tattered cassock that was recommended to be worn while taking a weekly shower (immodesty). All had "come out" to the U.S. and, through the enormously effective clerical network, were adopted by more tolerant bishops who, in one Los Angeles monsignor's words "were damn glad to have us." (One monsignor from West Virginia was working as a longshoreman on the New York docks when the man who would be his bishop walked right on the dock and said: "Put down that hook. You've got a vocation.") "I think," said another more reflective priest who had been told that he did not have a vocation for his Irish diocese because his uncle had committed suicide, "that it was the Holy Spirit's way of spreading us around." (Irish seminaries had no monopoly on clerical arrogance. The famous Father Flanagan of Boys Town was dismissed from New York's archdiocesan seminary because he showed little promise in a seminary culture that had new priests wearing top hats to their ordination.)

It would be difficult to calculate their numbers. For years, dioceses rarely even gathered, much less shared, such information. Although they had been meeting annually since 1919, serious data collection began only after the National Conference of Catholic Bishops was formally established in 1966, and would not likely include precise ethnic data on the clergy.

Whatever the case, Thomas P. Cahalane represents the last in a century-and-a-half- long procession of immigrant Irish priests who, to use another Irish idiom, "put the sign of their hand" on the American Church.

I go home across the pond every year. I tell my parishioners that it's my graduate course in the brogue.

My name is a rare one, very much confined to West Cork or Kerry. You can go anywhere in the world and, if you meet a Cahalane, he'll be from West Cork or Kerry. It means "battle full" or "battle ready" in Gaelic; it's pronounced "Cathlain" back home.

I'm from Glandore in the west of County Cork. It's a rural area, mixed farming. It's one of the most picturesque places in Ireland. It's near the sea. I grew up with a great love for the sea and now, here I am, in the desert. My mother is still back there; she was born in 1900; she lives with my married sister. I still have a bachelor brother there, another in London, and another in Cork City. There's another brother who died over there. I'm the only one to come out.

I went to one of the National Schools out in the country, an old school built after the Famine. It had an enrollment of only thirty to forty. When it came time for high school, I went to Farranferris, a diocesan seminary high school in Cork. It was just a glorified high school. Its basic purpose was to form potential vocations; only five to ten each year went on to the seminary.

I'm from the diocese of Ross, a tiny diocese that was suppressed in 1958. It had only eleven parishes, but the suppression caused a lot of controversy. The Diocese of Ross dated to 700 or 800. There are people back there now who still raise the issue. We're now called the Diocese of Ross and Cork, but it's not the same.

I had a desire to be a priest since high school, but not necessarily for the home missions. My sense was that there was a glut of priests in Ireland; we were overstocked. The diocese often sent the newly ordained out to England or some other place for four or five years until an opening came up at home. Then, they'd bring the man back.

In my final year of high school, I made up my mind to go to the foreign missions. I responded to the offer to come to Arizona because I had a priest cousin, Cornelius Cahalane, who came out here in 1950. He's retired now, back home. He came home that year and told me about Arizona. I knew very little about the place except what I read in *Arizona Highways* and what I heard from my cousin. It was a great leap of faith. The bishop of Tucson was Daniel J. Gercke. We had never met. I could have gone off to Australia; there was an uncle there. But I chose Tucson.

The bishops or someone from their dioceses used to come to the Irish seminaries and talk to us about the foreign missions. Often, the choice for a certain place was tied to the man who did the best marketing. The seminarians went with the bishop who could get the fish biting.

I went on to St. Patrick's Seminary in Carlow. It's the oldest English-speaking seminary in the world; they'll celebrate their two hundredth anniversary in 1993. The preponderence of the men there were for the foreign missions. Maynooth was the seminary for those preparing for the home missions, although St. Pat's had some, too. All Hallows in Dublin, St. Kieran's in Kilkenny, St. Peter's in Wexford, all prepared priests for the foreign missions. St. Pat's was supported by the diocese. There was some money from parents and from the adopting bishop.

Thirty of us were ordained in 1963. At least twenty came out. They're all over the place, England, the U.S., Australia, South America, New Guinea. I really don't know how many were ordained in Ireland each year for the foreign missions. At its height, there might have been two hundred from Maynooth and thirty to forty from each of the other seminaries each year. If you say that years ago Ireland ordained upwards of eight hundred each year for both the home missions and the foreign missions, I would have to say that eight hundred is a bit on the high side. Perhaps it was five hundred all told. I really don't know. But after Vatican II, the falloff began to happen.

In Ireland just now, they're trying to amalgamate the seminaries. There has been a great change in the life style of the country. The people are more affluent. There's been a much more radical change in the priesthood there than the changes we are coming to terms with here. The celibacy issue is there too. There might be a desire for the priesthood among the young people, but the permanent commitment is a challenge.

The clericalism that is part of the priestly life style there is more of a hindrance than a positive incentive. There's the clerical mind set, an exclusivity that is formed around the priest. The basic style of leadership in the clerical culture is very often the autocratic style, and that's both here and at home. Of course, there's more of it back in Ireland, but clericalism is alive and well in the U.S. It's still being passed on through the formation process. It's not deliberately focused that way, but it ends up that way. It's still not an open church with a shared model of leadership.

When I came out, I thought I was coming to a missionary area in the United States. I thought the Church was just establishing itself in the West. I thought I'd be dealing with Native Americans. I soon learned that the Franciscans did that.

I was ordained the week that John XXIII died. It was midway through the Council. I was ordained for a pre-Vatican II church. We weren't aware of all the changes that would come. For the first six months to a year, I said Mass in Latin with my back to the people. Then, the altar turned 'round and the vernacular came in. It wasn't as radical a change as some would let on, but it caused some upset. I remember saying a youth Mass one evening. The adults came into the church and stole all the folk songs. They came to me after Mass and asked: "Father, will you take away that ironing board you're using for an altar and give us back our old Mass?"

I was stationed in Scottsdale from 1963 to 1967. Then I went to a mining town called San Manuel, about seventy miles northeast of Tucson. There were three churches in three small towns there; it was a mixed population, miners, company people, Latinos. I was an associate in three parishes.

In 1967, I came to St. Augustine's Cathedral in Tucson. I took over the CYO, they called it "youth ministry" later, in 1971, and I became vicar for education in the diocese in 1983. During the mid-seventies, I did a masters in education, guidance, and counseling at the University of Arizona. In 1981, I was named the fifth pastor of Our Mother of Sorrows here in Tucson, and retained my duties in education.

This parish opened in 1958. We are around 2,500 families. I've got two other priests with me and we have five others on the staff. We're a unique community these days. This is the fourth year in a row that we've had an ordination in the parish. And we've got six in the seminary, four of them for the diocese. The man to be ordained from this parish in June is a former Lutheran minister who came into the Church in 1989. He took a sabbatical some years ago and took a course in Ireland with thirty or forty priests. He came into the Church soon after. I just visited a young lady, another convert from the parish, who had taken her first vows as a Trappistine sister.

Our Mother of Sorrows is a very active parish. I try to promote lay leadership. The greatest leadership potential is dormant within the body of the Church. Very often, when we pray for vocations, we pray with a one-track mind. We pray only for priests and sisters. God may be answering our prayers but we may not be listening. The greatest resource in the Church is the human resource. Unless we shift these human resources into leadership models, we're going to remain stranded with the clerical model of leadership. We'll be far less effective than we can be.

I'm not sure that I'm a liberal. I like to describe myself as open to the Spirit that is operating within the body of the Church. There was a time when I saw myself as having all the answers. I didn't have too many questions. I was the giver of God's grace to people. Now, that position has changed radically. I'm not a Lone Ranger priest anymore. I've found out that the Lone Ranger's place is a very lonely place to be. I've found that, by involving the laity, the support base I now have has broadened and strengthened me. Lay involvement has only served to enhance my role as a priest. In my own reflections, I've come to the conclusion that there is a great need to develop a trusting relationship between the pastor and his parishioners. The more I communicate, the more I feel I am building a linkage of trust. The more you invite, the more trusting the environment. The spirit of the Lord simply blossoms.

Now, all that translates into accountability, not only of financial resources but also of human resources. Here at the parish, in October of each year we have an entire process, one that gets people to renew or join one of the apostolates in the parish. Then, we have a formation process. Too often, you know, in the past we have simply pirated people. We've let them work until they've burned themselves out. If we are to succeed, we must have self-growth and spiritual growth. We try to spiritualize the process, to make volunteering an integral part of the baptismal call. It's the Lord who is calling them, after all. The call may come from the pastor, but ultimately, it is the Lord. He's in charge of the Church.

I'm thinking of John XXIII who would say before he went to bed: "Lord, this is your Church. I'm tired. I'm going to bed right now." That's how we must see it.

We've had as many as 700 to 800 people involved in some form of ministry. We try to have a turnover of leadership every three years. We don't want people to stagnate or get power hungry.

The foreign-born Irish priests are a dying breed in Arizona. We're moving toward our own priests. In Tucson, we had fourteen ordained for the diocese in the past three years. That's pretty good for a diocese this size. [Tucson has 294,000 Catholics, 111 diocesan priests, 63 parishes.] It's difficult to say why, but I think that a solid family life and Catholic schools are the seedbed of vocations. We have 460 children in our grammar school.

We have devotions. We have exposition of the Blessed Sacrament twice each week. It brings the people in. We try to create a prayerful environment. We promote the belief that God is present in the Eucharist. We asked our people why they stay Catholic and our poll validated all the things that Andrew Greeley says. They come because of Eucharist, because we are a sacramental people. God reveals himself to us because of the sacramentality of the Church. What we do here may not be the particular style of devotion for the pastor. That doesn't matter. Our job is to produce a smorgasbord for our people. We're not to decide for our people what's best for them. The Church has always promoted devotions. They adopted and adapted pagan rituals and blessed them. A parish can never create enough opportunities for the needs of the people. It doesn't matter how many people come, whether it's five or five hundred. Our job is to just do it and leave the rest to the Lord.

Since 1987, we've been doing a six-week process known as Alienated Catholics Anonymous. Quite a number of people who came to this wanted to be reaffiliated but didn't know how to connect. So, at Christmas and Easter, the two times that alienated Catholics are minded to come to Church, we announce these evenings. At first, it was only for three weeks, a meeting each week. But when it was over, they said they wanted more, so we stretched it to six weeks. It's a very simple process, little more than an open forum. We ask them to complete questions such as "I am here for . . ." or "My feelings about the Church are . . ." Then we develop a profile and that becomes our agenda.

People, you know, are looking for reconciliation. If we're not doing that, we're missing our main call. Then, there's marriages and remarriages. About a third of the marriages we see aren't blessed by the Church. I bring in the graduates of Alienated Catholics Anonymous and they tell the others of their experience. The program sells itself. When it's all over, we have a Mass and a party, a banquet for the prodigal sons and daughters who have returned.

I love these open forums and my random phone calls. Some nights, I simply pull a dozen parishioners' cards from the files, especially new parishioners, and I call them. It doesn't take an hour and I learn a great deal. They're always glad to get the call. It builds the community. I see them at Mass the next Sunday and they tell me that they appreciated my call.

I'm afraid that we're more concerned with preserving the institution than developing the potential within the Church. We seem to invest so much energy in making sure that everything is legally correct within the institutional framework. We forget what the Church is really all about.

As for my overall vision, I'm drawn to that statement by George Bernard Shaw, the one about people who see things and ask "why?" and those who see things and ask "why not?" The Spirit asks us to dream, to ask "why not?"

Clericalism as we know it today must die. The clerical structure must open its eyes. Isn't it the Lord who has the final say anyway? The Lord has time on His side. It may be difficult for us to accept all this, but this is the Church of the Lord. We must read the signs of the times and follow through.

We do a good job in talking about leadership of the laity, but we're not actually shifting our resources. We're turning out fewer trained laity than we need; we're not serious about developing lay leadership within the Church. We're simply not taking advantage of the lay resources that the Spirit is giving us.

My observation is that the larger dioceses have become so institutionalized with layers and layers of bureaucracies that they have little relevance to the grass roots. We're maintaining bureaucracies that simply aren't necessary. Here in Tucson, we've become a much simpler diocese. An investment in television that was washed away cost us a great deal of money, so we've had to simplify. Now, there is no bureaucracy to come down upon the parishes and the parishes are already getting stronger. People experience Church at the local level, not at the bureaucratic level.

The fullness of the priesthood is exercised in the midst of people. The longer it is isolated from the people, the more it will diminish. The power brokering and the formation of clerical kingdoms has nothing to do with the Kingdom of God. I've seen this from both sides. I've seen good men in the priesthood get isolated too easily. Their lives become unreal. We mustn't let that happen.

· 7 ·

Daniel M. Cantwell: Priest for the Laity

Most nights, Dan Cantwell eats alone in the rectory kitchen at Old St. Patrick's Church on the outer edge of Chicago's Loop. The seventy-five year-old monsignor lives there in active retirement. "I find it hard to believe that God takes pleasure in our loneliness," he observed in a manner that capsulized his views on celibacy. He has been speaking and writing about celibacy since the early 1970s. Always decades before other thinkers, he was writing about racial issues and the role of the laity in the Church by the early 1940s.

A half century ago, when a "pray, pay, and obey" Catholicism was preferred to social action, Cantwell was writing that it was much more important to ask if the Blessed Mother would sign a restrictive covenant or refuse to join a labor union than if she would smoke or chew gum. The pieties of that era placed more emphasis on chewing gum, especially for young women.

Monsignor Daniel M. Cantwell is a prophet with honor in both church and country. The honors, including five honorary degrees and Chicago's "Man of the Year," came years after his prophetic words and actions. Cantwell's priestly life has bracketed the most explosive period in the American church. Since his ordination in 1939, the church has evolved from a largely ethnic, missionary institution with a theological emphasis on piety and a muted voice on social issues to a post-Vatican II, socially concerned church that is still trying to retain aspects of its immigrant model.

After a year of parish work, Dan Cantwell was sent to Catholic University for two years of graduate work in sociology and the theology of liturgy. He returned to teach at the major seminary for five years, during which time he became involved with the Catholic Labor Alliance (later the Catholic Council on Working Life), Friendship House, and the Catholic Interracial Council. In 1947, the seminary faculty was taken over by the Jesuits and Cantwell moved to the Catholic Worker's Peter Maurin House, where he became involved full-time in social issues. It was decades before Martin Luther King, Jr. and the Civil Rights Act. It was still a time when a priest could get in trouble with his superiors by speaking in a union hall. But Cantwell picked his way through the minefields of political and ecclesiastical opposition. His soft-spoken but challenging words energized a generation of clergy and laity and nudged them out of their pious tranquillity.

When the late Cardinal John Cody arrived in Chicago, however, things began to change. Socially minded priests such as Cantwell found budgets cut and support staff vanishing. In 1966, he was named pastor of a black parish on Chicago's South Side, where he ministered for fifteen years. He wrote less but spoke more. His thrust was not only social justice in all its forms but also the freeing up of the laity to spread the kingdom of God. For over fifty years, he has preached that the service of the nonordained is every bit as important to God as the service of the ordained, a view that is so obvious that it seems impossible to believe that it continues to draw much opposition.

Dan Cantwell speaks slowly. There are often long pauses between thoughts, but when the words begin to flow, the content is so rich that it is difficult to get it all down. He remains a treasure of the American Church.

Yesterday, I had an interesting experience. I went to Mary and Tommy's house. The gathering was supposed to be about wine, but Mary had just gotten back from one of those shrines in Europe and she wanted to have a picture of the Sacred Heart dedicated. It was a ghastly picture. It would turn your stomach. I was uncomfortable just watching the ceremony and the picture, let alone being asked to lead it.

There was a college professor there. He saw himself as a great Scripture scholar or historian, something like that. He was expounding on what he had just discovered about Jesus. His speculation was so positive that it annoyed me. Perhaps what he said had merit factually. I don't know. But he shook everyone up, trying to show how far out he was. He was out of place.

So was I. I wanted no part of the Sacred Heart dedication or the professor. We belong to a community of such great diversity, I guess. We've got to learn to live with this diversity.

I just finished reading Dick Wesley's latest book, *Theology of Presence*. There are some awfully good things in there. He doesn't talk about celibacy directly. He talks about the whole mind set. It's in the human experiences that we find

God. Dick says that we're not just rational animals. We are incarnate spirits and we express this through our own bodies. Experience must be the important thing. If our theology books say one thing and our experience tells us another, then we've got to follow our experience.

It's that Holy Thursday revolution or something like that. Jesus was giving us a whole other meaning. He was doing away with structure. He was washing feet, but we never really accepted this.

Oh, I can't remember everything I read at my age, but I'm thinking of that woman and her husband who created a community of people, living a contemplative life. We've always had the monastic mindset. We couldn't believe that married couples could be contemplative. These are just some of the things that I've been thinking about.

After fifty-one years as a priest, I should know what a priest is, but I don't. Jack [Reverend John Wall, pastor] said once that what lights me up is liturgy. I do enjoy being the celebrant. But I can't do multiple liturgies the way we're expected to do today. I can do two. But after two, I'm just not with it. My homily suffers the most, I guess. I don't like weddings much now. But, after I get to know the couple, I get involved and, when the day comes, I come to like it.

You know, I wasn't in parochial work much at all until St. Clotilde's. I was trying to involve lay people and trying to get them to give love and service in the workplace all day. I wasn't doing things around a parish. It was laymen like Ed Marciniak and Russ Barta [Catholic lay leaders] who helped me to grow. They were my friends much more than the priests in my class. I guess that I never got into the clerical club. To this day, I have very few close priest-friends. And I don't know a lot of young priests. So, when I got to Clotilde's, I told the people that I was going to be the chaplain and that they would run the parish. But I didn't quite know how and I ended up trying to do everything. We didn't have any money. I wish I could have been like Jack Wall. He gets lay people involved at every level and turns it over to them. I've lived a happy life as a priest but it has not been a parish life.

I loved the years that I spent teaching at Mundelein [the University of St. Mary of the Lake, archdiocesan seminary]. But it didn't last long. The diocese put a lot of money in our education, but then moved us after a only few years. I suppose that if Reynie Hillenbrand had stayed on, we would have, too. We all enjoyed it. [Monsignor Reynold Hillenbrand was the legendary rector of the major seminary. He transformed seminary education in America, calling for an emphasis on liturgy and social concerns. In what is regarded as the worst mistake he made as archbishop, Cardinal Samuel A. Stritch, bowing to pressure from some priests and affluent laity, removed Hillenbrand from office in 1944. Cantwell was one of his chief disciples.]

Even after Reynie was moved to Sacred Heart, I enjoyed helping out there on Sundays and holy days. He had such taste; he got rid of all those terrible statues and replaced them with exquisite art. It was great to see how he went his way at being pastor.

I suppose that I could have branched out into other things but, when I was named to Clotilde's, I decided to make the best of it. I liked the people there. They were great people.

After Clotilde's, I went down to Moorfield, West Virginia, to be chaplain at the Vineyard, a self-supporting facility for retarded adults. Not long after I got there, the bishop asked me to be pastor of a small church. It was such a change from Chicago, where the numbers are so great. In Moorfield, there were only ninety Catholics in the entire county. There was some curiosity about me and some friendliness. I joined the local ministerial association and spoke in a Baptist church. But there was some animosity, too. When I walked through the hills, I didn't tarry.

In West Virginia, I had some health problems, including a little stroke. When Jack Wall wrote me, I felt it was time to come home. The cardinal [Joseph L. Bernardin] wrote me a nice letter and welcomed me home.

Priesthood and celibacy were one thing when I was ordained. Now, at this point in my life, I believe we were brainwashed. As I look back, I resent the whole thing. All those notions about women that were built into us are repulsive to me now, although it wasn't just the seminary training. I heard a woman say that Jesus would have nothing to do with a woman. Good Lord, what does she think of herself? When I think of the dirtiness we were told that we were; the dirtiness of our own bodies! And for years, I believed that and lived it! If there was pain in my life, it was caused by that. Yet, getting through it all was also a part of growth.

Now, I just can't understand the rationale of celibacy. Bernardin said that we've got to think this thing through and find a new rationale. But the pope still calls celibacy a closer way to come to Jesus. I challenge that. It's that mindset again. No human experience can validate what the pope said.

John Paul calls celibacy a sign of the Kingdom. As a sign, what does celibacy signify? That heaven is sexless? Am I to think that the resurrected body of Jesus is sexless? Is Mary's body sexless? Does Christian theology ask me to believe that? Are the loving human relationships established on earth and celebrated and deepened sexually to be terminated in the Father's house? If so, what is the point of the resurrection of the body?

You know, my first experience with married Catholic priests occurred in the Holy Land nearly thirty-five years ago when I lived for a few days with married Catholic priests of the Eastern Rite. Until that time, it was unthinkable for me that a man who went to bed with a woman, touched her, and was touched by her should then celebrate Eucharist. But in the Holy Land, there it was before my eyes: a Eucharist celebrated by a married priest every bit as holy, as valid, and as legitimate as when I celebrated!

Then, there were years of observing married ministers and married rabbis, as well as married Catholic couples, who by any human standard equal or surpass the work of the Kingdom that I have observed in my life or the lives of other celibates.

I search for the meaning of celibacy as symbol. I have yet to find it.

In the seminary, celibacy was presented in military terms. It was a discipline of the Church militant. I remember that the archbishop came and referred to the place as West Point. The full meaning of that symbol escaped me at the time. Yet, I can't help but recall that most members of the military exercise the option to marry without destroying the strength and security of the republic.

There is no superiority of one state over another. The Church proclaims that no married person is worthy to celebrate the Eucharist. The cause for this unworthiness puzzles me, spiritually, theologically, and sociologically. I'm also disturbed that, when married men serve as extraordinary ministers, they often dress up like celibate clergy.

I used to think that killing sexuality in my life gave a special glory to God. Celibates were special people; the Pharisees thought they were special people, too. But back then that was the only God I knew.

But the attitude remains. Some years ago, I heard a theologian address the presbyteral senate. He spoke of the ideals of the priesthood. There was no mention of the laity who were called to the same perfection. The holiness of the church is still in clerical hands! The unreality traces back to our seminary days when we never had to even do a dish, except on movie nights, when we did them so that the sisters could watch one of those stupid Mickey Rooney movies with us.

I like to think of the priests and laity as partners in the vineyard. Liturgy is the service of God, but so is the struggle for social justice. Priests are called to do Christ's work, but so are lay men and lay women. The sanctuary is a sacred place, but so is every factory, every workshop, every bus station, every crib, every bed.

Oh, it's been a good life, I suppose. I am now more convinced than ever that the secular is sacred, that the service of the nonordained is every bit as important to God as the service of the ordained.

No one can make you happy. You've got to make yourself happy. I still go to the reunions of my classmates. There is a sense of loyalty and we still have some theology in common. We avoid controversial issues; we generally just talk about our health. Bill McManus will always have something good to toss to us [William F. McManus, a classmate, is the retired bishop of Fort Wayne-South Bend].

I don't think that I would have bothered with a Golden Jubilee celebration without Eileen Durkin [a pastoral associate who coordinated the occasion]. I hate those concelebrated masses that only separate the clergy from the people. Thanks to her and all the others, it was a nice celebration.

Oh, I don't know. I suppose that I'd do it all again. The priesthood remains a mystery. It's been a great life.

I await new light.

· 8 ·

John C. Cusick: Minister to Young Adults

John Cusick has a salesman's hope and the intensity of a Little League coach. The mailing list for his young adult ministry now numbers 15,000. His "Theology on Tap" talks through the archdiocese of Chicago attract large turnouts. He may have the biggest "parish" in Chicago. His First Friday Club luncheons, sponsored jointly with the Center for Faith and Work at Old St. Patrick's Church, are sellouts. His newsletters are filled with cogent views and sensible solutions. He is an associate pastor at Old St. Patrick's in Chicago, a church that has increased from four registered parishioners to over 1,300 in less than ten years. Many are young adults, drawn to St. Pat's by Cusick's welcoming ministry.

I've said this before, but do you know what the Church needs right now for the Confirmation liturgy? They need someone standing next to the bishop. After he confirms each kid, this Confirmation minister can kiss each of them good bye.

We're losing them. And we're not getting most of them back. The level of their participation in the Mass and the sacraments sends many of their parents right up the wall. In the years between confirmation and getting married, young adults often don't see what the church has to offer them. I'll come back to that.

Just now, the institutional Church isn't paying any attention to its priests out in the trenches. After twenty years in the priesthood, I have no idea what the future holds. A priest ordained in 1940 could have guessed what the Church would be like in 1960. Never in a million years would I have guessed in 1970 what the situation would be in 1990!

As a deacon, I found myself in a rectory with seven guys and only six beds. So I moved. Today, the only place you're going to find seven priests living together is the cemetery!

I've been in young adult work since August, 1977. Before that, I spent nearly eight years at Niles [the college level seminary for the archdiocese of Chicago]. I was a residence hall director and was involved with recruiting and admissions. I was a fulltime body snatcher.

When I began doing young adult work, I found that I was doing the same things I did as a recruiter for the seminary. To young adults, I was attempting to call them to the Church. I've never had more fun. These are the people who at one time formed the basic activity of the Church. Priests worked with youths in Catholic organizations. It was the biggest part of their work. Today, young adults are the least present in the Church.

I think that young people just do not see the value of Church. It just does not speak to them. Sometimes what attracts young Catholics to Church can be found in their criticism. What they criticize is the preaching, the hospitality, and the music. They're not criticizing the word of God or the Eucharist. They want to develop the spirit side of their lives. They have been shaped and formed by television and rock music. Perhaps the secular pushes people to the spirit side. But when they come to church and find people who are there for over an hour with their coats on, they feel that they are just passing through.

Young adults are teaching the Church a lesson: they can live without us. The question is: Can the Church live without them?

I asked Jack Egan about this. [Monsignor John J. Egan, a priest of the Archdiocese of Chicago, was very active in Catholic Action movements during the 1940s, 1950s, 1960s.] His time was the golden age of young adult activity. He was in the Cana Conference and Christian Family Movement and urban affairs. He told me that the people he worked with were all young people, in their thirties at most. Today, those same people are still marching. They're in their sixties and seventies. They just changed the flags. But young people didn't follow them.

We've analyzed ourselves to death, but there is still no strategic planning. Now, the Church spends most of its energies trying to get out of a financial crisis.

People didn't get into these activities years ago without a reason. They had religious needs and the Church appealed to those needs. Look at the Christian Family Movement or the Catholic Interracial Council or the Holy Name Society. We got all these people involved and they were moved to do things and to write a check. Involve people and they will write checks!

Bill Clark was my first pastor. He is a saint. He's now in a nursing home. I recall one day that we got a letter from the Vatican via the chancery office and I was yelling about it. Then Bill said: "John, don't you realize that when you speak to your people on Sunday, you're more significant than the pope or the cardinal." He was so right. I can't fight city hall. I'm part of it. Now, I simply think of ministerial impact.

I deal with people who are wandering and who just want to rest for a while. Here at St. Pat's, we draw from the whole area. For the young people who come here, the Church is not an end. It is a means to an end. I use the Church to help people locate their God.

We've got to develop an attitude of welcoming, not grilling. We need an attitude of gracious hospitality, not interrogation. No clubbish questions. Jesus would never ask such questions. We must be able to say to our young people, "You are important here. Come join us." Then, we have to remember names; send a note; thank them for coming.

We gave young people the finest education in the world. We told them to be the best and the brightest and now we're having trouble putting the best and the brightest before them on Sunday. Now we can't get them to enter religious life or the priesthood, although other denominations can. We've encouraged their success without asking anything in return.

I was ordained to a Church that had become narcissistic. We never talked about the Church's mission. It was a Church aimed at older people. A good church is always other-oriented, always looking through the eyes of faith. It makes you look at something and say: "That's what I want to do!" A good faith is like a good pair of glasses. You can see clearly in three dimensions.

When Jesus said: "I will make you fishers of men," it was not a call to ministry. I hustled that line for years, trying to recruit for the priesthood. That call is a call to see what life can be. I use it now as a call to young people, a call to faith.

We simply call people to faith. The Church helps in this. It keeps the faith alive by providing a Catholic view of life. I'm really indebted to Andy Greeley for much of this. [Andrew M. Greeley is a priest sociologist, prolific author, and popular novelist.] He urges a strong and clearly articulated Catholic theology.

I didn't know anything when I was ordained, but I've been mentored by truly great priests. In those early years, we weren't sure what we were about. *Humanae Vitae* had been published. [*Humanae Vitae* is the papal encyclical on birth control, published in 1965.] Scripture wasn't working; the studies weren't that far along. I was looking for a pragmatic theology; I wanted results; I was scared. I was asking myself: "What good am I?" I started looking for mentors and I never had to leave Chicago. I found twenty truly great priests just a phone call away. I could just walk down the corridor of my rectory!

Again, I had Bill Clark who asked me: "Are you ready to give up and share some of your priesthood?" Then, Leo Mahon came in from Panama. [Mahon is a Chicago priest who worked at the archdiocesan mission in Panama.] He stayed with us for only three or four months. He filled the church! That was before *RENEW*. [*RENEW* is a popular evangelization program.] We were doing wisdom weekends then. Leo worked his magic. It changed my preaching and it gave me a practical theology that was later developed even more through Andy Greeley and John Shea. I also lived with Jake Killgallen, a great catechetical man. [Killgallen was a Chicago priest, catechetical expert, RIP.] We had an exciting house!

My dad used to say to me: "Say good things when you preach." Good preaching is saying good things. We have to be calling people to something. And Dick Westley [Loyola University of Chicago professor] always says that we don't need clerics, we need priests. When you're with a cleric, you just look at the top of your shoes.

I'm forty-four now. I've begun to understand my limits. I don't try to take on the seminary anymore, for example. When I was part of the seminary system, I brought Andy Greeley in to speak. He gave a powerful talk, not a hint of anger or criticism. But now, when I submit a list of fifteen great priests who could talk to the seminarians, they say: "Oh, isn't he the man who had Greeley talk?" I'm afraid that the seminarians wouldn't care what these men have to say anyway. The caliber of seminarian just isn't there.

Oh, I don't know yet. Perhaps we have to be like a potter who must work with the clay in front of him. Together with my own education and my years at Niles, I was in the seminary system for twenty years. Add to that the fact that my whole life was Catholic through and through. I was born in a Catholic hospital and I already have a plot in a Catholic cemetery!

Through those years, we were taught to think critically. Now, if you think critically, you could be burned at the stake! Perhaps I'm looking for too much, but I'm convinced that the problem of the priesthood is one of quality, not of quantity. The seminaries today are just not training people for pastoral ministry regardless of what they say. They're training for institutional survival.

If I were in charge, I guess I'd strategically develop about twenty showcase parishes. We wouldn't be arrogant or intimidating about them, but we could use them to show people how things can get done. Then, I guess I'd convene a monthly meeting of all my pastors for one year. You know, a local parish is only as good as its pastor. The tone is set, messages are communicated, all tied to the ecclesiology of the pastor. I believe that there's a great deal of goodwill out there among the pastors. It's just that they don't know what to do or how to do it.

We must train people to a whole new way of doing business. Four years ago, when the tax code was changed, every accounting firm in town took its people away to school and told them the new way of doing taxes. It wasn't an option for them. We need to teach our pastors to do ministry in a whole new way. Instead, we're bombarding them with forms. There's no time to do pastoral ministry.

We're trapped between a canonical system and a pastoral system. Sadly, when the pastoral system fails, pastors fall back on the canonical system. That's when all those horror stories about marriage preparation get real and we have to listen to statements such as: "Well, canonically speaking, Father is right." Priests get religiously schizophrenic, swinging between the canonical and the pastoral. It's the same problem that was raised in the Scriptures. Jesus tells us of the rich young man who wanted to be perfect. Keep the rules, Jesus told him. But we learn that rules are not enough. That's when we get into the pastoral approach. Jesus healed on the Sabbath. He wasn't saying that rules were not important but he responded to pastoral needs.

You know, I always get nervous when I hear someone say: "I know God's will." I put my hand over my wallet. They always want money, but never want intimacy. And intimacy is tied to pastoral approaches.

Greeley says that we have to celebrate people's moments of return. They're not returning from faithlessness or debauchery. It's often a return from a depth of love. We have to be empathetic.

You remember that Marine Corps ad? It says, "We're looking for a few good people." That's all it would take, a few good people.

᥅᧞᧐ INTERLUDE II ᥅᧞᧐

The bishop was an aged turnip. He ruled his small diocese with an iron hand, sometimes even calling pastors in the vast neighboring archdiocese to warn them that they should not permit people from his much smaller, steel-town diocese to attend Mass in their territory.

He sometimes sat on his episcopal throne, reading his breviary, while the priests of his grubby cathedral said Mass. He liked to keep an eye on them.

The newly ordained always spent a plebe year at the cathedral parish. "We're his prize cattle," one priest said. "He's got to put his brand on us." The first assignment to another parish was termed "the freedom train."

The latest young priest was giving one of his first sermons. He was nervous, especially with the fully vested turnip sitting there on his carved throne. He was angry, too. "Why doesn't the old goat take part in the Mass instead of reading his breviary and making those wet whistle sounds through his bad dentures?" the young priest said to himself.

The young priest mispronounced a word. Flustered, he paused, just long enough for the bishop to get to his feet and shout: "Father, that word is pronounced . . ."

The congregation tittered nervously. An electric pause followed.

"That's O.K. for you," the priest said to the congregation. "You don't have to live with the sonovabitch."

> Circa 1955. The bishop is in his grave. The young priest left active ministry during the 1960s and now is a painting contractor.

There were only sixty-eight priests in the vast, Canadian diocese. Many were so isolated that they did not meet a brother priest for months at a time.

The archbishop's silver anniversary brought most of them to the cathedral for a solemn high Mass. Frank Firth, not without reason, was pastor of two parishes on the outer edge of the diocese. Frank heard many different drummers and marched to all of them. He also had a speech impediment that made it hard for him to say his own name.

Frank Firth arrived late for the anniversary Mass. The priests crowded the sanctuary and, as Frank made his way to his place, he waved, winked, and shook hands.

The priests liked Frank. Like Jesus, he had a heart that went out ahead of him.

The master of ceremonies, a dedicated careerist, bowed to the bishop, then the altar. Hands joined in correct rubrical position, he approached Frank and whispered: "Father, please refrain." Then he bowed to the altar, to the bishop, and took his place at the bishop's side.

For a moment, Frank Firth stared in disbelief. Then, he walked to the credence table; took the red-leather Gospel Book; he bowed to the altar, to the bishop, and approached the master of ceremonies.

Frank Firth bowed and placed the book in the surprised emcee's hands. "Father," Frank Firth said. "Would you st-st-stuff this up your ass!"

Frank Firth bowed to the bishop and the altar and returned to his stool in the sanctuary.

Circa 1952

· 9 ·

Michael L. Donovan: Heartland Priest

Michael L. Donovan was picked almost at random. A brief item in the *Catholic Times* of the diocese of Columbus, Ohio, described a First Communion liturgy to which the then pastor of Christ the King Church had brought a live lamb. Phone calls tracked him to his present parish, St. Pius X in Reynoldsburg, a suburb of Columbus. Father Donovan offered to send copies of parish bulletins to serve as resources for a monthly newsletter, *U.S. Parish*, published by the Claretian Fathers. Soon, bulletins from some fifty parishes arrived. They provided valuable insights into the chemistry of parish life in a midsized diocese of east north central America.

The Diocese of Columbus covers an area populated by some 2,000,000 people, 202,000 of whom are Catholics. They are served by 213 diocesan priests, 155 of whom are active in 111 parishes. The diocese has 18 seminarians. (Source: *Catholic Almanac, Official Catholic Directory*) A priest of the diocese receives a basic stipend of $7,500 per year with a seniority increment of $60 per year, a professional allowance of $700 and a car allowance of $4,200, about enough to drive the car 16,000 miles annually for parish business or pleasure. His health insurance package is worth $1,920 and his pension is $7,200. A priest ordained twenty-five years has a total package of $15,760. (Source: National Federation of Priests Councils.) Columbus will lose approximately 40 percent of its priests during the nearly spent forty-year period between 1965 and 2005, the average for the country. A random sampling suggests that six out of ten parishes have only one priest. Parish staffs, or "teams" as they are often called, are largely laity and overwhelmingly female.

The parish bulletins detail the activities of a church that understands the Catholic in the pew. The "From the Pastor's Desk" messages, sort of second homilies, are moderately progressive messages of faith. The activities reveal parishioners who give to the poor, reach out to the aged, value religious education for their children, and invest a significant amount of their social life in the parish. Efforts are made to help those hurt by divorce, abortion, sickness, and death. Adult education is modest but self-help groups for single parents, blended families, senior citizens, etc., abound.

Michael Donovan may represent a more conservative approach to priesthood, but he is not alone, nor is he a reactionary. Many priests and laity share an Alexander Pope view of progress: "Be not the first by whom the new is tried, Nor yet the last to lay the old aside."

O h, I just love looking out the rectory window and seeing the parking lot filled with cars or kids. Sometimes, I'm not even certain what's going on. There are so many activities. Sometimes, I have to walk over to see what's going on. I don't like to miss anything. I think that priestly presence is a very important thing. There are so many activities. Why, we've got sixteen basketball teams and forty-four coaches. You know, Greeley [Andrew M. Greeley, priest-sociologist-novelist] was right. Schools are the heart of the parish. Our people are wonderful. They are family people, church people, job people. That's their life. Because of our people, I'm not in the survival position. You know, the last parish with a school in this diocese was founded in 1963. I understand the Church's problem. I could still build here, but I'd have to be concerned about this parish becoming building rich and financially poor. Still, in summertime, I miss all those kids playing out there. It's like a morgue.

I love my priesthood. It's a marvelous vocation. Sure, we can't get married and we don't make a lot of money. But I've never been in want. My meals are ready for me; my wash is done. My biggest expense is a car. In my old age, I'll be taken care of. My retirement plan is eternal life. I can't complain in the least. When you observe your parishioners who can't go through a line at the supermarket these days without spending about $300 on groceries, my sacrifice is nothing. I look at their crushing burden of debt and I have to ask who has the harder life. Certainly not me.

I was born in Columbus in Our Lady of Victory Parish. I went to St. Charles Seminary Prep High School and College and then to Mount St. Mary's of the West in Norwood, Ohio. That's in the Cincinnati archdiocese. I was ordained in 1964 in a class of seven from this diocese and a total of sixty-three from all the other dioceses.

St. Pius X here in Reynoldsburg was my first parish. I was stationed here from 1964 to 1967 while I taught at Bishop Hartley High School, a regional coed high school in Columbus. In 1967, I was assigned as a notary to the Matrimonial Tribunal, an associate at St. Joseph's Cathedral and secretary to

John J. Carberry [bishop 1965–68, now a cardinal and retired archbishop of St. Louis]. Bishop Clarence E. Elwell [1968-73] came in 1968 and I was sent to Rome where I completed my doctorate in canon law in 1971 at St. John Lateran. I returned to Columbus as vice chancellor. When Bishop Elwell died, Bishop Edward J. Herrmann [1973–82] came from Washington. I was named chancellor in 1978; Herrmann retired in 1982, and Bishop James A. Griffin came in 1983. I was pastor of St. Thomas in 1976 and of Christ the King in 1981. Last July, I returned to St. Pius X as pastor. Now, I'm vicar general and pastor here.

I used to go to the chancery office every day but I don't now. We're not a big diocese. And we get only a few marriage cases each week. Most of the time, I'm here in the parish.

We have the same problem with the priest shortage as elsewhere. The bishop is conscious of the problem. In my mind, there's no lack of vocations, just a lack of response. These are not religious times; there is a lack of generosity. I can't predict the future; I'm just looking at a crystal ball.

Consecrated celibacy has been a tremendous gift to the priesthood and the Church. I don't foresee any change in that discipline. If such a change were ever to come, I could accept it, but only after we had rediscovered the value of celibacy.

So many things were made optional by Vatican II that the value of them has been lost. Look at fasting and abstinence. They're observed only on Ash Wednesday and Good Friday. Fasting and abstinence are deeply rooted in the Judaeo-Christian heritage. Marriage and the priesthood are compatible, but the time for that isn't ripe yet. If celibacy were made optional, it would lose its value. I'm not at all sure that it would fill the seminaries anyway.

We need to make a little more room for the grace of God. Just look at the college campuses of the 1960s and look at them now. A complete turn-around, an about-face. There are all those psychological and sociological considerations. They could change just as rapidly as the thinking did in the post-Vietnam period. And, most important, we could turn this around if we priests could show a greater love for our vocation.

This is an upper-middle-class, white collar parish with about 1,900 units. I guess you could multiply that number by five to get the total number of individuals. We have a staff of about sixty-three people and a budget of over $1.2 million. Our collections run about $11,500 per week. The people are very generous. We have 628 children in the grammar school and there's a waiting list. The greater Columbus area is about 20 percent Catholic. There are 535 living units presently under construction in the parish and we're adding more and more families each month.

We have an associate pastor here, so I generally say only two Masses each weekend. I really don't think it's wise to do four or five Masses on a weekend.

You know, some of the old rules weren't so bad. They made sense. Three Masses on All Souls Day was considered a privilege. The Church didn't want a multiplicity of Masses. That can reduce their value. And they didn't want their priests to be burned out. Priests need to be protected. The bishops should follow the canons on the deans of a diocese. A lot of the work could be fielded out, especially if we believed in accountability.

I've been on the Marriage Tribunal for years. I believe that the judicial decisions we make should be respected. Of course, there are good conscience cases that priests can handle outside the tribunal, but I'm afraid that some priests are assuming that the good conscience is theirs and not that of the couples involved. I've had marriage cases in the parishes that I felt in good conscience were definitely invalid. However, the good conscience test rests with the couple, not the priest. We're not supposed to annul a marriage just because we think it's invalid. The couple must come to the decision that no marriage existed. In this diocese, we did over 460 cases this year. The administrative part is easy; the tough part is dealing with the people. A marriage case that goes through takes about a year. When the cases go through to completion, most rulings are favorable. The others tend to drop out. I'm convinced that we priests must respect the judicial process. Can't anyone say "forever" anymore? There's a lack of concern for the sanctity of marriage. As a result, people are making a lot of mistakes.

Bishops have lost their credibility. They have a tough job but they have caused some of their own problems. They've got to have some guts. A lot of priests reflect their hostilty toward the bishops by going around them. They write those pastorals and they make them so long! No one's going to read those things! And they should never have tried the one on women. With pastorals, you don't write about people. You write about issues. They should have written about the job discrimination women suffer or the lower income they get. The bishops would then have to deal with the issues and would have been slower to bury the pastoral. Issues, not people. They would have gotten a better hearing. As it is, I don't think the pastoral on women will see the light of day. I've worked with four bishops; they have a tough job. But I'm afraid the bishops are out of touch.

I don't mean that we should have any lack of compassion for our people. I think compassion is terribly important. Boy, I wish we knew everything that Jesus said to the woman at the well. He really laid it on the line, but we don't know all that he said. If we knew that, we'd have the answer to a lot of questions.

Vatican II gave authority to the bishops, but it stressed that the bond with the Holy Father is a strong one. The Pope is an excellent man, a significant influence in the opening up of Eastern Europe. We need to fully recognize the primacy of the papacy. The NCCB [National Conference of Catholic

Bishops] has been destructive of that bond with the Holy Father. It has weakened his authority as well as the authority of the local bishops. What pastorals are the local bishops writing anymore? Now, all they want to do is ask the conference to write the pastorals. I'm not against the conference but it doesn't have to be dabbling in everything to the point where the local bishop is afraid to take a step. Why are bishops going to the conference for decisions they should be making at the local level? That's not collegiality! What the bishops are saying isn't having an impact. That's not good, but the people have no reason to open their ears.

I believe that the priest's ministry is one of presence. You could put a priest in the middle of a field and people would gather around him. We can vitally influence their lives, and that contact is very important. I believe that it's important that the priest be there, present to his people. We don't have to go to every dog fight, but the people have to know that they can get you when they need you.

Priestly fraternity has gone through a dry spell. I think it's pretty good now. We gather in small groups here in Columbus. The nights we gathered at the close of Forty Hours and Confirmation are gone. But we still have our dinners and meetings. There are few prayer groups, but I don't see that as a good or bad sign. Most of the men still gather at the diocesan-sponsored retreat. I think that more priests are turning to their own spiritual director; years ago, we didn't have much of that. I do see an increased interest in Scripture reading. I certainly don't see the priests *not* getting together, but I do believe that their spirituality has to be better disciplined.

I read a great deal about liturgy and Christology and I'm a fan of C. S. Lewis. Perhaps my favorite book of late is *Jesus before Christianity* by Albert Nolan, O.P. I think I've read it six times. I also read Henri Nouwen and I do a lot of reading around preaching as well as the *Pastoral Review*.

The future? Well, the number of priests will decline, until we get a more positive press. The popular journals don't help. They show a negative side of the priesthood. The pedophilia issue has hurt us. And society remains too materialistic to think of priesthood. We've got to become more open to the public. The permanent diaconate hasn't caught on and lay ministry hasn't overshadowed the priesthood. But, along with the Church, we still have a credibility problem.

I love being a priest. I could never work for IBM or Xerox. I'd be fired in a minute. You know, we're hunting for heaven on earth. We forget that Heaven is for later. We don't serve Christ by trying to water things down. You know, the sum of all the theologies doesn't even equal the gift of faith.

Leonard A. Dubi: Recovering Alcoholic

The bishop arrived to address a group of recovering alcoholic priests. The auditorium was filled but less than half the priests were dressed in their clerical garb. "I can't talk to that group," the bishop said. "I was told it would be just priests, no laity."

"Bishop," he was quietly told, "they are all priests." (Some years later, the tense bishop would admit that he, too, was an alcoholic.)

Priests still occupy a special niche in the cathedrals of most Catholics' minds. They stand on fail-safe pedestals, apart from the rest of us. The reality is that they are no more immune from the disease of alcoholism than anyone else. Indeed, they may be more vulnerable because society protects them from the harsh conditioning of the lay world. Further, until recently, an unrealistic and myopic institutional loyalty has deprived many diseased priests from getting the support they need. A popular misconception is that, on the rare occasion, a fallen priest is found staggering along skid row. It is the stuff of which "B" movies are made—the tragic hero, the flawed saint, a victim of alcohol. The reality is quite different, just as it is with the population at large.

How many alcoholic clergy are there? The accepted national figure holds that 10 percent of the work force of 45 million, about 4.5 million, are problem drinkers. Add another 3 million teenagers from fourteen to seventeen, and 2 million homemakers. Then, consider that the number of elderly alcoholics is on the increase and that hundreds of babies are born each day with a predisposition to alcoholism because of one or both parents' addiction. The numbers rise dramatically.

Then, consider the fact that an alcoholic priest is nothing more than a man with a disease who has been gifted with a vocation. It helps a little, at least, to put a frame around the problem.

Few clergy would quarrel with the estimate that at least 10 percent of priests have a problem with alcohol. Sister Terese Golden, O.P., who works full time with addicted priests, brothers, and sisters believes that the figure is higher. A study done by Father Edward Royce, S.J. of

Seattle University suggests that the figure could be as high as 15 percent. According to Sister Terese, "Priests and religious are clustered very close to the medical profession which ranks as the highest addicted group."

Precise numbers are elusive because only one in ten priests with an addiction problem is getting treatment. Further, alcoholic priests leave active ministry either because they have been confronted or disciplined, or simply in search of a drink.

Government estimates say that about 70 percent of all alcoholics are among the bread-and-butter working class. They lead average lives; live in respectable neighborhoods; go to work every day; mow their lawn; raise kids. So with the alcoholic priest. The majority function at a reasonably high level. They get their work done, much the way the addicted physicians or lawyers do, at least for a while. Priests may have a higher rate of addiction because the denial, both on the part of the priests and the institution, runs higher. Rectory communities can become enabling communities. Non-addicted priests often cannot tolerate an addicted person in their midst. So, they tend to ignore the problem. Often, the intimacy levels are so shallow that confrontation is virtually impossible. Addicted priests will sometimes unfurl the "once a priest, always a priest" flag; wave it in the face of their bishops; blame the institution for their problem; even demand a canonical trial in place of treatment, or threaten to sue. Finally, successful treatment for some may mean resigning their vocations, and bishops are reluctant to invest in a potential defection.

Asked privately to evaluate their ordination classes and to estimate how many have a drinking problem, priests will generally give higher figures. Typically, one priest in an ordination class of twenty-two stated that "at least four and perhaps six" of his class have a problem, somewhere between 18 and 27 percent. "It's the only thing that wasn't a sin," one priest observed. "Drink is the first thing you're offered when you get upstairs in a rectory."

The roots of the problem among clergy are difficult to trace. Priests often come from ethnic groups with a penchant for drinking. One priest, an active member of ACOA (Adult Children of Alcoholics) stated that 50 percent of the clergy in his diocese were adult sons of alcoholics. (Alcoholism runs higher among ACOAs.) A likely oversimplification ties some clerical alcoholism with celibacy. (Clerical humor calls alcohol "celibacy vaccine.") Priests with sexual problems appear to have a high incidence of alcohol abuse, but no definitive studies have been published. Suicides are often committed by priests who cannot face their alcoholism.

Conversations with clergy reveal some encouraging changes. First, hardly a diocese in the country is not without a recovery program for its priests. A professional like Sister Terese states flatly that she has never met a bishop who says: "I don't need you." The National Clergy Council on Alcoholism was formed in the 1950s to deal with the problem of addicted priests.

As recently as 1953, Austin Ripley, founder of Guest House, a center for recovering clerical alcoholics in Lake Orion, Michigan, and Rochester, Minnesota, received a letter that stated: "All our friends here are opposed to any open, active identification with Alcoholics Anonymous. . . . I am entirely opposed to having our Catholics, with their magnificent treasure of the whole Deposit of Faith, making common cause with these men in their worship of the vague, amorphous Diety of A.A. I object to open, active identification of Catholic priests with A.A." Such a view among clergy is rare today. "There's still some rejection," Sister Terese said. "And nothing can break an alcoholic's spirit more than rejection. But it's getting better." Facilities like the two Guest Houses which have treated over four thousand men since their founding in 1956, are doing an outstanding job with their ninety-day programs. It is not uncommon today to hear priests asking their congregations for their prayerful support when they enter treatment.

About one-third of all priests, perhaps more, never touch a drink, and don't become alcoholic. Parish priests are encouraging the formation of Alcoholics Anonymous groups in their parishes. They are adapting A.A.'s famous Twelve-Step program and/or its Twelve Traditions for many other addiction programs. Inevitably, priests are affected by the groups they help to form. There is evidence that the rectory bar is fading. One hears less and less clerical talk about rectories with good bars. Evaluation-assessment programs that have been used successfully with business executives are now being employed for priests who give evidence of an addiction problem. The tests work better than a confrontation with a bishop; individuals asked to take them are more open to facing their problem because they don't feel that they are being evaluated by their bishops. The tests cut drastically on the denial. Finally, the recovery rate among priests is very high, at least 75 percent of those who get some form of treatment.

Len Dubi is pastor of St. Anne's in Hazelcrest, Illinois. His unvarnished and unfiltered honesty echoes Step Five of the Twelve Steps: "Admitted to God, to ourselves, and to another human being the exact nature of our wrongs."

I t's been eight and one-half years since my recovery. Things have never been better. I'm coming of age, although I'll be forty-eight soon and will be facing a mid-life crisis.

I don't know where you heard the rumor that I was leaving active ministry, but I'm not surprised that you heard it. I did write a pastor's message in the parish bulletin that got me in some hot water with the cardinal. He saw it as critical of the pope. It was. But it was the truth. And when word gets out that you're writing stuff like that, the next word is that you're leaving. And, no, I don't have cancer. I had a prostate infection, nothing more. But by the time it goes around the clerical grapevine, it's cancer.

You know, the Scriptures tell us that there is nothing hidden that will not be revealed. It's all going to come out someday. I told Joe [Joseph Cardinal Bernardin] that. He asked me to come down to his office to discuss my bulletin message. I went down. It was a strange experience. I walked down that long corridor to his office, past all those other offices with people in them, but with no sounds of life. It really got to me! Half way down, I broke out singing "Mother Dearest, Mother Fairest." I had to do something to break the spell! You know, you've got to sign in and sign out and get buzzed through locked doors. It all goes back to Cody's time [John Cardinal Cody, 1965–82, Bernardin's predecessor]. But you have to ask why they call it a pastoral center with all those locks and buzzers.

The visit was also a chance to talk to the cardinal about all the people with needs, people addicted to drugs or alcohol, Adult Children of Alcoholics, and others. At St. Anne's, we're using the Twelve-Step format where people can come together to talk about spiritual issues relating to their lives, and how God is empowering them to live faithful lives. We're working that Twelve-Step theme not only in our catechumenate but also along a whole range of issues, involving Scripture as related to other topics. We've done a "Quality of Spiritual Life" survey in the parish and we're introducing the Twelve-Step format to small groups.

It was a good visit. The cardinal has to do those things. People write him. We have a lot of CUF [Catholics United for the Faith, a conservative group] in the area. He gets pressure. So we talk and he can say that he talked to me.

I grew up in a dysfunctional family. My father was an alcoholic; so was my grandfather. My father was a steelworker who used to say, "All I want to do is drive a bus." He used to talk about my grandfather who came from Hungary. My grandmother came a few years later to join him. My grandfather would get drunk and beat up on my grandmother; my father raised his family the same way; I grew up in that dysfunctional environment. It was and is a dysfunctional society.

Grandpa died of liver cancer. In a way, he was a victim of those robber barons who worked him half to death. I really believe that some of these addiction diseases have their roots in social injustice. It's odd, but when Studs Terkel was doing his book, *Working*, he interviewed both my father and me. Dad and Studs were talking with a bottle of Chivas on the table. Alcohol was part of everything!

I got drunk the first time at eighteen. Later, in the seminary, I used to get drunk on vacations. During the year, we got Thursdays off at the seminary and we would sneak into town and drink. There was a guy named Emil who owned the bar. Boy, he retired to Florida on the seminarians' booze!

The seminary was an unjust place. We were expected to prepare ourselves to talk with people by not talking to each other. I was a kid from a dysfunctional family in a dysfunctional seminary within a dysfunctional Church. The Church brings so much trouble on itself. There's no sense of process, no real sense of theology. It tries to hold on to the future by holding on to the past. Anyway, I lived in such a spiritual vacuum that I didn't know what normal was.

I grew up trying to please everyone in the hope that the drinking and the fighting would stop. I blamed myself. I got good grades in school and I kept the house neat. My mother had to go to work when I was only four, so I learned how to take care of the house. I worked as an Andy Frain usher back when they were all at least six feet tall. I'm six-six. It was a prestige job in those days. I dated but had no desire to be married. Marriage as I saw it was misery. My father would stop at the tavern on his way home from the steel mill. He had a bad back and the pain was awful. Perhaps that explains some of the drinking—to kill the pain. But he'd come home drunk and there were fights. There were divorces in my family among my aunts and uncles. There were mentally ill people across the street who were married. So, I chose the priesthood. That would avoid marriage and please my mother, I thought. I guess I always tried to please my mother. I even shaved my beard for her funeral!

I was ordained in 1968. There were forty in the class—only about eighteen or nineteen still in. We get together for reunions, not much else.

I go to a lot of meetings. I'm addicted to relationships. I don't feel good about a relationship, however, unless there is some tension. I used to come home from school full of tension. I never knew what I'd find. I guess that tension is still with me. I guess it's why I push relationships to the point of tension. I simply never saw my parents talking lovingly and openly.

I see a lot of the basics of Adult Children of Alcoholics in all this. There is a desire to be in a close relationship but a fear of it, too. There is a lot of confusion between love and pity. Adult children of alcoholics become rescuers. I saw myself as a rescuer.

As an Andy Frain usher, I worked outside St. Peter's Church in the Loop. It was a Franciscan church. They used to get big crowds there for their lunchtime Masses. I used to go to confession to Father Cuthbert in my Andy Frain's uniform. I hadn't been to Mass for years. My parents were Catholics but didn't practice much. My father thought that priests ripped people off, coming around, asking for money. I felt that these Franciscan priests were really being helpful. It made the priestly vocation really attractive. I was also dating a Catholic girl who was praying for me. I had dropped out of active practice in the fifth grade. Didn't go to Catholic school. One night, I took Fran to a place named the Green Shingle. It was a place where we could all get served even though we were under age. Fran got bombed. She got terribly sick. I told her that I was going into the seminary. She cried. I ended up giving her my ring.

My father was active in the union. He gave me a love for justice that was nurtured by a wonderful teacher I had at Bowen High School. The poor soul has Alzheimer's Disease now. She had a lot to do with my vocation.

In any case, I was an episodic drinker, marijuana smoker, and drug user. I tried cocaine and lots of other drugs. I might not get drunk for two or three months, however. So, it was easy to hide. Once I was ordained, I had no trouble getting liquor when I wanted it. There are so many rectories around where you could get all you wanted. And I never had trouble getting marijuana or drugs. I got it from parishioner-friends. I smoked pot for at least ten years, from age twenty-eight to thirty-eight. Ironically, it brought back my inner life. I would smoke and write poetry.

In my early days, I was involved in a great many social issues. They included protests and Saul Alinsky-type organizing. But in those years, the church never supported us. The church is supposed to be free, but it is bound up more than the American government, always afraid, always prudent.

For my part, I saw myself as a fisher of men. It was a very manipulative role. The notion of a fisherman is one of a hooker and a stabber. It was enlightened self-interest. There were days when I was so involved in protest activities that I could hardly keep up with it. We fought the city about the airport, the stink of the sludge in the Sanitation District, housing, and lots of other things. It excited me. I loved fighting the alderman. To add to the problem, I was so stoned on drugs and alcohol that I didn't know what I was doing. I found myself a young leader, a role I wasn't prepared for. So, I'd get bombed and just plow my way through it. And, at one point in all of this, I had a pastor who was also very sick.

Going into treatment was very difficult. When I got to Guest House, I was so ashamed. Here I was, the guy who kept his room neat, the Andy Frain usher, the guy who was rescuing people and all that. Now, there I was, a whiskey priest. A disgrace. I can still feel the pain of walking in there.

I was in good shape. I was still young and in good health. You would never know by looking at me that I was an alcoholic. But there was an awful lot of pain inside.

I walked into the chapel. There was a statue of the Angel Raphael there with Tobias. And the message read: "Do not fear. You are safe." That experience meant so much. I felt safe at last.

The staff was wonderful. They joked with me, saying that I looked so good that I didn't belong there. But they put me through the program and got me into A.A. I've been back for two brief visits.

I was assigned to a parish with another A.A. It was a good assignment. We could pray together. When he retired, I applied for the job but didn't get it. Perhaps it was because they didn't want two A.A.s in a row. Perhaps some of the people saw me as too liberal. Perhaps I had caused problems by having A.A. meetings in the parish center, meetings that brought in some blacks who were in A.A. We never had any problems with meetings before, but the minute we let those blacks in, the local fire department inspected the building and said that it was unsafe for meetings.

In any case, when St. Anne's opened up, I applied. The process is completely clerical but I insisted on visiting the parish and talking to the people. "I'm Father Len Dubi," I told them. "I want to be your pastor. I'm an alcoholic."

The parishioners were wonderful. Again, all things will be revealed anyway. I average a call a day from someone in the parish, telling me that they are addicted to something.

I'm alone, and there are over 1,400 families. I could use help but, with the terrible shortage of priests, it's not likely. Part of me likes being alone. I grew up with lots of people. The seminary was filled with more. Now, I'm alone and it's not too bad. I'm busy but lonely. I thought perhaps that I might get a seminary deacon, but, when I inquired, a priest who didn't know me said: "They're going to be very careful with assignments. They're not sending any of them to pastors who are nuts or alcoholics." He didn't know I was an alcoholic. It hurt. It means I'll be alone.

It hurt, too, when the Vatican decreed that all priests had to use wine at Mass. That was an awful ruling. I had already received permission to use plain grape juice before the cut-off date. But it still hurt because it showed what a terrible lack of understanding there was. Well, the bishops made some noise and the terrible ruling was quietly buried somewhere.

We have so many things going on in the parish. The day-care center has been filled from the start. We simply asked the people what their greatest need was and they told us it was a day-care center. Now, we're working with other parishes, Catholic and Protestant, mostly black, on acquiring decent housing. The government is picking up these foreclosed houses through HUD. They sell them to the local banks. We're persuading the local banks to sell them to us at a low price and we're getting people to fix them up. It means that we can sell good homes at affordable prices. It means that we can do something about the apartheid in our society. It means that, maybe, we can cut down on the differences between Olympia Fields [a wealthy area] and Ford Heights [a poor area].

We pastors have got to cooperate more. We've got to think about merging our schools rather than closing them one at a time. We can link other parish services.

This priesthood is a good life. I try to remain very positive, in spite of the institutional fighting. It would be a good life even if they found Christ's body.

· 11 ·

Harvey F. Egan: Skilled Infuriator

Few Catholic communities in the country have attracted more attention than St. Joan of Arc parish in south Minneapolis. Its pastor for twenty years, Harvey Egan, or "Harvey the Heretic," served in a series of parishes before being named pastor of St. Joan's in 1967. (On being reassigned with depressing but not surprising regularity, largely because he marched to a different drummer, the man who has been dubbed "the skilled infuriator" observes: "This was the standard, decently handled soft-shoe routine, the dance of diocesan diplomacy.") When he arrived at St. Joan of Arc, he found "a ministry pressed down and flowing over with tremendous trifles." Gradually, he moved the parish toward a post-Vatican II community. Once known as "St. Jock's" Parish because of its emphasis on athletic programs ("Jesus was an athlete," one muscled parishioner said), Egan turned the parish into a haven for the disenchanted, the socially sensitive, the activists. "St. Joan of Arc became a mecca for colorful characters," he wrote in his autobiography, *Leaven: Canticle for a Changing Parish*. "It included a higher-than-average number of underachievers, overachievers, lovers of loose connections and geniuses with technicolored visions." Within a year, it was the most exciting parish in Minneapolis. Egan is puckish, witty, and unfailingly graceful. The exterior charm hides a piece of steel within that would not bend to social injustice, administrative nonsense, or pointless pieties. He had already marched in Selma; he had served time for his opposition to war and to nuclear proliferation. Anonymous letters, obscene phone calls, and chancery salvos didn't scare him. Retired from active duty in 1987, Harvey Egan lives in a two-room apartment in downtown Minneapolis. When asked, he serves in a variety of parishes as a Sunday "help-out" priest and is chaplain to a sixty-member group that meets monthly for liturgy and laughter. Now, in Leonard Bernstein's words from his "Mass," Egan's motto is "Sing God a simple song. Make it up as you go along."

(The interview took place at the Basilica of St. Mary Co-Cathedral and in the gardens of the Walker Art Gallery in Minneapolis. Some statements also appear in his autobiography.)

This cathedral was built by Archbishop [John] Ireland just after the turn of the century. Look at it! That's the way they did things in those days. Now, it has a load of problems. It's going to take $13 million to fix it up. Just a half a mile from here is a ghetto, crawling in poverty and loaded with drugs. There's a great pastor here, a good Roman. I'm sure that he does what he can for the poor, but he must spend most of his time fund-raising to save this great building. It capsulizes the problem of the church, trying to preserve the institution.

I retired four years ago when I was seventy. I love it. I should have done it earlier. I was ordained in 1941. As a seminarian, my efforts to play the monk's role were as awkward as they were arduous. I was supposed to live like a monk and be an effective parish priest later. I had my doubts, but I played the game.

As a seminarian, I sneaked the occasional cigarette. Once I was ordained, I could smoke. So, naturally, I quit. Years later, when I told that to a bishop, he said: "Father, that's the story of your life."

I'm busy enough now. I go where I'm asked, and I have a little group that meets a couple of times each month. We used to be underground, but now the underground has surfaced. Catholic people all across the U.S. have surfaced. They love their Church. They don't join another church because there's nothing there for them.

I'm downtown, near the public library. Just two rooms, but I love it. I've got an unlisted phone number because people still call to yell at me, but St. Joan's gives it out to people.

We have a retirement home for priests in the diocese. There may be one or two living in Florida or California, but most are at the home. I wouldn't be comfortable there. You know, we live our lives alone and get used to it. We grow a little funny. Even at the retirement home, they kind of stay to themselves. Some don't even gather for a drink! I couldn't do that. I can't sit in a room and stare at a blank wall.

I'm still looking for a community. Many failed because the bishop quashed them; some because the priest who founded them left the priesthood, and some because people quarreled among themselves. Democracy doesn't work very well in the nation or the Church. It doesn't make for a dynamic jump forward. Locally, there are a few groups, but it's difficult.

At Joan of Arc we were about 80 percent to 20 percent ecumenical. The 20 percent from Protestant churches came because they couldn't find answers to personal or global problems. It's sad but often people outside the church can do better than the church itself. It seems that as soon as you enter an institution everything becomes formalized.

When I'm not at the altar on weekends, I often go to two or three churches, some of them Protestant, looking for a good liturgy. But it's hard to find one. It's gone dead. Oh, Joan of Arc is still fine. It's bigger and better than ever. Harvey Egan is not the indispensable man.

In the early 1970s, there were 100,000 cradle Catholics in the St. Paul-Minneapolis archdiocese who were no longer affiliated with the church. In those days, there were few inspirations, meager consolations, and no surprises. Sermons were mired somewhere between ho and hum.

At St. Joan's, our liturgies began to improve. We used some toe-tapping love songs to replace dreary hymns and we put the prayers into understandable English. Gradually, we became a mini-magnet community. People asked to be married at St. Joan's. Before long the chancery sent us a letter saying that only people who lived in the parish could be married there. So, some people took up residence in our neighborhood.

Gradually, the pendulum began to swing from conservative to liberal. I began to feel almost at home. Now that I was welcomed, I became a welcomer. I began to hear "Harvey" more than "Father." Our church started to bulge.

We invited lots of speakers who addressed thorny problems both personal and public. We had pacifist Philip Berrigan, Senator Eugene McCarthy, theologian Anthony Padovano, and poets Robert Bly and John Berrigan. Then one day in 1978, a parishioner called and said that Gloria Steinem was in town. When she said she could get her to speak, I immediately said yes. I admired her. She was a heroine of the feminist movement.

Well, the place was jammed. The opposition, mostly from the pro-life movement was there with a loudspeaker that bellowed: "She is a murderer. Gloria Steinem is a baby killer."

She spoke for twenty minutes, but never mentioned abortion. She did say that it is a tragedy that most institutionalized religions have proclaimed and perpetuated a message of sexism and racism.

The next day the papers were filled with it. The event made the front pages in New York, Tokyo, and Rome. By Wednesday of that week, I was summoned to a meeting with Archbishop John Roach. The archbishop had been eminently kind in dealing with me and the parish. He told me once that, if there were not a St. Joan's, he would have to establish one. Later, when he was asked why there were not more parishes like St. Joan's, he said: "One is enough!"

Archbishop Roach had drafted a letter of apology to the local Catholics and a censure for the parish. We received hundreds of letters, pro and con. I learned a few new obscene words. I was called a "stupid, psychopathic Irishman." But one Catholic writer wrote that it was "strange to hear my church publicly rebuke a priest for allowing his parishioners to hear the other side of an issue that threatens to tear the church apart." I got so many calls that I finally shut the phone off.

You know, in the old days the priests fought for the big parishes, those with the huge church and school. Now, no one wants them. There are impossible situations with loads of problems and no more curates to help the pastor. Look at Joan of Arc. When I retired, there must have been 350 priests in the diocese. People were standing in the parking lot for Sunday Mass. Lately, they've added a sixth Mass on Sunday evening. The place is still growing, but no one applied.

Twenty years ago, Richard McBrien [chairman of the Theology Department, University of Notre Dame] called for small communities. McBrien is one of my heroes. He reminded us that a pastor is more important than a bishop. It's true. Bishops are administrators, too far removed from the community. McBrien says that the Christian community should seek to meet the unmet needs of the people. I've tried to do that. That's the role of a Christian. The unchurched, the young and the old—it's our job to find them and to serve them. We've got to tell them where their adult education needs can be met, tell them where the best is and send them there. We can't create a mental and spiritual ghetto. Otherwise, the church will become a second-rate cooking school.

We tried to combat racism at St. Joan's. We tried to do something about housing but it didn't work. We were involved in the women's movement from the beginning, but it seems to have waned. That second letter on women by the bishops is worse than the first. But the bishops won't repudiate it. It would be a miracle if they rescinded it. What we need is a letter written by women about bishops. [A few weeks after this interview, the Vatican asked the American bishops to delay the publication of the pastoral on women, suggesting that other countries be allowed to study it. The conference was held in May, 1991. The results were inconclusive.]

I searched, I wrestled with and, in large measure, I failed to find the effective formula for progress. I wanted to concentrate on the religious needs of our parishioners and the social problems of our society, but most of my days were crowded with a pressing parish agenda: attending meandering meetings, preparing bulletins, answering doorbells, supervising caretakers, visiting patients in hospitals, shopping, writing letters, finding keys, and creating an impression of orderliness. I was also expected to add a bit of clerical geniality at anniversaries, graduations, wedding receptions, and corporate takeovers.

Oh, we did get our people involved in social concerns. We helped at the

Dorothy Day Center with the Catholic Worker. I didn't want to duplicate what they were doing, so we simply tried to help.

In the pastoral ministry, it is not the wrong done that triggers personal uneasiness, but the good left undone. Sadly, I often failed to help people with pains and problems—a loveless marriage, a dehumanizing job, a lurking tumor, religious doubts, errant children. The pleas for help that I could not give were frequent and urgent; the delays and failures caused pain.

Personal counseling was not my long suit. I rarely knew what to say when a middle-aged wage earner for a family lost a job or when a teenager wept at Communion time every Sunday or an affluent woman shoplifted at a supermarket. I struggled when unprepared people volunteered to help a parish program or a shouter wanted a political platform. Sometimes a man with slipping plates wanted to be a lector, or a woman who believed she was already saved and could not pray "O Lord, I am not worthy" wanted to guide the prayer services in our church.

Our parish property became a nuclear weapon free zone, but it didn't seem to make a difference.

I rejoiced when a non-Roman became pope, but now his legalism has out-Romaned the Romans. The Vatican and the bishops are leaving the Church. Word has it that the pope's next encyclical will be on moral values and that he might lift the teaching on birth control to the level of infallibility. That would cause the separation of the leaders from the real church to grow even more.

Look at Richard McCormick [Jesuit, John A. O'Brien professor of Christian ethics at the University of Notre Dame]. He's hardly a liberal but he's going out on a limb. He's the biggest recent switch. He said something to the effect that "I'm changing with the changing church." I think his final line was: "I once considered that loving the church meant acquiescing. Now I see silence in a changing world as betraying the church."

Did you read Bernard Haring's [German Redemptorist, moral theologian] essays in the *Tablet*? He recalled that he was investigated by the Nazis three times and by the Vatican once. "I'll take the Nazis," he said! Our best theologians are being investigated and accused of moral relativism. And look at our bishops. After you've looked at Weakland [Rembert G. Weakland, O.S.B., archbishop of Milwaukee] and Hunthausen [Raymond G. Hunthausen, archbishop of Seattle], you've used them all up.

The celibacy issue is hurting us. Some years ago, a young guy would stay around for ten years after ordination and then start looking around. Now, the older men are doing it. There's a terrible need for companionship. Well, God bless them! There's so little for them. Anthony Padovano [Dr. Anthony T. Padovano, president of *CORPUS*, a group of resigned priests and others calling for optional celibacy and the ordination of women] tells me that it's going to change and that we'll have married priests within ten years, but I don't see it. I hope it comes today! The statistics are disheartening.

Our little group meets every month. We pray, discuss, sometimes have Eucharist. We aren't engaged in social causes. Perhaps we should be. Everyone in the group is a cradle Catholic, registered in a parish, but they don't subscribe to Church teaching on every issue, especially on birth control. That issue has turned the Church into hypocrites. Even the right-wing priests are absolving those who come to them. It's a gross contradiction, an impossible problem in the confessional.

Small, informal communities seem to be the pattern for the future for people who wish to remain Catholic. Hopefully, they'll have a priest to pray with them. But priests want to be more than eucharistic celebrators. They want to be multifaceted.

This is a wild prediction, but I believe that in the years ahead we will be like the early Christians. For the first three centuries or so, there were no priests. People simply gathered and broke bread with the head of the household as the leader of the celebration. The friends of the Lord met and prayed and something happened. There wasn't any formal priesthood and no bishops until about the fourth century.

Hans Kung raises the question of what happens when Christians get together. Does anything happen? He believes that it does. But do we need the priest? Parents can do baptism. In Penance we can ask God for forgiveness. Confirmation can become a Bar Mitzvah. In Matrimony the priest is only a witness and the perpetuity of marriage is being reconsidered. Extreme Unction has been long under scrutiny. Do we need a grease job at the end of our lives? It's the direction of our lives that really counts. And so it gets down to Eucharist and one must ask: "Is it really necessary to have a priest for Eucharist? The priesthood could disappear.

My mother predicted that I would travel alone most of the time. "But at some place along the road," she said, "you may find a family, or a family may find you." It happened. It happened at Joan of Arc. I found a colony of Christian friends who were in a zestful search. We danced for twenty years.

"Let the pilgrims march on without you," Mother also told me, "just before you get tired and stumble."

And that's what I've done. Now, I am more of a watcher than a marcher.

· 12 ·

John J. Egan: Pastoral and Social Ministry

When Monsignor John J. Egan was a young seminarian at Chicago's St. Mary of the Lake Seminary (now the University of St. Mary of the Lake at Mundelein), he came under the influence of the legendary Monsignor Reynold Hillenbrand, the man who transformed seminary education in America. Hillenbrand planted seeds of social activism that would cause Jack Egan to gravitate toward movements such as the Young Christian Workers and Young Christian Students, which he served as chaplain.

In early 1954, Saul Alinsky, a maverick social organizer that theologian Charles Curran believes had a most distinctive impact on the American Catholic social justice movement, called Egan. Alinsky's friend, the philosopher Jacques Maritain, had suggested that he get in touch with Egan in order to meet a Father Voillaume, the founder of the Little Brothers and the Little Sisters of Jesus. Voillaume was coming to Chicago and would be staying at a parish where Egan was a resident priest while directing the Cana Conference of Chicago. Alinksky called and the two met in Egan's office. They began a friendship that would last until Alinsky's death in 1972. In one of their hundreds of meaty conversations, Alinsky said to him: "Make up your mind, Jack, whether you want to be a bishop or a priest. All other decisions will flow from that one."

Jack Egan is not without ambition. He would like to have been a bishop. But a social conscience and a sensitivity that refused to see people pushed around would preclude any ecclesiastical ambitions.

Egan chose the picket line over the procession.

Jack Egan is a romantic pragmatist. He can cry in frustration at mindless injustice, but he can also cut a deal. When dealing with city agencies and independent groups, he caused them to see the archdiocese of Chicago and its priests as trusted and valuable resources, even while persuading some of the priests to set aside their own prejudices. Few priests are more loyal to their fellow priests, yet Egan has risked isolation from them in order to achieve a measure of justice.

Even at seventy-five, he risks isolation by going public on issues involving race and labor. His letters still appear in Chicago's papers and, although he did not agree with everything it said, he signed the controversial *New York Times* advertisement sponsored by Chicago's Call to Action calling for reform within the Church.

Monsignor Egan was unafraid to take on the powerful Richard J. Daley, Chicago's mayor, and the University of Chicago with its deep pocket financial reserves and media influence. The issue was race. It was a sad chapter in a great mayor's and a great university's history. Egan lost the battle but won the war.

There is much more. Jack Egan is in the history books now. Jay P. Dolan's *American Catholic Experience* and Sanford D. Howitt's *Let Them Call Me Rebel*, a biography of Saul Alinsky, are just two books that have appeared in recent years that cite Egan's work. His own biography, *An Alley in Chicago: The Ministry of a City Priest*, by Margery Frisbie, will be published in 1991.

Egan has been a priest since 1943. He is now assistant to the president for Community Affairs at DePaul University in Chicago. Born in 1916, he has survived at least one serious heart attack and two major heart surgeries. Yet, he continues to live and work in a parish and to serve on a half-dozen boards. He has been awarded six honorary degrees and a dozen other major awards for his humanitarian and ecumenical efforts.

The monsignor (everyone calls him "Jack") is the former director of the Cana Conference and the Office of Urban Affairs of the archdiocese of Chicago. Under Cardinals Samuel Stritch and Albert Meyer, Egan's work flourished; but when the autocratic Cardinal John Cody arrived in 1965, Egan's budget dried up and he was assigned to the ailing Presentation Parish on Chicago's westside. In 1970, Theodore Hesburgh, University of Notre Dame president, invited him to South Bend where he served as a special assistant to the president and director of the Institute for Pastoral and Social Ministry. When Cardinal Joseph Bernardin was named archbishop in 1982, he asked Egan to return home. He served as director of the Office of Human Relations and Ecumenism for four years before going to DePaul.

Jack Egan remains the consummate communicator. He is the master of the short but pointed letter and the perfectly aimed phone call. He can still work the back of the church and he remains a tireless cheerleader to his fellow priests.

Well, I've survived. I've hung in there. I love being a priest. It's been a great life. I still love wakes and weddings. I love the old parishioners. I love working the curb outside of church after Mass. I don't like calculated movements.

Jim Halleran was my first boss at St. Justin Martyr in 1943. Halleran told me to take care of the people and he'd take care of the parish. Oh, we counted the collection together on Sundays, but, for the most part, I took care of the people while Jim ran the parish. Jim Halleran taught me a great lesson. He was a comer. He was assistant chancellor or something and he crossed [Cardinal George] Mundelein on a matter of principle. He was out within a week and Mundelein moved in Bennie [later Archbishop Bernard J.] Sheil. Halleran's career was over but he never uttered a word of complaint. He did say to me: "You'll be a wise man, Jack, if you just stay in a parish. Stay away from the chancery office as much as you can. The work of the church is in the parish." Saul Alinsky told me the same thing.

It was George Higgins [Monsignor George G. Higgins, professor emeritus, columnist, now retired, at Catholic University in Washington, D.C.] who taught me that you have to learn to fight injustice wherever you find it, whether it's in a white or a black community. When Eugene Sawyer was mayor in Chicago, I went to him and told him that one of his aides was going to destroy him. And I said so in letters to the *Sun-Times* and the *Chicago Tribune*. Sawyer was black and his aide was black. That didn't matter. He spread untruths and hatred. You've got to speak out. You've got to pay your dues. (Sawyer listened; he fired the aide.)

It was no different years ago when I asked the late Bill Berry of the Urban League to talk at the American Legion Hall out at 69th and Paulina. We both talked on race relations and racial equality. It was met with complete silence. The guy who invited us vomited after the talk. Four guys escorted me to my car. "We wanted to be sure you got out safely, Father," they said. And these were guys I had been working with, Catholics! Afterwards, Bill Berry told me that he said the same thing to black audiences as he did to white audiences. I've always tried to do the same.

A priest has to realize that for reasons he cannot explain he has been blessed far beyond his desserts. He has to crawl into people's lives on the street or in the hospital room or on a plane. There are just so many blessings that come into a priest's life.

No one should be ordained who doesn't give clear indications of loving people. A priest has got to be vulnerable. He must be willing to let people take little chunks out of him. I made a vow when I was ordained that I would never say no. A priest must always be open to people.

The days of my priesthood have always been days of crisis. I was in the seminary during the latter part of the Depression. I was ordained during World War II. Much of my priesthood came during the period when racism and civil rights were issues. Then, there was Vietnam. Everyone of these crises touched individuals I was close to. It was issues like that which kept me in the priesthood.

Sometimes, one has to remain because the work must be done. Not long ago, I wrote to a young priest who was on a leave of absence and told him that he should never leave, that he should stay in there, that the work he was doing was simply too important, and that he was so good at it. Sometimes, a man should stay because the work is more important than the individual.

Again, it's the influence a priest can have, sometimes an influence he isn't even aware that he is having. I'm thinking of a woman named Mary whom I've known as far back as my days with the Cana Conference. Her daughter called me recently and told me that Mary was dead. I went to the funeral where I learned something that taught me a great deal about the influence of a priest. Mary and her husband—he was a physician—were very active in the Cana Conference movement. They used to make retreats with us up in Ontario and it was during these that I listened to Mary. She taught me a great deal about married love. In fact, she formed my understanding of married love.

What I didn't know was that, through all those years, Mary's husband was addicted to drugs. They were wonderfully devoted to one another but there was terrible pain there. Her daughter said that Mary used to keep a picture of her and me on her bedstand. Somehow, the picture sustained her when times were tough. I feel that way about the priesthood. There can be pain but, like Mary, you hang in there. I wish that young priest had. He had so many gifts. But he left and married and we all lost something.

There are the blessings and the sacrifices. It's really scaring me now, but the thing that is deep in my soul at this moment is that, every time I say Mass, two thoughts haunt me: first, how unworthy I am to represent the community and, second, the Mass means more and more to me, but it so tests my faith. You know, I look out over the people in the cathedral. I've come to know some of them and something about what they have endured. And I feel like Newman [John Henry Cardinal Newman, English convert, prelate, author, candidate for sainthood]. He used to pray "Lord, I believe. Help my unbelief."

I remember Reynie Hillebrand saying to us one time: "Life is so pitiably short and I have only a few years to live." It makes me sorry that they took the prayer "What should I give to the Lord for all he has given me?" out of the liturgy. It still means so much to me.

I wasn't too bright as a student. I really had to work my ass off to get things done. But I've been blessed with good assignments and good priests. I even had to overcome my father's opposition to my going into the seminary. He told me that he didn't want the same thing to happen to me that happened to him. I didn't know this for years but he had been a novice with the Irish Christian Brothers back in Ireland and, when he left, he was talked about as the spoiled brother, the one who left. It was a disgrace in those days. He never got over the hurt he suffered. He didn't want me to suffer.

I was lucky. I had the work ethic screwed into me. I had to work hard and I had to do it within my own skin. I had to learn my limitations and learn how to enjoy people; how to let them open up to me. Everyone is so exciting, you know, even the stinkers.

I wanted to succeed. I was ambitious. I had a driving force. I didn't always do things for the right motive. I think my crucial sin before God is pride. I wanted to succeed. I wanted to be wanted. And now that I've achieved everything I set out to achieve, I am left with the question as to whether or not I've become a holy person. I'm not at all sure.

Priests must have lay people in their lives. Laity must be there to affirm them, to be critical of them, to tell them the truth. The laity are there. They're in every parish. If you listen to them, they are a treasure. I had the parish and YCS (Young Christian Students), the YCW (Young Christian Workers) and the Cana Conference. These people brought me so much and taught me so much.

I had a priest friend in Baltimore. A Servite named Kevin Conway. He said to me years ago, "You know, Jack, you're not too smart, but you're smart enough to get good people around you." Well, I guess I've done that all right.

I've also found that it helps a great deal to have a few priests around you who respect you, guys with whom you can share stuff. Guys like Ed Conway over at Catholic Charities. We have dinner together and I can tell him things. It really helps.

You can't pass it on, you know. You've got to do it. Time is running out. I'm now passing over articles in the *National Catholic Reporter* about appointments of bishops and all that. Now, such news is no longer important. I have no vote and the area in which I can now do some good is the parish.

Now, I can do some good in the confessional. Now, more than ever, I realize that a priest must be kind in the confessional. When I was a young deacon, the man in charge of us deacons told us that the day that we were unkind in the confessional is a day we could never recover.

My best moments in the box come when I am struggling about what to say to a person. I realize my own frailty and that God must work through me. And then it's amazing how eloquent I can become!

You know, when you use the collar in terms of justice, that's when you really walk the walk. But you never walk alone. I'm really puzzled by all this talk about the loneliness of the priest. I've always had people in my life, even when I was involved in protests of one kind or another. A priest can make himself alone. I've always had a helluva lot of people in my life.

One of the worse things we're facing is retirement. Today, people are crying to be able to talk to a priest. We should be accumulating wisdom. We can retire from our administrative duties but not from the spiritual side. We're *never* retired from pastoral work!

I've been so lucky. I've been trained by the finest this country has produced. There were Reynie Hillenbrand and George Schuster [former president of Hunter College and chancellor of the University of Notre Dame]. There was John Ryan on social teaching and John Courtney Murray. I remember well being in Rome during the debate over the Declaration on Religious Freedom (Dignitatis Humanae) and having John Courtney Murray burst into the common room in the seminary where we were staying. "Jack, we won!" he said. I could feel his enthusiasm and love for the Church. I remember sitting in a kitchen in Paris with de Lubac [Cardinal Henri de Lubac, S.J., a *peritus* at Vatican II, once dismissed from the faculty of Lyons because of a misunderstanding of his book, *The Supernatural*; reinstated by John XXIII; named a cardinal by John Paul II in 1983]. I'd be an ingrate if I didn't try to pay them back through my priesthood.

Our ordination class meets faithfully three times each year. We've been doing it for forty-seven years. The same twenty-four out of the surviving twenty-eight show up; fifteen others are dead. Only one man left. He was a terribly shy man who probably never should have been ordained. We treated him contemptuously. It was terribly unfair. The poor man just couldn't answer back.

Two men have sustained me in my priesthood. Tim Lyne [classmate, now auxiliary bishop of Chicago] and Gerry Weber [classmate, author, now semi-retired in California.] Tim has been a great advisor. Years ago, while I was still at Notre Dame, Tim advised me not to come back to Chicago. He was right. It would have been awful. And Gerry was envious of me and I think correctly. I was getting credit for the work he was doing. His criticism of me brought me down to reality. He made me think. I'll never forget Gerry Weber.

But the most sustaining force for me over forty-seven years has been lay people. I'm thinking of the YCS and the YCW. We had four hundred volunteers and I was close to all of them. Then, there were all those national groups. I've had the privilege of working on national-level groups, helping them to put things together. Then, there's all the people I married over the years. I've gotten close to all of them.

Now, thanks to the national networking, I can go into any city and get a room for the night. I've come to know a network of priests and sisters. That's been a great force in my life.

Since late 1966, Peggy Roach [administrative assistant], has been a sustaining force in my life. She has a great love of the Church and respect for the priesthood. She has integrity and unbelievable loyalty. She has great wisdom. I trust her with anything. She is my closest advisor. Peggy knows how to love people in an appropriate way. When I get all steamed up about saving the world, Peggy will say to me: "Apparently, you don't believe that God loves the world far more than you do. He sent his Son."

I haven't been blessed with the ability to make friends. I've really had to work at it. As a young man I felt that there wasn't much in me to love. To some, making friends comes naturally, but not to me. It was only after I was ordained that I found the sustaining force of the love of God. I also discovered a sense of humor and an ability to take issues seriously but not to take myself too seriously.

I got into social action for the same reason Dan Cantwell did. He sensed the pain in people—the blacks and the poor—and I shared that feeling.

I'm glad that I'm feeling well because I've got some jobs to do. I've got to go to war again, this time with one union at a hotel that is being unfair. You know, there's very few priests to call on in the labor movement nowadays.

This world needs a deeper appreciation of the southern hemisphere. The northern part still tries to dominate the southern part. John Paul's message has gotten so truncated because of the Church's teaching on birth control. I'm afraid that his background is keeping him from seeing needs. He would have had an unbelievable influence if he had just stayed out of the sexual issues.

We've got to deal with the decline in our numbers in the Church. At the same time, we've got to deal with the fact that millions throughout the world are being deprived of the faith. We've got to deal with the fact that, with the decline of priests, those that remain are being overworked and this is tragic. We must help priests to understand the role of the laity. They can perform a multitude of duties that priests are now doing. We've got to bring back the old practices of so many organizations to observe, judge, and act.

We must ordain married men and we should ordain women. There is a place for optional celibacy, in fact there's a sacredness to it. It freed me to do so many things but in all other areas of life there are noncelibate people who are also giving completely. Sadly, too often celibacy just frees us to do what we please.

I'm thinking of Lorscheider [Cardinal Aloisio Lorscheider, O.F.M., archbishop of Fortaleza, Brazil] who called at the Synod on the Priesthood for theologically trained leaders from the community. He and I share the same thinking. We simply haven't handled well the training of lay people.

I recall Dorothy Day and Reynie Hillenbrand saying that priests must be poor, not just in spirit but poor financially. I think of the workman with his pail, getting on the trolley, and remember that he is supporting me. I think of the beggar who looked at me one day and said: "You're just a better beggar."

There's another thing. A priest has to be aware of when and how to pray and he's got to be convinced that he cannot do without it. The best prayer I ever heard came to me from the Chicago Board of Rabbis who wrote me at Mercy Hospital after my heart attack. "Dear God," their prayer said, "don't let me die because I have not loved enough yet." (Cries.)

LATER: I hope you weren't disappointed with the interview. You made me cry, you (bleep)!

· 13 ·

John Tracy Ellis: Church Historian

Monsignor John Tracy Ellis could be said to have educated every priest in America. For over fifty years, he has taught at the Catholic University of America. During that time, he has written some twenty books. His influence has been responsible for introducing church history into the seminary curriculum. His classic, *American Catholicism*, first published in 1956 and revised in 1969, is in its seventh printing. It is part of the renowned University of Chicago History of American Civilization series, edited by Daniel J. Boorstin.

John Tracy Ellis not only taught seminarians; he also influenced Catholics, Protestants, Jews, and nonbelievers, by, in Boorstin's words, helping them to "discover how narrowly Protestant has been the familiar interpretation of our history."

John Tracy Ellis's students are now among the hierarchy, the seminary rectors and professors, and the priests in the parishes. He has taught them that they can be faithful to their Church without setting aside their intellects. He has had the gift of time, over a half-century of teaching and writing, enough to have a profound impact. His students have reciprocated. Monsignor Ellis has received at least twenty honorary degrees and numerous other awards, including the Laetare Medal from the University of Notre Dame.

He lives in retirement at Curley Hall on the campus of Catholic University in Washington, D.C., where he was interviewed in his quarters, from which he rarely strays. A consummate gentleman, he reflects many of the virtues of one of his heroes, John Henry Newman.

N.B.: Characteristically, Monsignor Ellis had prepared for the interview. Some of his statements are taken from material he alluded to in his essay in *The Catholic Priest in the United States* (St. John's University Press, Collegeville, Minnesota, 1971). Other citations are from an essay in the same book by Michael V. Gannon, a former student of Monsignor Ellis. The essay is titled: "Before and After Modernism: the Intellectual Isolation of the American Priest." Still other notes are from Ellis's *American Catholicism* (University of Chicago Press, revised 1969), and from an article in *The Tablet* (October 6, 1990) by Sean McDonagh.

In the interests of simplicity and clarity, some of the citations have been paraphrased but I believe that they fairly represent what Monsignor Ellis pointed out.

I can still read, thank the Lord. I can still say Mass every day and that's a great consolation. I'm eight-five and I've had a stroke recently, and I've had diabetes for years. I'm pretty much confined to this apartment, thirty-two steps from end to end. I walk back and forth to get my exercise and I get my meals downstairs. There are about twenty of us here at Curley Hall. I taught here until 1989 and just quietly retired. I like it here. This is my home.

You are as wise as I am about the future. I'm a historian, not a prophet. Those who live until 2050 may see a change in the Church. I'm told that the seminaries in Africa and Latin America are filling up. Maybe my nephew is young enough to witness the changes that will come. But it will take time.

As for the reasons for the present problems in the American Church, it's all there in that book [*The Catholic Priest in the United States: Historical Investigations*]. You'll learn in my essay in that book that the American Church has always been short of priests. Between 1920 and 1970, the Catholic population grew from 17,700,000 to 47,800,000 and the number of priests increased from 21,000 to 59,000. That's an increase of 266 percent in population and 295 percent in the number of priests. We never met our needs completely and we never met them with American-born priests. We imported many of our seminary professors and many of our priests and seminarians. When Bishop Casper H. Borgess took up his duties in the diocese of Detroit in 1870, for example, he had eighty-six priests, only six of them native Americans. So, of course, we mustn't be surprised that our numbers are now down. Among other things, the foreign-born priests are simply not there.

But the main reasons for our present situation can be found in the essay by Michael V. Gannon. He was one of my students from St. Augustine, Florida. He's left the priesthood now. But you read that essay, "Before and After Modernism: The Intellectual Isolation of the American Priest." That tells it. The Modernist Movement simply snuffed out the hopeful character within the Church.

The early priests in America were only modestly educated. In 1819, Archbishop Marechal of Baltimore complained that of the ten Irish priests who had come to his diocese, eight turned out badly. Yet, when he sent men to France for an education, he was only concerned that they learn to preach and be submissive. Seminarians attended formal classes only a few hours each week and courses in Canon Law were considered "ornamental."

The immigrant priest may be judged harshly by the Protestant critics and by modern Catholic historians, but he was seen as nothing less than an intellectual giant by his people, not for his theology, but because he could give advice on politics, law, education, mechanics, pharmacy, banking, and social reform. De Tocqueville wrote in 1832 (*Democracy in America*) that the priest rose above the rank of his flock. Years later Archbishop Ireland [1838—1918] of St. Paul said that "Priests are officers, laymen are soldiers."

Anti-Catholicism was the pornography of the Puritan culture. It reached its height with the nativist movements of the 1840s and 1850s and the American Protective Association of the 1890s. Those movements put the Catholic Church on the defensive. The intellectual abilities of the American priests were devoted almost exclusively to the task of apologetics. As for the other writings, they were all heavily influenced by European thinkers. The Church remained on the defensive.

The Civil War changed some things. It brought the clergy into politics and bound them up with the nation. Catholics fought with their fellow Americans on each side. But it was no sooner over than Vatican I (1869–70) introduced the doctrine of infallibility. For the most part, the American bishops objected to it. It was seen by them as simply impractical because it served to separate Catholics from their fellow Americans. But they submitted.

Then, in 1871, after the close of Vatican I, Charles Darwin published *The Descent of Man* in which he made explicit what he had written first in his *Origin of the Species*. For the next thirty years, Darwin's theories divided Catholic thought. The bishops and the priests vacillated between granting the probability of evolution without fully accepting it, and rejecting it without fully condemning it. The issue really separated the Church from the intellectual community. After a while, evolution was associated with atheism.

Now, add to that the Sulpician piety that permeated the clergy for so long. It placed great stress on humility and obedience, a military subjection of priest to his bishop, and it cautioned against the "vanity" of learning. Further, immigrant priests tied their nationalties to their faith and cautioned against "Americanizers," including the Irish-American bishops. Rome even managed to issue a papal condemnation of "Americanism" in 1899. None of this did much for Catholic intellectual life.

The division between American Catholic thought and American scientific thought was fixed in the fight over evolution. It also influenced the whole tenor of American seminary education. The seminaries were founded in great numbers, without much planning and with bishops jealously guarding their own. Around the turn of the century, the average seminary had only about forty students. You can't have much quality with numbers like that. Besides, the seminaries were even more hampered by the pervasive belief that they held all the necessary truths of life. They saw themselves as a center for the diffusion of knowledge, not for research of new knowledge. Clerics rarely got in touch with authentic university traditions. The candidate for the priesthood was insulated from the natural or historical sciences. Scholasticism was the only discipline; the intellectual processes of the Thomistic system were the only ones approved. The value of a secular education was not even adverted to. When Walter Drum, a prospective Jesuit, applied to enter the society, for example, he suggested to the provincial that he might study at Harvard for his doctorate before entering. He was told not to "waste" two years at Harvard. That's how it was.

There was a lot of intellectual arrogance and cocksureness among the clergy, and it lasted for years. Not all felt that way. Bishop John Lancaster Spalding of Peoria, Illinois, called seminaries the "elementary schools of theology" and he called for a "high school" of philosophy and theology at the very least. But changes would be years away.

It was beginning to change for the better. In the early years of this century, the quality of seminary education began to improve. Intellectual publications such as the *American Catholic Quarterly Review* began to appear. We were ready for an intellectual renaissance. The Paulist Fathers began to work in universities and bishops began to appoint chaplains to secular universities.

But in 1907, lightning struck. The Holy Office issued a syllabus (*Lamentabli sane exitu*) that listed sixty-five heretical propositions, and in the same year Pius X issued an encyclical (*Pascendi Dominici*) condemning the errors of what he called "modernism." The encyclical cautioned against all systems of thought that expounded an evolutionary theory of religion; or suggested that the Church had reshaped eternal truths in every period of its history according to its understanding; or otherwise threatened the validity and the stability of dogma. The number of modernist heretics in the American Church was barely a half-dozen. Most of the fears were imported from Europe. The modernist teachings barely took hold. Only three priests left the ministry and married. That's rather an insignificant number to start a movement. But the paranoia the encyclical ignited spread rapidly. Seminary curriculum was often reduced to a series of questions and answers, questions that had not been asked in centuries. Students were expected to simply memorize everything. "Catholic philosophy alone has the whole truth," one professor wrote. He echoed what others thought or practiced. Students developed the weakest of all attitudes toward adversaries—one of contempt. The truth, they were told, put a stop to the swaying of the mind. Minds became fixed with mindless certainties. Men such as Cardinal Mercier and Angelo Roncalli (later John XXIII) would suffer because of Modernism.

The attitude lasted well into our day. The conceit of the clergy was terrible. Some priests, ordained between 1915 and 1929, and interviewed in 1969, stated that they felt that they had received a superior education, despite the fact that their education required little reading and less research. The seminary library was opened only two hours a day. The seminary was seen as another West Point or Annapolis. There were frequent analogies drawn from the military.

Here at Catholic University, we had to take the oath against Modernism every year. The fact that we took it once wasn't enough. If you missed the ceremony, then you had to go to the office of the vice rector who would administer it the next day.

I came here in 1935, three years before I was ordained. I taught part-time until 1938 when I became a full-time professor in church history. That was in the history department. In 1976, a new School of Religious Studies was formed with a department of Church History. It may be the only one in the world. There are twenty-nine in the Religious Studies school now, two of them full-time in Church History.

We have never fully regained the intellectual status that was beginning to take hold before Modernism. We frightened promising scholars out of existence. It has cost us uncountable vocations. I believe that there are only fifty seminarians here at Catholic U. and only thirty-eight at Dunwoodie (archdiocese of New York). There were 130 here in my time. I can't say that suppression of thought caused the present shortage of vocations. But it was an unhealthy atmosphere for growth.

There was a spirit about those days after Modernism. It was mostly bad. Now, we're largely out of it, but we are paying the price. The case involving Charles Curran isn't part of the old thinking. It's really rather complicated, not cut and dried. I couldn't agree with him on a number of his stances but his charity puts me to shame.

If the seminaries went to one extreme years ago, some seem to go to an opposite extreme today. Some seminarians are out on the streets to all hours of the night. We have young men in seminary going out at night to bars. We have a report of one rector turning the budget over to the students. Well, chaos ensued. Some seminaries have no daily Mass. Seminarians should be going to Mass every day. Well, I think that we may be getting back to a more moderate way of life.

The effects of Modernism aren't the only reasons why we are having a crisis in the priesthood. There are a great many pressures from outside. There's been a general breakdown of morals, too. We're living through a revolution that is turning society on its head. There just doesn't seem to be any moral sense; we've become very weak; I'm afraid that we yield to things around us. I was just listening to Beverly Sills speaking at the annual Al Smith dinner in New York last week. She was pointing out the terrible problem of child abuse. Isn't that terrible?

I don't want to sound too facile in blaming society. But I believe that Catholics who have attained riches have succumbed. I'm thinking of one Catholic family with fourteen children. They are multimillionaires. One of the children is dead and three others are unmarried, but the remaining ten have all been divorced. Two generations ago, this would have been unthinkable!

I think, too, of the support that rich Catholics give to charity. Catholic institutions just don't get that support. Look at that Catholic man who has given $40 million to Columbia and not one cent to Catholic U. We're all touched by these things. The Church, after all, doesn't exist on Mars. It's going to have an impact on us.

This priest crisis has happened before, but not in the United States. Priests have always been falling away in the U.S. as far back as John Carroll of Baltimore, America's first archbishop. He faced that as early as 1784. And it will be that way until the end of time. But we still have suffered nothing like the losses we had during the Protestant Reformation or the French Revolution, during which many left and many married to avoid detection. Now, as I wrote in *American Catholicism*, the monastic discipline of the seminary, the static scholasticism that so long dominated the curriculum, the authoritarian teaching methods, and the general Council of Trent tone that dominated the system for so long had to undergo a radical change. I believe that it's that change that we are experiencing now.

There's an article here in the recent *Tablet* [an international, lay-edited Catholic weekly out of London]. It's by Father Sean McDonagh, a Columban Father, who served in the Philippines and is now coordinator for justice and peace at the Columban Fathers headquarters at Navan in Ireland. It reflects some of my views. This recent Synod on the Priesthood isn't addressing the whole question of ministry. It's simply talking about priestly formation. The *Lineamenta* for the synod that was circulated in advance of it did very little to encourage church leaders to bring imagination to bear and come up with relevant and workable solutions. The document failed to look realistically at the dwindling number of candidates entering the priesthood and bypassed the emerging debate about ministry in the Church. The only context in which they wanted to discuss priesthood was within the old clergy/ laity or sacred/secular dichotomies. It all smacked of the damage control that politicians utilize. The bishops insist that there are signs of revival. But that is not an honest picture.

The document blames materialism and selfishness for the fall in vocations and, as I said, there is more than an element of truth in this. But it is simplistic and misleading. The studies show that there are a significant number of people willing to become involved in ministry, but these young people do not feel called to a life of celibacy, and John Paul II has ruled out any discussion of celibacy at the synod. How can a worthwhile debate on ministry take place unless the question of celibacy is addressed? The bishops could have begun by tearing up the *Lineamenta* and drawing on their own pastoral experience. Otherwise, we can expect more of the same: exhortations to pray for more vocations, glossy vocation brochures, and tighter control in seminaries.

My own background was very modest. My father was a Methodist; my mother's side of the family was solidly Catholic. My father wept when he learned I was going to the seminary, but he came around. In fact, his two sisters asked him about becoming a Catholic, but he never converted. He was buried from St. Patrick's Church back home with twelve of my fellow priests on the altar.

I was raised in Seneca, Illinois, in the Peoria diocese. My family is still there. I taught briefly at St. Viator's College before entering the seminary for the diocese of Winona, Minnesota. But I've spent all my time here at Catholic U. and, years ago, transferred to the archdiocese of Washington.

Yes, those are some of my heroes on the wall. That's Thomas More, John Carroll, James Gibbons of Baltimore, and John Henry Newman. I'd love to see Newman canonized and named a Doctor of the Church. But it will be difficult. Do you know that he wrote 20,000 letters alone? They fill forty volumes. They'll have to go through all those. It will take time!

Anyway, I am grateful for my life. I hope that I did some good. I get assurances in correspondence or in a call I got recently from a priest in San Francisco who told me how much he appreciated my work. I hope so. I want to bring God something.

· 14 ·

John Everyman: Every Priest

When Father John Everyman was contacted for an interview, he said: "I've written something about that very topic. I sent it to *The National Catholic Reporter* with the request that they publish it anonymously. They turned me down, saying that they don't like to publish anonymous articles. So, it's been sitting on my desk."

Everyman and I had lunch together. He didn't want publicity for a number of reasons, all of them understandable. Letters or conversations that sound like gripe sessions can backfire. He is a good priest who loves his work. His thoughts are faintly melancholy but they are echoed by many priests. They are what one hears in rectories, especially during discussions of the issues that affect the morale of priests.

During 1990, in the Diocese of Green Bay, Wisconsin, a group of thoughtful priests spoke openly of the issues that prompt weariness and low morale. They included lack of vocations, conflict with administration on policies, changes in the priests' role and identity, tensions caused by feeling forced into using unsanctioned practices, conflict with conservative groups (altar girls, group reconciliation services, etc.), loneliness and isolation, retirement concerns and other costs, undue expectations from hierarchy and parishioners, insufficient areas for advancement, less recognition, fewer rewards and promotions, ongoing universal supression of thought. Father Dennis Bergsbaken of Hortonville, Wisconsin, said: "When you're doing the best things, there are groups who are convinced that you're going to hell in a handbasket." Father Mike O'Rourke of Appleton, Wisconsin, added: "I feel like a mother robin cleaning out the nest and I have a worm in my mouth and I've got this one pelican that reaches up and grabs everything I bring. The pelican is the institution screaming for attention to support itself. And around underneath the nest there are grandmas and grandpas and little kids for whom I thought I was getting into the priesthood. I'm supposed to feed them, not for myself, but for them, but I can't get past the damn institution. It's taking everything I bring to the nest. It's frustrating as all hell." Reporter Kathy Berken of Green Bay who covered the seminar cited another priest, Harold Berryman, who described the frustration with this example: "General absolution was outlawed just when people were returning to the sacrament of reconciliation. We had a penance service and the place was overflowing, but now it's taken away."

So it goes. John Everyman's letter is not a catalog of gripes. It is rather a summary of very real problems that may be at the root not only of priests' morale but also contributing to the shortage of priests.

I t doesn't matter who I am. But it matters what I am. I'm a priest. I've been one for twenty-five years.

I'm a pastor. I serve in a city parish of one thousand families. I am its only priest.

I love the priesthood and I love my people. I pledged my life twenty-five years ago, and even before then, to serve God's people. I have given my life to help all people as best I can. To this end I have freely renounced marriage, promised obedience, and not expected material gain. Jesus is at the heart of my love and the source of my strength and dedication.

Still, I am a man and only a man. I say this because the people need to know that the Sacrament of Holy Orders did not bestow on priests special human powers. There are many things I cannot do, even if I have the heart and will to do them. There are also many things that are expected of me that are beyond my abilities. What I have I am willing to give freely in the best way I can. Priests can do no more.

I try to spend as much of my day as I can helping people. Helping them doesn't always mean making them happy. I'm sure every parent knows that. It's impossible to be all things to all people.

My first concern is to bring God to people and people to God. Everything else flows from that. God comes first in my life—not the parish, not the diocese, not even the Catholic Church. That is not simply my choice. It is the First Commandment.

Then comes my parish, the family God has given me to love and serve. Years ago, my parish had a pastor and three associates. The work was carefully apportioned so as to meet all the pastoral needs of the parishioners. Someone took care of the youth; another the Holy Name Society and Mothers' Club; another the other organizations. The pastor had the administrative responsibilities. Of course, all the priests were involved in the administration of the sacraments, visiting the sick, and counseling. It was pretty much the same everywhere.

Unfortunately, that has changed. I have a sister pastoral associate and a limited-time permanent deacon. As invaluable as they are, it has not changed the expectations of the people. They still expect to see the priest at every-thing. They try to understand but they are upset if I go to one meeting and not to another. If the sister goes on a hospital visit, they complain that the pastor didn't. Then, when I do go, they say that I'm showing favoritism by visiting some parishioners and not others. When the deacon takes the bap-tisms, they're hurt because I didn't "bother." When the pressure gets to me and I do these things, the sister and the deacon feel slighted. It's impossible for me to be everywhere and do everything that four priests did before. When I go to the bishop for help, he tells me that all the pastors are facing the same problems.

In the four years I have been pastor, we have experienced two major boiler breakdowns, the repair of the entire school roof, and the partial repair of the church roof. I have had to negotiate leases for rentals of classrooms and the convent. I've had to contract with the city about a parking lot and face three lawsuits against the parish. Needless to say, I have no background or training in any of these things.

The priest's life does not compare very favorably to that of others around him. When it comes to money, I am the lowest-paid member of the parish staff. The part-time janitor earns more than I do. In terms of what I am paid per hour, I make less than the minimum wage. It is truly a matter of indifference to me personally except when it is brought up to me that I get free housing and food. The rectory is used in all hours of the day and night for parish meetings and get-togethers. The kitchen is open to and used by everyone. I have no objection to this. After all, it is the parish house. It's simply that it's not the luxury people make it out to be.

Our working hours are expected to be twenty-four hours a day. Although regular hours are considered to be 9:00 a.m. to 5:00 p.m., people do call before they go to work in the morning and after they get home from work. Weekends are especially heavy. Because priests live where they work, they are expected to be there all the time. (Not the sister and the deacon, just the priest.)

I get one day off a week. The people are very understanding about this. However, on occasion, I have to come back for a funeral or an emergency sick call or an unavoidable meeting. I can't take another day off because the other days are all scheduled. You just simply lose it.

When I go on vacation, I lose income while I'm gone. Priests supplement their expenses with Mass stipends. They aren't much but they do help. Yet, while I'm away, I am penalized financially for each day that I'm gone.

In most dioceses, priests must buy their own cars, clothes (black as well as regular), and personal items. And contrary to what people think, we pay all federal and state income taxes.

Perhaps what pains the most is having to deal with a chancery office that has an entirely different agenda. After four years, I was called to the chancery on business. The chancellor told me: "You're doing a fine job, John. We've received only one letter of complaint in four years." Although they wouldn't tell me, I knew that the letter had come from a woman who had complained that I wanted to move the altar. The job was done with the prior approval of the parish council. Later, in fact, when she saw the finished job, she apologized to me. But the chancery had the letter.

Well, later, one of the pastors was named auxiliary. I went to the party and he greeted me with: "Good job, John. I hear there's been only one letter of complaint." And still later the bishop, with whom I've had some respectful differences, said: "You know, John, we used to get lots of letters about your predecessor. Only one on you in four years." It is that type of thinking that frightens and depresses me. That's what drains morale.

On top of all this, I am expected to keep the parish spiritual, solvent, and active. Is there any wonder that there is a vocation crisis?

Yet, in spite of it all, I repeat that I love the priesthood and I love my people. The only reason I have gone into all this is because Catholics need to know the pressures their priests are facing today. I am confident that they will respond with understanding and love.

These are transition times and all change is difficult. I believe that God is preparing us for a new, dynamic Church of shared ministry. I want to be part of it. I don't want it to happen over my dead body.

· 15 ·

Thomas R. Franzman: Blue Collar, White Collar

"Tom is the ideal institutional priest," one of his priest-friends said. It was meant as a compliment. Tom Franzman travels light. He is at home in the institutional church. He is not a careerist and Church politics only seem to amuse him. He doesn't reflect a great deal on problems. He simply tries to fix them. He is unfiltered, unvarnished, unaffected. While he was rector of Quigley North High School Seminary, a group of resigned priests asked to use their alma mater for a day of recollection. In the past, they had been refused the use of church property. Tom asked only one question: "What date do you want it?"

It has been observed that while priests receive an education that is comparable to other professionals such as lawyers, physicians, and professors, they tend to think and act like police officers or fire fighters. If this is true, then Tom Franzman is a good cop. He responds.

At Maranto's Hardware Store just a few blocks from Archbishop Quigley Seminary High School where Franzman was rector for eight years, the clerks know Tom as both priest and handyman. He spent considerable time and skills keeping the old French Gothic high school seminary building in good repair. He has a blue-collar worker's view of life and, although both his parents were teachers, a workingman's attitude toward his priesthood.

"What you see is what you get," says his close friend, Father Tom Nangle, chaplain to the Chicago Police Department. Franzman and Nangle own an ancient fire engine together. They have been restoring it for years. It is their therapy. "It keeps us from going crazy," the outspoken Nangle said. Franzman just laughed.

Guys will say that the priesthood is ten funerals for every one wedding but, when you get into it, it becomes very rewarding. I've been a priest for twenty years and it has been a happy experience.

I've always wanted to say yes to any assignment. That hasn't been hard. I travel light. Now that I'm out of Quigley, I would like to be given a parish in the city. I'm not ready for a suburban parish yet. I'd like one where you can walk around the neighborhood and visit with the people sitting on their stoops. Just now, though, the cardinal wants me to fill in for a guy who is going in for treatment. It looks like a good spot. I like the neighborhood. I'll be there about four months, then we'll see.

My seminary training was a rich experience for me. I experienced two styles of leadership. The first years under Mal Foley were very restricted. But I gained an appreciation of the old days and an understanding of some of the older men's hostility.

Some guys in my class couldn't wait to get out of there. Then we got Jack Gorman and the seminary opened up. Gorman was the John XXIII of the place.

At the major seminary, a group of us decided that, for better or worse, this was our home for a while. So we adjusted. We taught at Santa Maria del Popolo, a parish elementary school, not far from the seminary. We got close to the working people near Mundelein. They became part of our lives. A lot of us thought that the real work of the priest was in the city. I guess I still do. I like the city.

Thirty-three of us were ordained in 1970. There's twenty-seven still on the list. Not bad. As a deacon, I worked at St. Clotilde's and at Catholic Charities, about half-and-half in each place. My first assignment was to St. Bede's in Fox Lake. After seven years, I came here to the cathedral. I've been here since.

In 1982, Cardinal Cody named me rector of Quigley North. I told him that he didn't know what he was doing. He told me that God wanted me there. So, here I am. Quigley South has closed and combined with Quigley North. There's a new rector. So, here I am, between assignments.

We were sending anywhere from a low of 16 percent to a high of 24 percent of the Quigley grads on to Niles [a four-year college, affiliated with Loyola University; second phase of priestly formation]. In an average year, we would send fifteen or sixteen guys on to Niles. That's not many. The priesthood needs to be suggested more by priests to potential candidates. But priests aren't doing it. They believe very much in what they're doing but they're not comfortable with celibacy themselves. So they don't invite people.

Lifetime commitment is another consideration. Perhaps we could use a limited commitment, serve just a number of years. We would most likely get a good number of short-term vocations, but I would question limited commitments.

Hoge's figures are interesting, but they're just a guess. [Dean Hoge, sociologist at Catholic University in Washington, D.C., is the author of

Future of Catholic Leadership: Responses to the Priest Shortage.] It could change if we changed a few things. We should be looking at the possibility that not all priests have to be general practitioners. For example, does every priest have to know Canon Law? Twelve years is really too long a time to educate most priests. We could have priests with less training who would serve on weekends. A priest sees his people on the weekends. His contact is through the liturgy. If difficult situations arose, the weekend priest could refer the case to the full-time, fully educated priest.

We wouldn't have to sacrifice quality. We could still make certain that people's lives were being taken care of. Priests could end up doing only sacramental work or having one priest pastor of several parishes. Those responses are only stopgap measures. They're not realistic solutions. They aren't going to work.

I've always admired priests. It's a noble profession. I've admired priests who knew who they were. Look at John Ireland Gallery out on the South Side. He was a character, all right, but he thought nothing of walking into a tavern and confronting a guy who was spending his paycheck at the bar. "Is this what you're doing with your check," he'd ask him, "while your wife needs money to put food on the table?"

Take Cardinal Mundelein [George Mundelein, archbishop of Chicago 1915–39]. I think Rome wrote him a letter once expressing concern over the fact that his diocese had approved four or five annulments during the previous year. I guess they thought that was a lot then! Well, Mundelein just wrote them back and told them that he was the archbishop and that the decisions were made on the merits of the cases and that they ought to get off his back. They didn't bother him after that. He knew who he was. They respected him.

We will continue to lose numbers. We once had the luxury of almost too many priests. Now, we don't know who we are. Our job description has been clouded.

I've always wanted people to see me as I am. I'm comfortable with that. Sometimes, after a day at Quigley, I'd come here to say the 5:15 evening Mass. I'd be very tired and it would show. So, I let it show. My homily wasn't so hot. The people understood.

I heard about the report that said that, by the year 2000 or something, the majority of priests will be homosexual. I don't know if that's true, but it's sort of like the statements that all cops are crooked. Reports like that make people think that a priest is something he is not and you end up thinking too much about what people think of you. Again, I just want people to accept me as me.

Years ago at Fox Lake, I got involved with the local fire department. It was wonderful. The fire department is the secular church. They serve the entire community—people who have been displaced, people with heart attacks, people with troubles. I made hundreds of contacts through that fire department. Some have lasted to this day. It brought me to the people. I've learned that a priest is a symbol and that just by being a priest he can gather people.

I don't know where the Church is going to get the money to do all the things it must do. But I think that we could soften the hurt of having to close parishes by getting parishes to be neighbors first. We could get them to do more things together so that, gradually, people would gravitate together. My mother has been in the same parish since 1929. Moving to another parish would be very hard for her. But suppose we simply let people pick their own parish? Maybe, in time, the bad parishes would close. No one would go to them!

A parish is a place to be with people, to be part of their lives. If a priest gets close to the people, he won't have to go back to an empty rectory. If he can do well what he does well, he won't feel that gulf.

Oh, the fire engines are just for fun! I found one years ago. It's twenty feet long. It's a pretty old wreck. It belonged to the Itasca Fire Department. I parked it in a garage at DePaul University and I've been tinkering with it for years. Tom Nangle and I have another one we're working on, too. I prefer to build and tinker than to go out drinking. There are times when I can't go near it for months, but when I do, people come to watch and I get to meet them. Old Father O'Malley waves from the porch of the Vincentian priests' house at DePaul, and the engineer from one of the buildings comes over and talks. It's a chance to get close to people, and, someday, when it's restored, we can use it in parades.

I think it was at Fox Lake that I caught the phrase: "This day is a gift of God to you; what you do with it is your gift to the Lord." I try to live that out.

· 16 ·

Joseph Gallagher: A Sweet Mystery of Empty Hands

Joe Gallagher's name is on the title page of the Documents of Vatican II. With help from other experts, he had translated most of the 103,014 Latin words of the sixteen documents into clear, readable English. (John Courtney Murray, S.J., supplied the bulk of his own translation of the Document on Religious Freedom.) Gallagher received the 743 lines of the Document on the Church in the Modern World just five days before they were promulgated. It was quite a job.

There is hardly a priest in the country who doesn't own a well-worn copy of Gallagher's translation. But there is far more to Joe Gallagher than simply a priest and translator. In addition to the work he describes below, he has written articles for *The New Catholic Encyclopedia* and journals such as the *New York Times*, *America*, the *National Catholic Reporter*, and the *Catholic Digest*. More than two hundred of his columns have appeared in the Baltimore *Sunpapers*.

More important, however, is Joe Gallagher's emptying out. Few priests permit others to look inside their hearts and heads. Most prefer to quote Augustine, John of the Cross, or Teresa—all safely at rest—to describe their own or others' dark night. Joe Gallagher said that he is too far removed from everyday ministry to comment on its future. However, his account of the pain and the privilege speaks volumes about the price many priests pay for the power and the glory.

I'm sixty-one now, born in 1929, at Mercy Hospital in downtown Baltimore where I would one day serve as chaplain. I'm just two weeks younger than the Mormon Tabernacle Choir, born into a church that has all saints in heaven, all souls in purgatory, and all sorts on earth. Now, sixty years later, I feel like the priest in George Bernanos's novel, *The Diary of a Country Priest*. In one scene, he is comforting a family that has lost someone. "I who don't feel hope am giving hope," he says. And, as he looks down into the coffin, he reflects on "the sweet mystery of empty hands."

I am a priest who might have left active ministry as far back as 1978. But, in those days, even now, you have to declare that your sexuality is unmanageable, and I couldn't do that.

Humanae Vitae [Paul VI's encyclical on the regulation of birth, 1968] was a watershed for me. I had left the *Catholic Review* [archdiocesan newspaper] in 1966, in the middle of the Vietnam War and the Civil Rights movement. My local hero, Cardinal Lawrence J. Shehan [Archbishop of Baltimore 1961–74], and I had an almost infantile relationship. He was a sincere, dedicated, unselfish man, docile, childlike and unself-centered. He never did say: "What would you like to do?" But he never pressured me and certainly never punished me. I could write what I wanted. But *Humanae Vitae* did it. In this instance, the authority of the Church was not only wrong but wicked. And then this man [John Paul II] visits Manila and lectures the people on following the Church's teaching on birth control. There they were, living in shacks, with no water, piled on top of one another, and he was lecturing. It was obscene!

I've known something about poverty. I can recall sitting on a kitchen chair as a child, waiting for my mother to serve powdered potatoes and powdered milk. I've got to tell you about my family because it would be unfair of me to criticize the Church without telling you of the circumstances from which I came. It sort of puts a frame around my thoughts. My father was a strong, bright man, always the life of the party, and a gifted mechanic. But he was also an Irish alcoholic; you could mimeograph them, I guess. He died of pneumonia at forty-seven when I was a freshman at the local high school seminary. He was a violent man who spent time in jail for trying to choke my mother in order to get money for drink. We took in boarders to make ends meet. One was a woman who looked just like Olive Oyl, Popeye's wife. She was a protection for my mother. My mother was beautiful, kind-hearted, brave, and prayerful. She was a widow longer than she was a wife. She died of cancer in 1975.

My father wasn't a churchy man. When his first son was born, however, he announced that he was going to be a priest. But that turned out to be my brother, Francis Xavier Gallagher. He didn't become a priest but he did become a prominent lawyer and a member of the Maryland State Legislature. He became the attorney to Archbishop Francis P. Keough (1947–61) and Cardinal Shehan. That turned out to be quite a drama. Here I was, disagreeing with the cardinal, and my brother, the lawyer, was listening to the archbishop! Frank was a bright, witty, and gregarious man who, sadly, died of a heart attack in 1972 at only forty-three. His five children became a preoccupation for me for the next fourteen years, until the two eldest were married and the twins went off to college.

My brother Tommy quit high school and joined the navy, but received a psychiatric discharge after a short time. He worked for a while as a Batimore policeman but, after a disasterous fire in which he helped rescue some injured firemen, he suddenly left town and headed for California. He was married for a time but his emotional problems only got more severe. He's been institutionalized several times but he remains a turbulent paranoid schizophrenic, a homeless wanderer around the streets of Los Angeles. I've tried to keep in touch. There are people on the streets who know where he is. But it's difficult. He hears voices. God speaks to him. I used to send him money but he would say that God told him to give it away.

My sister Mary Jo married William Burdell, a long-time employee of Bethlehem Steel. They have a son and daughter, but the loss of their first two children added to Mary Jo's emotional vulnerability and resulted in several institutionalizations. She is sweet-tempered, excessively religious, rather reclusive, and slowed down by medication.

I mention all this because the strain of mental illness, derived mostly from my mother's side of the family in spite of my father's alcoholism, has had an impact on my life. Two of my mother's brothers spent long years in psychiatric wards. There was a joyless spinster aunt and another aunt who was married to an alcoholic policeman. I was named after those two institutionalized uncles, John and Joseph. Ironically, Gallagher means "the stranger who helps" and their ancestral home is Donegal which means "the fortress of the stranger."

I've had to live a stripped-down life. I'm an embodiment of Henry James's observation: "I've always expected the worse and it's always worse than I expected." (Laughs.) Like William James, I strive to be genuinely indifferent as to what comes out of it all. That's become my mantra. But I had to tell you about the shadow part of myself so that you could put it in a framework of my remarks about the Church.

I recall the rabbi who said that we don't see things as they are but rather as we are. I was never sure that I could lead a normal life with all that background.

Anyway, I grew up in a disturbed household. There were no books, just a copy of Defoe's *Robinson Crusoe* and Maugham's *Of Human Bondage*. I have no idea how they got there. I was never good at sports because I never had a bat or a ball, a skate or a bicycle. To this day, as far as I'm concerned, every sport in the world could disappear and I wouldn't miss it.

I had no idea where priests came from. I thought that they came from another world. I thought they were like archangels. Anyway, the Church brought me a sense of the holy that was so different from home. I can still recall moving around a great deal, especially as parental arguments grew worse. I used to hide the kitchen knives during them. I spent six happy months with a Protestant family in the Pimlico area. There I heard my first classical music and got disposed early toward ecumenism.

While at St. Ann's Elementary School, I took the exam for St. Charles College, a high school and junior college seminary in the Baltimore suburbs. I was supposed to be smart—tests indicated that I had an I.Q. of 142—but was very unsure of myself. St. Ann's meant a lot to me. The pastor, Monsignor Charles Morrisey, died in 1941. It was my first experience with death. He had given me money to buy galoshes and had forgiven me when I smashed a sacristy window and ran away. I recall shooing the late summer flies from his coffin, and an elderly lady who had given me a lace handkerchief to assist in my futile task. I recalled Sister Bernarde, who encouraged me to write, and writing a poem that ended with: "And if I try a little harder / I may grow up to be a martyr."

Anyway, I spent the years 1943–49 at St. Charles in Cantonsville. They were good years. I was president of my class for five years. I'm afraid that my classmates had more confidence in me that I did in myself.

In 1949, I won a three-year Basselin scholarship to the philosophy department of the Theological College, the seminary affiliated with Catholic U. But after a lonely and unhappy year, I switched to St. Mary's Seminary on Paca Street. That seminary is gone now; there's only St. Mary's in Roland Park, still taught by the Sulps [the Sulpician Fathers]. I went there in 1951 and did the usual seminary curriculum without pursuing any particular degree. St. Mary's has about 120 students now; Catholic University's enrollment is way down. Hickey [Cardinal James A. Hickey, archbishop of Washington, D.C.] won't take outsiders.

The theology, like the philosophy, was boring, but when my friend Joe Gossman, now bishop of Raleigh, asked me to return a book to the library and I glanced at its title, *Existentialism*, the mental fireworks exploded! People like Soren Kirkegaard and Gabriel Marcel were speaking my language, asking my kind of questions. Experiences like anxiety and dread were taken seriously in this new philosophy, so much more personal, concrete, immediate, and "existential."

As early as St. Charles, there had been the beginnings of emotional slumps. I was only twenty at Catholic U. when I had to leave the seminary program and finish my year there as a lay student because of my emotional slumps. It was the start of a series of nervous collapses connected with depression and religious confusions.

Even then, I hated the Church's teaching on limbo and hell and contraception. I took the issues of sin, guilt, and eternal rejection very seriously, and could much more feelingly believe in God's severe judgment and severe demands than I could in His Mercy and understanding. I dreaded the pressures of putting pressure on consciences and on fragile psyches.

Two years before ordination, I almost left the seminary; but one day, while doing my laundry, I felt a rebound of energy and dedication. Perhaps it came from my lack of desire, or ability, to be anything else but a priest. Anyway, my rector was aware of my turbulance. He postponed my ordination to the diaconate until two months before my ordination.

It was during those years that I discovered an interest in writing and worked at my Latin. My first dictionary was a Latin one and it started me on a lifelong love affair with the etymology of words.

I was ordained in the old cathedral in 1955 in a class of eight. One has since died and two have left, I think. Not bad. Even the total class of 109 for all dioceses has held up pretty well, although we've had twenty-one deaths.

I was assigned to the old cathedral, the Basilica of the Assumption. They knew that I liked to write, and they thought I could help the archbishop with his speeches. Actually, the help I gave with speeches turned out to be minimal. In 1957, I was placed in charge of the archives, a job I had until 1966. It was a great experience, sifting the records of the oldest diocese in America. In 1959, I began writing for the *Catholic Review*. I also appeared often on the radio and television. Shehan arrived in 1961 and, at my own request, I was sent to be chaplain in an orphanage and a teacher in the newly opened St. Paul's Latin High School in addition to my work on the paper.

I was the priest-editor of the *Catholic Review* until 1966 when an editorial clash with the cardinal led to my resignation. It had been an exhilarating period for me, before and after Vatican II. In 1965, the Jesuit editor of *America* magazine asked me to translate the sixteen documents of Vatican II. The task took me to Rome for the final weeks of the council. I was privileged to attend the final session of Vatican II. I borrowed another monsignor's robes and ended up on the altar very near the pope. I listened to the translations I had worked on being read. The translation was an awful lot of work but I enjoyed it. The earlier translations were awful, filled with clumsy phrases and unintentional double entendres. The translation with expert commentaries was published in 1966. It sold over two million copies before I lost count.

I had written editorials questioning our position in Vietnam and I had taken a strong civil rights stance. It led to a painful break with a good man who had been pastor in my family's church when he was auxiliary bishop. I had written an editorial against an Irish-Catholic candidate who was preaching "Your home is your castle." It was a clearly segregationist position. And my anti-Vietnam War position came in the middle of a big fund drive. Yet, in 1965, the cardinal named me a monsignor. I respected him. We were friends.

But by the fall of 1966 I resigned as editor because of our differences. The traumatic episode crystalized serious doubts I was having about my vocation, and even about my affiliation with the Church.

That crisis intensified two years later when Paul VI published *Humanae Vitae*. I was in Jerusalem when the encyclical was issued. I returned to Rome. In response to that document, I resigned the honor of being a monsignor. I didn't even wait until I got back to Baltimore. Cardinal Shehan was upset that I had resigned the honor in Rome. He was very tied to the papacy. Back in Baltimore, seventy priests signed a document protesting the encyclical, but Shehan didn't do anything. Over in Washington, O'Boyle [Cardinal Patrick O'Boyle, 1948-73, archbishop of Washington, D.C.] was firing guys right and left.

My resignation had some ripple effect. I ended up a fictional character in two novels. I also wrote my memoirs in 1979 and raised the issue again. Image Books published them in 1983 under the title *The Pain and the Privilege*. Paul VI lived another ten years after that document. He said after: "We bless those who accept our encyclical; we bless those who do not." I guess I have the same trouble making up my mind. In fact, during the following decade, I seriously considered applying for laicization. I had even completed the paper work when Paul VI died in 1978. Obviously, I have been double-minded on that subject for many years.

When I left the *Catholic Review* I was given permission to work as an editor with Corpus Books, a new Catholic publishing venture in Washington, which had been founded by a priest-cousin of mine. But I was so demoralized that I couldn't concentrate on religious or theological matters.

During Holy Week of 1967, I made a retreat at St. Mary's on Paca Street and found much-needed emotional nourishment in the friendly welcome of the faculty and students. I ending up staying two years as a teacher of philosophy and poetry. When Paca Street closed in 1969, I went to St. Mary's at Roland Park and taught there until 1976, when some budget cutbacks and the arrival of a teacher with a doctorate in communications caused me to leave. The doctrinal issues still gnawed inside me but those midlife years of contact with gifted and idealistic seminarians enriched me with some of my most treasured and enduring friendships. In fact, I must say that, even today, there are first-class men in the seminary. I don't know why they are there but they're every bit as good as the best of my generation.

In 1975, I inherited a house on Park Avenue in Baltimore. I fixed it up and lived there until 1982 when I undertook a series of house sittings around Baltimore and D.C. In 1986, because of my failing health, I received a retirement pension. Now, I live in a little efficiency apartment in the Northwood area of Baltimore. The bishop has been good to me. I'm on a pension of $800 per month and find that I can live on that. I've discovered that I can manage on $13 a day. You could say that I've backed into evangelical poverty! I had no savings.

I've turned into a writer again. I keep coming back like Banquo's ghost. It's an apostolate and a way of supporting myself. In 1983, I translated Archbishop Dom Helder Camara's *Symphony of Two Worlds* from French into English for its English premiere performance in St. Louis. In 1988, Christian Classics published a collection of eighty essays I had written over the previous twenty-five years [*The Business of Circumference—a Kaleidoscope*]. In 1987, the *National Catholic Reporter* published a lengthy article called "Voices of Strength and Hope for a Friend with AIDS." It became a cassette and booklet and caused me to get involved in helping people with AIDS. I did it until my own health wouldn't permit.

In 1979, I had a heart attack. It led to a quadruple bypass operation. A second bypass was recommended but I refused. I'm now attempting to treat the condition with drugs but they have a bad effect on my diminished energies. I find myself increasingly lethargic, irritable, absent-minded, unsociable, disinterested, and even slower in reading, absorbing, and remembering.

There's more—a blood condition, an esophageal ulcer, and a potentially cancerous condition known as Barrett's Syndrome. Somehow, it's a comfort to know that I can't win!

In addition, there have been numerous periods of psychotherapy. As early as age twelve, I was cautioned by a doctor to just be Joseph, not try to be St. Joseph. And, years later, a psychiatrist told me that I had enough anger in me to blow up the city of Baltimore! I've had to rely on a lot of antianxiety and antidepressant pills.

Now, I find myself floating in an undogmatic world. I've built a comfortable nest. Facing death has caused me to live a very simple life. My prayer gets very simple. From writing poems about popes as a kid, I now write about simple acts of the will and the mystery of being. You come to note colors and tastes and to appreciate the sound of music. You learn how many things you have no power over; you don't let what you don't have spoil what you do have. It's as if you discovered the world late in life. I still look out my window and see kids with their fathers going to the park to play. There's still some rage there. I never had a daddy to dress me up in a baseball uniform and take me to the park. Oh, how hard it is to change memories!

I've gotten used to celibacy. I did propose to a woman once, but it came to nothing and that's good. Now, I don't know how the pope can be pope or how bishops can be bishops. I'm reading a book about a priest now and I don't know how one can be a pastor. The tensions are so hard. I've moved away from all those intellectual props. They only made me tired. Today, when I listen to young priests, I try to guide them to an unstructured life, one without a need to campaign.

I've ceased to care about the future of the Church but only the people in it. I keep in touch with priests and family, especially former students. I no longer function as a priest, except the rare funeral, and I find it more peacifying not to. *Humanae Vitae* liberated me from pope worship. It shook me to the roots. Now, my serenity is inversely proportional to my theology system. The older I get the more mysterious life becomes. I see the plus side of negative things and vice versa.

I've found that there is no longer any need to be angry with the Church. I think of Cardinal Shehan and the many things that were on his mind and I feel sorry for him. It was a stormy life in a stormy Church in a stormy world. Now, I accept the shadow part of myself.

In spite of the fact that I've almost become a nondenominational Buddhist, I come to believe that some men like myself must be priests so that a priest can be there for the people. I have befriended so many good and decent men among the priests. The Church has treated me very decently.

Gerard Manley Hopkins's lines have become a model of my own experience. "Good grows wild and wild, has shades, and is no where none."

❧ INTERLUDE III ❧

I was a chaplain at a huge state university in California. I really liked it there. Stimulating people. Always something to do. It was clean work. But things were slow during the summer and I was scheduled to go back to Catholic University to take some courses. I also wanted to do some parish work, just to put my toe in the water. In those days, the provincial could move your checker on the province board pretty easily. I wanted to be ready.

After summer school, I was sent to help out in a parish in Fairfax, Virginia. It was a good-sized parish. Four priests, including the pastor. I was supposed to fill in for six weeks while the curates took some vacation.

The pastor was a decent administrator, a good man on the phone. He provided pastoral service because he wasn't afraid to assign his curates. He rarely took sick calls himself. For that matter, he never took a vacation. It took me a week to realize that he seldom left the rectory because he didn't want to be too far from his medicine cabinet where he kept his bottle.

The assistants said nothing. Diocesan priests in those days rarely shared war stories with order men. Besides, he wasn't a falling-down drunk. As far as we knew, he never touched a drop before five, and that met clerical code.

I took a ride up to Catholic U. one night, just to have dinner with some of my own men. Two of the curates were on vacation and the third was out somewhere. I came home around eleven and let myself in.

The pastor must have thought that he had the rectory to himself. His door was open, a rare thing for him.

I tried to pass his room and get to mine without disturbing him. I could have done it but I stopped dead in my tracks when I saw him, standing in the middle of his study with one of his Waterford crystal glasses in his hand. It wasn't the drink that got me. It was the way he was dressed. He was in full regalia—a tailored black cassock with purple piping and purple buttons. He was dressed like a monsignor! He even had a biretta with one of those purple balls on top.

It was weird! When he saw me, he said, "Hello." I didn't know what to say. I had always called him "Father," and he never suggested otherwise.

He was drunk, all right, but not sloppy. Now I could see that he had his pajamas and slippers on under the fancy regalia.

"Father," he said, "I didn't know you'd be home. These are mine." He was talking about the vestments. "I was named a monsignor by Tom Farrell, the present man's predecessor. Tom Farrell was a fine man. A gentleman. If he told you something, it was gospel. Our present man isn't that way, I'm sorry to say."

He was talking about the bishop, of course. You don't have to know the bishops to understand the stories. When you're a priest, the plots are all the same.

"Tom Farrell told me with his own lips that I was on the list. I was a chaplain, you know, during the Second World War. I never left the country, but I was able to help the Vatican get certain supplies through our military over there. They were grateful.

"It took a few years but friends I made over there showed their gratitude by suggesting to the bishop that I be made a monsignor.

"Then Tom Farrell retired and the new man came in. I went to his installation and was invited with all the other pastors to attend the dinner after. Perhaps I overstepped my bounds but, when I inquired of the new bishop's vicar at the installation about my appointment, he told me that I was being entirely inappropriate.

"When I got back to the rectory, I was so furious that I called the vicar. Later, he said that I said some very bad things and he hinted that I was drunk. He called it a moral lapse.

"I had already bought these robes. They cost me several thousand dollars. I even bought them from the recommended tailor in Rome.

"But I never got the letter. I should have been a monsignor. George Wesphalt was made one the very same year. He's never done a day's work in his life, but he's that fat little vicar's uncle.

"Now, I've just got these vestments. Would you care for a drink, Father?"

From a former Paulist priest, now a public school administrator in Los Angeles.

Dennis J. Geaney, O.S.A.: Clerical Prophet

When Dennis Geaney attended the first Mass of a young priest friend, he listened to the young man's exhuberant homily. "I've been ordained only one day and I'm already angry at the Church," the newly ordained said. He proceeded to list his grievances, most having to do with injustices. Geaney listened with the quiet patience that comes only with years. "Well, he put his cards on the table," he whispered after. "Now, let's see how he plays them."

Dennis Geaney has been putting his cards on the table for nearly fifty years. He is a reporter and participant. His most recent book, *Quest for Community*, profiles twenty parishes that successfully help people to build community. Geaney calls for an end to the consumer parish in which people look to a largely clerical staff to meet a demand for the minimal rituals of Masses, baptisms, weddings, and funerals. He wants to change the notion of the pastor as manager, a cleric dealing with lights, leaks, locks, and leases. He calls for community parishes that focus on liturgies, places where the Jesus Story is heard in a manner that touches people's lives.

Geaney's views are highly subjective. He visits parishes and collects impressions. He can sort out the parishes that are held together by the personality of the pastor and those that are building genuine community. He is invariably on target. He believes strongly in small groups as the basis for the strength of the larger community. He has a nose for a good parish and an enormously generous ability to give credit to others. His books are all about other people.

"Community is friendship writ large," he says, but then immediately quotes Sam Keen's *To a Dancing God*. "Roots must intertwine, time be wasted together, crises weathered, celebrations shared before the relationship reaches maturity." For Dennis Geaney the parish community process is much the same—"a shared story, told in a faith community context that gets us through the shattering experiences of life."

I see the pope as the "alcoholic" father and the Vatican officials and bishops as codependents. The Church is an addicted family. The codependents may complain in private about John Paul's behavior, but in public they defend him. The people who complain in private about the system, but support it in public, are more responsible than the members of the Church who are so dysfunctional that they cannot tell night from day.

At the first session of Vatican II, the bishops were given the working papers for the commissions written by the Vatican people. The first motion on the floor was to reject all the papers and start from scratch. The members of the Synod on the Priesthood that was held last October (1990) seemed unaware of the Church's long tradition of dissent. It dates to the day that Paul confronted Peter.

You know, some time ago, we had a half- dozen overnights on celibacy in this diocese. Priests both straight and gay opened their hearts to one another. Michael Jamail, a priest from Beaumont, Texas, spoke to them. Later, he wrote an article for me that said that celibate people are different, that they live in a way that almost no one else on earth does, and that that decision radically alters the way priests experience being alive, loving others, being intimate with others, touching others, and being there for others. He said that we are not celibate for the sake of irresponsibility, though celibacy is liberating. He said that he was available to others because he was celibate. He wasn't sure what that meant but he knew it was true, and he knew it was important, and he knew it was different. For him, Christ held the mystery of his life in his heart and to be celibate was part of that mystery.

O.K. But since then a score of priests in this archdiocese have left the priesthood because of the burden of celibacy. The overnights may have helped some priests to heal the dualism that splits their sexuality and spirituality, but it hasn't stopped the resignations and it hasn't increased those who are being ordained.

I had hoped that Cardinal Bernardin would tell the Synod on the Priesthood that the priesthood must be opened to married people and women if the Church is to survive. Instead, he spoke eloquently on the subject of celibacy and the need to get this message out to priests and prospective candidates.

I don't just want to score John Paul and Joe Bernardin. The same intransigence is at the priests' level. I have yet to hear a single priest say publicly that we must abandon our emphasis on the seminary as the only way to prepare priests for the future. It is estimated that it costs us one million dollars to ordain a priest. We have a fully staffed and financed high-school seminary for young men who are not capable of making a decision for priesthood. We have a seminary college where seminarians could interact with ordinary folks. And we have a major seminary that could offer an M.Div. [master in divinity to lay people]. Instead, we maintain a system that employs nearly 150 people to ordain a few people each year. (Chicago ordained five in 1990; in early 1991, there were sixty-two seminarians for the Church of Chicago at the major seminary.) We're just not reading the signs of the times that decisions for the celibate priesthood are not made before age twenty-five.

How many parishes have line items on the budget appropriating money for the education and training of lay people? I have yet to hear a plea from pastors that half the annual seminary collection be devoted to the education of lay people who will replace priests even as pastors. Lay people will definitely replace us. We are simply not going to survive. Without the theological education and experience priests presently have, we will have fundamentalists running the Church at the local level. We still have not prepared the next generation of teachers—the laity. The fundamentalists among us will bring us back to a pre-Tridentine era of uneducated people.

We almost do less than nothing for the laity. Even if the laity offered to pay full tuition in order to be educated, we still would not accept them in the seminary. We are still following the dictates of the synod: future priests trained in isolation. We will do as the synod says: no women as spiritual directors. We still will not admit that there is a clergy shortage. There is still a lack of psychosexual development.

Priests complain that they are not consulted or listened to downtown. Parishioners complain that they are not consulted or listened to by their pastors. Pastors have as much difficulty in allowing people to take ownership of their parish as do the pope and bishops. But there'll be no turnaround in this Church until we face up to the fact that we priests are part of the problem. We've got to recognize that we are codependents in a dysfunctional family.

But let me go back. I've been here at St. Victor's since 1979. I had been prior of the student community and director of Field Education at Catholic Theological Union until I suffered a coronary. I figured that it was time to move on. So, I called Leo Mahon [then pastor of St. Victor's] and he said to come on over.

I'm an Augustinian, still close to my community. But I'm practically a diocesan parish priest. Even since I came to Chicago in 1943 and Ted Hesburgh [later president of the University of Notre Dame] got me involved in the Young Christian Students near St. Rita High School where I was teaching, I've been caught up in the Chicago movement and the diocesan clergy. The move alienated me from my community. They were more traditional than the priests coming out of Mundelein [St. Mary of the Lake

Seminary]. These were the Hillenbrand priests [Monsignor Reynold Hillenbrand, rector of St. Mary of the Lake]. They didn't see themselves as radicals, just parish priests, but they anticipated Vatican II. They wanted to get priests out of the sacristy and into the world. My mentor was Bill Quinn. He brought me to the diocesan priests' parties and the Hillenbrand readings. Those experiences lasted into the seventies.

I was formed and shaped in the liturgical movement by Tom Carroll [Boston priest, died 1971]. He was my liturgical mentor. I was ordained in 1942; came to Chicago in 1943 and worked at St. Rita's until 1947 when I was sent to St. Thomas High School in Rockford, Illinois, where I spent the next twelve years. I taught social studies and typing. I was never a great teacher, but the typing came in handy.

It was during those Rockford years that I started writing. Bill Quinn and Bill Rooney introduced me to Godfrey Diekman, O.S.B., at *Orate Fratres*. That must have been around 1950 or 1951. In any case, he told me that I could write anything I wanted. I wrote a piece called "Keeping Things Together." It had to do with keeping liturgy and social action together. Well, it became the most publicized article of my life! That article put me in business. Since then, I've written fifteen books and hundreds of articles. Most of what I have written has to do with parish life.

My last book profiled twenty parishes around the country, parishes with a future. They're not parishes that are just meeting minimal needs; they're helping people build a genuine community. For the last eleven years, I've been editor of *Upturn* for the ACP [Association of Chicago Priests]. I call priests; get them to write brief observations. It gets some dialogue going.

Cardinal Suhard [Emmanual Suhard, former archbishop of Paris] used to say: "Do something about liturgy." Well, Cardinal Stritch [Samuel Stritch, archbishop of Chicago] was permissive. We were able to combine liturgy and social action. We were able to experiment, to ask if Catholics who went to Holy Communion only once a month and who threw rocks at race riots in order to "protect" their neighborhood would do the same thing if they went to Holy Communion every Sunday.

It was an era of Joe Greer type priests. Did you read that book [*In Mysterious Ways* by Paul Wilkes]? Well, Joe Greer is a tremendous priest. Paul Wilkes was looking for a modern priest like the one in *Diary of a Country Priest*. He didn't find quite what he was looking for, but he found Joe Greer, a Boston priest who took a parish and really turned it around. Then, he got cancer and nearly died. Half the book is about his battle with cancer, but the other half is the story of a shrewd, caring priest with great instincts. That's the way priests were in the forties, fifties, and even the sixties. Priests will like that book; they should. But the Joe Greer model is over. It's finished. Joe Greer couldn't delegate authority. He didn't have to, until he got sick.

Do you recall the young seminarians interviewed in that book? Did you notice the difference? Those young men weren't pastoral types. They're institutional types, tied to institutional thinking, not pastoral thinking. Joe Greer had problems with closeness, with intimacy, but those seminarians had much deeper problems. Wilkes quotes George Bernanos's hero to the effect that, if you want love, don't put yourself beyond love's reach. Well, Greer wanted love and, like most priests, put himself beyond love's reach. But those seminarians wouldn't even understand what the statement means. It's changed. The Joe Greers of the Church are dying out.

My first two books were winners. *You Are Not Your Own* and *You Shall Be Witnesses* went into three printings during the fifties and sixties. I had a constituency in those days. There was a grapevine. People talked to each other about ideas and books. Now, my constituency is gone. We're now in a different era. Personal stuff sells now, you know, spiritual development—that sort of thing—but very little of the new stuff has any thing to do with parish. The liberal Catholics of a few decades ago had a network throughout the country. Now, there's no such group. The liberal Catholics out there now aren't interested in parish renewal.

Future chroniclers will not speak fondly of us. We have not prepared the next generation of ministers. We could have had an orderly transition. Instead, there'll be nothing to pass on.

I can't predict the future. I can only say that the present model of Church is dead and that it's not changing. I don't see many parishes changing, either. The pastors understand the words, but there are few parishes where people genuinely operate, where people are brought in at every level. We're not preparing for the future in any way, shape, or form. The charism just isn't moving.

There are some model bishops out there. I like Rembert Weakland (archbishop of Milwaukee, Wisconsin), Kenneth Utener (Saginaw, Michigan), Raymond Lucker (New Ulm, Minnesota), Walter Sullivan (Richmond, Virginia), Thomas Gumbleton (auxiliary, Detroit, Michigan), and Frank Murphy (auxiliary, Baltimore, Maryland). They are men of vision and courage.

In the future, we'll have some strong parishes that will be filled on Sundays. But the others will be dull and lifeless with only pretty good attendance.

We'll keep tightening up. And people will go away. Look at us here, a parish right on the border of another diocese that is already dead. People from that diocese come here on Sunday in the hope of finding some life.

I sound cynical. I'm not. The Church has served me well. I owe it a great deal for what it has given to me. I'm seventy-six. Officially, I'm a resident emeritus or something like that. But I'm still active. I work the crowd before and after Mass on Sunday; I go up and down the aisles playing the jester or clown, warming up the people for joyful celebration of the Eucharist. I play with the children, asking elderly people about their lumbago or fallen arches—or more seriously, how they are managing the recent death of a spouse. I simply try to bring people from their private commerce with God into a worshiping community.

Until recently, American Catholics made the Eucharist a private devotion, like prayer at a shrine rather than fellowship at the table of the Lord. Like those Italian mothers who created family warmth at table with their special spaghetti sauce, I am trying to build community out of the love and caring in the worshipers' hearts. Those are ingredients that crave expression. It's what John Shea writes: "Gather the folks, tell the Story, and break the Bread." Or it's what Jodi DeBais, a pastor in West Virginia, said to me about his goal as pastor: "To create a community of friends."

Liturgy, you know, tends to be paralyzed by rigid parish structures that haven't adapted to contemporary life. People over forty are inclined to hold on to the precious moments of their youth, but in the process deny their children the opportunity to reshape the liturgy and express their own religious experience. Liturgy may simply have to die and be reborn again from the life experiences and cultural demands of younger people. Parishes need to be converted and live or become museum pieces supported only by precious memories.

Those first-century Christians found strength in the missionary spirit of the Church. They had one goal: to tell the Jesus Story, to spread the Good News about a life that has a future, a life that death changes but does not take away. But that story is carried in vessels of clay and from time to time these vessels need to be broken and recast. We need to renew the Church and the parish in a way that creates new vessels that will carry the Story into the future.

I still do my articles for the parish bulletin; I do the occasional funeral. I like it here. I can't go elsewhere. I'm here until I die.

I still have energy. I put more time into diocesan priesthood that I do into religious priesthood. I have a room at St. Clare's, an Augustinian parish on Fifty-fifth Street. I spend a night or two a week there. I enjoy talking to the young men. It heals the hurts of years ago when I was moved around because of my stand on race. The Augustinians are still my family but it is my interest in diocesan priesthood that gives me energy. I have a deep love for the priesthood.

· 18 ·

Dominic J. Grassi: Urban Parish Rejuvenated

St. Josaphat's Church was one of the old national churches, officially suppressed in 1910 when territorial parishes were established. However, ethnic parishes endured for years because their roots were intimately entwined with their religious traditions. Since it was organized in 1882, St. Josaphat's has had about four distinct lifetimes. Initially Polish, and still having about 30 percent Polish names on its roster, its first parishioners were Kashubes—Poles who lived under Prussian domination in their homeland. Eleven of its thirteen pastors were Polish. Although located within the borders of an English-speaking parish and surrounded by two German parishes (Kashubes speak German and Polish), by 1902 St. Josaphat's had over 5,000 parishioners.

The gradual breakup of the national parishes and the shifting demographics as immigrant Americans followed the American dream to the suburbs, saw St. Josaphat's decline to only 600 parishioners by the 1970s. Most of them were living in other parishes. When Dominic Grassi became pastor in 1987, there were only 250 registered parishioners. About 20 percent are Hispanic, but their numbers are dwindling as increasing real estate prices force them to move. Townhouses, selling at $200,000-plus are being built on every available lot. The old homes are being renovated. The neighborhood is going upscale. There are now 625 registered parishioners and 250 kids in the elementary school. Grassi has two part-time associate priests, a full-time secretary and a largely part-time staff.

Grassi bills the parish as "A Church to Come Home To." The young, urban professionals are getting the message. They are "reconnecting" in increasing numbers. Grassi and other urban pastors are proving that a mix of good evangelization and pragmatic marketing can keep urban parishes alive.

I just got out of the hospital. It was a heart-attack scare. I was only in a few days. I really had to get out because I couldn't get a bath. The nurses' aides were all Filipinos and they wouldn't give a priest a bath. I had to come home! Well, it was just a scare. My blood pressure was sky high and I was close to a major attack. I've got to realize that I'm not Jesus but that I am forty pounds overweight and that I've got to slow down.

I'm only forty-three. Ordained in seventy-three. There were about forty of us and thirty-seven are still in the priesthood. Other classes are almost wiped out. No one wants to research why this happened, but I believe that it's because we were given extraordinary freedom. Jack Gorman [former Rector of the University of St. Mary of the Lake and now an auxiliary bishop] let us make mistakes. We grew up a lot. Jack wasn't afraid of losing control. Now, Wilt Gregory's a bishop [auxiliary, Chicago] and the rest of the class are doing some very fine work.

We've got to look at why guys are still leaving. Thirteen this year, I think, and we ordained only five. And we're not losing marginal guys anymore. We just lost Ken, an enormous talent, and Tom. Now there is a genuinely spiritual guy. Gone! What's wrong?

Our class reunions used to bring out at least two-thirds of the guys. Now, we only get twelve to fifteen. They can't be there. They're nailed to their parishes. Too much work and too few priests. They look tired. Yet, one guy who works at the chancery told us that our problem was that we cared too much about people! You know, when they gathered us together to talk about the parish closings, they called us "managers." Lately, I've been involved with a support group of eight or nine pastors. Meeting and praying with them really helps. And I can talk with the people on our staff. They're mostly women. You know, when I was twenty-five, I saw sex as an important part of the celibacy issue. Now, I find that companionship, or the lack of it, is the most difficult.

Anyone who wants to be a pastor these days must be crazy. The gap between the Chancery office and the parish just seems to keep growing. We never know where we stand. We get the enrollment in the grammar school up to 200 and then we find they've raised the guideline to 275. I never realized that the Church could get so political. I became a priest to get away from politics!

I'm so blessed! Great parents. My father owned a grocery store. He taught us that a man expressed his love for his family by hard work. And my mother, well, you know that every Italian considers his mother a saint. Mine is a saint! My three brothers feel the same way.

I love the Church. I love being a priest. When we were in the seminary, speakers would come up there and tell us we were heroes. That's nonsense. We do what we do because we like it. I'm no hero.

Many of the church's pronouncements are a joke. How could they be against the Human Rights Amendment, for example, because it mentions rights for gays?

It seems to me that half of our ministry is spent sweeping up after other priests. I think of an uncle of mine who was away from communion for years because he got a divorce and his priest told him that he couldn't go to communion. That's not Church teaching! And I have a woman in my parish who can't go back to her hometown to get married because she doesn't live in her parish. That's insane! She lives in Chicago. She just wanted to be married in her home parish. Ugh!

Sure, I get the reputation of being a McDonald's Parish. Just pop in. It isn't true. What I ask people to do is often more difficult than being made to do what they're told. I ask them to think about what they're going to do. I wasn't ordained to judge people. We are trying to protect a church that's going to be empty. Even now, the amount of hurt we cause people is extraordinary. I have a young woman in my parish who was engaged to a man who had been married before. I counseled them both and we filled out all the annulment forms and sent them downtown. Can you believe I got a call telling me that they couldn't take the case because his home address was in the Joliet diocese? Her parents and grandparents are in this parish and they turn the case down because he's a couple of blocks out of the diocese. I told them: "You're going to lose them." They told me that there's nothing they could do. So, I refiled in Joliet. They told me that they would have to interview his first wife. I told them that he had asked us not to, and he had good reasons for asking. They said: "Father, we do things right out here." I begged them. "They're good people and we're going to lose them," I said. "There's nothing we can do, Father," they said. So they got married in a Lutheran Church. We've lost them and we didn't have to.

We've got pastors turning away funerals. Some of these men just don't like people. Some have serious problems. But there's no evaluation. No accountability. If they goof, we reward them with an even bigger parish! It will all come to the top in years to come. We just have to learn to help people celebrate important moments in their life in their own way. Even funerals are important celebrations. The sacraments are the greatest evangelization moment. That's when we can do our best work. I'm thinking of a couple in my parish who buried their baby. They were both physicians. She was a pediatrician. And she lost her own child partly because she didn't check out a symptom that she couldn't believe her daughter would have. They were devastated. They hadn't been practicing their faith for eight to ten years but they wanted their baby buried in the church. Hey, that's not my call! I just thank God that I was there for them when they needed the church. Now, we talk often. We have lunch together. They've had another baby and he's been baptized. They're in the parish.

We are a sacramental church. We've got to make changes or we're going to lose it. I'm not just someone who can say the magic words. I can't consecrate five thousand hosts and then go on vacation! That's crazy!

After all, it's each person's call. It's their conscience. That's not situation ethics. Most people are good people. We burden people with rules. We break their hearts.

I don't know why we do this. I don't understand some clerical thinking and ambitions. You know, it reminds me of the NCAA basketball tournament. Lots of teams, only one winner. Those careerists play the clerical game for years. They turn off people, drive them from the church. Then, only a few of them ever get to be bishops. The rest get big parishes and spend the rest of their lives being bitter or drinking. It doesn't make any sense.

· 19 ·

Andrew M. Greeley: Sociologist, Author, Novelist

Andrew Greeley's office at the National Opinion Research Center on the campus of the University of Chicago belies the fact that he is the author of over a hundred nonfiction books and nineteen novels that have over 20 million copies in print. The two-room suite is extremely modest. It is cluttered with cartons, stacks of books, and God knows what else. If, as his critics charge, Greeley makes vast amounts of money on his books, he clearly does not spend it on creature comforts. The fact is that his personal life is much like his office—very modest. I haven't the faintest idea what Andrew Greeley earns, but it isn't as much as his critics would have one think, and he gives a great deal of it away. He isn't in the priesthood for the money.

Andrew Greeley can stir up any thinking Catholic. I have been a participant in long discussions during which Greeley's thinking and personality have been the only topic. They were good discussions. Greeley makes people think. His books are not penny catechisms with their catalog of questions and answers.

Since we both live in Chicago, our paths cross often, sometimes simply in a bookstore near his Michigan Avenue apartment. He spends part of each year in Tucson, Arizona, where he is professor of Sociology at the University of Arizona, and as much time as he possibly can at his home in Grand Beach, Michigan, an hour or so from Chicago. I've listened to him talk at liturgies and groups such as the Midland Authors and at Old St. Patrick's Church in Chicago where he is a perennial guest. Although I have known him in a casual way for over twenty years, I wasn't going to contact him for the book. I didn't want to take advantage of a thin relationship in order to have his name on the dust jacket blurb. When I met him at a reception honoring a mutual friend, I took advantage of a mere acquaintanceship to introduce him to a clutch of people who wanted to meet America's most famous priest. He was most gracious, answering some questions, including mine, again and again. But I didn't ask him for a formal interview.

The next day, Jean met him on Michigan Avenue. She told him of the project; he responded that he would be flattered. I called him immediately.

Greeley's gifts make an interview book easy. They also explain his popularity with his fellow clergy, including bishops who would never admit publicly that they read him. He has the ability to make the complex clear. He talks in whole paragraphs, with topic sentences and conclusions and an enormous amount of data in between.

I found Greeley's books in virtually every rectory I visited. Opinions of his fellow priests varied. He was alternately described as "my hero" and "contentious." But the overwhelming majority of the priests interviewed stated that his research must be taken seriously by the hierarchy and that, sadly, it was not. Greeley's data on the Catholic in the pew and the priest working the back of the church doesn't tie in with increasingly centralized authority. His analogy that a parish closing is like a steel plant shut-down implies criticism of authority. His writings on the Catholic imagination represent some of the best work he has done, but they leave ecclesiatical bureaucrats unsettled. They prefer mounted butterflies to those in flight.

Greeley's priests, both in his novels and his nonfiction work, are human. His critics would prefer a more prudent portrayal—one of priests who are so correct and so holy that, if they were any closer to the Almighty, they would need a harp. His priests are flawed. His fictional characters are sometimes larger than life. ("Most fictional characters are," Greeley responds.)

Greeley's Catholics sometimes lose their beliefs but never their faith; his people go to confession to tell the priest they have lost their faith. They belong to a church that is filled with faults because it is filled with people.

A proper interview with Father Greeley, who has studied the priesthood and the parish church more than any other other sociologist, would take days. We had only a few hours. However, he supplied me with five talks and articles that he had just completed and which have subsequently been published. He also pointed to copies of his more recent books and, as he left his office for a luncheon with a friend, said: "Help yourself. Take anything you want." I did.

Greeley's observations have filled books and have been the subject of innumerable articles. I have confined myself to his views on priesthood, parish life, and the Catholic imagination. What follows are observations from our interview, from some scattered and brief earlier conversations with him, and from the lectures he supplied to me, material he subseqently mailed to me, and his 1990 book, *The Catholic Myth: The Behavior and Belief of American Catholics.*

I guess I agree with Hillaire Belloc. He said: "Let it be said that his sins were as scarlet but his books were read."

No, I'm not any of my characters in my novels. There are bits and pieces. But Father Laurence O'Toole McAuliffe [hero of one the most recent novels at the time of the interview, *The Cardinal Virtues*] is from Seventy-ninth Street; he's 6'3" and has green eyes. I'm not like that. (Smiles.) There's a bit of Leo Mahon in him [Mahon is a Chicago priest; pastor of St. Mary of the Woods Parish where Greeley is frequently a Sunday presider]. You just watch Father Lar in the new book. It will be out next year. He doesn't even drink coffee or tea or anything that would disturb his sleep.

Catholicism means "here comes everyone." In spite of attempts by the right and the left to restrict who is Catholic, it simply hasn't worked. The Spirit flourishes through people. Today's liturgical literature is innocent of that notion. Its authors are aprioristic. They're just like the Curia. They ignore the Catholic religious sensibility. The Catholic spirit is alive but it cannot be expected to pass all the tests or to jump through all the hoops. That's why I'm put off, for example, by the RCIA (Rite of Christian Initiation for Adults), which dismisses candidates after the Gospel. Just another pointless hoop.

When I criticized the RCIA program, the response from the defendants was that I didn't know anything about a parish. The fact is that I've been in parish work all my life and I would stack my experience against anyone's. I also have my "Mailbox Parish," which puts me in touch with all those who write to me.

The bishops and others restrict the spirit; they reduce the faith to magisterial teaching. Imagery and imagination are ignored.

If I could use a metaphor, the faith is like those electromagnetic waves. We can see the band but, above the ultraviolet waves, we can't see. Yet, it's in those vast areas that we must pay attention because that's where the Holy Spirit works; that's where you must pay attention.

When I did the research on religion for the *Chicago Sun-Times*, I found that families wanted a faith to pass on, something to sustain them, to bind families together, and, of course, the sacraments. David Tracy [noted theologian, now at the University of Chicago] was right. It's the sacraments that fire the imagination, yet even these are seen by the Church as reward for passing tests instead of a use of the imagination.

I am convinced that religion is imaginative before it is propositional. It begins in experiences that renew hope; it is encoded in images or symbols that become templates for action; it is shared with others through stories that are told in communities and celebrated in rituals. My sociological theory of religion as imagination parallels Tracy's theological theory that is contained in his book, *The Analogical Imagination.*

We are reflective creatures; we must reflect on our imaginative religion. Because we are creatures who belong to communities which have heritages we must critique our imaginative religion. Creeds, catechisms, theological systems—even teaching authorities—are an inevitable and essential result of reflection on and critique of experiential religion. Religion must be intellectual, but it is experiential before it is intellectual. Most of the transmission of a culture takes place through narrative before it takes place in nonfiction. Jesus was a story teller; the parables are the essential Jesus; they share with us Jesus' experience of the generous, hope-renewing love of the Father in heaven. The Catholic tradition is passed on especially in the stories of Christmas and the Christian passover. I often think that maybe half our heritage is transmitted to children around the crib at Christmastime.

Let me put it this way: Theology is the manifestation of the superstructure of the religious enterprise, but the infrastructure is the religious sensibility. Aquinas's writings are a rationalization of his imaginative instincts, not the other way around. I am always impressed by the ongoing debates within Catholicism between the magisterium and the theologians. Both sides think that they are terribly important. Both pay little attention to the third party—the laity—who listen but little to either of them.

I don't mean to suggest that the sociologist who uncovers all this is more important than the theologian. What I am saying is that both become equally unimportant, though still equally necessary, when compared with the poet, the artist, the storyteller, the mystic, or the saint. Catholic poetry antedates and exceeds Catholic prose. Remember your religion classes? You heard the poetry before the prose; you listened to the stories before you encountered the institution. Thank God for that!

Theologians must treat the orientations and behaviors of the ordinary faithful with more respect than they do. The critic who understands sympathetically those whom he is criticizing is likely to be far more effective than the one who simply denounces. If you write off your own people as materialist, individualist, consumerist chauvinists, and polluters, it may be great fun, but don't be surprised that they don't listen to you.

It's a serious mistake for those who attempt to educate to think that because the faithful are illiterate in the terminology of contemporary theology that they are also religiously illiterate, graceless, and spiritless people. You may modify the religious sensibility but you won't eliminate it. If you try, it will eliminate you. The prose writer must listen to the poet; the institutional leader and the theologian must listen to the storyteller.

Catholic social theory is nothing more than a formalized and generalized articulation of the instinctive response of those in the grip of the Catholic imagination. The politician who believes that political power grows not out of the barrel of a gun but out of voting decisions in the precincts has an organic image of society even if he doesn't know the word. The good precinct captain and the good parish priest have the same image of social action, that is, one must be out on the streets listening more than talking, out with people in the smallest units of society in those places where men and women live, love, raise their children, reconcile, worship, and die.

I wouldn't have any formal testing for First Communion, for example. I would gather kids around and talk to them about their First Communion. There wouldn't be any test. The gathering around is very important.

Our research on Catholic schools shows that there are ties to the institution. They are informal links, such as the schoolyard. It's there that you can see the priest. There are no formal barriers. Again, it's the priest inserting himself into the natural community. His ties are sustained.

Leo Mahon is trying to build a teenage club at St. Mary's. He's finding it hard because it hasn't been done there. But it will come. It just takes time. We priests must still be prepared to waste time with kids. That won't be easy because we now have one priest to do what three did years ago.

We priests must look for our spirituality among the people. I took part in a lot of funerals this year. It was very painful but very inspiring. There were two young mothers; I listened to what their children said. I am finding God among the laity. I suppose that one has to be at it for a while. It takes that long to get over the excessive rationality of seminary training. I'm reminded of my mentor, Peter Rossi, who said that he left the church at twelve and didn't return until he was forty-two, and then he discovered that the boundaries had been changed! Well, I've experienced some of that. It has caused me to change. Throughout our education, we wrote off lay people as spiritless, graceless consumers.

Yes, I know I'm accused of priest bashing. But the real issue is not whether or not I priest-bash but whether or not it is true. The priesthood is in terrible disarray. The morale of the priests is awfully low. They're battered, they're hurting, they don't have much hope for the future, and they're not terribly interested in recruiting young men to follow them.

There were four important findings in the 1970 study on the priesthood sponsored by the National Conference of Catholic Bishops. The study showed that between one-sixth and one-fifth of those who are still active in the priesthood were planning, with varying degrees of certainty, to leave the priesthood. It showed that more than four-fifths of the clergy did not insist on the acceptance of the official birth-control teaching in the confessional. Catholic priests were much less likely in 1970 than they remembered themselves being in 1965 to engage in active recruiting of young men to be priests. And, finally, the occupational satisfaction of associate pastors is no higher than that of semiskilled workers.

Those four findings point to a loss of nerve, a loss of discipline, a loss of sense of identity in the priesthood, and a decline of job satisfaction among the younger priests. When any professional group loses interest in recruiting replacements, that professional group is in considerable trouble.

But the bishops were more embarrassed at the discovery that the majority of their priests had rejected the birth-control encyclical and the further embarrassment that four-fifths of the priests in the country believed that married men should be ordained priests and the priests who left the active ministry to marry should be permitted to return. The bishops were more concerned about the impact of the study on Rome. They ended by setting up a committee to worry about the problems of the priesthood, a committee whose impact on the priests appears to be nonexistent.

The celibacy rule is not likely to be changed. My suggestion of a "priest corps" like the Peace Corps in which men—and women, too—would serve in the active ministry for limited terms of service is generally ignored, although there is no theological reason someone should have to serve in the active ministry all his life. Up until a century and a quarter ago, the average age of a priest at death was thirty-five. Now, most priests live to celebrate their golden jubilees. A priest who can put up with the many and varied demands of the ministry for his whole life may be unusual. By forcing men to stay in the priesthood when they're worn out, the Church runs the risk of their becoming bitter and cynical and taking out their frustrations on the laity.

Unfortunately, priests have little regard for the importance of their own work. American Catholics may complain about the quality of preaching and the quality of counseling and sensitivity they encounter in the rectory, but they still have considerable respect for the sincerity and the diligence, if not the professional competence of their priests. The most powerful single influence in facilitating the return to the Church of someone who has drifted away, particularly a young Catholic in his or her twenties, is a relationship with a priest. Priests are at least as important in the lives of lay people as they used to be. But priests are not inclined to regard their ministry as important as it used to be. So, they're not inviting others to join them. The laity aren't going to leave the Church, but the priests are committing collective suicide because they do not have enough confidence in themselves and their work to actively recruit young men to follow them into the priesthood.

It is difficult to find anything in the evidence available to us, either from studies of priests or studies of lay attitude toward the priesthood, that would justify optimism about the present condition of the Catholic priesthood in the United States. The laity seem convinced that priests are important and are certainly not anticlerical, but they do not give the priest high marks on professional performance. Priests have lost confidence in their ministry. The hierarchy, for its part, is apparently resigned to a continuing vocation crisis. The priest shortage is still not being felt. By the time it is, in the next fifteen or twenty years, it may be too great to do anything about it.

Vatican II did something to the priesthood from which it is yet to recover. I don't know what that is. The crisis in the priesthood today remains to a considerable extent inexplicable. Until we understand better than we do now why the council was such a severe blow to morale, the self-esteem, the self-confidence, and the self-respect of priests, we will have to accept the decline in the number of priests and the mounting problems for the laity because of this decline.

One possibility for the decline is the narrowness of the clerical culture. Priests may be trapped in a culture that still causes them to worry more about what their fellow priests are thinking or what their bishops are doing than about the needs of the lay people they were ordained to serve. Another possibility is the loss of respect for their leaders. Increasingly, Rome has appointed "safe" and conservative bishops. Many of the new hierarchy are not only conservative, they are incompetent and stupid. It's difficult to sustain morale when you believe that you are not only governed by fools but that their folly is increasing.

Hedrick Smith has written an update of his book called *The New Russians*. In it he makes a comparison of the Soviet Union and the Church. Smith speaks of Gorbachev and the foundational church. Gorbachev initiated the changes in the Soviet Union. We could have a Gorbachev in the Church. I think that someone in the church bureaucracy will make the changes but I'm not certain who and when. I don't see the bishops doing it. I got a letter from a friend who observed that the bishops simply don't have enough nerve or enough courage.

In my book *The Catholic Myth: The Behavior and Beliefs of American Catholics*, you can read about E. F. Schumacher, the author of *Small Is Beautiful*. Now, I don't subscribe to the notion that everything must be small. You can't run an airline for a hundred people. But I do believe that an institution should be no bigger than necessary. That's why I support the aldermanic system such as we have in Chicago. The wards are sufficiently small to get the job done. So with the parish. It is the most ingenious community ever invented. That's what worries me about the priest shortage. It is causing a lack of respect for the genius of the neighborhood parish. The only thing that gives me hope is the people.

Catholic social theory vigorously argues that nothing should be done by a larger organization that could be done as well by a smaller one; and nothing should be done by a higher bureaucratic level that can be done just as well by a lower level.

Back in the old days, people chose their priests. In the early Middle Ages, they picked their popes. When a name was announced from the balcony, the people would cheer or boo. If they booed, the electors would go back inside and look for another candidate. I think we need something like this. People should have veto power over priests.

Oh, yes, I've studied how my work has been received by the priests. About one-third are positive, one-third negative, and the rest are in between. That's not a bad split. Yes, I've made some enemies. But there's no one in this world that I wouldn't forgive. I'll be reconciled with anyone who wants to be reconciled.

The future? I think we could see the notion of priests giving a limited number of years of service. We'll ordain married men and have women priests. I think these changes will come with a rush. Celibate priests still get support, but when they don't get it, they will look elsewhere. The parishes will support these changes; the people so love the priests.

There are four important religious socialization experiences, four sets of influences that shape your religious life—your parents, your spouse, your parish priest, and your children. The parish priest is not as important as either parent or spouse, but he's still important. As for the pope, the Vatican, your bishop, and the chancery, they simply don't matter in your ordinary religious life. I mean no disrespect for the Vatican or the chancery or the people in charge of those institutions. I am simply asserting that the parish and the home are where the religious action is. Church leaders are only effective if they help the spouse and the parish priest do their work. Otherwise, they should forget it!

No, I haven't mellowed. Just read my columns!

· 20 ·

Edward J. Griswold: Vocation Director

Ed Griswold is executive director of the National Conference of Diocesan Vocation Directors (NCDVD). A professional organization for diocesan vocational personnel, NCDVD represents 175 of the 185 dioceses in the U.S. and has associate members in Canada, Australia, and Britain. Founded some twenty-five years ago with assistance from Serra International, it functions under the umbrella of the National Coalition for Church Vocations which also embraces the National Religious Vocation Conference, an organization that promotes vocations to congregations of religious sisters, brothers, and priests. The office prepares quantities of mailing material for churches, schools, and organizations. It is supported by membership dues, grants from Serra International, and sales of vocation material.

According to Schoenherr and Young's study, *The Catholic Priest in the United States*, the number of diocesan priests dropped from 35,070 in 1966 to 28,240 in 1985. By 2005, the most optimistic projection states that there will be 23,040 diocesan priests; the most pessimistic projection indicates a drop of 53 percent to 16,653 diocesan priests by the same year. Some dioceses could lose upwards of 68 percent of their active diocesan priests; most show a drop of at least 50 percent and only a handful show an increase between the years 1966 and 2005.

Of the forty-nine remaining theologates (major seminaries) only twenty-one showed an increase in enrollment in 1990 and only eleven of these showed an increase of ten or more candidates. In 1990, there were 2,617 seminarians in the final years of study in the diocesan seminaries, a drop of 117 from the previous year. (Overall enrollment in diocesan seminaries, including high school and college, was 5,531 in 1990. If one folds in the numbers in religious and unaffiliated seminaries, the total enrollment in 1990 was 8,394.)

In addition to the dwindling enrollments, seminaries are finding that many candidates have little philosophical training and only a casual acquaintance with traditional church teaching and spirituality. This is particularly true of minority candidates—Afro-Americans, Asian-Americans and Latino-Americans. While minorities may be the most needed, their numbers remain small: 68 Afro-american, 282 Hispanic, 205 Asian/Pacific, and three Indians (1990 enrollment figures from National Center for Education Statistics). There is a need for a pre-theology program not only for minority candidates but also for candidates of all racial and ethnic groups who come from dysfunctional homes, especially those troubled with drug and alcohol abuse.

Dean Hoge's thorough study, *The Future of Catholic Leadership: Responses to the Priest Shortage*, states that the vocation shortage is long-term, not just temporary, and that the social pressures causing the downturn in vocations are pervasive and strong, and that the Church is powerless to correct them. Hoge views the shortage of priests as an institutional problem, not a spiritual one. Yet, the most widely discussed solution, optional celibacy, is still not permitted to be discussed in official church circles. Hoge's research shows that if celibacy were made optional by 1990 there would be a surplus of diocesan priests by the year 2000. Yet, months before the world's bishops gathered in Rome for the Synod on the Priesthood in the fall of 1990, Pope John Paul II announced that optional celibacy would not be on the agenda.

Opinions on the present shortage vary widely. One bishop criticized the research as biased and suggested that more prayer was the only answer; a pastor cheered the sad state of vocations saying that "priesthood as we know it has to disappear before new forms of ministry can develop." Most took a more moderate view suggesting that the institution would change "within the next generation or so." The changes varied from optional celibacy through the ordination of women to "battlefield commissions," i.e. ordination by the parish community of selected parishioners with or without episcopal approval.

Hoge's research confirms that parishes will continue to be the basic units of Church structure and they will require full-time, stable leadership. Ed Griswold continues to identify and recruit such leadership.

I'm from the Trenton, New Jersey, diocese. During my last year in Trenton, before taking this job, I was vocation director for the diocese and president of the Priests' Council. Ironically, our research at the time showed that the person most likely to encourage vocations was the vocation director and the one least likely to do so was the president of the Priests' Council. I had both jobs. It was confusing!

This isn't much of a building, but it's being rehabbed and our rent is only

$7.50 per square foot. We just couldn't afford anything closer in. We came to Chicago over twenty-five years ago because Serra International is here. They once provided free office space and still give us grants. For the rest, we rely on dues and the sale of materials. We're doing O.K. but we could use some assistance with ethnic and minority vocation literature.

Our literature is geared to promote vocations to the diocesan priesthood, but it also can serve to remind priests of their own vocation.

What am I doing here? I'm here because I believe that there are still people who are interested in diocesan priesthood and who are willing to live a celibate life. The numbers have decreased dramatically but lately there's been a slowdown in the decrease. It's sure a long way from the days when I started first theology at St. Mary's in Baltimore. There were 106 in my class.

I'm afraid that there are a lot of priests out there who are still very unhappy that the ideal has been diminished.

I have to chuckle about the tension that is going on among the different ministries. Some priests are very uncomfortable. They're watching some of their jobs being taken over by the laity and they're asking "What's left for me?" There are plenty of things to do. Priests can do leadership; they can provide a vision.

I love ministry. I was an associate pastor for eight years and later was an administrator of two parishes. When I got involved with this vocation conference I was vocation director for Trenton. I came on the board and, later, became president. When the executive director post opened two years ago, I was encouraged to apply.

It isn't easy to change, I know. Priests who used to do "x, y, or z" are now watching lay people doing these tasks. Now, after seventeen years as a priest, I'm beginning to understand how some of the older guys feel.

I share Andy Greeley's thinking that priesthood is a powerful symbol. It's an invitation into people's lives. [Andrew M. Greeley has written extensively on priesthood, including *The Catholic Priest in the United States: Sociological Investigations*, a work commissioned by the United States Catholic Conference and published in 1972.]

You know, we're not very good at managing our priests. They get very little feedback or evaluation. We don't even seem to have graceful ways of easing people out. We sort of go with the latest way of doing it. We're really not like Ford or GM and, as a result, the bruises tend to stay.

Priests need to sense that they are having an influence. Instead, a relatively few are calling the shots and those who are are just are not paying any attention to the ground swell. We're not here to make Chevettes. But the Church still fears a loss of control. So, they continue to try to get the toothpaste back in the tube. There has to be a new mind-set.

Cardinal [Joseph] Bernardin [archbishop of Chicago] really tried a few years ago. He started with all the priests who had been ordained ten years or less and he listened. He brought them up to Mundelein [University of St. Mary of the Lake, archdiocesan seminary] and he listened. The priests called them "pajama parties," but they helped. Bernardin listened. He heard the young priests say that they didn't like where the Church was going; that it was getting more institutional; that it was putting on the brakes. The priests spoke of their reluctance to invite others to live a celibate life. They spoke about women's issues and about their own personal problems. Nothing was solved, but people were heard. The priests felt better. As parish priests, we don't feel that we are being listened to and there's frustration in that.

I recall a friend who left from Trenton. He said that he saw no hope that things would change. Now, I know that he had a girlfriend and I'm sure that this colored his decision. But after he left and took a job with Blue Cross, he told me that he had received better treatment from them in six months than he had during his entire sixteen years in the priesthood. We've got to change that.

Priests get isolated. It's partly because they don't want to get hurt anymore. They want to walk with people in their parish; they want to love their people and have their people love them. People in the parishes are looking for personalism and for caring. If the people get a sense that the priests care about them, the isolation is going to dwindle.

Some years ago, when I gave a retreat at a parochial high school, I broke the students up into discussion groups. One of the questions I was asked a lot was: "Hey, when is Monsignor (the pastor) going to take off his white gloves?"

What we do as priests is wonderful! The role of the priest is to bring the Tradition to the people and the people to the Tradition, and that isn't always done by following the book. It's not just making rules and keeping rules. We ought to just leave the Canon Law to those who just want to keep Canon Law.

In real life, the issues get very complex. When you're trying to bring Jesus into people's lives, it gets sloppy. But sloppiness is very human. We can't turn our backs on people. I'm a priest so that people won't think that the Church has turned its back on them. Priests have got to be more compassionate, more present to people. Rigid decisions have never brought anyone closer to the church. We must speak to people about God and eternal life even if it makes us vulnerable.

I think that our present circumstances may remain for the next two or three generations but we still need to see that the sacraments are celebrated authentically. We still must ask ourselves: "What's the most compassionate thing to do?"

The dedication is there. I just can't count the numbers of young people who join the Jesuit volunteers or other groups. Somehow, we haven't been able to share that vision.

I'm optimistic for the Church. It can be a very vital community. The institutional structures? I don't know. People will continue to come forward. It won't be what the institution wants but even today there are good people coming into the priesthood. It could all mean a great change in our spirituality. We may become more like Protestants with less emphasis on the Eucharist. Bishops are already saying: "I have parishes with no one there." [Presently some 10 percent of parishes, about 1,950, are classed as "priestless." The figure does not include the hundreds that have been closed, in part because of the lack of priests.]

Bringing in foreign priests just isn't going to work. They bring another culture. People won't respond. We just have to take another look at this. The permanent diaconate has come in for a lot of criticism lately, but it may be one step toward change.

I'm still filled with hope. That's partly because of the quality of the priests that I know. We can work it out. We just need to do things differently.

· 21 ·

Martin J. Hegarty: A Resigned Priest's Apostolate

During the late 1940s, a book appeared that was a quiet best-seller among clergy and educated laity. *Shepherds in the Midst* by E. Boyd Barrett, a former Jesuit, was the saga of a "spoiled" priest, a man who left the active ministry, married, and went into business. The slim book was about his return to the Church, although not to active ministry.

("He has to take care of that woman," one priest said at the time. "That woman" was Barrett's wife, referred to as if she were evil incarnate, a betraying bitch who had lured him from the sanctuary. Before Vatican II, the Church was in its prepubescent stage, viewing women as early elementary schoolboys view girls. Subconsciously, the clergy believed that it would have been better for women if they had remained ribs.)

Barrett's book sold because it was unique. Resigned priests were simply not written about except by those who leaped over the wall and formed sects of some kind. While the book treated priestly defection as the ultimate betrayal, it at least brought the subject into the public domain.

Priests have been departing the active ministry since Father John Carroll (America's first bishop in 1789 and archbishop in 1808) was made made superior of the American mission in 1784 and the country had twenty-four priests. However, they did so under cover of darkness; their flocks were often told that "Father has gone out West." They were never mentioned again. Until years after World War II, even former seminarians were regarded as "spoiled priests." Scripture was invoked incorrectly to warn that anyone who "put his hand to the plow" must not look back (an argument for faith, not vocation).

Canon Law once required dispensed priests to remove themselves from the diocese. If they married, the ceremony was performed in a rectory or in a locked church. It didn't matter that they were properly laicized. Any priest who had been "reduced to the lay state" was to be considered clerical offal.

Not many years ago, a prominent Catholic layman, addressing a clerical banquet, described with great relish his response to a priest-friend, now resigned, who had called at his office. "I told my secretary to tell him that I knew *Father* So-and-So. I didn't know *Mr.* So-and-So." The faithful clergy applauded.

Resigned priests have been denied pension benefits they had accrued, in some cases after over twenty-five years of service. There are instances in which they were refused employment after the bishop had "put in the word." They are generally not permitted to be employed by the Church, especially if they are married. Some have been denied Church burial, largely because of invalid or canonically illicit marriages.

But there is another side. Resigned priests, especially those with addiction problems, often get substantial help from their bishops even in cases where there is no evidence that the priest will return to active service. Bishops have presided at the funerals of resigned priests; attended quiet meetings of prayer groups founded by resigned priests; opened their seminaries for retreats for such groups; arranged pensions for those with years of service. In some dioceses resigned priests are heading agencies such as Catholic Charities. At the very least, bishops have retained close friendships with many departed colleagues.

Until the early 1960s, the close of Vatican II, and the death of John XXIII, departures from active ministry remained rare. Then, when Paul VI eased the restrictions for dispensations, the floodgates opened. A study of U.S. diocesan priests shows a 20 percent decline in numbers from 1966 through 1984, most of them through resignations. The study, with sponsorship by the U.S. Catholic Conference and funded by the Lilly Endowment, was conducted at the University of Wisconsin by Richard Schoenherr and Lawrence Young. The research showed that resignation was the most critical "exit event" in the study. The data revealed that by the time members of a typical class ordained during this era reached thirty-five, 19 percent had already resigned. By age forty-five, 34 percent had resigned. By the time the class celebrated its twenty-fifth anniversary of ordination, 37 percent had resigned. In other words, an ordination class of forty in 1965 had twenty-five surviving members by 1990.

Resignation rates in the mid-1980s had dropped to about half what they were in the early 1970s, but the rates have bottomed out at relatively high levels. Between 1970 and 1974, for example, 1.71 percent of diocesan priests resigned from active ministry on an annual basis. During 1980-84, only 0.86 percent resigned annually.

Looked at another way, the report shows that from 1966 through 1984, entrances to the U.S. diocesan priesthood through ordination and incardination (priests arriving from other dioceses in other countries) amounted to 15,000 priests. Exits through leaves, resignations, and natural losses totaled just over 22,000. The net loss was a little under 7,000. The number of diocesan priests is expected to decline from a high of 35,000 in 1966 to 21,000 by the year 2005.

In his book on resigned priests, *Shattered Vows* (an unfortunate title in the opinion of some resigned priests, but one picked by the American publisher, not the author), David Rice, an Irish journalist and former Dominican, states that one-quarter of all active priests in the world, over 100,000, have resigned. Rice adds: "Those one hundred thousand shepherds did not shuffle into the mist with downcast heads. Most of them marched resolutely out, vowing to take no more; others stormed out in fury and disgust; many simply got up from their knees, made the sign of the cross and walked quietly away." Rice calculates that, by the turn of the century, there will be only 15,000 diocesan priests in the U.S., about the number there were in 1925. The vital difference is that the U.S. had 16 million Catholics in 1925 and is expected to have 65 million by A.D. 2000.

Rice's figures are lower than those in other studies. However, some observers claim they are more realistic. The figures cited are about diocesan priests. Most studies include religious priests and show that their numbers are declining at an even higher rate.

CORPUS figures claim that there are at least 17,000 resigned priests in the United States. Dioceses that attempt to project ordination rates tend to estimate slightly higher figures than they actually ordain. There is prayerful hope in such projections.

There is little evidence that resigned priests are returning to active ministry under the present structure. In an interview with *The Catholic Observer* of the diocese of Springfield, Father John Gray, provincial of the Missionaries of Holy Apostles in Cromwell, Connecticut, said that more than sixty priests have inquired about returning. Only five, however, have made formal application. CORPUS reports that, if the Church made celibacy optional, over 3,600 of its members would be interested in returning to ministry.

Clearly, the declining numbers have put the American Church in deep trouble. David Rice cites Jesuit scholar John A. Coleman: "Any profession for which the following facts are true—declining absolute numbers in the face of the growth of the larger population, significant resignations, a declining pool of new recruits and an aging population—can be referred to as having a deep-seated identity crisis, whatever the internal morale of the group."

The majority of resigned priests are like Marty Hegarty. They remain faithful Catholics; many are actively involved in their parishes. Their closest friends remain priests with whom they were ordained, whether or not they are in or out of the active ministry. Indeed, their wives often must bear patiently their clerical gossip and old war stories. They retain strains of bitterness but such strains generally run no deeper than those of active priests, or any male-dominated professional group.

Marty Hegarty is special among resigned priests. He devotes enormous amounts of time and substantial personal funds to helping his fellow shepherds. His ordination classmates count on him to organize their anniversary Masses and parties. His clerical friends call St. Gertrude's East "Marty's Parish."

I got a letter from Tim Cloonan (pseudonym) the other day. He's a fascinating character. He wrote me in the early eighties. He was an army chaplain and an alcoholic. He left and got married; no kids; they got divorced; he dried out, and he wanted to come back.

There's a lot of cruelty involved in getting back. He wrote a lot of letters but most of the bishops didn't want him. Cloonan wanted to stay at his job. He needed the money. But the bishops willing to accept him would do so only with the clear understanding that he would have to resign his job. The bishops just can't afford to have their priests independent.

Well, one bishop took him. He sent him to a small parish with a bastard of a pastor. It's harder to get back in than it is to leave!

I was ordained in 1954. I resigned in 1969. Carole and I have been married twenty-one years. I loved those years in the priesthood and I love married life. I've been very happy in both lives, but one is about intimacy, and there's a big difference. You could say that my life has been on an upward curve since 1954. Everything is better now.

I'm an industrial psychologist and I work out of our home. I started WEORC in 1976. At least that's when we got our not-for-profit status. In reality, WEORC was in existence since 1969.

WEORC is the Anglo-Saxon spelling of "work." We needed some corporate title in order to get our corporate status. First, I thought of "Omar" after the tent-making ministry of St. Paul. I thought I'd be real subtle. Would you believe, I found out that "Omar" was registered all over the place? So, I just picked WEORC out of the dictionary.

WEORC is about jobs. We're not trying to do anything else, just help people in transition. I learned that some other guys were offering job counseling. They were charging resigned priests money and giving them advice that contradicted everything that I had learned. My experience as an industrial psychologist and my experience as a resigned priest looking at other resigned priests told me one simple thing: Get a job. Priests are capable people. They move up rapidly. They were being told by others to wait for just the right job. Some priests in transition do have inflated notions about their marketability. Other have poor work habits. But a lot have a low self-concept. They got discouraged.

Jim Wilbur's mailing list had 456 names on it [Wilbur is another resigned priest. He has been Hegarty's cohort in WEORC since its inception].

We did a questionnaire to all those resigned priests and asked them to describe their experience in getting their first job, working their way up, etc. We asked if they got any counseling from their diocese, and we asked what's happened to them since.

We found that resigned priests do very well. Most go into service jobs. Most like what they're doing and earn a good living. Some of the entrepreneurial types have done exceptionally well. Around 80 or 90 percent had advanced to a job level they were comfortable with and were stable in their jobs. And virtually all found that their status as resigned priests made no difference to their fellow employees or their bosses.

I never found anyone who had gotten job help through his chancery office. A lot of chancery office people and bishops have my name in their Rolodex but I'm afraid there isn't a lot of high-mindedness in this. I never get a direct referral. One chancery office official, now a bishop, told me: "Marty, I have your WEORC directory. I'll keep it on my bookshelf, but I won't share it with anyone who is leaving."

Chancery offices rarely keep track of their resigned priests. It's as if they were dead. I've been asked by chancery officials often about the location of a resigned priest. As I said, there's a lot of cruelty in all this.

In the second part of the questionnaire, we asked personal stuff—marriage, earnings, etc.—all of it anonymous. Again, we wanted to see how they were doing. There weren't many rich guys, but most were comfortable.

Finally, we asked if they would like to be in the WEORC directory, a listing of people and their jobs. Being on the list means that you are willing to help others find jobs, especially jobs in your field. Over 250 of the initial 456 contacted said that we could put them in the first directory.

We had 500 copies printed. We assembled them by hand; mailed them to the 250 members, and used the others to pass out.

The first effort really worked. I got a mention in the *Wall Street Journal* and the *National Catholic Reporter*. That first edition was really used up fast.

Our second directory had 1,000 names; we printed 1,800 copies. The third edition was 2,500 copies and they're all gone.

The directories set up a great deal of networking. They also prompted an occasional newsletter that we mail to our membership. We've never charged a fee. This is not a part of my business. We rely on the contributions of the

WEORC members themselves. Some counselors of resigned priests use the directory and then charge a fee! When two former nuns came to me for help, I gave them a lot of time. Now, they have a counseling service of their own. So, I asked them to help at one of our sessions and they said that they would have to charge. Isn't that something!

There are 2,075 names on the list now. Ninety-five percent of them are resigned priests; about twenty-five priests on the list are still active.

We do some other things. We hold a day of recollection and an annual retreat for WEORC members in the area. We use some of our funds to help resigned priests in third world countries who have a terrible time. We help a few widows in this country. Most priests don't accumulate much during their years in minstry; when they leave and die relatively young, it can put their widows in a real bind.

The fourth directory will be the last one. I'm getting old. The young guys don't seem interested. Young guys who leave today aren't staying close to priesthood or even to the Church.

You know, when a guy walks out of his chancery office, when that door closes, I'm afraid that the bishop just says "next." There isn't a lot of feeling in all this. I've noted that there are just two ways to get removed from your ordination class listing: death or resignation. Either way, you no longer exist. The chancery just issues a correction to the diocesan directory that simply says "delete."

My years in the active ministry were very happy ones. They were filled with the ordinary ups and downs of human life. There was a lot of anger at pastors, a lot of frustrated ambition. But they were good years.

As I look back on my priesthood, I think that the one flaw in our training was the terrible competitiveness of our seminary education. Both the priests and the priesthood are victims of that competitiveness. It stayed with me after ordination. I found myself competing for the approval of my pastors and the love of my parishioners. I wanted to be the most sensitive of confessors. My ego was such that I was always doing it.

I think that the replacement for intimacy in the priesthood is power. Power comes in many garbs. There's the power that comes with needing to be the best, the power that comes with having needy people, and the power one feels in wanting to help them. Oh, we often invent all sorts of altruistic terms for all this but often it's nothing more than a needy person like myself trying to meet the needs of other needy people.

I've managed to leave all that behind. Now, people still come to see me, lots of them. I can be empathetic. I still try to help. But I don't need them. The intimacy of my marriage has removed all that.

This is a hard story to tell. It gets into that intimacy I've been talking about. But it's important to what I'm trying to say. I hope I can say this right.

The other day, Carole was terribly upset. "The people at my school are just eating me up," she said. She's been teaching and counseling at the same school for over twenty years. It's in one of the poorest neighborhoods of Chicago. Carole has the seniority; she could ask for another school in a better neighborhood. But she cares about the kids in this school and this neighborhood. Recently, she challenged the top man at St. Ignatius, the Jesuit prep school not far from her school. She asked him to give scholarships to the kids in her school. She got scholarships for five of them. Carole could be a principal; she's got the degree and she has passed the principal's exam. But she stays where she is because she feels that she's doing some good.

But dealing with the mindless bureaucracy is very painful. They take all her energies and they don't give anything back. She's just coming back from a bout with cancer and she just doesn't have the strength.

Anyway, not long ago, I was frightened that she was near a breakdown. She just doesn't have the same energy since her operation. The other morning, while we just held each other, I recognized that I could be strong for her. I don't need her to be dependent upon me, and she knows that. She said that I'm the most independent person she ever met, but it's nice to know that she can count on me. I guess I wasn't invited as a priest to share Carole's life, so I don't need my Messiah complex. Our intimacy isn't based on need. I do keep telling her to quit. We don't need the money. But that's up to her. Intimacy doesn't mean that you run another person's life.

I said once that, if Cardinal Bernardin [Joseph L. Bernardin, archbishop of Chicago] announced that the Pope had changed the ground rules and that all resigned priests who were married could return to ministry, and that all who wanted to do so should just gather on his front lawn the next morning, that there would only be a half dozen guys on his lawn. I still believe that, but I'd modify it slightly.

Lately, you know, I've been helping with the liturgy at St. Gertrude's East, not far from our condo. The people are older; they can't make the trip over to the church, so we have this Sunday liturgy at Sacred Heart School on Sheridan Road.

I'm very comfortable getting there a half-hour early. I like puttering around, doing things. I try to see that everything's in place. I suppose that I'm in charge, but I no longer feel that way. The sisters from the school and the other people are good at getting things organized. So, I find myself gravitating to the door and greeting the people as they come in. I ask them how they're feeling. I ask about the regulars who aren't there. I want to know how they are, to find out if they're sick.

I'm someone in that community; it's my community and I love them. I do the announcements and acknowledge the people who are there. I ask for prayers for the sick. They're such good people, so calm in the face of all the turmoil in this world.

I gather the community and I call them to prayer. There is something about me that still loves to call a community together and to bring them to prayer. At those times, I feel of sense of wanting to proclaim the Word again. I feel that something is happening to me. I feel that I'm communicating well.

We do the responsorial psalm and we read the responses rhythmically. It's kind of a sung prayer. And I look out there and everyone is really praying and responding with the verses, and it has a great grip on me. It's that wonderful return from the community. It reaches inside me.

I'm describing a role that is essential for a pastor or priest, to bring the community to prayer. I think I do that, too. It's not phony with me. I suppose that *if*—and I can't imagine it as anything more than an *if*—but *if* the community did call me to return; *if* they wanted me to preside, I would. I'd do it with great joy. This would be the best priest I could be.

I'll give you another example. Carole's family is from northern Wisconsin, at Pelican Lake. There's a little parish there, maybe a hundred families. During the summer, when the tourists are there, the church fills up twice each Sunday. Well, some time ago, when Carole's father died, I preached at his funeral. The pastor invited me to give the homily. Now, people still come up to me after Mass and ask: "When are you going to be our priest?"

Well, I can almost see myself in such a setting. But if word came down from on high, if the bishop insisted on control, I couldn't do it. I'd have to work for nothing because to take money would make me an employee and I believe that employees should obey their bosses.

I'm only talking about myself, of course. There are others who would rush back to full service. I know that groups like CORPUS are pressing for full service for married priests. I guess I share some of their goals but not their approach.

I believe in the ordination of women, for example, but I'm not going to stump for it. I don't have to support the Church's teaching on birth control, either, or announce whether I'm pro-life or pro-choice. The teaching on birth control is fine with me as long as they leave it in the theology books. I can accept Church teaching in good conscience, but if the bishop is going to ask me specific questions, then I'd have a problem.

I don't know about the future. I'm not very good at projecting. I'd just like to see happen what we're talking about, that is people choosing the person they want to lead them, the person to be their presider and their leader in prayer.

I want to continue the tradition. I want to preserve the tradition of handing things on. There is no stronger tradition than the Eucharist, and part of that very tradition is the handing on of the custom of calling certain people to Christ and sending them forth. That tradition dates to the earliest days of the Church. It's very important to me.

I don't think that gender identification is all that compelling. Yes, Christ called only men to be his first disciples, but, if Christ called people today in the twentieth century, women would be represented. It isn't what Christ did then, but rather what he is doing now. If the congregation called people to be their presider today, women would be called as well as men. That's what Schillebeeckx [Edward Schillebeeckx, O.P., distinguished Dutch theologian] would say. He writes about the community calling people to ministry, a calling that is always in relationship to the larger Church, the Catholic community.

I've got a strange thought. You know Andy Greeley's novel, *Cardinal Virtues*. [Andrew M. Greeley and Marty Hegarty spent twelve years together in the seminary and were in the same ordination class. They remain good friends.] Well, his novel is a fanciful bit of pastoral theology, filled with wonderful ideas. No priest is ever as good as Father "Lar," the novel's hero, or as bad as Father Simon, the vicar general, the novel's bad guy. Andy's characters are larger than life but they're pointed in the right direction. There's a lot of Canon Sheehan's style there. [Canon Sheehan was a well-known Irish novelist. His best known work is *My New Curate*.] Priests in *My New Curate* and Sheehan's other novel, *Luke Delmege*, are larger than life, too. They are romantic heroes in the style of other writers of the period, and in Greeley's novels, too. Greeley is a kind of modern day Canon Sheehan. There's no real model in the priesthood for pastor or for the young curate in Greeley's novel. There are bits and pieces, of course, but mostly they exist only in the highly creative and highly idealistic mind of Andy Greeley. These are priests who love God, love their priesthood, their country, and, most of all, their people. I think every priest—and the Church itself—aspires to that, but we fall short and have to make do.

I suppose that the Church and the priesthood is a lot like another novel, *Gone with the Wind*. That novel says that there is no one as evil as the South nor as noble as the North. It's much the same with each of us, and with the Church.

· 22 ·

J. Bryan Hehir: Scholar, Professor

Bryan Hehir may be one of the brightest men in the American Church. The Joseph P. Kennedy Professor of Ethics and International Policy at Georgetown University is not as well known as other scholar-priests but his influence on America's bishops and the thinkers in Washington and academia is significant.

In a Chicago address in 1990, Hehir stated that "the Catholic moral vision runs from womb to tomb. It cannot be reduced to a single issue." He attempts to bridge the gap between the Catholics who live at the edge and those who live at the center of the Church and society. Hehir sees America's 54 million Catholics as being at the very center of American society. With three times more representatives in Congress and more corporate CEOs than any other religion, he sees American Catholics as moving more to the center, even as their immigrant Catholic brothers and sisters are still arriving. "We worship with the new people at the edge but it is the people at the center who are making the limited choices." Hehir looks for ways of joining these two groups.

Bryan Hehir often has to address what he calls "the question of limited choices." His task as an ethicist is to lead people through the maze of limited choices that so often define people's lives. Referring to America's vast defense system, for example, he asks: "When you can do almost anything, how do you decide what you're going to do?" Hehir's task is to find answers to the hard-choice questions of allocating resources for a society that must wrestle with cutbacks in vital medical care for the elderly while increasing expenditures for weapons of destruction.

Hehir's words echo the sounds of the seamless garment language of Cardinal Joseph Bernardin. The fifty-year-old priest maintains that the quality of our faith is dependent upon the quality of justice in our land. For him, the genuineness of Catholic faith is linked, not only to the abortion issue, but to how we treat the children, the widows, the aged, and the homeless in our land.

Hehir is a resource for the bishops in their efforts to form pastorals. Most likely, he provided much of the phrasing and knotted the paragraphs together for their pastorals on the economy and nuclear weapons. He is a regular columnist for *Commonweal*. Between classes at Georgetown and work at the NCCB/USCC, he lectures throughout the country. His thoughts are as organized as a librarian's desk. Clearly, much of his learning is shared with other academics and influential people who turn to him as a resource on the complex questions of ethics and international relations.

While other clerical academics find parish life tedious and rarely venture into the day-to-day doings of a parish, Bryan Hehir finds that it is an integral part of his life and thought. "I learn a great deal from the parishioners at St. Anthony's," he said. He presides at parish liturgies and takes his turn in the confessional. The experience of parish life gives a pastoral flavor to his thinking.

W̶e shouldn't ordain anybody who can't read a federal budget. It has the moral quality of a secular encyclical. It defines our priorities.

I was ordained for the archdiocese of Boston in 1966 but I've been away from Boston for seventeen years. The cardinal [Bernard F. Law] has been very good to me. "I'll never call you back," he told me. "But I want you to know that I'd welcome you back." I told Cardinal [Humberto] Madeiros [archbishop of Boston, 1970-83] that the local church had educated me and that I felt an obligation to Boston. But he said: "You serve the local church by serving the Conference" [National Conference of Catholic Bishops]. So, I'm here in Washington, but if the cardinal appointed me to a parish in Boston, I would go back.

I did my doctorate at Harvard. It's in ethics and international policy, but I did about one-third to one-half my work in divinity. Over half of the students at Harvard's Divinity School are Catholics. Many of them are women. They don't talk about ordination; they don't have much time to talk! But I don't think a lot of them are seeking ordination. Still, it's clear that they are at Harvard for a purpose. They will emerge somewhere in the Church or have an impact on it.

In looking at this priest situation, I think that we have to distinguish between the short term and the long term. I'm not very good at numbers but I read all of Andy's [Andrew M. Greeley, priest, sociologist]. They have a fundamental dimension about them. I don't become pessimistic. I do want to look the numbers in the eye. And, short term, I want to recognize the reality of the numbers. I take them as a challenge to creativity.

Now, obviously, you could change the ground rules. We could ordain married men and we could ordain women. Karl Rahner says it's possible. But I see no change in this pontificate.

The present situation challenges us in two ways. First, there is a certain conception of our work. Priests are expected to do more and more. We may not live until retirement. We have to do something about this. Second, we are being challenged to create ministry. There are a lot of possibilities. We can have a really good parish even with only one priest. My own diocese of Boston is expected to have at least 165 parishes with only one priest by 1995. Now, maybe that's too static a view, but I believe that it's real.

I'm thinking of Cardinal Suhard, who was Archbishop of Paris during the time of Pius XII. He structured a diocese in such a way that it was successful even under the tightly controlled regime of Pius XII. There was lots of creative activity. There were men like Yves Congar who were allowed to flourish. I'm thinking of Jack Egan [Monsignor John J. Egan] in Chicago who was able to do extraordinary work at a time when there was a lot of control. We need some Suhardian vision in bishops, priests, teachers, and lay people—people who are not overcome by facts.

There's one great thing about this job. It means that you're on call to dioceses around the country. You get to see these places. You find names that rarely surface in the headlines. You meet bishops and priests with imagination. I believe that the examples of Suhard are there. I think that Congar and John Courtney Murray are two examples of theologians who did extraordinary things in challenging circumstances. There are bishops in this country who have that Suhardian vision. I don't want to name them, but they're there. They have the potential of coming to the forefront.

Now, you can't do these imaginative things on the presumption that you will live to see them flourish. But you've got to go about your work that way and figure that the Holy Spirit will use it.

We just buried Shawn Sheehan [Boston priest]. He was a great friend of Godfrey Dieckman [renowned liturgist] and William McManus [former bishop of Fort Wayne-South Bend]. He was another one with creativity and vision. I used to meet with him on Saturday afternoons back in Boston, before I entered the seminary. He made a great contribution to social action. Later, he taught me incarnational theology. I entered the seminary in my third year of college. I found it a prison, but I was able to read the *New York Times* and I got to know Sheehan. Richard McBrien was four years ahead of me and, through Sheehan, I got to know him. Sheehan introduced me to Congar's writings and he sent me to liturgical conferences. He had a great impact on McBrien, too. It was men like Sheehan and Dieckman who took us through *Mystici Corporis* [Pius XII, 1943, On the Mystical Body of Christ], *Mediator Dei* [Pius XII, 1947, On the Sacred Litury] and *Pacem in Terris* [John XXIII, 1963, On establishing universal peace] and, of course, *Rerum Novarum* [Leo XIII, 1891, On capital and labor], and *Quadragesimo anno* [Pius XI, 1931, On reconstruction of the social order]. These men prepared all the material for Vatican II and they didn't even know there was going to be a council.

We had good resources in those days but within a less open context. We've got to take all that stuff now and use it creatively. We've got to take it to new stages of development. I don't think that the Holy Spirit is going to do our work for us.

John Paul II is a major figure in international politics. He should have shared the Nobel Peace prize with Mikhail Gorbachev. Communism began to die with the first visit of John Paul to Poland. I think that it was a fitting tribute to the end of Communism that the pope and Gorbachev met. John Paul has a design for Europe. He has been talking about it since 1980. I don't think it's transferable to this or other countries. It's his model of Church discipline. His social teachings are great stuff, but he remains a conservative theologian.

You may know of the historian George Williams who has written a book about the mind of John Paul II. Williams is a Congregationalist who met Karol Wojtyla at Vatican II. Williams got to know him; he even learned Polish. When Williams got him to come to the U.S. in 1976 to lecture on phenomenology, Williams declared: "There's the next pope."

The long term view of his papacy gets fuzzy. Some variants are possible between his approach to mission countries and industrialized countries. He has enormous political instincts. He's a politician, an actor, a philosopher. He has lived under great pressures and he hasn't flinched. I'm sure that he takes numbers very seriously. He understands them in depth. Personally, I like him. He's a major figure in this century. We may disagree with some of his judgments, but his place in history is guaranteed. However, I think that we have to accept the fact that some things aren't going to change.

I think that we have to work with our American strengths. We need to go to our congregations and to ask them for their skills. We need to foster a conception of Church that says it's all ours. I think that there is a danger that we could get captured by these internal questions. We may get turned inward and exhaust our energy on political or institutional considerations. That would be bad for the Church and bad for our country. The American Church can influence a wider society; I believe that it has through its statements on the economy, Latin America, and the letter on peace and nuclear weapons. I think that the bishops have had an influence in helping the government to avoid the temptation to use military force.

I live at St. Anthony's Parish in Falls Church, Virginia. The parish is central to my life. It's fundamental. I'm in ethics and international policy but the work I do here at Georgetown is influenced by what I learn from the parishioners of St. Anthony's. It would be a dangerous thing for me not to be in a parish.

· 23 ·

Eugene Hemrick: Pulse Taker

Gene Hemrick joined the National Conference of Catholic Bishops/
United States Catholic Conference in 1978 as director of the Office of
Research. Since that time he has turned the office into a state-of-the-art
research facility, capable of doing sophisticated studies and networking
with at least fourteen other pastoral planning organizations. The office
assists the bishops in their role as educators and acts as a counselor to
members of the conference. Its research has appeared in fifteen magazines and Hemrick has written over five hundred columns which have
concentrated on the results of the studies produced by the conference.

Hemrick was interviewed four times, twice in Chicago and twice at
his Catholic University and NCCB/USCC offices. Much of the data that
appears in this book comes from his files. Hemrick is an academic with a
strong belief in the importance of parish ministry. Like Emmanuel
Cardinal Suhard, his writings portray the good priest-pastor as one who
subtly emphasizes the qualities of intellectual-spiritual responsibility. He
is concerned that the need for priests could cause the Church to recruit
men who are too status quo oriented and afflicted with an outdated
educational process. "One of the wisest principles of spirituality is that
we must never opt to maintain a middle ground," he writes. Hemrick
appears to live that gospel fully. Priest, researcher, writer, teacher,
already in his fifties, he is also a superb triathlon athlete.

W e've just gathered some impressive data about young
priests, men ordained five to nine years, guys who range in age between
thirty-four to forty. I think it's good stuff.

We learned that most priests would be priests again if asked, and they
would definitely encourage others to consider the priesthood. They receive
their greatest identity from celebrating the sacraments, especially the Eucharist, and they are most inspired by the spirituality and faith of the laity.
They have a high satisfaction with their present work and are moderately
satisfied with their personal health, spiritual life, psychological well-being,
and living a celibate life.

We've learned that satisfaction is high with respect to working with laity and women religious, but a bit lower with regard to working with fellow priests, bishops, or superiors. Two-thirds of these priests are in favor of continuing to allow married Anglican priests to become Catholic priests.

They're very comfortable celebrating the sacraments, and fairly comfortable with Church social-justice teachings, with the spirituality of the priesthood, with the increase of nonordained persons in ministry, and with permanent deacons. They're least comfortable with the governance of the Church and with its moral teachings.

The younger men see the Church's biggest challenges as the need for stronger evangelization, responding to the priest shortage, and working more closely with the laity.

There's a lot more. I find it exciting and important. This office of research was set up in 1978. We're here primarily to assist the bishops to better understand and respond to the sacramental life and evangelization efforts of the Church. You know, every study we've done could be put under one of the sacraments. It's really evangelization. We don't spin off any particular model. We try to see these studies through the eyes of priests, through sacramental language that they understand. We don't like to give just numbers.

We've done over thirty studies, studies on holy orders, penance, matrimony, evangelization, black seminarians, seminary life, nuns living in poverty, the permanent diaconate, the rite of reconciliation, and studies on active and retired bishops. We've published them everywhere we can.

Sure, some of the bishops blew up at some of the findings. They wanted to send me to a doctor. But our data confirmed what is really happening. The bishops support this office but have no control over it. They could close the office, of course, and they might do that because of budget restraints. Ironically, our own research shows that bishops react badly to research and financial data. Often, they simply don't know how to read the findings. Some of them got very upset over the study on the future of the priesthood. We still must find a way to lobby the bishops. We have to find a way to place this data within a pastoral context.

I've moved a lot myself in the fourteen years I've been here. My thinking and my writing have changed. I've had to combine the data with practical and pastoral considerations. I've found that my own priesthood gets very involved. It washes off me like ocean water.

I got my B.A. and M.A. from St. Mary of the Lake Seminary in Mundelein, Illinois, and was ordained for the Joliet diocese in 1963. Later, I got another masters in religious education at Loyola University of Chicago and a Ph.D. from the University of Notre Dame.

I guess I really got into research while at Notre Dame where I worked on the "Study of Man" project. Anyway, I worked in religious education for the diocese and, later, set up and directed a school of catechetics at Illinois

Benedictine College. I came to Catholic University as a prof and I've been a visiting professor at Villanova, Notre Dame, St. Thomas, St. Louis, and Fordham universities. Now, I'm full-time here, doing some teaching, writing a syndicated column for CNS (Catholic News Service), and helping as a weekend parish priest.

Anyway, the bishops are growing more and more respectful of this office. They're not ready yet to say much publicly but they do tell me privately. If we have to move, I've been talking with people here at Catholic U. and at Georgetown. Perhaps we could set up a national center for theologians, politicians, and researchers—an office that would ask a lot of questions. The politicians in this city have an enormous amount of information to share. Senators and representatives gather tons of data. The center would have to be interdisciplinary, not simply a sociological point of view. When we moved into a question, we would have to bring a concrete grasp of the tradition.

When we started all this years ago, we tried to make a mosaic of the Church in America. At first, we simply went to the bishops and asked: "Hey, do you know something we don't know?" We started to write brief things, sort of data minus the jargon. It was all kinds of stuff woven together. Then, along comes the Lilly Foundation with a grant of nearly half a million to help with the Schoenherr study [*The Catholic Priest in the U.S.* by Richard Schoenherr, University of Wisconsin, director of the project] that went off like a loose cannon. We got lots of cooperation from the bishops and we were able to send them back lots of data. But some of the bishops found the data pessimistic; they suggested that because Schoenherr was a resigned priest the study was biased; they questioned my confidence in the report; some said that we omitted the influence of the Holy Spirit. It got messy. All of a sudden because of the publicity and the outside funding, some questioned who owned the report. In retrospect, we should have had an oversight committee.

I believed that the data was correct. In fact, I had to push Schoenherr to finish in a timely fashion. I wanted it out; I didn't want it silenced. Nothing was done behind anyone's back.

Well, it was sent to all the bishops and caused a bit of an explosion. But they're taking the data and they're using it.

I want these studies to be a catalyst to creative thinking, not a cause of controversy. But we've gotta make sure that the bishops feel that they have control.

That recent study on the five- to nine- year men should prove encouraging. They showed themselves to be open and frank, not threatened, more positive, and able to work with women. The priests with the cushy jobs are not the parish priests, not the ones doing priestly work. Some of those other men get locked into these special ministry jobs and, after a while, they're unable to tell the difference. I'm finding that pastors are increasingly doing their own thing. They're being pastors. They have good vision and they're working well.

I use the questionnaire to help priests to find out where they're at. We're able to tell them, for example, that they're reading Karl Rahner, Henri Nouwen, and Thomas Merton. We're able to report that the magazines *America*, *The Priest*, and *Origins* and the weekly newspaper, *National Catholic Reporter*, are the publications that help them in their ministry. Continuing education or being an educator seems to correlate favorably with their personal happiness. And men who have had a good first assignment have a higher morale, and are more comfortable with their bishop. Such men don't mind being assigned by the bishop rather than picking a rectory.

The priests support the ecumenical movement but they remain somewhat concerned about too many interfaith marriages. The notion that Christianity is already being preached to people does not deter them from wanting to introduce Catholicism. A good third of them are concerned that Catholicism is becoming less distinguishable from other denominations. When they hear, for example, that evangelization is a major future challenge, they tell us that there is a need for Catholicism to better define what it means to be a Catholic in a modern society.

The men are celebrating Mass on a regular basis but the recitation of the breviary is sporadic. The sacrament of penance is a biannual practice and a good number do not avail themselves of a spiritual director. However, they do a lot of Bible reading, gathering for renewal days or support groups, and making frequent days of private renewal.

They fault the system for not training them adequately in working with Hispanics, Afro-Americans, and in administration, and they didn't feel that celibacy was discussed adequately or treated frankly. In fact, they stated that an improved seminary education would be a good first step in meeting future challenges.

But don't overlook the positive side. These priests have reflected the same concerns as those of world-renowned anthropologists, historians, and theologians. They revere the heart of Catholicism, with its sacramental life, especially the Mass, and worry about its availability. There is less of a clerical mentality distancing them from the laity. They're comfortable with changing Church structures, but they're restless over present church governance and moral teachings.

This was just the first go-around. It's positive, but there are indicators that, if certain issues are not addressed now and acted upon, we might not see some of these priests in the second go-around. If fact, it just can't be a second go-around. Something has got to happen between now and then that will cause the Church to grow with a new enthusiasm that defeats sameness.

It all means that this is a time for prudence in the best sense of that word. It demands that we take a good, hard look at reality, get at its truth, and act on that truth. Prudence strongly emphasizes a volition that leads to follow-through. The opposite of prudence is irresoluteness, thoughtlessness, hesitation, being wishywashy, know-it-allness, and closed-mindedness. Prudence means being clear-sighted and having the strength to stay in there and sort it out when all looks like chaos.

Most priests say that they would still recommend the priesthood to others and the studies show that those who enter the seminary have had a close relationship with the parish and/or the parish priest. The program Called by Name seems to be working. At least it's producing inquiries.

We know that there is a correlation between priests who further their studies and their personal happiness but we're still not granting enough sabbaticals that permit them to be better educated and happier.

We've found one startling item: priests were often badly scarred by a bad first assignment. (NOTE: It was not uncommon, particularly in large dioceses, for priests who had notable seminary records to be sent to difficult pastors in order "to teach them humility." The priests learned nothing of humility; they were only humiliated.) We found that children of alcoholic parents (ADOA) often need counseling later in adulthood because they have received permanent damage. It can be much the same with young priests who are assigned to a neurotic or psychotic pastor.

Nearly three-quarters of the priests wanted to move away from the rectory concept. You know, the great architect, Frank Lloyd Wright, was famous for designing homes best known for the use of light and space. They were homes that produced happiness for their owners. Maybe our priests need more light and space.

We really have to ask a lot of questions. Are we in need of some kind of evaluation of rectory life? What is the level of our professionalism? How much hospitality is reflected in our rectories? Are support groups a substitute for spiritual direction? What are we really saying when we say that priests are uncomfortable with the Church's moral teaching? How much discontent is there with the directions of the bishop, the personnel board, or Rome itself? Are we hearing a restlessness that is common in most large institutions? Are priests caught between the pastoral and institutional worlds? Are they overwhelmed by the media coverage on the Church? Is it causing them to flinch? Is the media causing them to think only in political terms?

I love the research. I'm a one-man office but, over the years, I've involved over a hundred people in the projects. You know, it's like canon law. Some of the most pastoral people I know are canon lawyers. They're down there dealing with cases, working with people, day after day. The best ones are always more pastoral. I think that, properly understood, research can have the same effect.

I work seven days a week. On Saturdays, I ride my bike to the Washington Mall or to the Library of Congress. It isn't crowded on weekends. And I try to sit outside while I write my column or my Sunday homily.

My dream, again, is to combine research with a university, to have an Institute for Catholicism and Culture. I believe that something like this is what the Church needs for its future.

We couldn't do it with university types alone. They're naïve; they couldn't write for the bishops; they can get locked into one school of thought; if they run into opposition, profs will be inclined to take their name off the project and to go home. Then, there are the bishops who will say that they don't know about all this pastoral stuff. What they mean is that they are in charge. But I really think that, after all these years, I know how to bring out the brilliance on all sides.

Our Catholic population is more educated than ever. We've got a highly mobile population, and we're finding a vast cultural pluralism. We've got to have the data that will tell people where the parks are, as it were. We've got to be able to tell them what their kids will be facing and what to do about it. Right now, we're doing a study on the readiness of our seminarians for just that purpose. We've got to insure that they can read and write in the best sense of those words.

Numberwise, the data indicate a probable decline of 40 percent in diocesan priests over a forty-year period. You've seen the figures. The number of active diocesan priests, which was 35,000 in 1966, will fall to approximately 21,000 by the year 2005. Currently, for every ten priests who leave ministry by resignation, sick leave, retirement, or death, only six are replaced by ordination. Two out of every five positions are going unfilled in dioceses. It means that the ratio of Catholics to priests will double from 1,100 Catholics per priest in 1975 to 2,200 in 2005. That's a conservative estimate, since the growth in Catholic Hispanics could not be calculated.

The number one cause of the decline isn't resignations, retirements, or even death. It's a decrease in ordinations, a lack of candidates. For the sixth straight year, we've had a decline in seminary numbers. In 1990 the number of first-year theology students dropped from 919 to 819; in fourth year from 723 to 659. The numbers are nibbling away.

And what is the effect? Well, look at the bishops' document, "Reflections on the Morale of Priests." The bishops said: "Each presbyterate and community has always had its share of men who were limited in their energy, skills and even on-the-job presence. . . . Today, limited energy and regular absenteeism are not so easily disguised or replaced. Bishops and personnel boards find themselves giving full and total pastoral responsibilities to men who could serve well and happily only in carefully limited capacities."

And the bishops added that the probability of retirement was being lessened even while some solutions to the clergy shortage are precluded from discussion. This can really cause lowered morale. We could quadruple the number of chaplains needed today and triple the number of campus ministers. Both places are places where we could reap vocations.

It's not unlike our pool of scientists. Research has shown that half of our scientists will retire within the next decade. Look at nursing and government jobs. All are on the wane.

We will have older candidates. Even now, one-third of our seminarians are over thirty. In 1966, less than one-tenth were. And that will change the nature of the clergy. The older men see themselves as ombudsmen, set apart, preserving the institutional life of the Church. There is both a difference in attitude and energy levels. Will this cause a polarization of the clergy?

And all this while congregations change from agreeing on most things to disagreeing on most things. Now, in light of the "multi-persuasion syndrome," a priest must be able to distill the best out of the many worlds he enters and then create a new synthesis. Can our priests do this?

Seventy dioceses now have priestless parishes and another ninety foresee them in the very near future. These changes have altered parish organizational charts. The old code of canon law of 1917 saw a parish as a number of priests presiding over the people; the new code of 1986 now calls a parish a "definite community of the Christian faithful which is established on the stable basis within a particular church." Note how the emphasis has shifted from pastor to people.

The new administrative model isn't line/staff anymore. It's a collaborative model. Business people call such models "team-oriented cooperative environments." I think the message is clear. Pick up our pace, change, or be left behind.

I see a lot of changes. We'll be forced into new models of church. We've got to come up with new ideas; get the brain power going and explore these ideas. Research is an educational tool that creates dialogue. It gets the agenda going. It gets something done.

I suppose that the real challenge is to understand more fully what our times are telling us when they move us in new directions. Emily Dickinson writes that "our outlook should be circumference. It is in the total aspect, the total form that one finds the essential character of things and people." I think that the more we look around and compare the better we will avoid pining for the past, or worse, becoming matter-of-fact. To the degree we can expand our world, it is to that degree we avoid "sustain eminent," being eminently locked into closed thinking to the point of being victimized by a vicious circle.

⧈ INTERLUDE IV ⧈

I guess I'm a fringe priest. Downtown (the Pastoral Center) is tolerant of what I do but I'd never be invited to talk to the seminarians about it. It just isn't mainstream. I suppose some recognition would be good. But I've got my morning Mass. That means a great deal to me. It's what I was ordained for. After Mass, not much can happen during the day that can really hurt me.

An airport chaplain.

The bishop had just arrived for the Confirmation. He was in the pastor's bedroom, sitting on the edge of the bed, changing his socks from a black pair to a purple pair. The bishop's socks were a joke around the diocese. Like most episcopal regalia, people wondered where the socks came from.

The pastor was there, a reserved man, someone stronger men could strike matches on.

"Tell me, Charles," the bishop asked. "How long were you in Rome?"

"Twelve years, Bishop."

"My, my," the bishop said. "Twelve years in Rome and not a bishop yet. My, my."

Circa 1959.
Vatican II (1962–1965) would follow.

In fifty years, he had accomplished a great deal. At the top of his form, he was one of the best-known priests in America, a prophet of the laity movement within the American church. He had been careful. His speeches were liberally seasoned with papal sources. But he had taken risks, too, and often had to duck when the mortar fire came his way.

Asked how he succeeded, he said:

"Oh, I learned that it's always easier to ask forgiveness than permission."

Yes, the rumors are true. I'm married. I have a wife and children (from her earlier marriage). I'm a grandfather. I have a family. I'm not going to be lonely anymore.

> From a telephone call of one priest to another.

I've been an auxiliary bishop for twenty-one years. It's obvious now that I am never going to be an ordinary (bishop of his own diocese). Years ago, I came to the conclusion that it wasn't very important.

> Auxiliary bishop giving a talk at a midwestern Catholic university.

"Father, don't you recall your ordination day when your hands were bound and you put them in mine and you pledged obedience to me or my successors?"

"Yes, Bishop."

"Then, why do you disobey me?"

"I thought it was a multiple choice question."

The teenage kid was hanging around the parish. He shot baskets on the school lot. The priest asked him if he was going to his high-school prom. The kid said he was but that he was feeling uncomfortable because his only pair of good shoes were brown. He didn't have a pair of black shoes and his father wore a size 13.

The priest took off his black shoes and gave them to the kid. The priest walked into the rectory in his socks.

That was years ago. The kid is now married; he remains a faithful Catholic.

· 24 ·

Terence M. Keehan: Young Priest, Old Church

Terry Keehan is an associate vocation director for the archdiocese of Chicago. He is part of a four-person office that works with priests in the parishes to recruit for the diocesan priesthood. Much of his work has to do with introducing older men to the major seminary.

Keehan believes. He has a lighthouse smile, warmth, and enthusiasm. Once a star basketball player, he is well over six feet tall, still trim and as graceful as a college-level athlete. (He dances as well as he plays and can generally clear the floor at a wedding party.)

Although he works in the chancery office, he reflects none of the vaunted chancery mentality. (Ironically, few chancery priests do any more. "Hell," one priest said, "the only power they have is the power we give them.") "But working here," Keehan said, "I do see things differently."

Keehan is a blend of realism and optimism. Concerning monies being poured into a seminary system that nets less than ten priests a year, he cites companies that often have to pour money into sagging areas in order to help them develop. He feels that leaders will emerge and that the numbers will improve. "We had seventeen young men visit the seminary recently," he said. "They are seriously considering priesthood. The cardinal came to talk with them and they were impressed. When I was in sales, I learned to sell opportunities. I still see tremendous opportunities."

I was one of the new system guys in the seminary. We were older. At thirty, I was the youngest of the new crowd. I was ordained in 1986. Altogether, there were thirty-six in my class; twenty-one of them for Chicago. About half were old system guys who came through the seminary structure. The rest of us had done our high school and college elsewhere and had some work experience. There were teachers, managers, bankers. Now, at least half the class are in special ministries. I'm in the vocation office for the archdiocese and in residence at John of the Cross in Western Springs.

After my schooling, I worked for Stuart Pharmaceuticals of Wilmington, Delaware. My territory was on the north side of Chicago, selling to doctors, hospitals, and pharmacies. I was what they call a detail man, selling drugs. I liked it, but the thought of being a priest had been with me since grammar school.

We're an athletic family. My older brother, who is now a dentist, played for Serra High School in San Mateo, California. We moved there when our father was transferred out there by International Harvester. Jack was a good basketball player and, pretty soon, coaches began coming to the house and telling my dad that they wanted Jack in their school. He eventually went to Dayton and is now a dentist. I was only in the fourth grade but, after hearing those coaches, I set a goal for myself: to get an education and to be an athlete. It sounded great. It was.

We came back to the Chicago area and I went to St. Viator's High School. When the recruiters came to visit me, I decided on the University of Nebraska. It was a clean operation. I got my B.S. there in Speech Pathology and stayed on to get my Master's degree in organization management.

In school, I think I dated more than any of my friends. I dated one girl for at least three years and, in college, I dated another for at least four and a half years. I just assumed that I was going to get married. I was still dating in graduate school and took the best job I could find back here so that I could be close. I really loved her, but I guess not in the way that says "get married." Anyway, she's married now and has a baby coming.

At St. James Parish in Arlington Heights, I helped to start a young adult group. Again, I was meeting other women and enjoying being with them. But the work at St. James brought me close to the priests. The experience with the priests helped me to demythologize the church and the priesthood, but it brought me into new myths.

Salesmen spend most of their time in their cars, you know. I made seven or eight calls a day, and, as I drove around, I thought more and more about the priesthood.

The thought just wouldn't go away. Of course, Noreen noticed it and said that I wasn't going to be true to myself unless I did something about it. "Maybe you don't *have* to get married," I began thinking to myself. The thought had nothing to do with the priesthood. It was a new insight, a freeing insight. All of a sudden, I began to see things in a different light.

Working with the young adult group strengthened my faith. I began asking myself how I could live out my faith. What job do I take? How do I best love? How do I give love to other people? How do I share intimacy in the best way for me?

It's odd, but I tell this story all the time:

I had been dating Noreen over three years when a cousin of hers got married in Detroit. In fact, Noreen was the maid of honor. At the wedding party, an aunt came up to me and says: "You should marry someone who is like you." And a little while later, her uncle comes up and says: "You should marry someone different." That was confusing!

Yet, even those times when I was most in love, the priesthood still came to me as a possibility. I took a ministry weekend with Jack Wall [now pastor of Old St. Patrick's, Chicago]. We're old friends since 1972. It pushed me a little closer, but even my final entrance to the major sem was conditioned. My company promised me my job back if it didn't work out!

Jim Keleher [now bishop of Belleville, Illinois] was the rector. Again, half of us were adult men with worldly experience and shared values. There was some tension with the younger, system guys, but basically we got along. There was a blending.

I guess my best friend was Ed Fealey, now over at Holy Name. He had been a junior high school principal for ten years. Ed and I shared a lot of discernment together. We often asked each other, "Do we want to be priests?" I think that's the purpose of the seminary. People should come to the seminary, then commit to the priesthood. That's what it's for. My seminary did as good a job at that as any other place.

There was nothing new out of that Synod on the Priesthood [held in October, 1990]. I would like to have an honest discussion about priesthood rather than a synod with subjects such as celibacy and the ordination of women closed to discussion.

It's not true that celibacy and sexuality were closed topics in the seminary. We talked about it a lot, too much in fact. We hashed it and rehashed it. It was good, healthy, honest discussion, all through the seminary system. I think I came to terms with it. Now, I go places and everyone wants to talk about celibacy!

You know, when I was in the seminary, I went to a bar where I met this woman. She was my age, separated, with a one-year-old daughter. "You're going to be lonely," she told me. "Why make such an odd commitment? How can you chose *that*?" We talked for over an hour. Gradually, I realized that *she* was lonely—projection on her part, I guess. She started to cry. "Good, now," I said to her. "Now we can be honest."

Lots of people feel lonely as a consequence of their decisions. I remember once, while I shared some of my struggles with my mother, she asked: "Are you lonely?" I told her that I was a little but that it wasn't an overwhelming feeling. She said: "Honey, you're very lucky." I guess I am.

Hey, who instituted celibacy? The people of the Church did. They wanted some sort of commitment from the priests who were going to celebrate the

Eucharist each day. So celibacy grew along with the monetary concerns that made adherence to celibacy very practical. Celibacy was asked for because it is tied to the sacredness of the Eucharist. I can't think of a better way to capture sacredness.

If we let go of celibacy, we let go of a lot. Celibacy is needed for some. So, let's make it optional, but at least talk about it. Will it change? I don't know. But did the Berlin Wall come down?

It's the Church's job, however, to listen and to *do* something. Now, the Spirit may be moving us in another direction. Clete Kiley [now rector of Niles Seminary College of Loyola University] used to say that there is a tension between celibacy and the Eucharist and that, so far, celibacy is winning.

We've got to be true to the movement of the Spirit. Celibacy doesn't guarantee health; just look at all the alcoholism. But it has wisdom; it has intrigue; it has benefits.

Anyway, there are three important things about what I do as a priest. I articulate, celebrate, and suggest the presence of God in human life. I articulate because I've been trained to articulate this wonderful power and mystery that is God. Many people don't have enough interest in God to talk about God. I articulate in order to give people both a public and private moment of the Spirit.

And I celebrate. That's basic human instinct, to celebrate. I celebrate the presence of God and the word of Christ. You know, as Catholics, we celebrate well, and I like that.

Then I suggest. A lot of people, you know, live their lives without really experiencing the presence of God. We need people to suggest God to them.

These are self-serving questions and perhaps self-serving answers. But they must be asked. I must continually ask: "Can I be a priest?" and I must follow with: "Can a priest be me?" If I can't answer them in a positive way, then I am going to stumble. Again, I find celibacy advantageous for these tasks because it frees me to be in the wider Church, to celebrate in a more public way, and to make suggestions to people.

I have looked at the celibate commitment as being a unique one, counter-cultural. Yet, in the last year, I've gotten closer to my three married brothers than I have ever been. We've shared a lot. We've asked each other: "How do you live out these adult commitments?" Mine is less difficult than theirs. And yet, I feel a lot of pressure because everyone wants to talk about my commitment! I respect my brothers for the faithful way in which they've lived out their commitment. They are spouses; they have families; they have their professional lives. That's a lot.

Life is difficult. Being an adult is difficult. We travel by different paths but our struggles are very similar. In the seminary, I got a little myopic about all of this. Now that I'm out among people, I see other people's struggles. Priests share powerful things with people and those things bring us together. Because of the way that people bring you into their lives, I learn that the meaning of what they are doing brings them together. Greeley [Andrew M. Greeley, priest, sociologist, novelist] writes a lot about this and he's right.

I love women. I come alive when I am with them. They give me life and I need those relationships.

I'll be forty-nine years old in 2005, the year all those terrible numbers about priesthood are supposed to come true. I don't know how it's all going to turn out, but I believe that priests can still be enablers, organizers, managers. They can do what John the Baptist did. "There's your Lamb; there's your Savior," they can say. I'm confident that I'll be able to do that. As Ray Carey, a priest-psychologist says, I'll be involved in the enterprise of "preaching the good news about the risen Lord."

Those are the things I get most excited about now. The human spirit is most pliable, flexible, and strong. When human hearts get around their mission, it's amazing what can happen.

The Church has always been an instrument for the future. I worry about it sometimes, but it will work out. If we really embrace the spirit of Vatican II, I think we'll become more critical. We need to get into a discussion that really captures the spirit of our Church, a discussion about leadership and the different charisms of leadership. In that way, I'm confident that the Spirit will thrive. We might become smaller, but that may not be so bad.

Let me say one more thing. It puts everything in perspective for me. It's the Epiphany story. Those soothsayers, or astrologers, or wise men, were seeking the Lord. They journeyed across the land, following the star. They knew a lot about astrology but they never confused *the* star with others. They journey with others. They hold gifts in their hands. The star leads them to the Savior.

The priesthood is my star. It enables me to give my gifts away.

· 25 ·

William G. Kenneally: Valuing the Things That Really Matter

"I try to support those people. I believe in the causes they represent. But my pastoral experience doesn't connect with what they're doing. They're angry at the Church and it consumes their energies. My parishioners just aren't there."

Bill Kenneally was referring to a well-known lay Catholic group that is generally associated with liberal causes. In conversations with him, it became equally clear that his pastoral experience didn't connect with conservative causes or even some of the institutional Church's directives.

Pastors represent the Catholic Church to their parishioners. They have about as much impact on their people as parishioners do on their priests. They must constantly search for a delicate balance between official Church teaching and what they hear in the rectory office, the reconciliation room, and the sidewalk outside the church. While Church leaders wrestle with politicians over the abortion issue, for example, pastors must form groups to help women through post-abortion traumas. While the Church decries divorce and remarriage, pastors must deal with couples who have done just that. St. Gertrude's parish bulletin does not hawk the sinfulness of this world. It announces meetings of Al Anon, Families Anonymous, Overeaters Anonymous, and Adult Children of Alcoholics. In short, the parish deals with people where their souls are rubbed raw.

St. Gertrude's is always in need of money. The asbestos removal cost $30,000; repair to the church floor was another $30,000. The rectory roof is leaking. "We don't want wet priests, do we?" Kenneally asks his people with his usual good humor. These are all unexpected and un-budgeted items, so Kenneally is pushing a cash raffle on the front page of the parish bulletin. There's the usual thermometer in the vestibule showing two hundred tickets have been sold. "But we'll take off like a space shot," he is saying, "the first two hundred feet of lift-off is the toughest. We'll accelerate like crazy!" It's what a pastor must do, especially when Sunday collections are below budget. Pastoring means begging.

In spite of the leaks, Bill Kenneally lives in a nice rectory, much of it now used for parish business. His two-room pastor's suite is filled with books. Most have to do with a search for sanctity; the others are about pastoring. There isn't much light reading. Priests take their reading seriously.

At fifty-six, Bill Kenneally is about the average pastor's age. His parish has one associate, one Sunday help-out priest, and one pastoral associate. His congregation is a mix of urban professionals and immigrants, wealthy families from lakefront condos, and unemployed people from Chicago's uptown. He has implemented all the right things—parish council, committees, and clubs—involving laity at every level. Basically, however, he is seen as the parish leader. When the chancery calls, they ask for him. His name is on the signature cards at the bank. When parishioners come to the rectory or telephone, they want to talk to Father Kenneally. It's still that way in virtually all of the 19,620 parishes in America.

I've just turned over as pastor. I'm in for another six years. I was ordained in 1961. There were thirty-four of us; twenty-one are still in. We're part of that pre-Vatican II generation, trained in one era and doing our priesthood in another. It's hard to get guys like us to talk about ourselves, at least the personal stuff.

I haven't the faintest idea, for example, as to who is heterosexual or homosexual in my class. The percentages I'm hearing are meaningless to me. One guy in the class died of AIDS. He was clearly gay; his partner came to the funeral. But for the rest these are things our generation didn't talk about. We still don't.

Some time ago, they held one of those overnights at the seminary for groups of classes. The priests call them "pajama parties." They brought in a guy from Texas, a priest-psychologist. We were supposed to confront celibacy and the sexual issues. "O.K., you guys, I'm going to put it on the table," he said. But he didn't tell us anything, and we all kept our cards close to our chest. Nobody in the class spoke. There was no revelation of any sort. If someone in my class is involved with a woman, I'd never know. I couldn't even guess.

Maybe we don't need to be that honest with each other. I'm not close to Sipe's figures [A.W. Richard Sipe, *A Secret World: Sexuality and the Search for Celibacy*, a study of sexuality in the priesthood]. Sipe must have his sources, but they're not in my class.

I think that celibacy is about over with. Certainly, it's over in the Philippines and Africa. It will soon be here.

No, I don't call the chancery office unless it's a problem with the roof. I've got an asbestos problem just now in the grammar school. You've got to call on that. But they sent this idiot out, a man drunk with power. He bragged to me that he had closed one school last year. It was just a week before Christmas and there was no evidence that the asbestos had caused any problem. But he shut the place down and they had to spend $50,000 to clear it up, even though the school was scheduled to be closed in June! Now, that's institutional thinking. He's going to delay the opening of our school now. There's nothing I can do about it. We're paying a fortune to clear up a problem that may not be a problem. Well, I'm not going to say anything. Some people down there are helpful but the lay people can get just as arrogant as the old pastors years ago. I'll get even later.

I just don't do all that wedding paperwork anymore and I don't do the endless annulment forms, either. The bishop and the others down there must face Rome. Now, if they want to be effective, they must face us. They are simply not an intermediary between grace and truth.

I'm fifty-six now. I'll be seventy-one in 2005 when all those figures you talked about come true. I'll be retired. I'll want to be downtown somewhere, in an apartment. I don't want to live with other priests, but I don't want to be alone. That's very significant about Mike Cleary (pseudonym). He retired as pastor and got married. The approval of the priests was almost universal. Maybe we'll see more of that.

Remember Sertillanges's book, *The Intellectual Life*? I'd like to have some energy left at the end of my active priesthood to go back over books like that. I'd like to have some friends to share them with, and I'd like to be able to throw good parties, and maybe give a talk.

I liked my seminary years at Mundelein [University of St. Mary of the Lake]. The education was poor; the profs were poor, but it was a chance to do some talking. The profs just didn't open things up for you. They took a certain self-satisfaction in their own "rightness." I discovered after I was ordained that there was more to philosophy and theology than the manuals. We were midwestern nonintellectuals. The intellectuals at the University of Chicago weren't helped very much by our presence in the area.

Remember that statement that someone made about selecting U.S. senators? It was something to the effect that we could go out on the street and pick a hundred people at random and come up with as good a group as we'll find in the Senate today. Well, the basic principle might apply to the priesthood. We should select our priests from the lower and middle classes. We could make it a kind of lottery process in which we pick from the good people in the parish. Then, we could simply let them pick other people. I have five or six people in my parish now who could be priests. One of them is an Evangelical Protestant, but he should be a priest. There are fathers of families and women. I wouldn't pick some of the sisters. I'm afraid that they're as screwed up as us priests. Besides, I would want married people.

In my age group, most of the men in the seminary were from lower-class working families. The seminary didn't do a very good job in helping us to build our self-image. Part of the very spirituality we were given was to beat up on people, not to find their lightness of being. It carries over to our pastoral work. To this day, when my class gathers, much of our conversations are about how people were beaten down.

It wasn't done to me. I was able to smile. I didn't look for approval. When the profs announced: "Here's your marks; you don't have to come up and get them," I would never go up. They were just using marks as a way of beating us up.

About seven guys in my class still meet weekly; three or four others meet occasionally, and the others only once a year. It's an old boys' club. There's a lot of support, but how often do you need a booster shot? There's some drinking and a lot of negative talk, but it looks and sounds a lot greener compared with the young guys. With celibacy on the books until we retire, we're at least a lot closer.

I meet regularly with four other guys and we work on self-revelation. We work on the talking part of it; we ask questions of each other. There's no formal prayer at such meetings. I do belong to a prayer group. We meet at 6:15 on Friday mornings, before the guys go to work. Sometimes we meet outside in the grotto, but for the rest we're inside. About thirty in the group. Ten regulars. A good mix of economic and educational levels. Most are Catholics but we have a local minister, some Evangelicals, and Fundamentalists. It was formed by a guy who was trying to get through a goofy marriage; he doesn't come anymore. We do a lot of scripture; use the lectionary. We stay clear of academic differences. The experience is good for me as a believer. I'm not certain that I can get to that with priests anymore. We priests have all those layers to get through and it isn't very helpful.

I make the coffee at these prayer meetings. Only occasionally will the conversation turn to me. We used to have more ministers coming but they dropped out. Some of the Evangelicals have an awful way of using scripture. One of the ministers had to move because he danced at weddings.

We've turned the convent into a kind of shelter. I wanted to make the place into a home for unwed mothers who were going to college, but some people in the parish screamed. "Couldn't have those kind of women around here," they said. I was confronted by one parishioner who said: "Father, we know why you want those women here." It nearly broke up the parish. So, after that, I made up my mind that no one was going to tell me what to do with the convent. I didn't even ask. Now we've got a burned-out social worker in there with a minister, a Baptist volunteer, a youth worker, a young mother and her kid, some Nigerian and Indian priests. There's a street guy named Brother Joe who monitors all this. It's a stopover place for them. The Nigerian guy was cooking a goat the other day, and the Indian was preparing curry. We've got to have a common meal for them! Someday it's just going to explode, but so far it's O.K.

We're not bothered much. We don't have those CUF [Catholics United for the Faith, an ultra-conservative group] coming around. Sometimes, when Patty [Sister Patricia] gives the homily, people complain. They call. I listen and say "thank you." I just do not engage in conversation on those matters.

Why don't you stay for dinner? Dan Cassidy is cooking. He's the new associate. He can stretch the food. There'll be enough. I've got a meeting now, but let me get you a drink.

· 26 ·

Joseph E. Kerns: To Live Is to Be Loved

Kathy and Joe Kerns live in Fairfax, Virginia in a modest, immaculately kept house. The first thing one notes about their relationship is the sincere civility. Joe's strong statements about ecclesiastical authority belie a gentle manner marked by a touching cordiality toward his wife of over twenty years. Theirs is a shared life in which compliments go back and forth as easily as thoughts on the Church. Their unofficial motto, "To live is to be loved," is drawn from their wedding ceremony which was written by Joe. In fact, he has drawn a once painfully shy Kathy out. On some issues, she is now more outspoken than he is. He loves to talk and he's good at it. But he listens with an ear that has been tuned by experience. His Jesuit education is both broad and deep. Joe's book, *Once and Future Church* (Winston-Derek, Nashville) was issued in 1991. Joe and Kathy insisted that Jean and I share their home for this interview. After a good bottle of wine during a delicious meal, we talked until my notes became a rosary of unfinished sentences. We were their overnight guests and, the next morning, we followed Joe through D.C.'s rush hour while he led us to the Catholic University campus. The Kernses are that way about everyone.

These interviews were supposed to be limited to diocesan priests, active or inactive. But Joe Kerns's views on priesthood are so compelling that they require a place in this discussion.

No, I don't even want to be known as a priest. Now, you can't believe what it means for me to say this. No one was more invested with the idea of priesthood than I was. I'm still a priest, but I refuse to play the bishop's game and to pretend that I am not a priest. I left the Jesuits but I never left the priesthood. For that reason, I didn't even go to my mother's funeral. I just couldn't sit there, away from the altar, pretending that I was not a priest. Kathy and I had our own funeral liturgy for her.

The bishops simply don't care how much they are roasted. Remember the old Chicago politician who said that it's better to be roasted than ignored. It's their authority that concerns them, and by acknowledging that authority, we give them status. And to think that I used to believe all that!

Ignatius of Antioch [bishop and martyr, died circa 110–18] didn't see himself as anyone special. He was one of our first priests, but he never believed that he had some magic power not shared by the group. He simply had a sense of order. He felt that, if you had a lot of people in a room, someone had to be in charge, and that did not convey any particular status to the person in charge. He simply saw the role of the presider as someone who told the group what the Lord was trying to do. Ray Brown [Raymond E. Brown, S.S., scripture scholar] has written that you just can't make any historical argument for a priestly class. And Brown is just one of many scholars who hold that position. In fact, the early Christians were unique in that they were the one group at the time that didn't have priests. We read in the letter to the Hebrews that Christ did the sacrificing once and for all. There simply isn't any need for a priest.

Paul is misquoted. The expression "This is my Body" is a compact idiom. It's a mistake of Jews trying to speak Greek. They were still thinking like Jews. It really means: "This sharing of the one piece of bread shows that you share me." The sharing of the cup means a sharing in life. It means that we're all in this together. The Gospel writers took what Christians were doing and put the words back in Christ's mouth. The Last Supper narrative is an essay on theology during which we explain the meaning of the sharing. By sharing the same cup, Christians were saying that they would stand by one another and share one another's good times and bad times, and be willing to have the same kind of life that Christ had. In Philippians 2:5, we read: "Have among yourselves the same attitude that is also yours in Christ Jesus." That passage goes on to say: "Who, though he was in the form of God, did not regard equality with God something to be grasped. Rather, he emptied himself, taking the form of a slave, coming in human likeness; and found human in appearance." The sharing of the cup reflects that mentality, just as the bride and groom at a Jewish wedding still share a cup. Paul finds great good coming from all this. It's the same with us. We feel better because Christ is there. Our reason for sharing that bread and wine is because people are better for having shared Christ. So, whenever people are doing things that they could never do themselves, then Christ is obviously there. Sharing the bread and the wine made people care more about Christ and about each other. Paul writes that he will come and look for the power of the Holy Spirit. He tells us that God cannot be commanded to come. The spirit of Christ is not happening to us by accident, but it is not confined to the priests.

I was working on my book for nearly ten years when it hit me: the so-called Sacrifice of the Mass would not have meant a thing to Paul, or to most of the early Christians. Bread and wine was always shared among Jews and early Christians. Now, with our Sunday Bunch, this belief all came together. We do things as a group. Our group moves around to each other's houses. Generally, each host presides, although some will defer to the priest. There are a number of resigned priests among us.

In Augustine's time [354–430], daily Mass was still vague. When they talk about celebrating often, we're not certain whether they meant celebration in a public or a private place. When it did move from the small group in the home to a public place, it changed from a celebration to a performance. Once the change was made, people stopped coming to the altar. Chrysostom complained that we stand here and nobody comes, and the Fourth Lateran Council tried to make them come by ordering them to do so once a year.

Over the centuries, people began to gather where their friends were. Many were members of the same guilds. They worshiped together. In time, the people began to see the church as their building, the place where they gathered. It was where people met each other. Even when they moved to the cities, they would pick the building where their friends were. Even when they stopped going into a building in the fifteenth century, they gathered outside the building. The test of who to be with was how much the people cared about each other and how much they were like you. The priest presided from a distance, however, and the system fell into place. It has remained so ingrained that most of us were programmed to it even before we started elementary school. Since Vatican II, we have moved the altar and all that but there's still a significant distance between the priest and everyone else.

For Kathy and me, the biggest change from priesthood and religious life was finding our roots. We needed to stand back and look at the whole picture. We needed to know where we fit. You know, historians have blown the Church apart by showing it like it was. We are, after all, a historical religion. We can nail these things down.

I'm from Philadelphia. I entered the Jesuits in 1942 when I was just out of high school. I was ordained in 1955 and left the Society in 1969 and married Kathy the same year. We met on a blind date in New York. I had left only a little before and was in New York to see my literary agent for a social meeting. Kathy is a former Mercy sister. She was teaching in a Catholic high school in New York and had only one conviction about marrying: she was never going to marry a priest! We were married six weeks after we met!

I earned my S.T.D. from the Gregorian, so I wanted to teach theology. I also tried to write a book on marriage and realized that I didn't know what I was talking about. (Laughs.) Anyway, I could have stayed in Wheeling, but there was no market for a theologian in the non-Catholic colleges. I applied to St. Mary's in Winona. I wasn't married at the time but I told them that I might get married someday. The Christian Brothers there were Christian in the best sense of the word. Even after I married Kathy, they made no effort to throw me out. The Brothers simply said that my personal life was my own concern. As far as they were concerned, I only had to be a good teacher. I didn't advertise my priesthood. I didn't hide it, either. Two of our closest friends weren't even aware of my background. In fact, I was picked to be the next dean. I had a great year there. However, a local banker who was on their board of trustees and was chairman of their annual fund drive protested my being there. He was being egged on by the local bishop, especially after I gave a day of recollection to the Brothers and word of my status filtered out. I didn't want to cost the school $250,000. So I decided to leave St. Mary's.

We went to Holland. I wanted to look at the Dutch church. We thought that we would learn a great deal about a changing Church, but instead we learned that the Dutch church was not for export and, in some ways, was not as advanced as we thought. Teaching positions at universities are plums, passed on to favorites, not available to foreigners, especially to one who was an American and therefore rich. Outsiders just aren't tolerated. In the Dutch culture, everything is done by consensus. That's why they have so much trouble with Rome, which prefers to dictate.

So, we came back here to the Washington area and I became the headmaster of a private school. Two years later, I was named an administrator of a home for problem children. I was there about a year and a half and that's how I got involved with the federal government in a teacher corps effort that tried to help teachers deal with problem kids right in the classroom. I've had a number of government jobs since, including one working with the Native Americans. It's been good. I've had my ups and downs when administrations and budgets changed, but basically it has worked out. Presently, my job is to evaluate the accrediting agencies for colleges. In a sense, our agency polices those who police higher education. I'll most likely have to work until I'm seventy; those twenty-seven years in religious life take a big chunk out of one's earning. It's hard to catch up in a race when the other runners are already halfway around the track. (Laughs.)

Yes, I still witness weddings when I'm asked to do so. I love doing them. For many of the people involved, marriages represent a return to religion or, at the very least, a religious moment. The bishops have no authority in marriage. In fact, they would have no authority at all if we did not give it to them. The bishops don't speak for the true Church; they speak only for themselves. Marriage is a gift of self that one adult makes to another. While I was still teaching, I used to skip that part of the marriage course that dealt with the Church's authority in marriage. Now, we've fallen into a rabbinical syndrome, a fascination with marriage cases. Our chancery offices all have tribunals that do nothing else, asking intimate details concerning marriages that they have no right to ask.

Somehow, it all reminds me of a woman I knew who commented that she heard lots of public sinner stories but that I was the first one that she actually knew. When I left Wheeling College, now called Wheeling Jesuit, I wrote a letter to the faculty and students. It wasn't an angry letter. Far from it. I was simply telling the students of my very personal decision. Well, somehow, the local paper picked it up. Then, the local chancery office felt obliged to respond. Some chancery official there was asked about my status and he responded: "Well, of course, he's a public sinner."

Our Sunday Bunch has been gathering for seventeen years. We don't get any heat from the local parish. Most likely, they don't even know we exist, although we have had a television presentation of our liturgy. Some of our members still go to a regular church on Saturdays and come to the Sunday Bunch the next day.

Our format is very simple. We have prayers and singing, along with the readings. They're followed by a discussion and the petitions. Then, we have the Eucharist and end with our version of the Our Father. It varies, of course, with the host, but that's basically it. We've lost some members in recent years, mostly because people have moved. And, like any group, we've had our differences.

I also belong to the Society for Serious Loafing. We meet for dinner once a month. Someone reads a letter or article and we all discuss it. A couple of them are resigned priests. I enjoy their company.

KATHY: Resigned priests still gather as priests, not like our friends in the Sunday Bunch. Woman are still secondary among those ex-priest groups. Joe isn't like that. They should prepare priests to leave—at least teach them to put a nail in the wall!

JOE: Personally, I've come to think of the priesthood as an aberration. It now seems to be in the process of disappearing. I hope so. One struggle today in our society is the pyramid structure versus the concentric circle structure of administration. The Church continues to try to be the pyramid while other structures change. Christianity is a tremendously complicated thing. Each Christian has one circle after another going out from him or her, circles that embrace intimate people, all the way out to total strangers. Basically, there are only three things we seek: nearness to people, to people like you are, and to people who care about you. The whole success of Christianity is built on that. The institutional church is at best irrelevant to this model and at worst harmful.

Oh, I don't mean to imply that there are not good people in the Church. On the contrary, they are everywhere in the Church. But Paul would not have known what we are talking about today and a Francis of Assisi and the many other saints did what they did quite apart from the institutional church. To me the institutional Church only proves that Christ has a sense of humor—that all these good things could go on through the centuries in spite of all those people fighting for power and playing at being Christian.

Patrick R. Lagges: Canon Lawyer

Jesus gave only one command: Consider the lilies. In the centuries that followed his death, the necessity of codifying and organizing an institutional Church caused a body of laws to grow. By 1234, Pope Gregory IX issued five books of "Decretals" and later additions were made. However, the canons were largely uncodified until 1903 when Pope St. Pius X ordered a codification, a task that took fourteen years and resulted in the first organized code of 2,414 canons. The canons (the Greek root means rule, measure, standard) were divided into general principles, categories of persons, means employed by the Church to achieve its purpose, canons on procedures, and penal codes.

At Vatican II, it was decided that the code had grown cumbersome and was in need of revision. In 1983, a revised code was published, consisting of 1,752 canons in seven books. The new titles are general norms, the people of God, the teaching mission of the Church, the sanctifying mission of the Church, temporal goods of the Church, penal law, and procedural law.

From one point of view, the number of canons is remarkably small. Some fraternal organizations and numerous religous congregations have many more by-laws and constitutions.

Yet, the code is often viewed as prohibitive and negative. It is seen as contrary to the Gospel of Love. In the apostolic constitution, *Sacrae Disciplinae Leges*, that forms the introduction to the revised code, John Paul II wrote: "It appears sufficiently clear that the Code is in no way intended as a substitute for faith, grace, charisms, and especially charity in the life of the church and of the faithful. . . . Its purpose is rather to create such an order in the ecclesial society that, while assigning the primacy to love, grace, and charisms, it at the same time renders their organic development easier in the life of both the ecclesial society and the individual persons who belong to it."

While the pope recognizes that the code must not supplant the gospel message he points out that the code is extremely necessary for the Church. "Since the church is organized as a social and visible structure, it must also have norms," he wrote, "in order that its hierarchical and organic structure be visible; in order that the exercise of the functions divinely entrusted to it, especially that of sacred power and of the administration of the sacraments, may be adequately organized; in order that the mutual relations of the faithful may be regulated according to justice based on charity, with rights of individuals guaranteed and well-defined; in order, finally, that common initiatives undertaken to live a Christian life even more perfectly may be sustained, strengthened, and fostered by canonical norms."

John Paul II said that the new code appears at a time when the bishops were crying out for its promulgation "almost with impatience." The pope's observation highlights a syndrome in any large institution: leadership likes rules, policies, guidelines; it make their burden easier. "They can point to the manual," one observer said.

Father Pat Lagges would agree with the pope's sentiments. He represents both the wisdom and the spirit of the canons. His preparation for his position is vastly superior to those of an earlier generation. He exhibits no clerical ambition. (Thirty percent of the present archbishops have a J.C.D. degree, the doctorate in canon law. Most earned it in Rome while following the yellow brick road that would ultimately invest them in the watered silk.)

Today, while some clerical resentment toward canon lawyers surfaces in conversations, the fear they once inspired is largely gone. (Present anger seems more directed at diocesan auditors—"bean counters" in search of the pastor's cookie jar.)

It would be very difficult to resent Pat Lagges. His manner has none of the arrogance sometimes stereotypically associated with bright canonists. He is as jovial as he is learned. He does not take himself seriously. He remains a servant of God, not of an institution.

Oh, yes, we still have priests telling us that it's different out in the trenches. That's an old charge still thrown at canon lawyers and people who work in chancery offices. It isn't true but you learn to live with it. Canon law can be pastoral. We try to make it that way here.

I like canon law. I guess I've always been intrigued with minutiae. (Laughs.) You know how it is with us priests. We live alone and develop our eccentricities. For us celibates, our projects become our progeny. Perhaps that's what canon law is for me.

I'm a product of the entire seminary system—four years of high school, four in college where I majored in biology, and four in the major seminary where I earned my masters in divinity, the "M-Div" that we all got.

I was ordained in 1977; thirty-one in the class; twenty-seven still active, most of them in parish work.

I spent five years at St. Genevieve's, then two years at St. Patricia's in Hickory Hills, while I worked at the Marriage Tribunal. Then, there were three and a half years at St. Paul's in Ottawa. I didn't go to Rome because, if I'm ever going to lose my faith, it would be in Rome or the Holy Land. (Laughs.) St. Paul is run by the Canadian Oblates. It's affiliated with the University of Ottawa. Each recognizes the other's degrees, so I graduated with around six of them! Actually, it took two years for my licentiate and another year and a half for my J.C.D. and Ph.D. in canon law. It all means that I enjoy both a church and civil degree, kind of like one for the office and one for the home. (Laughs.)

St. Paul's was wonderful. Most of the students were older men with substantial parish experience. One guy had been a priest for twenty-five years. The approach to canon law was very pastoral. The profs could tap into the experience of the students.

Things are different in Canada. The clergy are much more ecumenical and low key. It's such a vast country with so few priests. Up there, a priest wouldn't move into a territory where an Anglican priest was working, for example. He'd be respectful of the fact that Christianity was being brought to the people. He'd go somewhere else. The Canadian Church is tremendously creative. Just look at Hurley [Francis T. Hurley, archbishop of Anchorage] during the recent meeting of our bishops. He was pleading for permission to let the laity preside at funeral services in the absence of a priest, and, as you know, he got voted down. They turned the resolution down even though he told them that parts of his diocese were hundreds of miles and hundreds of dollars air fare from the nearest priest. Well, the Canadian church has permitted this for years. Their focus is on getting the Gospel preached, not on politics. They get away with a lot more because they don't advertise what they're doing. You can feel it at the conferences. They are much more together and you sense it in the spirit. Much fewer tensions. It's not unlike parts of this country. As you go West, things get looser.

I came back here with all my degrees and was assigned to the tribunal and to residence at Our Lady of Mercy with a great pastor, Don Headley. It's a mixed parish. Right behind us is a Lebanese meat market, a Korean newspaper, Kaufman's Bakery, and a driving school. We have a little bit of everything. I keep learning from the people.

There are about 1,800 canon lawyers in the country, at least that's about the membership of the Canon Law Society. We get four to six hundred at our meetings. The majority are still priests but we're getting other members, especially religious sisters. Just now, in fact, the president of the Society is a Dominican sister, Lucy Vazquez, who heads the tribunal in Orlando.

Canonists in general are seen as suspect in this country. We take a lot of direct hits about not being in those trenches. Many of our people are on career paths. That does get in the way. And lawyers in general are suspect.

I don't fault the priests who do it their own way. It's not the right way to do it, of course. It would be better, I think, if they came to the tribunal. But the priests of this archdiocese have always been tremendously creative. Furthermore, the entire process is made up of ecclesiastical law. The process can be changed. They can make pastoral decisions. Even here at the tribunal we sometimes don't go by the books. It isn't so much that we bend the rules. It's just that we sometimes take a creative approach to them. So do some of the priests.

We have a common law concept in this country. We Americans see a law and we observe it. But Rome sees a law and interprets it. The problem now at the Vatican is that a lot of people in the Curia have adopted a Western mind set, but that's not the tradition. We don't bend the rules but we do occasionally interpret them. On the rare occasion when the Vatican is involved, they will ask us for our interpretation of a given law or give us theirs.

It isn't all that complicated. It really doesn't take a canon lawyer to rule favorably in an annulment petition involving a woman who was married at sixteen because she was pregnant and who was sexually abused as a child by her father. The majority of the cases just aren't that complicated. The people down here are concerned not just for the institution of marriage but also for the welfare of the people. It's true that most of the people who follow the process through to the end will get an affirmative decision. That's because a good number drop out along the way, partly because they are anticipating a negative decision.

One of the real problems in the code is that marriage cases are treated as contentious cases. As often as not, both parties in an annulment case are agreeable to the annulment. According to tribunal procedures, petitioners for an annulment must first obtain a civil divorce, a procedure that generally covers the contentious portion of the procedure. So, who is the contentious party? The man? The woman? The Church? It's very unfortunate that the rules are so complicated; you have to go through all the details, as if the case were a contentious one.

When we're finished with the case, it goes to the Court of Appeals for the Region. For us, it's just down the street. They'll review it. If they have any questions, they'll call. Technically, if there's a real problem, both canon lawyers, the defender of the bond and the canonist for the petitioner, are supposed to be present. But we're fairly casual about some things. There's a lot of integrity in the people here. There are seven full timers here. We trust each other.

There's never any clout here. It's simply not necessary. In fact, I'm mostly unaware of who the people are in terms of their social standing or their standing with the Church. Sometimes, long after a case is closed, I learn that the people were VIPs. As for the cardinal or one of the bishops injecting themselves into a case, it simply doesn't happen.

The process still suffers from bad press. Recently, the diocesan paper printed a story that said, in effect, that an annulment costs $850. Well, that's true. Those are our costs per case. And we do write the petitioner and ask them to think about that. But we take whatever they can pay. It's no different than setting the cost of a wedding in a church. Many parishes tell the couple what their costs are and ask the couple to give what they can. In my parish, we actually get more than our costs. No one wants to just give cost! But we don't seem to be able to get that across in this office.

We're never asked to pass on the canonical correctness of cases involving the archbishop's office. He has his own people up there. We do occasionally get involved in cases regarding Church property. And I've heard of cases of canonical trials involving priests who are being kicked out. But they're rare.

I used to be more conscious of rules. Now that I'm steeped in canon law, I don't feel that way. Now, when I do a wedding, I let the couple celebrate in a way that lets them demonstrate their faith. We have a lot of Filipinos in the parish, for example. It's their wedding custom to bind themselves together with a colorful ribbon. They bring sponsors to the altar in addition to the best man and maid of honor. The sponsors are generally older people who may have been involved with the courtship or the families. They signify wisdom and experience, so I talk to the couple about sharing that wisdom and experience. At first, I thought all that stuff was hokey. Now, I understand the symbolism of it for the couple. Now, when coins are exchanged, I know that it means that they will share all aspects of their life.

Canon law and liturgical rules don't have to be rigid. We're often blamed for rules that aren't even a part of canon law! A prime example in recent years is that nonissue of altar girls, or Mass servers. If one looks at the previous code, it's clear that females are banned from the sanctuary. A literal reading of the new code would still prohibit females, but an interpretive reading would show that females are really not banned. Sadly, many of our American bishops are falling back on the old code. They simply don't interpret. In fact, the biggest nonissue in the church is altar girls.

No, there's nothing in the code about flags for funerals. That's liturgical practice. But the prohibition of national flags on the coffin at funerals has been in a long time. It makes sense. The Church is anxious that no distinctions be made at funerals. It asks that the only "flag" be that of baptism, the white pall placed over the coffin. The Church doesn't object to an American flag over the coffin before entering the church or after leaving it. In this country the flag doesn't bring out the emotions set loose in Lebanon or Northern Ireland. But the white pall says we're all like kids in Catholic schools, in uniform, without class distinction.

Laicization of priests is another matter, however. Here's where the Church uses the code to discipline; and that's not good. In effect, the laicized priest is reduced to a role that takes away his very baptismal rights. He cannot read the Scriptures, be a catechist or a Eucharistic minister. Resigned priests become less than a lay Christian. The very word "laicization" becomes a misnomer. They're not reduced to the lay state; they are actually reduced to something below it. That's incorrect and unjust.

There are provisions for declaring nullity of sacred ordination. Just read codes 1708 through 1712. But we've been told not to use them. That's unfair, too.

Two things are very important in understanding canon law: what the code says and what the code doesn't say. Properly applied, the code is very pastoral. When I hear of cases regarding Church property, the Vatican always seems to be asking pastoral questions before granting permission, questions about the needs of the people and the effect on the community. If a hospital is going to be closed, for example, the Vatican will always ask: "What effect will this have on community health care?"

We're fortunate here. Our tribunal has a good reputation. Some dioceses don't. Our parish people are overworked; the last thing they need is someone telling them what to do.

This chancery does make mistakes. You'll recall the big drive to get kids into the high-school seminary, a drive that was going on even while they were preparing to close the place. When the rug was pulled, the priests were angry.

We're undergoing a transition in the Church. It's one that won't turn around in our current society. The priesthood is not a life that is very appealing or easy to sell these days. How would you feel about it? Long hours. Low pay. Loneliness. I genuinely enjoy what I'm doing. I'm happy as a priest. But it's got to change.

We're stuck in a transition period. Our people still see priests as people one sees to arrange to have a Mass said, or one to whom we donate clothes for the poor, or one to whom we go for a handout. Now comes a new understanding of the priesthood—a role of leadership, a person who seeks unity in a community, one who is comfortable with co-ordination.

Here in this office, I listen to or read about people's troubles each day. There are days when what I hear makes me physically ill. I always have to remember that these people are here because they want to rebuild their lives. What I see is their strength, their resiliency. I see God's grace working through them. I try to help them to rebuild their lives. By the judgments I make, I hope that I can help them put their lives back together. Then, it's not as bad as you might think it is.

The future? There'll be fewer priests. They'll have a different role. But the last priest in America will be in a parish, not a chancery office. We really don't belong here. We belong in the parish. However, if I can help the priest in the parish do his work, then what I do is worthwhile.

You know, local communities found creative ways to deal with annulments. They'll do the same with Eucharist. The Vatican won't have a role in the change, but the change will come.

You remember Tip O'Neill, the former Speaker of the House? He used to say that all politics are local. All church is local, too.

· 28 ·

Rollins E. Lambert:
Black Priest, White Church

The first three Afro-American priests were brothers, sons of Michael Healy, an immigrant Irishman, and a light-skinned slave named Mary Eliza, whom Healy had chosen as his mistress. Because she was a slave, the Church would not bless the marriage. Michael Healy was from Roscommon. He fought with the British army in the War of 1812 and later joined a distant cousin in Georgia, where by 1831 he became a wealthy plantation owner. He sent his children North for their education, most likely because their black blood would close school doors to them in the South.

Three of his first four sons became priests. James Augustine Healy was ordained in 1854. He later became chancellor and vicar general of the Boston diocese and bishop of Portland, Maine (1875), a state that lists only a hundred black Catholics in 1991. Alexander Sherwood Healy was ordained in 1858 after a brilliant academic career. Shortly after his ordination, his bishop almost nominated him as the first rector of the newly founded North American College. However, the bishop was cautious. In spite of impeccable credentials, Alexander Sherwood Healy was described as having "African blood"—and it showed. Sherwood became a theologian at Vatican I and was later named rector of Boston's new cathedral. He died in 1875 at only thirty-nine. Patrick Francis Healy was ordained a Jesuit in 1864 and, ten years later, was named president of Georgetown University. (This appointment was doubly ironic: Georgetown kept slaves for years and did not admit black students until the 1920s.)

All three Healys had brilliant careers, but, in the words of Cyprian Davis, whose book, *The History of Black Catholics in the United States*, provided most of these details: "They never used their position to champion the cause of their fellow blacks."

Augustus Tolton was the first recognized black priest in America. Born in Missouri in 1854, a son of two Catholic slaves, his father escaped to St. Louis and, later, his mother to Quincy, Illinois. Although a devout Catholic, her children were initially rejected from Catholic schools.

As a young man, Augustus expressed a desire to become a priest but no seminary would accept him. He was eventually accepted to what is now the Diocese of Springfield, Illinois, but with the understanding that he would become a missionary in Africa after his education at the Urban College in Rome. He was ordained in 1886 at thirty-two. He said one of his first Masses at St. Benedict the Moor Church, a black parish, on Bleeker Street in New York. A week later a crowd of 1,500 (500 of them black and mostly non-Catholic) witnessed his first Mass in Quincy. He was immediately appointed pastor of a black parish. His parish had only thirty-one Catholics. When whites began to attend, he incurred the jealousy of his fellow priests. Desperately lonely and feeling that his bishop had abandoned him, he went to Chicago in 1889 at the invitation of a group of black Catholics who had been worshiping in a church basement since 1881. He became the founder of St. Monica's Parish in 1891 and ministered to Chicago's black Catholics until his death in 1897 at forty-three. His parishioners were Afro-Americans who had often been denied entrance to white churches. His Chicago years were spent in poverty, living with his mother, isolated from most other clergy. While en route home from a retreat, he collapsed and died. (One report says that he was rushed to a nearby Catholic hospital, which promptly turned him away.)

The American Church's record on blacks is not an inspiring one. The Benedictine monk and historian Cyprian Davis reminds us that America's first bishop, John Carroll of Baltimore (1789–1815), was a slaveholder. Davis concludes: "His dilemma and his failure became the dilemma and failure of the American Church."

It would be forty-five years after Augustus Tolton's death before the archdiocese of Chicago accepted Rollins Lambert into its seminary in 1942. Ironically, Chicago was considered a progressive diocese, a pacesetter for the American Church, birthplace of a number of Catholic interracial movements. In 1945, Cardinal Samuel Stritch (1939–58) wrote to a number of Southern bishops, urging them to accept black students into their seminaries, although his own diocese had only one. Somehow, while preaching equality to others, and at a time when vocation recruitment was at its peak, little effort was made to attract minority vocations. Would-be candidates were often steered to religious congregations such as the Josephite Fathers and the Society of the Divine Word, which had opened a seminary for black priests in 1920. It would be nearly a century after James Augustine Healy's appointment before the second black bishop in America was appointed as auxiliary bishop of New Orleans. (Today, there are thirteen black bishops. One, Joseph L. Howze of Biloxi, is an ordinary. The remainder are auxiliaries. Eugene A. Marino, a Josephite, remains an archbishop, although he resigned as archbishop of Atlanta in 1990; James P. Lyke, O.F.M., one of the thirteen black bishops, has been appointed to succeed him as archbishop of Atlanta.)

Had Cardinal Albert Meyer, archbishop of Chicago, 1958–65, lived longer, Rollins Lambert might also have been a bishop. Lambert stoutly denies that he was ever approached. This is probably true, but clerical box holders believe that Meyer would have put him on his *terna*, the candidates' list submitted by bishops, and that at least one other bishop would also have done so, had not Lambert urged him not to.

Rollins Lambert is a cross between the intellectual Healy brothers and the pastoral Tolton. Formerly one of Chicago's sixteen deans, he was an oil can to twenty-seven parishes, dealing with everything from cooperative pastoral efforts to the pastors' wild pitches. He has been pastor of two Chicago parishes and Catholic chaplain at the University of Chicago. He spent twelve years at the United States Catholic Conference, the administrative arm of the National Conference of Catholic Bishops in Washington. At sixty-five, he returned to Chicago where he served as dean until August, 1991. He is now retired.

Rollins Lambert's convictions are buried deep but they are no less strong. One has to listen to his gentlemanly wit and pinpoint observations to sense his commitment to ending racial injustice. Confrontation just isn't his style. A picture of him presiding at a Mass at which another black priest and the ubiquitous Reverend Jesse Jackson vied for pictorial recognition shows him measurably uncomfortable. Yet, in his over forty years as a priest, he has accomplished as much for racial justice as those who would sound the cymbals. One example: Following the assassination of Martin Luther King, Jr. in 1968, Lambert was asked to preside at a memorial Mass in a Catholic high school of 2100 students on Chicago's segregated Southside. The students gathered in the school gym with palpable reluctance. Barely 800 placed hosts in the ciboria indicating that they would receive communion. Lambert said nothing until his homily. It, too, was gentle but pointed. Following the homily, at least 1,000 students rose to place a host in the sacred vessels.

Black Catholics are spread unevenly over America. Six states have only fifty to a hundred. Louisiana has 210,000, 17 percent of the state's black population. New York and California have over 200,000 black Catholics each, but, after that, the numbers drop. Black Catholics are largely in urban areas where they share a religious heritage that is often termed

"Baptist" but is, in fact, a black tradition. One urban priest stated that 60 percent of blacks have no mainstream religious roots. All told, the U.S. has 1,294,000 black Catholics out of an Afro-American population of 26,495,000, or 4.9 percent.

I'm finding a lot of angry priests in the deanery. They're saying that they think the focus of priesthood these days is raising money. They resent having to face the people and put the squeeze on them. Stewardship is basically a good idea. The lay people in the chancery office have tried to put the stewardship idea into a spiritual framework, asking people to give of themselves with no thought of money. But what it seems to have come down to now is capability, national statistics, and income zip-coding. Something's been lost. I'm afraid we'll be having a drive every year. It's going to take heavy giving and it's all tied to evangelization. More warm bodies in church so each can give less. Wilton Gregory [auxiliary bishop and vicar] must present figures for each parish. The actions seem to contradict the preaching. The pastors are very angry about all that. They're not beyond anger, as you suggest; they're still angry.

As dean, I'm the one who has the first go at a problem. Even if someone writes the cardinal, it will come back to me for an initial effort. If I can't resolve it, they can appeal to the vicar or to the conciliation board. If no one can solve it, it goes to the cardinal, but that's very rare.

When I was a kid at Senn High School in Chicago, I was urged to go to the University of Chicago. I used to go to U. of C. on weekends to do research. I loved Henrietta Hafmann, a favorite teacher at Senn for a lot of us. I learned how to do research. It was a great introduction to art. I was able to put on a slide show on the art of a period; I used slides from the library. I was about two years ahead of schedule in school. I entered the University of Chicago in 1938 at sixteen and graduated at twenty with a degree in political science. I was pretty good at languages; I was thinking of foreign service.

At the time of my entrance to U.C., I was a nonpracticing Christian Scientist. I had gone to Sunday School until college but, in those days, the Christian Scientists required that you pass an exam for membership. Well, during the exam, I was asked if I thought that the work of Mary Baker Eddy could be improved upon. I thought that the Bible was the only book that couldn't be improved upon, so I said that Mary Baker Eddy's writing could be clearer. So, I flunked. They recommended that I study more and come back. I didn't go back.

When I got to the University of Chicago, I found a part-time job in an office I shared with a guy who was a Catholic. He knew I was interested in music and he invited me to Holy Name Cathedral for the Easter liturgy.

Stritch [Cardinal Samuel Stritch] didn't have an orchestra but the music was good and I discovered that the liturgy was in Latin. I had done four years in high school and my scholarship at U.C. was based on how well I had done in Latin on the scholarship exam. I found a St. Andrew's Daily Missal in the library and took it out on permanent loan and started to go to Mass occasionally.

Then I met Jerome Kerwin, an advisor to some of the Catholic students. I began hanging around the Calvert Club, the Catholic club at the University. The Cardinal wouldn't allow a Newman club there, so this club was founded by Catholic lay people. I talked especially to one girl; we often went to Calvert events together. I met George Dunne, a Jesuit, who was a graduate student in international relations, and who did chaplain stuff with us. I started going to Childerley House, an old mansion in the country, that was used by the Calvert Club. There I ran into Johanna Doniat, an old teacher at Senn High School. She had taught me art and stagecraft and I had done yard work for her family. I began going to Mass regularly and praying the Divine Office. One year, I was reading Matthew 16:18—"you are Peter, and upon this rock I will build my church, and the gates of the nether world will not prevail against it"—and it struck me that the "church" I studied since high school was the Catholic Church. Jerome and Johanna asked me if I wanted to take instructions and, when I said I did, they arranged for me to go to the Dominican House of Studies in River Forest. Later that year, Stritch appointed Joe Cunnerton as the first official chaplain to what is now Calvert House. I had already pretty much decided to become a priest, but the guys in the Calvert Club didn't know the difference between a religious priest and a diocesan priest and I sure didn't.

Sara Benedicta O'Neill was very important in my conversion. She ran the St. Benet Bookshop and loved converts. I was her special catch. Later, there was Dan Cantwell [Monsignor Daniel A. Cantwell] and Nina Polcyn [now Nina Polcyn Moore]. We had tea in Sara's shop every Saturday afternoon. We met visiting abbots and I got interested in the Benedictine life. It was contrary to the Dominican spirit at the University of Chicago. I even visited Portsmouth Priory in Rhode Island where I was encouraged to enter. It was the full monastic life; we praised God seven or eight times a day.

I knew that I couldn't join. I had my mother who was independent but there were just the two of us. She was involved in my life all these years. She died only last year at the age of 102. She never became a Catholic but she learned to tolerate us. During those years before my conversion, she thought I was being deceived or duped. When I entered the seminary, she was shocked by the awful visiting rules. We had no car; she could only take the train up and then hope to get a ride home. After a year, she decided it would be better to go away. She went to California and was there many years. I thought of changing to a California diocese, but I listened to Dan Cantwell speak on urban life and I decided to stay.

I was baptized on Christmas Eve, 1941, and received my First Communion from Cardinal Stritch at Midnight Mass. Soon after, I told Jerome Kerwin that I wanted to go to the seminary. He told me that I didn't have a chance. He knew of a black guy just before me who had a Ph.D. and had been rejected. There was a very snobbish attitude toward the seminary at that time. The church had priests to spare; it was very cavalier. And I was black.

I learned that another black had applied in 1940 or 1941. He was rejected. I don't know what they told him, but the real problem was race. Kerwin was a friend of the then archbishop of St. Paul and of the rector of their seminary. I was accepted there, but I wanted Chicago. The acceptance to St. Paul gave me courage; I figured I'd apply and let my own diocese throw me out. I met Reynie Hillenbrand [Monsignor Reynald Hillenbrand, rector of St. Mary of the Lake Seminary]. He took the matter to Stritch and Stritch said that, if it was O.K. with Joe Connerton, it was O.K. with him. I entered Mundelein in the Fall of 1942, the first black in the seminary.

There was no overt prejudice. I never felt it. Oh, one day, while we were working on the grounds, some of the guys were goofing off and the groundskeeper was trying to urge us on. I was working just a little ahead of the pack when I heard him shout: "Look at Rollins, you guys. He's working like a nigger!" There was just silence. No one said a thing. Neither did I. The man obviously felt terrible. It turned out great for me. For the rest of my time in the seminary, he couldn't do enough for me. (Laughs.)

My Latin was as good as or better than the other seminarians, but I had no Greek. Hillenbrand arranged for me to have a tutor. I had some difficulty with philosophy, just understanding the philosophy profs. Hillenbrand was very kind to me. I was his protege. He let me skip classes I had already taken in college and he put me to work as one of his secretaries. We got to be good friends and remained so until Vatican II. Reynie just couldn't fit into the post-Vatican II church. The church just passed him by. He had a helluva time with young associates. Just couldn't work with him. Eventually, he had to use ex-patriate priests. I had no contact with him in his later years. That was sad.

Anyway, Reynie Hillenbrand was removed from office after I was in the seminary for only two years. Mal Foley took over and everything changed. The next five years were tough ones for me. Mal was suspicious of me for having skipped some courses; he had no faith in my secular education; he was suspicious of converts and, maybe, concerned that I was black. I don't know. He made me do the whole curriculum. I was at St. Mary's for seven years, even though I already had my degree and the normal term for a college graduate was four years. Mal would have liked to see me go, but I was a good student who kept the rules, and I was good at Gregorian chant. He couldn't find a reason to boot me out.

Priests, before and after my ordination, do not seem to have had any difficulty accepting me. There might had been a few, but very few. I've heard the stories of other black priests being refused permission to say Mass, especially when they traveled, but it never happened to me.

I was ordained in 1949 and was appointed to a black parish, St. Malachy's on West Washington. Stritch saw me as an experiment, his first black priest. He asked often about me. I was unique, I guess. Jim Lyke [James P. Lyke, O.F.M., now archbishop of Atlanta, Georgia] heard about me. He didn't believe that there was a black priest in Chicago. He made a trip to St. Malachy's just to meet me. But the people accepted me with open arms. It was a good first assignment. The parish had a little high school then. It was all black and I had a chance to teach a class in black history, a real innovation in 1949. Just across the street was a another school, run by the same nuns. It was all white; they never did take a black student. Black parents tried to get their kids in, but they were never accepted.

I was there for seven years, all of them with John F. Brown, who was pastor from 1938 to 1962. In 1956, I returned from vacation and the housekeeper told me that I had been transferred to St. Dorothy's. I was there with two pastors. There were two associates, Tom Raftery and myself. The parish was 80 percent to 90 percent black. It was middle-class black. We priests tried to bring the people into an integrated society. At one level, there appeared to be little discrimination. People had help from the federal government; they were able to get loans for their houses. We got a lot of good work done at St. Dorothy, in spite of the fact that the pastor was a pain because of his drinking.

In 1961, a chaplain's job at Calvert House opened up. Tom McDonough needed an associate. He was doing a lot of publishing. He needed some free time. I was anxious to get back to the University of Chicago and the academic life. The negotiations took some effort. It was still pre-Vatican II. But I got the assistant chaplain's job, got a Danforth grant, and tried to do a Ph.D. in Anthropology part-time. But I was too busy. I was named chairman of the Art and Architecture Commission for the archdiocese and became president of the National Black Clergy Caucus, which I helped found. There were only about twenty or thirty of us then, mostly from religious orders. We just wanted to promote the integration of black priests and people into the Catholic Church.

We worked for better uses of black clergy and religious. A real spark plug was Herman Porter, a black priest from Rockford, Illinois, who was vice president of the organization. We circulated a letter to all the black priests in the country, urging them to attend a special caucus in conjunction with the Catholic Clergy Conference. The invitation was prompted by Chicago's mayor, Richard J. Daley's "shoot to kill" order. Our theme was "Black Power and the White Church." It upset a lot of white priests, especially when we issued a manifesto saying that the church was racist. There weren't a lot of us. Maybe only fifty or sixty. But our statements made for change. The bishops became more sensitive. They stopped asking us if we wanted to work in the black community. We found many priests, black and white, who wanted to work in the black community. They became rectors and superiors, all in a period of five years. It reflected the mood of the country.

But Meyer died in 1965 and Cody came in as archbishop. A lot changed for me. I got a lot of heat from him. He told me that if I ever wanted to be a bishop, I had better give up all this race stuff.

McDonough and others agitated to have me appointed chaplain at Calvert House but Cody appointed me pastor of St. James, an old Irish parish that was now mostly black. I was there only a few months when a crisis broke out at my old parish, St. Dorothy's. The old pastor was changed to Waukegan and Cody appointed me pastor in order to block the appointment of George Clements, then a young associate pastor, who was black. The people wanted George. So did a lot of political activists and some clergy. I was no longer president of the Black Clergy Caucus and they were backing George. The people weren't against me as much as they were for George. It was a tough time for me. I felt very much like a pawn. It was all over the papers. A *Chicago Tribune* reporter asked me if I thought that Cody was a racist and I replied that I thought that he had some racism. That did it for Cody.

I was pastor but George was getting the support. The situation got very hot with George. If Cody had had his way, he would have burned the place down. All the publicity was a challenge to his authority as pastor of the Church of Chicago.

I was pastor of a divided parish. George Clements was still stationed there, but was spending time touring campuses. George was eventually appointed pastor of Holy Angels; things cooled down; gradually I was able to restore law and order. But two of the associates left the ministry, and young associates kept coming and going.

All I wanted to do was get back to the University of Chicago. Finally, in 1970, Cody appointed Jim Sweeney as pastor and I went back to Calvert House as chaplain. I was much more comfortable there.

In 1975, I thought it was time to make another change. I had a connection with the NCCB/USCC and I knew some D.C. folks. So I wrote and asked for a job. I knew that they wanted someone for African affairs in Bryan Hehir's department. I met with him for twenty minutes and Bryan gave his O.K.; Cody quickly gave his, and I was there for twelve years.

I came back to Chicago in 1987. I was sixty-five and had to retire from the USCC, but Chicago lets priests retire at 70. I would just as soon have stayed in Washington but my pension is back here and I needed the money.

Being dean is no great fun. I must go to an endless number of meetings.

Officially, I'm only in residence but I do a fair amount of parish work. I try not to do weddings, unless there is a special request. They take too much energy. But I do hospital calls. I see some scary things in the parish, especially about the Church's relationship with youth. We don't seem to be getting to them. If we don't have young people, what's going to happen? Our hope for the future must be in lay ministry. We just lost a fine young associate and he wasn't replaced. We now have a layman for the youth program and that's getting to be the pattern.

The Church will survive, but I don't know how. (Laughs.) I think it's inevitable that we'll have some married clergy. In fact, they may be just around the corner, including the restoration to ministry of married clergy. But I'm not sure about females. Maybe the door will open for ordaining married permanent deacons and permitting those under thirty-five to marry. And maybe they'll permit ordained permanent deacons to remarry. [Presently, if a permanent deacon is widowed, he cannot remarry.] All these rules are mainly to protect celibate clergy. Our permanent deacons at St. Joe's are doing a superb job. They give great homilies, and they're all working men, none retired.

Well, I'm nearly there. Seventy next year. I'm tired. It's been a good life. But I worry about the priests burning out. We're aging too fast; we seem to be caught in a downward spiral: fewer priests, more work, more burnout. We still have to find a way to relieve that burden. There's also a lot of time wasted in ministry. We could actually do more work without endangering our health if we made better use of our time.

I'm getting used to getting up on the altar again. All those years in Washington, I said Mass in parishes only twice. Now, I'm doing it all again. I'm at St. Joseph's in Homewood now. I like it there. I'll most likely stay there and help out after official retirement.

Raymond A. Lucker: Rural Bishop

"Ray Lucker can afford to be an outspoken bishop," a knowledgeable bishop watcher said. "He isn't going anywhere." The statement was meant to be a compliment and an indictment. The compliment recognized Bishop Raymond A. Lucker's integrity; the indictment defined the episcopal system that can turn earnest priests into sycophants and careerists.

Bishop Lucker is termed "one of the good guys" even by his fellow bishops. In a world where the Machiavellian principle that it is better to be respected than loved applies, Lucker is both loved and respected. He may, indeed, be envied by some of his fellow bishops who pay for their power and prestige with a terrifying loneliness. Some, forced to be bishops every waking hour, have long since lost touch with their own feelings.

According to the 1990 edition of *The Official Catholic Directory*, there are 458 American bishops. Nine are cardinals; 57 are archbishops; 151 head dioceses; 104 are auxiliaries; 30 serve outside the U.S., and 106 are retired. Over half of the active bishops have been appointed by John Paul II. Given their age, an average of sixty-two years, turnover is very high, in spite of the fact that mandatory retirement age is a comparatively old seventy-five. At the present rate, should John Paul II live another decade, there is a good possibility that he will have appointed 100 percent of the active bishops in the U.S. Like the Reagan-Bush Supreme Court and its interpretation of the Constitution, today's bishops will continue to have an impact on the American Church well into the next pontificate. John Paul's appointments have been described as conservative. He leans toward men who are liberal on social issues and conservative on doctrinal and moral issues. Of late, it would seem, his appointees are conservative on both counts. Administratively, his "office managers," as they have been described by a bishop himself, tend to hold power close to their vestments. They remain strongly clerical; lay involvement in their administrations is largely cosmetic or confined to positions that do not involve genuine decision making.

At the annual meetings of the National Conference of Catholic Bishops, the laity have no voice. While some listening takes place outside the sessions, the hierarchy remains a closed society. Voting follows predictable patterns, not unlike the boards of directors of large corporations. Few bishops wander too far from their sponsors. Less than a dozen bishops could be described as liberal; perhaps a few dozen more could be classed as moderate-progressives; the remainder are verbally moderate but functionally conservative. Among the megabishops of New York, Philadelphia, Boston, Los Angeles, Detroit, and Washington, D.C., the operational philosophy is strongly conservative. Chicago and St. Louis are examples of moderately liberal regimes and only Milwaukee, Seattle, St. Paul-Minneapolis, and a handful of dioceses could be termed liberal.

Overall, bishops are liked by their priests and laity who know them. (A grumpy pastor once said to his bishop: "Harry, do you realize that over half the people in this diocese never heard of you?" He probably wasn't far off the mark. A *New York Daily News* poll revealed that only 20 percent of the Catholic population could identify the present, highly visible archbishop, Cardinal John O'Connor.)

Bishops are kindly, prayerful caring men with decency and tact. They are a stable group. In recent memory, only two have left active ministry and married. A few have been treated for alcoholism; one was involved in a highly publicized affair with a woman, and, a decade ago, one was almost indicted for misuse of diocesan funds. But, for the most part, they are the kind of men one would be pleased to have as a next-door neighbor. They would shovel their sidewalk and offer to help you with yours.

There is ample evidence that they are well-informed about the problems within the Church, but they cannot bring themselves to act on the very data they gather. One archbishop visited with one of the NCCB's top researchers and informed him that his work was high quality and that it tied in with his own observed experience, but that he would have to differ with it publicly. Some years ago, when a careful study of the theological, psychological, and sociological aspects of priesthood were studied and reported in depth, the bishops rejected all three findings when they were at variance with the clerical culture. When the Canadian bishops announced that they were going to petition the Vatican to place optional celibacy or some form of married priesthood on the agenda of the 1990 Synod on the Priesthood, the cautious Americans declined to join them. Even when they are incensed with Rome, the bishops will say nothing publicly. (Challenged with this, one bishop answered simply: "I have an oath as a bishop. Before I will differ with the Holy Father, I will resign.") When Archbishop Raymond G. Hunthausen of Seattle was publicly humiliated by the Vatican, the bishops remained silent, although they were privately fuming over the clumsy treatment of a much admired colleague. The only way they expressed their anger was to refuse to elect Cardinal Bernard F. Law to a number of important NCCB committees when it was learned that Law supported the Vatican in the Seattle case. At the 1990 meeting, the bishops applauded Milwaukee's archbishop, Rembert Weakland, O.S.B., for the slight he suffered in having an honorary degree withdrawn because of pressure from the Vatican. But they did so behind closed doors. When an ultraconservative careerist bishop was inflicted on a diocese of over 350,000, six bishops spent an overnight in another's rectory. Throughout their evening meal, they joked quietly about the appointee's conservative ways. But they continued on their way to his installation. Bishops don't break rank.

In the past two decades, they have produced some outstanding pastoral letters, especially the ones on War and Peace and on Social Teaching and the U.S. Economy. (A third pastoral on women is caught in a political and emotional limbo and is not likely to appear.) In spite of strong opposition from Vatican officials unhappy with conferences such as the NCCB, the bishops have tried to address important issues without blinking. There have been credibility gaps as bishops fail to practice what they preach, especially on labor issues. Further, the gap between what one priest termed "the Cathedral Church and the Pilgrim Church" may be widening as, in one layman's words, "priests face their people while the bishops face Rome."

The bishops are not unaware of such observations, and they are stung by them. Privately, they sound beleaguered. It is as if they pine for the old days when a bishop had only to raise his ringed hand to silence further talk. But they would also like to delegate their responsibilities, especially financial ones, if the Vatican would only let them. They are uncomfortable gathering at an expensive downtown Washington hotel for their annual meeting instead of a college campus or a large monastery. But, when they go to the monastery, they are accused of hiding out from the media. At their episcopal retreats, they listen to speakers who generally represent critical and forward-thinking ideas. They even watch pivotal movies with the same thrust. But when they meet to translate ideas into resolutions, the votes tend to be very cautious. They enjoy the anonymous protection of a group vote but bristle that their individual discretion is being lessened by having to bring matters to the floor of the Conference, only to have the Conference timidly defer to Rome. At their

1990 meeting, they applauded their leader, Daniel E. Pilarczyk of Cincinnati, for the efficient manner in which he conducted the meeting, but confessed to missing his predecessors, James W. Malone of Youngstown and John L. May of St. Louis, because of their more casual and openhanded approach. Little wonder that they often feel trapped between the proverbial rock and a hard place.

Raymond Lucker lives somewhere on the outer edge of bishopdom. He has a diocese he can get his bishop's mantle around. He knows his priests and his people. He can be what a bishop is supposed to be—and he is.

The population of this diocese has stayed the same for the past thirty years. We're about ninety-five miles from St. Paul; we used to be part of the St. Paul-Minneapolis Archdiocese. New Ulm used to be the largest town, about 13,700. There are about 269,000 people in the area covered by the diocese, 69,000 of them are Catholics. We have eighty-eight parishes; only two or three of them have more than 1,000 families. Others have only two or three hundred; some have less than a hundred. But you'd be amazed at all the activity! I just finished a visitation in a small parish today. One hundred families. There were eighty-five at our closing Mass on a weekday. I met with the parish activities committee and there were forty-five people there. The CCD must have had forty-five, too. Practically everyone listed in the parish is involved in the parish. Only a few will tell you that they're not active because they had a fight with Father or something like that. It's just amazing how many are there, and even more amazing is the level of faith, the beautiful devotion, the way they pass their faith on to their children. This is an area where the children know their grandparents and the grandparents have an active part in raising them. These people have been on their land for generations. The strength of this diocese is in its small communities.

I'm still convinced that the most serious problem we have in the Church in America is the lack of commitment on the part of adults. We still need to evangelize adults. There are still too many whose commitment is only on the social level. A lot of our people just want to follow the rules, little more.

I spend a lot of my time visiting parishes. I started about eight years ago. I visit forty or fifty a year for Confirmations alone. We visit each parish for a weekend or for several days during the week. We teach classes; visit with the parish councils and other organizations. I ask them what it means to be a living parish. I tell them that they are supposed to be a visionary group—planners, people who need to come together and pray, not just for building and repairs. I tell them that they must make a commitment to social justice. I ask the social concerns committee how they are reaching out, how they are working on the social sins of our time. After a few years, the groups begin to find direction. I ask the educational committees how they are handing on the faith. I ask how they are worshiping God and about the devotional side of the Church.

I spend considerable time on the road. When I get to a gathering, I ask them to break up into small groups. It's just amazing how open they are! At the close of visitation, we have a Mass and an anointing of the sick. That anointing is one of the most beautiful celebrations to come out of Vatican II. I try to visit some shut-ins and the handicapped. Of course, I go through the sacramental books and the finances and, if it's a weekend, I preside at the Sunday liturgy. Then, there's the pot luck supper, recognition with medals of service to the parishioners or the local politicians who may have done something for the betterment of housing or some other need.

I've been here fifteen years. The people have come to know me. During these years, I've done about eight hundred Confirmations. I believe that I've talked to 75 percent of the people in the diocese. I get to some fifty of the parishes every year; perhaps twenty others every two years and a few at least every three years. I'm there for anniversaries, talks, and the like. I love meeting the people.

I believe that it takes at least 125 families to make a parish. I've found that the ideal size is 300 to 500 families. With that number, you can have some staff. As I said, we now have 88 parishes. We used to have 93. We'll close some more in the years ahead.

We're very committed to a planning process in the parishes. At the diocesan level, we've had people clarify our mission statement and our goals, and we organized our diocesan offices toward those goals. Our first priority was the spiritual renewal of adults. We found RENEW and were among the first to adopt the process. Every member of our staff is involved with RENEW and there is a heavy flow from our diocesan offices to every region. We spent a year or two going toward that process and most of the parishes adopted it. We ask the people to spend time at each meeting in prayer and adult formation, then to get to the business of the meeting. That's our education. We have no universities, colleges, seminaries, or formation houses in this diocese, so we have to supply all such education.

Oh, we've had to make changes. We started out with about thirty-five goals and then realized that was far too many; so we narrowed them to seven and made them more specific. We gathered all kinds of data. We even looked at shopping patterns and telephone installations. But in the end, the major factor was the number of priests.

Our task force met monthly. We sent our data to the parish leadership. We did a twelve-minute video in which we ask the people what a viable parish was. Then, we ask if they saw themselves as closing, or whether or not they could form a cluster. The priests of the seven regions we formed met and went through the same process. We tried to tell everyone what a cluster would look like, and then we asked them to meet with all the people.

We had seventy-five priests. We're down to sixty-five now. By 1995, we expect to have fifty priests. At that point, it should level off, but we're prepared for as few as forty-five priests. We've decided to close ten parishes and cluster others, so that we'll have about fifty parishes. We continue to meet and plan. Now, we're meeting with five parishes which will someday be served by only two priests. We need to discuss what to do with the rectory and the church. There's so much beauty and goodness in these small parishes. There's a lot of denial. "Let us have a priest," the people say, "and we can make a parish." But there are no priests. It hurts. There's some real grieving.

We hear talk that we should get priests from Africa or some other country where they have a modest surplus. But I'm not convinced that it would work. People ask: "Why not ordain a celibate male who can say Mass for us?" It's not a problem for them. They ask about ordaining married men. They want priests. What's needed is a start, a willingness to discuss this. If the recent Synod on the Priesthood had permitted at least a discussion of optional celibacy or married priests, it would have made an enormous difference. There is no incompatibility between priesthood and married life. Clearly, it's just a Church law. The celibate clergy have served the Church exceptionally well. I'm not against celibacy. I want to affirm it. But I believe that the Church would be well served by married men, particularly where men must be married in order to be accepted. If we had optional celibacy in this diocese, I'm sure that we would have all the clergy that we want. We could use twenty more priests right now.

This diocese is only thirty years old. It was carved out of St. Paul-Minneapolis. When they first came here, a lot of priests were just starting their pastorates. Now, they're retired. I'm the only one from my class of 1952 in this area. I'm sixty-four; the average priest is in his early fifties. Presently, we have six seminarians in theology. The next three years, we'll be ordaining only one a year, but the year after that, we'll have three. That's a good number. Some dioceses that are ten times our size have proportionately fewer. The people-to-priest ratio here is still pretty good, about one to 1,000. We're only 93,000 square miles, not very far from one side of the diocese to another. There are places where people can see the steeple from one church to another. It's just that they have gotten used to their own parish.

I'm in good health but I'm not sure that I'll be able to keep up the pace of the parish visitations in the years ahead. That's the most important thing I do. There are monthly meetings with the priests, and personnel and financial meetings. We have a staff meeting every two weeks and I'm involved in a clergy support group. Of course, I'm involved on committees of the National Conference of Catholic Bishops and I'm active in the Catholic Theological Society. In June, I'll deliver a paper at a symposium on Catholic Social Teaching. I accepted the topic of justice in the Church, of all things! It will be published by Orbis Books in the fall. Finally, I do a lot of reading.

I live in a community of five people. When I came here, I found a rather large building that included a residence for the bishop [Alphonse J. Schladweiler, 1958–75]. There were rooms for other priests and a convent. There was lots of space, but the previous bishop lived here all alone. There were three or four diocesan staff people and a retired priest, all living nearby. We found a lady who could cook an evening meal and we asked a Jesuit to come in and talk to us about how to share our faith and our lives. We all told our stories. It was very powerful. We were all laughing and crying. We got into each other's lives. We got involved in tasks. We had Mass every day; we joined the sisters in praying together. We still try to pray together for thirty minutes each day, and we try to say vespers together after supper. At least once a month all of us are home for dinner together and we take turns conducting meetings. We've brought the Jesuit back from time to time. Now, it's been fourteen years. The community has been a lifesaver for me. This year, we're having some troubles. The chemistry may not be right. Perhaps we still need the Jesuit to coach us. Perhaps it needs more time. I'm going to bounce with this. Maybe the Lord is leading me in a different direction. Perhaps by June it will be time to build a community again.

There's no turning back now. Vatican II set us on a trajectory in scripture, theology, liturgy, ecumenism, and lay ministry. Every single member of the Church is called to active participation. Once you've started on a path of personally taking responsibility for your faith, there is no way you can put it back into a bottle. There is no way we can return to the clericalism we once had. We're still clerical, but it's changing, just like our liturgy. There is no way that we can go back to the days when the priest did everything. Renewal has been set in place.

Now, many renewal movements have been slowed by Rome, especially ecumenism and theological development. I'm very optimistic, however, the Church is being guided by the Spirit. It's been the same for social justice. We've made enormous steps. There has been a great increase in the involvement by lay people. I am discouraged by the shortage of priests and the low morale in the priesthood. Again, there are some areas that should be freely discussed and are not being discussed.

I've been deeply touched by the spiritual movement in my life. When I was ordained in 1952, I was very much a part of the clerical church. I was imbued with the clerical culture. I knew all the questions and I had all the answers.

There was a kind of arrogance about it all. We were all set up during our six years in the seminary. That's the way it was.

Early on, I got involved in lay movements—the Confraternity of Christian Doctrine, Young Christian Students, Christian Family Movement, and the like. I went to summer schools of Catholic Action, followed Dorothy Day and Catherine de Hueck, read *Today* and *Integrity*. I read about the priest workers in France; I read the spiritual writers of the day. I got involved with the Legion of Mary and the Grail. In 1964, I got to Rome, just in time for the third session of Vatican II. I had been the assistant director of the CCD in the archdiocese. Later, I was professor of catechetics at the seminary in St. Paul. I got a master's in history and started on a doctorate in education at the University of Minnesota. It was interrupted when I went to Rome to study for my S.T.D. at the Angelicum. When I returned from Rome, I was named director of the Department of Education at the United States Catholic Conference. I held that job from 1968 through 1971, with some time off to complete my Ph.D. at Minnesota. In 1971, I was named auxiliary bishop in St. Paul-Minneapolis and in December, 1975, was named the second bishop of New Ulm. Those were the sixties and seventies, with the deaths of the Kennedys and Martin Luther King, Jr., and Watts and Detroit. And here was this incredible renewal coming from Vatican II and the growing peace movement here. I went through a personal conversion; got swept right into it. I got involved in theology and catechetics. I learned three words—God loves me—that summarized the whole of salvation. For me, love summarized living. Love was the Beatitudes and the Sermon on the Mount. You can explain all the mysteries with those three words. There are still a lot of grays, but when I returned from Rome, I wasn't threatened.

All these experiences opened up a whole new world. I got involved in the Cursillo Movement in St. Paul. I learned that I could pray without a piece of paper in front of me. This has all been a wonderful and exciting time.

Then, there's been the bishops in Minnesota. Every year, we make a retreat together. Those retreat days have opened my life. I made a thirty-day retreat. It was a marvelous experience. My own spiritual life has been blessed. I still meet with my spiritual director every month. So now, when I go through periods of depression, I realize how much the Lord has touched me. When I admit to my needs and turn myself over to Christ, I find that I can rise with Christ. There is a presence and the power of God in my life now. It's a very different outlook than the priesthood of nearly forty years ago.

· 30 ·

John R. Lynch:
Seminary Prof, Psychologist

John Lynch is a seminary prof at two seminaries: Niles College of Loyola University of Chicago in Niles, Illinois (a four year college seminary for the archdiocese of Chicago, with an enrollment of about 106 students), and the Sacred Heart School of Theology, Hales Corners, Wisconsin (a special seminary for delayed vocations administered by the Sacred Heart Fathers that accepts students nationwide and has an enrollment of about 190). He is a clinical psychologist, a trustee of the Chicago School of Professional Psychology and a weekend curate, still involved in parish work. He moves easily among three modest quarters, at the seminaries and the parish.

According to the *Official Catholic Directory*, there are sixty-nine diocesan seminaries in the U.S. with a combined enrollment of 4,311. College seminaries such as Niles number about forty-four. Lynch's primary home is at the seminary where he is a house moderator to a small group of older seminarians. Neither a philosopher nor a theologian, he is not a typical seminary professor. Seminary teaching remains a popular pursuit for many priests. Most simply enjoy teaching, finding it less stressful and more intellectually satisfying than parish life. When a seminary position is posted, it invariably draws a number of applicants, even as parishes go vacant. The vast majority, however, do weekend help-out work at local parishes. One reason that diocesan seminary committees continue to vote for the retention of the system is that they like what they are doing, find satisfaction in their work, and believe that, if they are not turning out a great many priests, they are forming a core of Christian laymen.

I like working with students. I'm not certain if I like the seminary, however. I think I may have done all I can here. I'm looking around.

I made a thirty-day retreat this summer. It was part of an effort to see where I'm going and where the Church is going. I am really going to try to give up my agenda and let the Lord speak to me. It's frightening, you know. It's dangerous!

I love being a priest. I love the work and I get good feedback. Yet, there's the institution. This is clearly not what Jesus had in mind. There's so much narcissism in the Church; so much trying to look good. This priesthood is what I want; I'm real sure of that. But the Church is impeding my happiness.

I'm not part of the club, I'm afraid. I'm somewhere on the outer circle; I'm looked upon as an oddball. If you're not part of the "in" group in the seminary system, you simply won't get in. It doesn't bother me. I feel like Martin Luther King, Jr. I have inner peace. But I'm convinced that I must get out of here when my contract is up. Dennis Geaney [Augustinian, parish priest] told me that I should have listened to my body. It tells you things. The whole situation has really depressed me. I gotta get out of here.

I was ordained in 1967 after five years in the junior seminary and seven years at the major sem. Those were interesting times, before and after Vatican II. If anything could have happened, it happened during those times. My first rector was a good, honest person, who believed that what he was doing was right. I respected him because I understood him. But my other foot was in a life that said: "This is all wrong. This isn't where the Church is going." The poor guy. Some of the seminarians thought he was Satan. Our class once staged a pray-in. It was 1920 versus 1965. There were seminary issues, but there were Church issues, too. Much of it was focusing on our own suffering, but there was a lot of CYA (cover your ass) in all of this.

Jack Gorman [now auxiliary bishop of Chicago] was a savior. When he took over the seminary, he helped us to live. He opened the windows. It was life giving. It was life preserving. Jack struck a balance. I feel a kinship with him. We're both hyphenated priests. He's a priest-psychologist, too.

In 1967, I was assigned to Our Lady Gate of Heaven. I met Harold Bush [psychologist] there. He was a mentor to me. Because of him I pursued my education; got my masters at Roosevelt University and worked together with Harold in the community.

Then, I started my doctorate. I went to Old St. Patrick's. It's flourishing now, but at the time there wasn't much happening there. So, I had some free time. I took my classes nearby and interned at Illinois State Psychiatric Institute Hospital over at Taylor and Damen. I used to go over in the morning, then rush back for the 12:10 Mass at St. Pat's; then go back to the hospital.

I wanted the experience of psychology so much that I put up with the running around and the criticism. Cody [John Cardinal Cody, archbishop of Chicago, 1965-82] called me in twice. He didn't understand psychology. He thought I was in medical school. I was paying my own tuition, so he had little control. But he bawled me out for a half-hour and then stood up and said: "This meeting is over." But I managed to say to him: "No, this meeting isn't over! I have something to say!" Well, by God, he came back and sat down. I said my piece and thanked him. He thanked me and I left and he never called again. Later, Pete Shannon [resigned priest, now an attorney] told me that it was the smartest thing I had ever done. I was simply accessing my honesty. We need more of that in the Church.

Cody backed down. It took five years to finish my doctorate. I got licensed in Wisconsin first because I was offered a job as an adjunct prof at the Sacred Heart School of Theology in Hales Corners, Wisconsin. It's a seminary conducted by the Sacred Heart Fathers for delayed vocations. They're doing quite well. I think there are 190 students, one of the largest seminaries in America. Just last week, they ordained six. One was a physician, another an accountant, one was a nurse. They are all seasoned people; some are widowers. The future for priesthood may be in these seasoned career people. There was a widower from Davenport, Iowa, in this last class. I watched as his two daughters helped him to vest. It was beautiful.

Chicago isn't serious about second-career vocations. I think they have one up at Sacred Heart. They're much like other large dioceses, very suspicious of second-career vocations. They want control and that's hard to achieve with older men. There were guys in my time who went through the system for upwards of twelve years. The expense of educating them was enormous, and some of them lasted six months or a year out in the parishes. Now, take a man who is fifty-six today. You could ordain him in four years at a fraction of the cost and he could serve for twenty years. The dropout rate in the seminary system is staggering, but they still prefer the present system. There's a whole other agenda at work here: many seminary profs and administrators want to be bishops. In fact, they're often appointed to the seminary system so that they can be positioned to be bishops. The present pope leans toward conservative seminary profs. That was his background. It affects all their actions.

People say that priests are leaving because of celibacy. But I think that's said too quickly. I don't think it's true. I think celibacy is part of the picture, but it isn't the whole picture.

My problem is not with celibacy. It's isolation, including isolation from the Church itself. Something is terribly wrong with the institution. It's Mark versus Mike, individual vitality versus a run for a bishopric. It's saying that one is unafraid to love but afraid of being engaged. The system fosters fear of engagement. It still fosters the illusion that being in the inner circle is something to strive for. You know, if Jesus were here, and got into a conversation with a careerist like "Luke," he'd tell him to get lost. Yet, these are the very people being moved into the inner circle.

I help out on Sundays over at St. Gertrude's. Bill [the pastor] and I have coffee together between masses. He likes to read aloud to me from Andy Greeley. Greeley drives me nuts, but, you know, he's right! He points out things that must be changed. He cites the abuses of power and the failure to face issues. It's all CYA again. Greeley's right when he says that the inner-circle guys act as if it were their own Church and that they are not account-able.

When I was a kid, I was an Andy Frain usher. In those days, they looked for tall people. I think you had to be at least six feet tall; I'm about six-six. Anyway, I liked it. We were given a tradition of service. We were taught to be nice to people. We learned social skills. Being an usher helped me to under-stand what priesthood should be about. It's giving service.

It's all over for Rome. And they don't know it. The Church has moved off the Euro-American axis. I've traveled a great deal. I've been to Africa, Asia, the Philippines. I've talked to missionaries in Asia, Africa, and India. Theirs is a different Church altogether.

I was at a five-day conference in Manila. It was mostly about evangeliza-tion. Well, after a couple of days, Cardinal Tomko [Jozef Cardinal Tomko, prefect of the Congregation for the Evangelization of Peoples] got up to tell everyone how to do it. A significant number of the bishops from Southeast Asia just quietly walked out. "The Church is not Rome," they said. "It's ours." The Vatican had nothing to say to these countries, other than to remind them of their authority.

In 1990, some African, Southeast Asian, and Canadian bishops at the Synod on the Priesthood asked the Vatican to do away with mandatory celibacy for the sake of the Church. They went hat in hand, respectfully, and were told in advance that the topic could not even be discussed. But my scenario holds that they might go back in 1991 or 1992—anyway, soon. And this time, they'll leave their hats at home. They'll still be refused, of course. But they'll come back and ask again. And then the year will come, soon, I think, when they won't come back at all. They'll simply change the rules for the sake of the Church.

It will be like Thomas More [1478-1535, English martyr, chancellor under Henry VIII, canonized 1935]. Someone will step up and ordain a married man or woman. He will choose his priorities and decide to be loyal to Jesus, even though it means that he will lose his head.

It's all over. The bishops remain faithful to a tradition that simply isn't there. It's the Church from below that will take over. It may be the poor that will save us. They are actually richer than we are in terms of the gospel. They will have the Eucharist, even if it means that a married priest will preside at the Eucharist. The bishops are good men. Mine visited me when I was sick; he came and buried my father; he was faithful to an older tradition. But

American bishops are spineless. Yes, they're office managers of an old tradition.

I don't like to sound pessimistic but the situation is bleak. We hyphenated priests are going to have a hard time. We're too educated, too seasoned, too independent, at a time when they just want functionaries to fill spots. Our independent attitude filters down, so in time they will have trouble with the younger priests.

Just look at the guy we met at lunch. He's running around putting no parking stickers on cars on a campus that has more parking spaces than you can imagine. Now, the spaces will all be parceled out on some silly rank basis. He's a nice guy, but he's playing a game in a divided Church. The Church is not a conveyor belt.

Again, I'm on the outer circle. You ask if there's any politics. Not long ago, I applied to give a lecture at a major seminary. I never even got a call back. No one talks there unless he fits in. Look at some of those great men of years ago. They could give wonderful talks to the seminarians about priesthood, talks that would excite them about ministry. But they're not asked. Isn't that politics? Yes, there are lots of hurts and slights. It isn't pure and innocent.

A priest has got to make a decision on his ordination day that this will be his only ordination. If he doesn't, it will color his entire life. I've seen it. When we have get togethers for our class, some of the guys in special ministries just don't come. They only go to parties that are safe. They've cut themselves off.

The future? Oh, I'm a firm believer in not making up answers. But I will say this: I was part of a group of separated and divorced people who gathered in Milwaukee not long ago. They talked a great deal about pain, the pain of their marital breakups and the pain they experienced with the traditional Church.

"Jesus is bigger than the Church," I said to them. "Now, let's talk."

· 31 ·

Richard P. McBrien: Theologian *sans* Ivory Tower

Most theologians practice their craft in isolation, teaching small classes in seminar rooms, writing articles for learned journals, and books that will be checked out of university libraries fifty times in fifty years. Richard P. McBrien practices his profession the way Notre Dame plays its football—in the open field, under the critical gaze of millions.

McBrien is a consummate American Catholic—open, honest, hardworking. Had he opted for politics, he would likely be the Democratic Senator from Connecticut, his home state. (If McBrien has any reservations about becoming a priest, there are dozens of bishops who wish that he had chosen politics. He makes them uncomfortable. He tells them to stop facing the Vatican and start facing their people. One prelate said quietly: "Oh, I like him. But I wish he'd be more temperate.")

Richard McBrien, the Crowley-O'Brien-Walter professor of theology and chairman of the department at the University of Notre Dame, South Bend, Indiana, is an American of Irish-Italian heritage from the archdiocese of Hartford. He is the past president of the Catholic Theological Society of America, and in 1976 he received the society's John Courtney Murray Award "for distinguished achievement in theology." He may be the best known theologian in America, partly because he often serves as a commentator on the American Catholic Church for network television. He has an ability to make the complex clear. He can translate theological niceties into practical realities without talking or writing down to his audience.

McBrien remains an ardent supporter of Father Charles E. Curran but would not likely have gotten caught in Curran's bind—i.e. differences on minor aspects of moral theology. He has publicly supported Curran and thus incurred the Vatican's wrath. But no Curia official wants to take him on, at least publicly.

McBrien's curriculum vitae fills fifty-three pages. He uses two offices and considerable clerical backup to plot his schedule of appearances, classes, writings, etc. With over a dozen books and hundreds of articles, exclusive of his syndicated column which he has been writing for twenty-five years, he is a theological industry. His major work, *Catholicism*, earned him the 1980 Christopher Award and the 1981 Annual Book Award from the College Theology Society. Described as a "magnificent vision of theology in the post-Vatican II context," the reference and discussion book may be the prime resource of thousands of Catholic discussion groups.

McBrien holds an S.T.L. (1964) and S.T.D. (1967) from the Pontifical Gregorian University in Rome and has studied at the Pontifical Biblical Institute in Rome and the Harvard Divinity School in Cambridge, Massachusetts. He has taught and lectured at Harvard, Weston College, Yale, Cornell, Purdue, Wisconsin, and other universities, and is a former trustee of the Boston Theological Institute, the largest ecumenical consortium in the United States.

McBrien is one of the central figures in the dialogue about religion and public life. His book, *Caesar's Coin*, remains a classic study of religion and politics in America. It is a book made important not only because of what it says but because it unravels what others have said.

If Edward Schillebeeckx represents the modern Dutch theologian at his best, and Hans Kung or Karl Rahner represent the Swiss-German thinkers, then Richard P. McBrien is the epitome of the American theologian at work—unvarnished, unfiltered, unafraid.

McBrien was interviewed in the theology department office at Notre Dame.

N o, I would not become a priest today. If I had known what I know now about the priesthood, particularly the demands of obligatory celibacy, I would not have gone to the seminary. Now, don't misunderstand. I've enjoyed my priesthood. It has been an exciting and fulfilling life. I have no regrets. It is not unlike my decision to come here to Notre Dame. I'd give you the same answer. I came here in 1980 from Boston College. I'd rank Boston College as a strong, B+ university. They're very good. But Notre Dame is the major leagues and I experienced a big difference, especially in terms of administrative and financial support. My job was to reshape the Theology Department. There were lots of difficulties. If I knew then what I know now, I would not have come. I got great support from Ted Hesburgh and Tim O'Meara [Theodore M. Hesburgh, C.S.C., past president of Notre Dame, and Timothy O'Meara, provost of the University] but it was a rough decade. I'll be out as chairman at the end of this academic year (1991). It will be easier. Again, like the priesthood, I don't regret coming to Notre Dame, but if I had known what I would face here, I wouldn't have come.

I guess I would have gone into politics. I like politics. I've been a priest for twenty-nine years, since 1962. I'm from the Hartford, Connecticut, archdiocese but did my major seminary at St. John's in Brighton, Massachusetts. Bryan Hehir was just four years behind me. In fact, I may have helped him decide his vocation. One of the faculty asked me to speak with him. We talked during seminary summer camp and he decided to continue his studies for priesthood. I preached at his first Mass. I can't compare us. Bryan's specialties are ethics and international relations. He's a very bright guy, more traditional than I am. I'm not comfortable with comparisons like that. Let's just say that many of the bishops like me. My theology isn't radical. It's just that they may feel safer with Bryan. His spirituality is more traditional, and so is his way of relating to the institution.

You should be asking specific questions of those conservative priests who still view celibacy as the "jewel in the crown" or as "freeing them up to serve." That's nonsense. They're denying something. You show me a heterosexual priest of my generation who doesn't tell you that he has real problems with celibacy and I'll show you a man who is not telling the truth. You've got to ask them specific questions. You've got to say: "Haven't you been seriously troubled at one time or another?" Ask someone more liberal like me and we'll admit it. But these conservative guys will hide behind that "jewel in the crown" language.

Celibacy can work for some. You look at Ted Hesburgh. There is an extraordinary example of healthy sublimation. He has turned his religious vows into very, very positive activities. Ted is a healthy, blunt, honest person. Chances are, if celibacy were made optional, Ted wouldn't marry. He is a member of a religious order. But a healthy man like him would welcome optional celibacy for others. He would support men who chose to marry.

We have a right wing pontificate now. O.K. We all know that. But what is more ominous is that we have an American episcopacy and others who won't speak up for the people who are demoralized by the present state of affairs. Just look at the Charlie Curran situation [Reverend Charles E. Curran, highly regarded moral theologian, was dismissed from the faculty at Catholic University after a long and highly publicized case. He has since taught at the University of Southern California, Auburn University, and is now at Southern Methodist. Curran has written a book about the merits of academic freedom and the Vatican's working relationship to the theologian, especially as revealed by its handling of so-called dissenters (*Catholic Higher Education, Theology, and Academic Freedom*, University of Notre Dame Press).] After Curran left Catholic U., Catholic universities should have scrambled to get him. Instead, nothing. We need voices. We need people in this Church with voices like Charles Curran's—and mine—who are committed and yet willing to say: "This is not right!" Charlie Curran should have oodles of honorary degrees. But no. Instead, he is treated like Weakland at the bishops' meeting. [Archbishop Rembert Weakland, O.S.B., of Milwaukee was offered, then denied, an honorary degree by the University of Fribourg because of Vatican opposition]. In executive session, the bishops gave him an ovation; publicly, they said nothing. That's ominous.

Bernard Law [Cardinal Bernard F. Law, archbishop of Boston] is not the leader of the American bishops. Just look at the bishops' meeting a few years ago. He was nominated for about eight different positions and didn't get elected to a single one. He backed the Hunthausen decision and the bishops were sending him a message. No, he's a court bishop. Some bishops are theologically conservative but politically liberal. Law is both theologically and politically conservative. He's an army brat. His father was military. The Old Testament prophets would have cringed at the way he sees the Church. Sure, he probably has links with the White House. And I can understand why he enjoys the access he has to the President. Those connections are very seductive. However, I don't think that Law has made any deals with the White House to be silent on El Salvador, Nicaragua, Panama, and all that in exchange for White House support on pro-life issues. No, Law is just naturally that way.

O'Connor [Cardinal John J. O'Connor, archbishop of New York] is the number one bishop in the eyes of the Vatican. Sure, his style can be off-putting, but he's the single most influential American bishop in the eyes of Rome. In fact, his standing may have grown lately. In one sense, he's a living cliché. Did you see his comment on that German theologian's book [*Eunuchs for the Kingdom of Heaven*, by Uta Ranke-Heinemann, a critical examination of the Church's attitude toward women and sexuality]? O'Connor condemned the book while admitting that he had only read the book jacket's blurb. Talk about judging a book by its cover! Anyway, O'Connor represents the American Church at the Vatican. Boston and Chicago aren't seen as the major American sees in Rome. For them, it's New York.

But back to celibacy. Yes, if the pope changed the ground rules and made celibacy optional I would seriously consider exercising my option. (Laughs quietly.) It's just pathetic to see what is happening to some of our older priests. You know, in the old days, "Monsignor" McBrien would have remained a pastor until his death. Even if he could no longer distinguish the housekeeper from the senior curate, he'd never get kicked out. Now, they have terms of office and, in many dioceses, aren't even allowed to remain in their parish after retirement. Is this a sign of the kingdom? Shoved out to live alone; to stare at blank walls? The old sisters get better care and they deserve it. At least, they continue to live in community. Diocesan priests don't even have that.

Again, people who are sexually immature see all this as a matter of lust. It's not that. It's the friendship, the intimacy, and the mutual caring. You know, you could tell a lot about priests by the jokes of years ago. You could hear their stories of going to a family for dinner and finding the kids all over the place, making noise, interrupting, sometimes misbehaving. And after, when they drive away, the priests say: "Boy, thank God for celibacy!"

Do you hear it? They're reflecting the reality of celibacy. It isn't being free to serve. Celibacy is not caring. It's freedom from care! There is no understanding of the closeness and love these kids bring to a family or of the emotional support they will provide in the years ahead.

They talk about celibate priests being free to provide more effective service. Lay people don't believe that. That's baloney! It's a slur on ministers and rabbis. If celibacy were all that crucial and beneficial, we would not have a Martin Marty [Martin E. Marty, Lutheran theologian, church historian, professor at University of Chicago Divinity School]. Look at him. He's been married twice. He lost his first wife and is now married again. He married wonderful women. And he has academically and ministerially outproduced us all!

Celibacy is one of the most serious problems facing the American Church today. It is keeping good, heterosexual males from the priesthood. It has increased the number of gays who are entering the seminary. But perhaps far more problematic, it has created a lot of priests who are sexually neutral. It sends a negative message to the rest of the world, a message that says that sexual intimacy and marriage somehow detract from one's relationship with God. It says that the ideal form of life is one that is lived without intimacy.

Why is it so important for priests to be unmarried? Obligatory celibacy is unhealthy. It can even be destructive. It forces healthy men to live in unhealthy ways. We American priests try to keep the rules. In Latin America and Africa, celibacy isn't universally observed. People know that the parish priest is living with a woman. They know he has children. They consider it more acceptable than if he lived alone. The Vatican knows this and accepts it. They play the game. And people, especially bishops, in this country help them to play the game. We give those canned answers about that "jewel of celibacy." You don't get canned answers from me. If you really used a can opener on those priests who give canned answers, you'd get different responses. Priests are normal people and normal people should be allowed to marry. Obligatory celibacy has no theological status; it's an aberration, an abomination, and the single most important reason why we have a vocation crisis today.

Abandoning mandatory celibacy is very threatening to many in the Church, more than any other reform measure. It goes to the heart of the very life-style of the clergy. Optional celibacy would blow the cover of some of our homosexual priests. Presently, the celibacy discipline affects only heterosexuals. If two gay priests go to a conference and share a hotel room, the bishop praises them for saving money. But if a heterosexual priest shared a room with a woman! Ha!

Authority is another major problem. The Catholic Church is now behind the Soviet Union. It's authoritarian. It still names all its bishops in secret. It still votes in small groups, when it votes at all. It still has one man who rules unquestioned.

Why should you enter a profession where you can't get ahead on merit? Look at Wellstone in Minnesota [Senator Paul David Wellstone, a Democrat from Minnesota defeated incumbent Republican Rudy Boschwitz in an upset election]. That would never happen in the Church. A Wellstone would *never* be a bishop. If you choose a career elsewhere, you might have a chance to advance, but not in the Church. Independents are simply not picked.

John Paul II's pontificate is reminiscent of Pius X's (1903-14). Power is too often exercised aggressively and punitively. You know, the Italians value the *bella figura*, a way of making things look good. Take the Hunthausen case. If an Italian pope such as a Paul VI wanted to send a message, he would have brought Hunthausen to Rome, made him a cardinal, and given him a meaningless job in the Curia. Not this pontificate. Hunthausen was publicly humiliated. It's an example of the *brutta figura* versus the *bella figura*. Denying the honorary degree to Weakland [Rembert Weakland, O.S.B., archbishop of Milwaukee] is another example. An earlier Vatican administration would have let the degree go through, then quietly called the University and told them not to do it again. Not this pontificate. It acts brutally as in *brutta figura*. That's very counter-productive. And, unlike Reagan's, a papal term doesn't end after eight years. We are already in the thirteenth year of this pontificate.

At some point in the future, the Church will need a *perestroika* (restructuring). It has got to come. My sense is that the next pope is going to have to be a realist, a man who knows that the Church cannot continue on its present course. He's going to have to be a Gorbachev, one who will acknowledge the need to restructure the Church. Mandatory celibacy will have to go. The appointment of bishops must change. The next pope will have to be a charismatic figure, inviting dialogue and consensus, not one who dictates all decisions.

Perhaps the unhealthiest thing is that the extreme right wing has not been kept in check. Just look at Opus Dei. Paul VI tolerated them. I agree with that. They should be permitted to express their views. Paul let them in the yard; he let them bark and didn't call the dogcatcher. But he didn't let them in the house. Now, Opus Dei and other ultra right-wing groups are in the house. That's ominous.

If I have a ministry today apart from my academic work, it is to keep the light of hope burning for those who are discouraged. Again, I've been a priest for twenty-nine years and a theologian for twenty-five years, teaching, writing books and articles, and doing a weekly column. In all that time, I have *never* had anyone come to me or write me in order to say: "Thank you for giving me the courage to leave the Church." But thousands have come to me and written to me and thanked me for keeping them *in* the Church. I'm very proud of that. It's my ministry.

Yes, I've been threatened. But, theologically, they can't get anything on me. My book *Catholicism* (a synthesis of the Catholic tradition) is squeaky clean. It's very middle-of-the-road. It was referred to the bishops' Committee on Doctrine because of some questions, but, well before I appeared before them, many of the changes had been made. Bill McManus [William E. McManus, former bishop of Fort Wayne-South Bend] and I had worked on the revisions. I agreed completely with him. The book didn't get an imprimatur but it didn't need one. If bishops wanted to get me on the grounds of orthodoxy, they just couldn't come up with the evidence. Besides, many of the bishops like me. The issue wasn't doctrine. It was authority.

No, I don't say Mass every day. I don't see the Mass as a priest's private devotion or as something to be celebrated on every conceivable occasion. It's not a clerical preserve, not a priests' thing. It should not be celebrated to reaffirm the power that we have. It's a public celebration. It's the Church's act of worship.

I'm not the big guru here on campus. I teach only one undergraduate class and that's got 150 students in it. There might be a waiting list, but I'm unaware of it. I'm more aware of my graduate ecclesiology class. That's coming up next semester and already has thirty-five in it, not counting some priests and religious.

I like teaching. Theology has made me happy. I'm not a theological policeman. Theology should help people. I teach people that God is a forgiving God. I try to save them from an angry God who, in reality, is the God of angry people. My God is not the God of the scribes and pharisees. I try to tell people that they can be good Catholics *and* be critical of their Church.

Again, I don't regret having been ordained, but I would not commit myself to this life again unless some things were to change, like obligatory celibacy. I have ability, creativity, and imagination in an organization that doesn't value those qualities. But I keep telling the people how the magician does his tricks and they don't like it.

↜∾ INTERLUDE V ↜∾

"You have to be nuts to go into the priesthood. It's an awful job. The pay is terrible, the hours are worse. People not only don't look up to you, they look down. You have to love God, and if you don't, it will grind you up. Remember, no trumpets will sound and you're going to spend more time being a carpenter than a priest. . . . I had another thought: this Church would have gotten a lot further if Christ had chosen twelve women as his disciples."

> Father Joe Greer, pastor, St. Patrick's,
> Natick, Massachusetts, cited in Paul
> Wilkes's book *In Mysterious Ways*.

What's happening? What are we doing to ourselves? We're getting advice from big bankers and doing management studies and we're hiring public relations firms. No wonder the priests' morale is gone. No one listens to us. Why can't we just sit down and make these decisions ourselves?

> Older priest, at the curb
> after Sunday Mass.

The class had gathered each year for over forty years. They took turns. This year it was at Matt's parish. Mass and dinner was a tradition for these men. Some knew that it shouldn't be. Eucharistic celebrations are not the property of the clergy, but old habits are hard to break.

Everyone was invited, including Jim, who had resigned from the active ministry over twenty years before, but who rarely missed a class reunion. Jim was a daily communicant who prayed his breviary every day.

The class included two bishops. They concelebrated. Jim was the only one in the congregation.

At the Canon, Matt looked down at Jim, kneeling alone in the large church, his classmates in a semicircle around the altar. He whispered something to one of the bishops.

"Come up, Jim. Come up and join us," Matt said.

The pastor was the scourge of the diocese. He had come from a family with connections. There was a brother who worked for the mayor and an uncle that had been an early chancellor. Very thin credentials, but years ago, such thin-sliced ham counted.

He couldn't keep a curate. They lasted about a year and then pleaded for reassignment on the grounds of conscience. (Allegedly, one man had whispered to the bishop that he was attracted to the cook, a rhinoceros, just to get out.) The pastor created his own reality, boasting that young men were sent to him for "training."

But Steve was no trainee. His oils had dried up years ago. He was the oldest curate in the diocese; no parish was decayed enough to merit his appointment as pastor.

The night Steve arrived, the pastor took his place at the head of the table and, as always, his dog sat just to his right, not on the floor but in one of the nicely carved chairs that had been donated by the pastor's affluent family.

The pastor carved the roast, placing a choice end piece on the dog's plate, then his own, and, finally, Steve's.

Steve fixed his plate, rose and walked toward the kitchen. "If that dog is sitting there tomorrow night, I'm gonna shoot the sonovabitch," he said as he carried his plate to the kitchen table where the rhinoceros was eating.

The next night, the pastor took his seat and, with some ceremony, carefully seated the dog. Steve rose without ceremony, pulled a gun and shot the dog in the head.

First, the pastor voided. Then, he ran to the phone to call the bishop.

"His excellency cannot come to the phone now," his clerical secretary said. "He's at supper."

"There's been a shooting," the pastor wailed. The bishop was on the phone in under a minute.

"No, Bishop, it wasn't a priest. It's my dog. Father Steve shot my dog!"

"It's a wonder he didn't shoot you," the bishop said.

(The pastor never got another associate or another dog. He died a few years later and lies buried with his wealthy family. Steve was traded to another diocese out West, where, at last report, he was chaplain to an unsavory union local. Several priests verified this story; one resigned priest said it is nothing more than clerical lore.)

· 32 ·

William E. McManus: Retired Bishop

Bishop McManus's rented retirement home is indistinguishable from others on the block. It is a modest ranch house on a wide suburban street in Mount Prospect, Illinois. It could be the house of a widower. There are even "family" pictures of what could be children and grandchildren. (They are, in fact, pictures of single mothers and their children, whom the bishop calls "my support group." In some strange way, the grouping of color photos of mothers and children brought to mind the bishop of Victor Hugo's *Les Misérables*.)

Bishop McManus dresses in casual clothes, the kind countless grand-fathers wear when puttering around the house or yard. There is no episcopal ring; when he does wear it, it is barely distinguishable from a layman's wedding ring. The crosier and miter are neatly stored in a closet with an incongruous box of diapers for the children who come.

His furnishings are functional, anything but elaborate. There is the mandatory clerical La-Z-Boy with the formica sidetable for breviary, magazines, books, and mail. It's diagonally across from a portable televi-sion set, with its wires curling under it. The art work is modest; he could have used some help in hanging the pictures. But it's a comfortable place. The hall closet has only a coat or two in it. Some clerics have summer homes that are far more elaborate.

Bishop McManus was born in 1914; entered Chicago's high-school seminary in 1928, and was ordained in 1939. Cardinal Samuel Stritch sent him to Catholic University in Washington, D.C., for graduate study, together with now Monsignors George Higgins and Daniel Cantwell. He later returned to Washington where he spent eleven years in the education department of the National Conference of Catholic Bishops. Back in Chicago, he was appointed archdiocesan superintend-ent of schools. He presided over an unprecedented expansion of Catho-lic schools that made the archdiocesan school system the third largest school system in America with over four hundred elementary and ninety-eight secondary schools.

In 1967, he was named an auxiliary bishop of Chicago while retaining the superintendent's job and being named a pastor. Nine years later, he was named Bishop of Fort Wayne-South Bend, then a diocese of over 140,000 Catholics in an area that is 14 percent Catholic. He was there for nine years when, as he puts it, "a much improved heart condition" inspired an early retirement in 1985 at seventy-one. His motto: "Leave while you can walk out."

Bishop McManus has been described by one bishop watcher as "one of the brightest bishops in the country." He is not the plodding intellectual; his mind is more lawyerly. He would have made a successful politician, a U.S. Senator. But he is also a dreamer, a highly imaginative thinker, unafraid to take risks. Indeed, it is this side of him that has inspired any criticism he has had to endure. He can be tenacious in combat, but he never holds a grudge. He is not a bishop that ever felt the need to be protected by his staff. "To be a good priest," one observer wrote, "you must first be a man. Then, a Christian, and, after that, a priest." William McManus fits that definition.

I like this house. I wanted a ranch-style house like I had in Fort Wayne. When I went to Fort Wayne in 1976, I found myself in an enormous old mansion. It had nine bathrooms! When winter came, the place was freezing; in some rooms, there was only a little heat. One winter night, I telephoned the man who looked after diocesan properties; he advised me to flush all the toilets so that the pipes wouldn't freeze. Well, that did it! I didn't become the bishop of Fort Wayne-South Bend in order to go around flushing toilets all winter. (Laughs.) So, I learned of the availability of a ranch house; made a deal and moved in. I lived there until I retired in 1985.

When I returned to Chicago, I wanted to live in a similar home. So, I put an ad in the paper saying: "Retired priest wants to rent modest ranch." This place is perfect for me. "You're a good tenant," my landlord tells me. This house is near my sister's place. It's near St. Raymond's, a parish in which I am a registered parishioner. I say Mass there every day that I'm here. They're very kind to me. There's always a Mass server assigned. The neighbors are wonderful. The kids are wonderful. I've had a few of them help me with the housework. They're beautiful! They are so fresh and bright! They give me energy. The young helper I have now is just over thirteen. We negotiate everything. If she does the kitchen right, I pay her so much; if she does another job, she earns more. I have to get after her occasionally, but she is so resilient!

When my ordination classmates come here for lunch, there isn't much drinking at all; most of us have given it up. We just get right down to eating and talk about each other's health. (Laughs.) No politics! I may be too liberal for some of them. (Laughs.) We all talk. Joe Kelly is the best talker. His stories are wonderful.

But let's get down to work; we can talk about all that later. I've got a good dinner prepared, including some salmon I caught up in Alaska when I visited with Frank Hurley [archbishop of Anchorage]. He's one of my best friends. I'll tell you about him.

Last Priests in America? That's an awful title! When the book comes out I'm going to review it and give it a bad review!

Let me tell you something. Since I have retired, there have been days when I've spent an hour to two on the phone in search of a place to say a scheduled Mass. I make call after call, and I'm politely told that all the Masses were covered. Oh, yes, they'll welcome me, but it simply means that one of the priests doesn't have to binate [preside at two Masses.] We still have over 53,000 priests in the United States and just over 19,000 parishes. I maintain that, allowing for the fact that priests, particularly on Sunday, can say more than one Mass, we still have more priests available to say Mass than we have Masses said each Sunday.

Sure, there's a problem. We do need more priests, but presently the problem is distribution. I'm aware of the pattern that has developed—aging priests, retirements, deaths, resignations, shortage of young men coming in. And if there is no radical turnaround, we'll be desperately short. But, right now, we're not facing the problem squarely. At the conference [National Conference of Catholic Bishops], there's a standing committee on distribution of priests. I don't think it's met in ten years. In fact, there are four committees of the conference that deal with priesthood. There are vocations, priestly life and ministry, formation, and distribution, all still acting independently. They need to get together. They need to do some planning.

When I was ordained in 1939, I was required to sign an agreement that, for a period of five years, I could be sent outside the diocese, anywhere the bishop wanted me to go. That was the custom for years. The idea was to share priests when and where needed. The system wasn't used, but it was in place.

I'm not close to all that data anymore, but it would seem to me that there are enough priests available to provide Sunday Eucharist in all existing viable parishes. I just haven't seen any analyzed data on the distribution of priests that could make this a reality.

Now, I don't think that the celebration of the Eucharist is the sole measure for determining the need for priests.

When I intervened against a bishops' conference resolution for the approval of the proposed ritual for Sunday Eucharistic rituals in the absence of the priest, I may have sounded as if I were completely against it. I wasn't. I simply wanted the ritual to be available to those who needed it, but I opposed having it become a standard procedure in many parishes. I feared that the bishops' formal approval of this ritual might give priests the blues, making them feel dispensable—nice to have around but not necessarily needed. I also was afraid that formal approval of the ritual might demoralize the laity by leaving them priestless even though what they wanted most is to have a priest celebrate their Sunday liturgy. In discussing this matter, I used the term "priestless liturgy." I didn't coin the term; it's widely used. My good friend, the archbishop of Anchorage, Alaska, Frank Hurley, has asked me never to speak of a liturgy without a priest as being a priestless liturgy.

Let me explain:

This past summer, I went to Alaska for a vacation and stayed with Archbishop Hurley. He gently berated me for my public use of the word "priestless" during the NCCB meeting. Frank is a real frontier bishop. He's been in Alaska for twenty-one years; for him, the clergy shortage is real. He has had to be innovative. He sent me to Cordova as a supply priest for a weekend. He's got five parishes with full-time parish administrators, all of them completely qualified for all phases of parish ministry, except the administration of the sacraments, which require an ordained priest. No resident priest, but in each of the parishes, the Eucharist is the center of the parish's worship and devotion.

Once or twice a month, over a weekend, an ordained priest celebrates the Eucharist. It's a big event, prayerfully anticipated, faithfully continued.

I met Sister Peggy Glynn, a Sinsinawa Dominican, in Cordova. It's an isolated village, a six-hour ferry trip from Valdez. It's on Prince William Sound, one of the fishing areas. Her parish has two hundred Catholics, fifty of them active. The others aren't really alienated; they're just slow to come around, and people like Peggy are more patient than priests. She loves the outdoors and, where the sisters used to carry a rosary, she now carries a .22 pistol! She needs it to scare off the bears.

Now, she devotes at least an hour a day to working on her Sunday sermon. When the priest comes to the parish and baptizes a child, he presents the child to Sister Peggy and she presents it to the community and then places the baby in its mother's arms. She presents the child to the community. Now, that's priestly!

To call these situations "priestless" is a gross misnomer. It denigrates the supreme priesthood of Jesus Christ; it glosses a doctrine, emphasized by Vatican II, that baptized Christians play an active role in the Risen Lord's priesthood; it rejects the extremely important fact that these parish administrators, like Sister Peggy, have a vocation, one they have accepted, to assume a leadership role with all the dedication and self-sacrifice required of priests. In my mind, these parishes are extraordinarily priestly.

I feel about vocations to the priesthood as I do about fund-raising. We must exhaust all remedies before we close schools or parishes. Back in South Bend there are two parishes, St. Patrick's and St. Hedwig's, staring at each other across the street, as I used to say. They're both ethnic and in a changed neighborhood that isn't served that much by either of them. It would be far more efficient to close one of them, but for now they are meeting their needs. My predecessor should have closed one of them; I should have closed one of them, but I didn't, and now my successor may have to make that decision. But, for now, as long as they are making their way, perhaps there isn't a need to close one of them.

It's much the same with vocations. We haven't examined all the remedies. There are alternatives that deserve at least a glance. We need to consider the ordination of married men and the ordination of women. Just now, I think just a few of my fellow bishops support me in this. I can't read the minds of the others.

I have no great quarrel with the statistics about priesthood that have been generated, but I think we are all just guessing. I would like to see some experimentation. Take two parishes, for example—one with a celibate priest, one with a priest who has a wife and children. Let's watch them a while. See how people respond. Among Protestant ministers, for example, I believe that they have found that marriage can become a two-edged sword, both a help and a burden.

I believe that the American Church's leadership appreciates the desire of the laity for full eucharistic celebration. Even though attendance at Mass has dropped, respect and love for the Eucharist still continues. I believe that many who are away from the Church would return, if we made some modifications. I believe strongly that we must retain the Eucharist as a central value in our program of worship. There is no substitute for it, no novena, no service, no partial liturgy. The lurking danger in this trend away from full eucharistic celebration is that the substitute may become more attractive, particularly here in the U.S. where people go for novelty. Believe me, I lived through that novena period in the Church and I saw how it captured the attention of thousands.

I learned something about all this while giving a retreat to priests in Superior, Wisconsin. I was giving a fairly routine talk when I noted the expressions on the faces of many of the priests. I wasn't reaching them. I broke away as soon as I could and asked them to join me for a bull session. There I was, talking to them about their celibacy, instead of talking to them about their real concerns—the dwindling number of ordained priests, no foreseeable hope of having enough priests for all parishes. "Not our celibacy but celibacy itself," they said. "This is the problem the bishops ought to address." That's what they were interested in.

The Mass is the distinction between us and Protestant worship. We are losing something that we've had for centuries. Our people, coming to this country, hardly had their feet dry before they built a church. That's how strong the Eucharist was in their lives.

We need to take a good, clear, long look at distribution of priests. We need to see where the priests are situated. They need to be in places where they can fulfill a set of priorities for their ministry. When the day comes when Chicago is like Anchorage, Alaska, or New Ulm, Minnesota, one with a priest shortage already and the other facing one, then we should bring in lay people we have been preparing and use them for Sunday services between full eucharistic celebrations. That day is far off, I hope.

You know, we are an auto culture. We have good highways. Our parochialism is so dominant that it has become almost irrational. People will often drive five or ten miles after Sunday Mass for brunch, but get upset if they have to drive the same distance to the Mass itself.

In the United States as a whole and dioceses in particular, we simply haven't restructured. This is the twentieth century and there are roads and shifting populations. I know it isn't easy. Look at the hysteria around Chicago when the church closings were announced last year. There were deep-seated attachments. But we have to look at the situation.

The worst thing in my judgment is to call in some management company to tell us how to do this. You just can't let everything go like that. I recall that when I was at the NCCB, they brought in Booz, Allen, and Hamilton to restructure the place. I had worked there eleven years for its predecessor, the National Catholic Welfare Council, and I had lots of ideas. But when I tried to tell their representative some of my views about the nature of Christianity, I was told, "Oh, we never get into that."

I believe that we still need to pursue a think-tank concept. The Church needs fresh ideas. Dullness is one of our worst miseries. I'm retired, but we retired bishops can still speak and I exercise my option every time!

I guess I became an expert on giving to the Church when I did the book with Andrew Greeley [*Catholic Contributions*, Thomas More Press, Chicago]. Andy is controversial, I guess, but that has not been my experience with him. His hand of friendship has always been longer than mine. He has responded to any request I have ever made of him for any kind of help. He has invited me to celebrations and to his home where we have discussed often controversial matters just for the pleasure of it. He finds me reasonable and outspoken, I guess. In his autobiography, he called me one of the best bishops in the country. That's not true. He's been called a bishop basher. But he should be bashing me. I hold him in high esteem. His social science research is good and sound and his data *are* very important. I've learned *never* to question his data. With Andy, you'd be better off questioning his morals or his faith. Just don't question his data! (Laughs.) And, I've seen an impressive collection of letters in his "Mailbox Parish" that reveal that a good number of people have found their way back to the Church because of his writings. We don't see much of each other, but I count him as a friend, and I must point particularly to his research on Catholic contributions. He's on target. Read the book.

Raising more and more money each year can involve a great deal of pastoral pain, but the money is there. I think that the gross income of the people of this parish, for example, is over $120 million each year. They do give over a million to the parish and school, and that's not bad, but it's less than 1 percent of the gross income of the parish. I believe that Catholics can support the churches and the schools and that we can pay our people decent wages. We have to make justice our paramount virtue; we must pay what we owe, including just wages. If there is anything missing in the Church today, it's a sense of justice.

We need to go after the freeloaders. You know, in a large parish like St. Raymond's, there may be a thousand registered households that give nothing. We must find ways to get them to give. We keep talking about evangelization, getting the people into church. I believe that if we can get them giving, they will come to church. Again, it's that business of the heart being where the treasure is. If they give, they'll come around.

I think we must keep spending until we're broke; then we stop, but that's very rare. We've got to stop the emphasis on *post factum* financial reports in the parishes. We must tell the people not what we have spent but how we plan to spend the money. Show them budgets, not reports. Then, if we're spending it right, we can get their interest and their contributions. We need to give them optional ways of giving, everything from the traditional weekly envelopes to credit cards.

I'm a Chicago boy, born and raised in Oak Park. I entered Quigley High School Seminary in 1928, right out of Ascension Grammar School. Then I went to the Seminary of St. Mary of the Lake in Mundelein, Illinois. In those years, the seminary system was shot through with politics and rackets. The common question among the seminarians was how you rated. There was pressure to conform from the very first day. "Look good," was the guideline. Privileges were based on looking good. The immaturity was appalling. Do what you were told; learn only what you were taught. In the major seminary, I was isolated from my family who were suffering from the Depression. Families were treated horribly. Expected to visit at inconvenient hours, to make that long trip up to Mundelein, to sit in a big room for ninety minutes, without so much as a drink of water offered to them. The rector would pace up and down the room, watching to make sure that no contraband such as magazines were passed. All packages were put on a table, subject to inspection before we got them. I still seethe at the way the families were treated. There was only the slightest difference between the seminary at that time and

Statesville Prison. At 3:00 o'clock, the parents were told to go and we went off to Vespers. It was cruel. I guess you can still hear it in my voice. After over fifty-five years, the anger and the hurt remain.

After three years in the major seminary, we went to the Villa up in Clearwater Lake, Wisconsin. It was a vacation place for the seminarians. There, thanks mostly to the men in the class of 1936, I had my first experience with a democratic way of life. Those men tried to be a real brother to me; they gave me a sense of my own dignity. Two years later, when I was the class leader and in charge at the Villa, I tried to follow their example. The experience of those men in the 1936 class came in handy. The worst assignments were often given to the class duds. I had a chance to take some of those assignments myself when I was in charge.

Reynie Hillenbrand [Monsignor Reynald Hillenbrand, rector of St. Mary of the Lake Seminary, 1936-44] came in as rector in 1936. I was thrilled by his attitude, his courage, and his vision for a decent world, influenced by the Gospel. It still hadn't changed much on the outside. There were good guys out there who didn't think much of Hilly and his system. Reynie wasn't liked for what he did. But he told us before we left the seminary after ordination: "Even if you can't do anything in your parishes, keep on thinking."

I have loved my priesthood; I still do. But I think that the seminary system never let me acquire a good understanding of the support system for priests so necessary today. They didn't prepare us for the full use of our talents. I was so glad to be free of the place that, even years later, as a bishop, I thought that I had done my duty by simply telling my priests that they were free to develop their talents. "You're free!" I told them. That didn't encourage them. They hadn't come from such a structured past. I didn't realize that they were looking for support. I should have visited them more and asked how they were doing.

You know, I love my present life because it isn't organized. All my life, everything was organized. There are just over a hundred retired bishops. We're all up there in years. I don't see much of them and I have no desire to organize them! (Laughs.) We can step aside at seventy-five; I retired a little earlier. I'm all chemicals. I have to take those beta blockers. They give me nightmares, but they keep the heart going. I often wake in a cold sweat, but then I can go back to sleep and when I awake in the morning, I just say, "Thank God!"

Those pictures are my new family. They are single mothers. I'm a friend to all twelve of them. I've managed to do a little for them. We've even had two marriages. They're just wonderful. My main goal is to give friendship, not money. Again, what I love most is the lack of organization, but we do have one rule: no credit cards! I lend them what they need, and I've never lost a cent. I try to teach them to be fiscally responsible. They come here with their children and we talk. I try to offer friendship. That's very important. I was so lucky with this house. There are swings in the backyard, so the kids can play there. And having twelve of my own gives me credibility with others who volunteer. I also collect clothes for Marillac House [a Chicago inner city agency, conducted by the Daughters of Charity]. I search the newspapers in the morning for sales. Then I go over to K Mart or another of those discount stores and I grab boxes of diapers and anything else on sale. I insist on a 40 percent discount, plus my senior citizen discount! It's wonderful! I love it! When the summer clothes go on the counter, I try to buy the leftover winter clothes.

For the rest, I keep busy. I'm asked to do a few Confirmations. I help out with Masses when I'm asked. Oh sure, I get asked to give an invocation at a banquet down at the Drake Hotel for a group of cement manufacturers or something like that. But I don't mind at all. It gets me out of the house; I meet good people, have a good time, get a free meal, and come home with a few bucks in my pocket that I can use for the poor.

I still get to meetings of the bishops. We retired bishops can have our say and I exercise my option.

Not long before I retired, I made my last *ad limina* visit to Rome. First, I saw the pope alone. When I went into his study, he had a large U.S. map on his desk. His finger was on Fort Worth, Texas. I moved it to Fort Wayne. "McManus," I said to him. "Fort Wayne-South Bend." Then, I added "Notre Dame." "Ah, Notre Dame," he said. "Notre Dame. Do the students go to Mass?" he asked. I assured him that, at Notre Dame, there were some twenty-nine Masses every weekend and that 80 percent went to Mass regularly. "Eighty percent? Eighty percent! That's good," he said. "That's good."

Later, we shared a meal with him. I figured that this was my last visit, so I ignored the nervous protocol people and sat directly across from him. He looked at me, pointed his finger, smiled and said: "Ah, eighty percent!"

Now, this interview is over. I'll get dinner. Wait until you taste the salmon I caught. . . .

Peter B. McQuinn: Seminarian

Peter McQuinn was interviewed in the rectory at St. Mark's Parish in Chicago. He was still so new to the parish that the volunteer from the St. Vincent de Paul Society knew him only as "the new priest." Peter had met the rectory cook who was already breaking him in. "You don't have to carry your laundry all the way back to the seminary, Father," she said with her Mexican accent. "You can do it here. We have machines. And, after you are ordained, Father, I will do your laundry."

Peter McQuinn just smiled and took the laundry to his car, which he had just bought. He would drop the laundry at his mother's if his new car would get him there. The two-door Oldsmobile cost $1,000. It made a lot of noise, but a "gear-headed" friend of his father's had assured him that it would run well. (The night before the interview, the police had stopped him because his car still lacked plates. As he tried to explain to the police that he had just purchased the car, it rolled backwards, striking the police car. McQuinn can talk. His Irish face exudes sincerity. They let him go.)

St. Mark's Church is in the heart of Chicago's Latino neighborhood. Founded in 1894, it has seen Irish, Germans, Poles, Bohemians, Italians, and Hungarians. It is a parochial Ellis Island. Since the early sixties, it has become almost completely Latino.

St. Mark's was lucky to get an associate pastor. The number of priests is declining steadily because of death, resignations, and retirements. Statistically, a megaparish of 10,000 parishioners will produce only one priest every six years. Less than one-fourth of 1 percent of Catholic males become priests, and that figure is dwindling.

According to the Washington-based Center for Applied Research in the Apostolate, for the sixth straight year the number of U.S. Catholic seminarians has dropped at all levels. The figures suggest that the pattern will continue for at least a few more years. Hoge's research states that the vocation shortage is long-term, not just temporary. His studies have demonstrated that the social pressures causing the downturn in vocations are pervasive and strong and that the Church is powerless to correct them.

Hoge views the shortage of priestly vocations as an institutional problem that can be solved through institutional measures. The greatest single change would be to permit optional celibacy. The introduction of this one change alone would result in a surplus of priests by the turn of the century.

At the start of 1990-91 school year, there were 7,523 seminarians, down 871 or 10.4 percent from the previous year. The new figures represent a 15.4 percent decline over the past two years and a drop of more than 43 percent since 1979-80, when there were 13,253 seminarians in the United States. In theology, the traditional final four years before ordination, the number of seminarians dropped from 3,698 in 1989-90 to 3,609 in the 1990-91 school year, a loss of 89 or 2.4 percent. The number of college seminarians dropped by 8 percent in 1990-91 and the drop in the past two years has been 15 percent. The biggest drop was in the high school seminaries with a loss of 28 percent.

In Peter McQuinn's 1991 ordination class of fifteen, only two had graduated from the seminary high school and only six from the college-level program. Seminary recruitment programs do not seem to be working. Certainly, their success ratio is far out of proportion to the amount of money and human effort expended. The number of seminarians remains woefully short of the number needed. The research clearly shows that a core of ordained, full-time priests is still necessary in the Church; but there is no evidence that the Church will act on its own research. Indeed, the bishops appear to be growing more defensive, issuing statements that proclaim that youth lacks generosity and that the research ignores the influence of the Holy Spirit. Neither statement addresses the issue. The institutional Church will continue to spend enormous amounts to maintain a seminary system that educates only a fraction of the priests it needs. The attrition rate remains high. The Church continues to speak of involvement of the laity in ministry but spends only a fraction of its budget to educate lay ministers, who far outnumber the seminarians. Without dramatic changes, the result may be a diminishing corps of aging priests attempting to preside over a growing corps of willing but poorly educated laity. Clearly, something has to give.

Peter McQuinn has heard all this. He is a good listener. He listens well but is impatient with all the rhetoric on each side of the issue. When he responds, he grows animated. His curly hair waves and his hands move as he makes his points. But he has an internalized serenity that seems to balance his feelings. He just wants to be a priest and to preach the Gospel. "I'm not concerned about my living conditions, or vestments and all that," he said. "Don't we dream anymore? Don't we put any stock in the Man who was murdered?"

I wanted a chalice made of wood. I saw the one your wife made for Matt Thibeau. My mother tracked her down through the parish. I just wanted a plain chalice with a gold-plated lining in the bowl. Yeah, I suppose it does have something to do with the time when the Church had men of gold and chalices of wood. But, mostly, I just wanted a simple chalice.

My folks are immigrant Irish. They came over from County Kerry in the mid-fifties. My father had a sister here; someone in my mother's family had a ticket and wasn't going to use it. Mom didn't want to waste it. So, she took it and came over. They met and married here. Dad is an operating engineer; Mom works in our parish. I've got three brothers, two older, one younger. They're all in the area. My folks still have a load of relatives back in Ireland. Some are coming over for the ordination. My parents are making an awful lot of the ordination. I just want to get it over with and get down to the priesthood.

I grew up in St. William's in Chicago and, later, St. Celestine's in Elmwood Park. After grammar school, I wanted to go to Quigley [seminary high school], but the pastor said no; so I went to Holy Cross High School, which was just a few blocks away. High school didn't work out all that well for me. My closest friends were at Quigley and I wanted to be a priest even in high school.

My priesthood started early for me. My brothers and I were servers; we had young priests in the parish whom we could talk to. One of my brothers is a musician. He had a guitar band that played a lot in the parish. We shared a lot with other parishes and I was very involved. I liked priesthood; I liked what they did. I think I've always wanted to be a priest.

I entered Loyola-Niles [college seminary] in 1983. I spent one of the college seminary years at Loyola's Rome Center with about seven other guys from the seminary. Rome was a great experience for me—not the Church part, but rather the travel and other experiences.

I graduated from college in 1987 and entered Mundelein [seminary of the University of St. Mary of the Lake). I have been there four years and I'll be ordained on May 18, 1991. I can't say that Mundelein was a great experience for me. What sustained me was that I was getting out soon. A lot of good guys there, on the faculty and among the students, but I tried to spend as little time as possible there. I just wanted to be in a parish, especially a Latino parish.

I think that the collaborative model you mentioned is the norm in the seminary. There are a few seminarians who are ambitious, who follow the careerist model, but not many. A lot of seminarians still follow the guild model, that is, they are loyal to each other and to the profession. I guess I'm part guild and part collaborative model.

Yeah, I suppose we are like cops in some way. I guess we develop a little of the cop mentality. We have to do a lot of troubleshooting. We are expected to maintain order, to lay down the law, at least part of the time. So, perhaps that is why we sometimes think like cops. As a matter of fact, if I hadn't become a priest, I would have gone on the police force.

I think that there is a growing awareness of the collaborative model. We have been taught in the seminary to be more sensitive to the development of unity with the laity. It's brought up all the time. We have to be more interactive, especially with regard to women. There is a real effort to use inclusive language. The majority of the seminarians would not oppose the ordination of women, but they support it with the conviction that it will never happen anyway.

There are fifteen for Chicago in my class; thirteen of us will go into parishes, two others will stay for another year to do a S.T.L. [Licentiate in Sacred Theology]. There are twenty-nine others from other dioceses. There are guys from Salina, Kansas; Tulsa, Oklahoma; Lexington, Kentucky; Omaha, Nebraska; Green Bay, Wisconsin; Memphis, Tennessee; Indianapolis, Indiana; St. Joseph, Missouri; Springfield and Belleville, Illinois; Billings, Montana; Orlando, Florida; and other places I can't remember. The guys from other places are different. They are more conservative. It's not that they're overly ambitious, but many of them are going to be pastors in less than three years. The Chicago guys are seen as too casual, too quick to leave the seminary, not as serious as the others.

I think that seminarians may be more conservative than in recent years. There seems to be a feeling that, after Vatican II, some things were done too hastily. I'm sensing a slight shift back, especially in the area of liturgy and devotions. Some of the seminarians come from the Bible Belt where the only difference between the Catholic Church and other churches is the liturgies and the devotions. I've found myself in the poor and Latino parishes; there is a real call for devotions. We mustn't neglect the things that mean much to the people.

There is a great emphasis on spiritual development in the seminary, and that's very important. We can't kid ourselves; we can't believe that something else, like working with kids, is going to substitute for a deep, personal prayer life. I think that they tried real hard to help us to develop a good personal spirituality.

There is still a lot of hope among the seminarians. They want to preach the Gospel. We look among ourselves for someone we can talk to and we ask that person to check us out. It isn't easy. Guys are still leaving the seminary. It's hard to find someone you can really talk to. But I've found a few guys I can say anything to. We've made an agreement: if any one of us is acting like a jerk, we'll confront each other. We'll remind each other that all we really wanted was to preach the Gospel.

Most of us come from middle class homes. Some, like myself, have old-country parents who bring a lot of values with them. For them, life is simple. You simply live it. It's kind of like that Bo Jackson ad: "Just do it." I just want to be a priest. I just want to help people make sense out of their lives.

I guess that I'm not typical of my class. I'm going to sound like a jerk, but, although I'm only twenty-six, I think I've had more experiences than most of the other guys. Their average age is thirty-one, but I've been exposed to more things. I've lived in Rome in a coed school; I've traveled through Europe and lived briefly in Ecuador and Peru. I've experienced the violence and the traditions of the Latino culture. They're a lot like the Irish.

Anyway, a lot of guys in my class haven't had those experiences. For many, their first experience of seminary or parish was after they entered. I practically grew up in the rectory; I visited the seminaries; I knew many priests; I felt at home.

Don't get me wrong. They are good guys. Real solid. It's just that many of them are very into being "Father." They're getting their albs and stoles made and are really excited about ordination. There is a real interest on the part of some about what's going on in the chancery office. Yeah, there is a certain cathedral-church mentality among some of them. But not too many.

In the classes, there were a lot of questions that asked: "How do I do it?" or "What do I say?" It's as if they needed to be told what to do, to learn the party line on everything. They weren't willing to rely on their own instincts. But then a lot of them had never been in a rectory. I was freaked out by some of those questions! The influential priests in my life just aren't that way. I guess I'm more interested in priests like Don Headley and Leo Mahon, two guys who work with Latinos, and who are great pastors.

I really don't think that the numbers in the seminary will grow. Perhaps ten to sixteen ordinations a year will be the norm. But if we can keep that number, we should be able to hold on.

I think we got good coverage of the celibacy issues through the spiritual direction classes. They brought guys in to talk about it. Leo Mahon came and gave an excellent talk, although some of the guys didn't know how to react. They also covered the pederasty and alcoholism issues. I don't know if these issues were covered adequately, but the guys did talk about these things among themselves. The best talk is one-on-one with a close friend to whom you can say anything. You've got to have someone you can be truly honest with.

The gay issue is hard to define. Sure, there are seminarians who are gay. I've been in the seminary system for eight years. If you're in the system long enough, you see enough. But it just doesn't come up and it isn't overt. No one is going to sit around a table with other guys and announce that he's gay. It isn't talked about, at least in groups. There are some guys who are effeminate and they're not gay. Yet, they were harassed because they were gay-looking. They were asked to reconsider their vocation or drop out for a year, or something like that. It wasn't fair. The whole gay issue is treated differently. I hear the same figures you quoted. I don't know. It's higher than the national average which I believe is 10 percent. Maybe it's 30 percent. Again, I haven't gotten too close. My Mundelein experience wasn't that satisfying for me. During my first year, I almost left six times.

About half the class will be assigned to the suburbs; the other half will be in Chicago. They had this elaborate system for placing us. When it was all over, we had twenty-two parishes to pick from. I asked for an inner-city Latino parish. St. Mark's was the only one that made the list, although a few have partial Latino congregations. I met Ed Maloney, the pastor, and he's a good man. We've got Placido Rodriguez, [auxiliary bishop of Chicago] living here. He's a fine man. I think I'm going to like it here. Yesterday was my first time at Mass here; the place was crowded; the people were very friendly.

The seminary offers a whole lot, especially for small dioceses who could not put together a faculty such as we have. They should bring in other people to talk, people who are doing genuine pastoral work. Too often, only the acceptable guys get in to talk, and these guys get to know the seminarians and become their spiritual directors once they're out. So, the system perpetuates itself. You know, safe guys come to speak and create other safe guys. But I look at Casa Jesus and Imani House, two preseminary places to help Latinos and Afro-Americans to become culturally adapted to our present system, and I can see changes coming. Time will tell.

Oh yes, there are still problems that divide the pilgrim church from the cathedral church. I suppose that it's our bigness and the money problems. We say we're for the poor, for example, but we close the schools and churches in the poor neighborhoods. Even before we leave the seminary, we hear that we mustn't trust downtown (the chancery). We hear stories that they call guys and ask them to take a parish because they don't want someone who has applied to get it. I've heard at least two cases like that. That's not good for morale. They forget that such things could be said of us. Soon, you don't trust them. I get the impression that the chancery lacks sincerity.

I just want to stay in the city, to work with Latinos and the poor. I just want to be able to follow my gut. Perhaps in fifteen years, I'd like to go to the missions in Peru or Ecuador.

I really don't know what's going to happen with the Church. Maybe, as

Bill Stenzel [Chicago pastor] says, we will have to fall on our face financially so that we can build up again.

I still ask: Why can't we just accept the human church? Most of our people live very hard lives. Why can't we just be satisfied to welcome people on Sunday and pray with them and sing with them and listen to their concerns about their jobs and their children? We have enough programs of all kinds. We only need a caring ministry.

Whatever the case, I like what Bill Stenzel says: "The Holy Spirit keeps on working."

· 34 ·

Jose Luis Menendez: Latino Dreamer

Jose Luis Menendez is pastor of Corpus Christi Parish in Miami, Florida. "Next time we talk," he said, "you must speak to the others here. I am not alone. I wouldn't be anything without them. I am only a dreamer."

According to Father Gary Riebe Estrella, S.V.D., there are about 1,600 Hispanic priests in the U.S. As of late 1989, twenty-one of them were bishops, all of them named since 1970. Two were archbishops, eight were heads of dioceses and thirteen were auxiliary bishops.

Estimates are that there are 20 million persons of Hispanic origin, most of them from Latin America, with between three and six million undocumented in the U.S. Seventy-one percent are native-born citizens. Through birth and immigration, their numbers rise by several hundred thousand each year. It is estimated that by the year 2000, the U.S. will have 30 million Hispanics. About 80 percent claim to be Catholic by baptism. Hispanics now represent 25 percent of the Catholics in the United States.

In a 1988 address to the National Conference of Catholic Bishops (NCCB), Archbishop Pio Laghi, the previous pro-nuncio to the United States, said: "It is important that we speak to Hispanics in their own language, but it is no less important that we know what to say and how to say it. Our success will be measured to the extent that Hispanic Catholics truly feel welcome in our churches and institutions."

The Notre Dame Study of Parish Life estimated that there was a significant Spanish presence in 2,900 parishes and that Sunday Mass in Spanish was warranted in 2,500 parishes. The study also reported the presence of 1,000 or more local leaders in 130 dioceses in such movements as the Cursillo, the Christian Family Movement, Charismatic Renewal, and various kinds of *encuentros*.

A national secretariat was established by the United States Catholic Conference, the administrative arm of the NCCB. The office now has seven regional offices. In the Southwest, fifty-five Mexican-American priests organized PADRES in 1970 to help the Church identify more closely with the pastoral, social, economic, and education needs of the Hispanics. Leadership development is now one of the principal concerns of PADRES. (PADRES is an acronym for the Spanish title, "Padres Asociados para Derechos Religiosos, Educativos y Sociales.") In 1987, the National Pastoral Plan for Hispanic Ministry was approved by the NCCB and an Ad Hoc Committee for Hispanic Affairs was made a permanent committee of the Conference.

In 1989, during a celebration of Latin American heritage, the Hispanic bishops of the Northeast called on Hispanics to form a new culture by blending the best of their traditional heritage with the best of what they find in the United States. In the same year, Father Rosendo Urrabazo, president of the Mexican-American Cultural Center in San Antonio, called on the Hispanic community to employ the "base community" approach to the evangelization of Hispanics. "The traditional parish structure was good for its time," he said, "but now it is just too big to serve the purpose of evangelization."

Jose Luis Menendez does intuitively what bishops and other administrators are urging. His English is charmingly adequate but, in the interests of clarity, some changes have been made.

The Lord did not send us here to care for a white elephant. I was not ordained to be a museum keeper. Corpus Christi is the biggest church in Miami. It holds 1,500 people. It's bigger than the cathedral!

Let me tell you the sociology. We have 17,500 Catholics in the area. We get 1,200 at Mass on Sunday and a third of them are old parishioners who come back here for Sunday Mass.

When Corpus Christi church was built in 1959, this area was like a Miami suburb. The parish was opened in 1941, only about twenty-nine blocks from the center of the city. Miami was a small city then. The parish is still small houses with small gardens. It has changed a great deal but, after nearly three years here, I feel as safe as in any other part of Miami.

In 1959, this was a White-American community. I never know what to call people who aren't Hispanic! (Laughs.) Is it White-American? Or Anglo-American? Anyway, the Cubans began coming about thirty years ago and gradually the Anglos moved. The Cubans were here for a while but then they got better jobs and made more money and, just like all Americans do, they moved to better neighborhoods. That is the American way. Here I am, a Cuban, who came here to work with Cubans, and now there are only a few Cubans left in the neighborhood!

In 1965, the expressways came, one on each side of us. Then, they began to tear down some of the homes to build warehouses on one side. There were railroad tracks on another side. So, in a few years we were a ghetto. Only the poor came in—Central Americans, Haitians, Puerto Ricans, people from the Dominican Republic. Very little English speaking. We are nearly 100 percent Spanish speaking with about 80 percent of us Catholics. Few jobs. A lot of drugs. We are no longer a suburb. We are a ghetto.

I was ordained for the diocese of Madrid in 1977. My family roots are from Spain, but I am a Cuban. My family came to Miami in 1960, but, after a year, we moved to Spain. I was only about twelve at the time.

In Spain, I joined the Congregation of the Sacred Hearts of Jesus and Mary. But those were the days of Vatican II and many of us did not stay. We wanted to do something right away, I guess! I left the seminary and became a worker. I worked with Cuban refugees for four years, working during the day and studying theology at night. Yes, you could do that in Madrid. It was hard, but it is a wonderful idea. Seminarians should be put to work with the priests.

I was ordained on December 17, 1977, and stayed in Madrid for two years. Then I asked to come to Miami. I always wanted to return to work with Cubans. So that is how I am here.

In this neighborhood, we cannot stay behind our walls. We must go out from our white elephants and knock on doors. People are proud to have a priest knock on their door. The rich lock their doors. They have things to keep. But the poor have nothing and so they are not afraid. Sometimes, they are frightened that you are a Jehovah's Witness, but when they learn that you are Catholic, they open their hearts. They are humble people. You are received with their heart. These are people of the Third Beatitude (Blessed are the meek, for they will inherit the earth).

We have to abandon the big church. It will be a mission like the others. Now, we have five small communities, all of them at different stages, including one that, thanks God, will start on October 15.

One is now called Our Lady of Alta Gracia. It is mostly people from the Dominican Republic. San Juan Bautista is in a shoe shop for weekday meetings, but we use a public school for Sunday Mass. St. Francis and St. Clare is one we use for A.A. (Alcoholics Anonymous) and for catechesis and prayer. It's mostly Central Americans and some White-Americans. In October, we will open Our Lady Queen of Peace. It will be 50 percent Cuban but will be very mixed.

Oh, thanks God, for those who help me! There is Oscar Casteneda and Pedro Corces (both priests) and we have five sisters. Our elementary school is struggling. We need a subsidy from the diocese. But it is the only subsidy we get and we offer the only good education in the area.

On Saturday evening, we get only twenty-five people in the big church for an English Mass, and at 9:00 a.m. on Sunday, we get 100 for another English Mass. There are about 500 for the Spanish Mass at 10:30 and maybe 110 for the 6:30 Sunday evening Mass. On Palm Sunday and Good Friday, the church is filled to the doors. So they are there. We must invite them to come.

We must go out from behind the walls! So you see we need to go out and knock on doors. We need small communities that people can walk to. They have cars, most of them, but they need their cars for work. They must be able to walk.

We're at different stages with each of our communities. The numbers aren't getting bigger just yet, but the quality is much better. You know, I ask myself when I talk: "Did they understand?" After all, I have much more education than most of them. Some have been only to second grade. In a small community, I can ask them to ask questions and they do. They get to understand. Our people understand Scripture. Most of them come from an agricultural background and they understand words like "seed" and "flower" and "birds." The teaching has gotten so complicated! We must keep it simple. We are at the level of Creed and we must try to recapture the simple truths of Jesus! Then, our people can grow from passive to active parishioners. The problem is not to put it all in a book, but to make it meaningful. Then, they will not just be ushers for ten years. You multiply the needs and you multiply the services and then you must multiply the commitments!

This is a challenge and an adventure. The Holy Spirit is working. The Holy Spirit will show us the way! For us Latins, when you touch the heart of a Hispanic, you win that person. You don't convince us with knowledge. You do when you touch our hearts.

Sometimes we forget to dream. When you dream, things will happen. Look at Moses. He could stand in front of the Red Sea and believe that he could cut it in two parts. One day, we will have a new church here in this neighborhood. One day, all our people here will embrace the Lord!

I think Jesus was a dreamer. Bishop McCarthy [Edward A. McCarthy, archbishop of Miami] is a dreamer. He is very supportive of us. When we started our first small community here, we invited Bishop McCarthy. You know, some people are afraid to talk to their bishop. But we are not afraid to talk to him. We asked only for his blessing. No money.

I took a pilot area in the neighborhood and picked a place. I put a cross at one end and a cross at another and found a place in between, one that people could walk to. But then I learned that the Pentecostals had already bought the place. But then one day, a woman came and told me that her husband was thinking of buying a piece of property. I saw the place and told her, "Tell your husband to buy the property and we will buy it from him." We had no money but our people prayed and we put up a cross and a statue of Mary and the Bishop came and blessed the spot and by November I was knocking on the bishop's door with a check for $50,000! It came from a man who had been granted a favor from God. You see how God works!

With the money, we can build the shell of the place, but our people must finish it so they will feel ownership. Our architect has donated the plans and the Rotary Club will give us money because they will use the place, too. It will be a worship place but also one for people in need. So we must involve the community.

We have an organization called PACT. That means People Acting in Community Together. It's made up of mainline Protestant churches like the Lutherans and the black Baptist churches and us. Just about everyone except the Pentecostals. They are very anti-Catholic. That is sad because many of them are Catholics. They are very bitter. They tell their people that the pope has eight women and that he owns the CIA and the KGB and that all priests are evil! They tell them that Mary had other kids and that the pope is the devil. After a while, many of the Pentecostals fall away but they don't come back to the church because they still have these anti-Catholic thoughts or they feel that they are sinners because they left the church. We have to heal their hearts and tell them to come and rest. The mainline Protestants are not that way. Just the Pentecostals. But we must go to where the people live. Otherwise, a hundred denominations will get there before us!

I really don't know about Hispanics in this country. I think that 64 percent of the Catholics in this archdiocese are Hispanic and that about 80 percent of the people in Dade County are Hispanic. But I am a priest, not a sociologist.

We need vocations to the priesthood to help with this. We need more of everything! If only the pope would see the reality of what we are doing! It must be very difficult to rule from one place. This is no longer a Church with the pope up top and then the bishops and then the priests and then the people. We are one body, like St. Paul said. One part cannot say to another that I don't need you.

We need married men to be priests, at least as a first stage. I don't believe that priests like us should be married, but we could start by ordaining married men. We have so many wonderful married men. And ex-priests who are married could be brought home.

If a Protestant pastor can survive with a community of two or three hundred, why can't we? Instead of closing churches, why can't we form small communities?

We are fighting social issues. We are working with the city to clean up the crack houses and to clear the empty lots. The church must take the offensive. We cannot live in a castle!

Our finances are terrible! But we have a festival every year and we must make people more conscious of the good that is here. We must knock on doors or our parish will not survive and others will take the place of the church.

We must always dream, thanks God. I will be a dreamer until I die!

Thomas J. O'Gorman: Creative Survival

St. Malachy's is billed as the poorest parish in Chicago. Actually, it is meeting its needs because of support from other parishes as far away as southern Illinois, an energetic fund-raising effort, and a dwindling but still generous subsidy from the archdiocese.

Established as an Irish parish in 1882, it remained a lace-curtain community until the Depression when the neighborhood "turned," as the old residents used to say. By 1930, parish membership had dropped from 1,400 to 300. In that year, the diocesan paper, with veiled racism, commented that "the sturdy old Irish are being replaced by shifting numbers of Negroes." In less than a decade, St. Malachy's went from a clout parish to one in need.

The first building in the parish was erected in 1882, eleven years after the great Chicago fire of 1871. In the aftermath of that fire, the city had passed a strict fire code that forbade wooden buildings. But the first pastor got a permit out of the city as easily as Mother Catherine Feehan, a Mercy Sister, got permission to build the school. (Her brother was the archbishop.)

St. Malachy's made an unsuccessful attempt to be the "actor's church" in the manner of St. Malachy's in New York, the Actors Chapel. Later, it became a "printers' church" with a 3:30 A.M. Sunday morning Mass that catered to the men who worked on Printers' Row.

Several ethnic parishes serving Italians and Slovaks were carved out of the parish but, in the code words of the archdiocesan paper, *The New World*, "their places were taken by a different class of citizens." Translation was easy. Blacks were simply not greeted in the same way as other immigrants.

By the time the first Afro-American priest arrived in 1949, he was given a broom and set to work cleaning the school, not because he was black but because the parish's resources were woefully bad. The pastor and the other associate also swept floors and washed windows.

Although 30 percent of the people living within the parish boundaries were white as late as 1970, St. Malachy's has been a black parish since the 1930s. While determined efforts were made to homogenize the ethnic parishes as consolidations took place, St. Malachy's parish borders were actually expanded. The expansion only emphasized its blackness and its isolation.

In earlier days, however, there were at least three priests to support each other. If the parish didn't have much "business," at least it had some clerical community. An earlier pastor, in fact, added another floor to the rectory. It contained a large rec room and porch. The upper room became a clerical Las Vegas where visiting priests could gamble to their hearts' content.

St. Malachy's history is echoed in literally hundreds of parishes in the urban areas across America. Their first parishioners, with little but the parish to serve their religious and social needs, had built great monuments to their faith.

When the automobile replaced the streetcar, however, their children discovered the suburbs. The education provided by the excellent Catholic elementary and high schools made it possible for them to ascend the economic ladder with its split-level homes and its backyard barbecues. The butcher, baker, banker, barber, and funeral director left early. Soon after, even the grocery stores and mainline Protestant churches were gone. The Catholic churches became the last survivors of the changing neighborhoods.

For a time, the Catholic churches prided themselves on their presence in the community, but now even these magnificent old buildings stand empty. Signs and symbols of their Catholicity were removed with unseemly haste, much the way a failed Burger King or other franchise is quickly erased. Some have been sold to other churches, others converted into centers for the homeless or senior citizen centers. (A few old churches have been converted into restaurants; one still bears the parish's name; another, called "The Refectory," has waiters dressed as Franciscan Friars and the sanctuary is a waiting area with a cheese bar where the altar once stood.)

Tom O'Gorman serves alone. He is part of a rapidly growing number of pastors of one-priest parishes, now common in the rural areas and the inner city. It is difficult to estimate just how many one-priest parishes there will be by the turn of the century. Frequently, the one-priest status is the final step prior to closing a parish. The official Church still prefers to point to dwindling congregations, aging buildings, and shifting populations as reasons for closing a parish. Only rarely are officials candid enough to state "priest shortage." Chicago, for example, closed forty-two parishes in 1990-91 alone. Consolidations reduced the loss to thirty-eight parishes. The archdiocese still has nearly four hundred parishes, more than the entire state of Florida. Barring further declines, the Chicago Church will have six hundred priests by the year 2005. Four hundred will be active, one for each parish. Clearly, the archdiocese will have to close more parishes. The Chicago experience will be repeated in other dioceses. Only Seattle with its redoubtable Archbishop Raymond Hunthausen, has pledged to keep every parish open. It is clear that Hunthausen is willing to turn parish leadership over to laity.

In some large dioceses, there has been talk of forming communities of four or five priests who will live in a single rectory while administering at least one parish each. The theory is that they could be a support to one another, taking each other's duty hours, and providing some relief from the crushing loneliness.

Tom O'Gorman survives creatively. He goes out to people. He brings them in. His rectory is reminiscent of *You Can't Take It with You*. Two brothers, Bill Tomes and Jim Fogerty, the only members of a fledgling religious order, live in the rectory and work for peace among the rival gangs. Josephine McCord and Clara Sanders, pastoral associates, work on the first floor. Demetrius Ford, a handyman and vital link to the projects, often negotiates the endless disputes of an angry community. An aging Mercy sister, the last in the parish, with the marvelous name of Maud McGreal, walks fearlessly through the projects, visiting the aged and the sick, using the last remnant of religious clout to wave down police cars to take her from place to place. Mother Teresa's Missionaries of Charity staff a shelter around the corner; Cloteal Butler runs a Helping Hands Center in the projects.

Tom O'Gorman is an activist for his people. He works with an ecumenical and racially mixed group of local ministers who seek some equality in a terribly unequal world. But he also knows how to survive as a priest.

O h, I knew you'd bring up Stritch! [Cardinal Samuel Stritch was archbishop of Chicago from 1939-58, a period during which the archdiocese of Chicago was a powerful force in the American Church.] Yes, I suppose he's my best friend. He's my hobby. He's been dead since I was a kid. But I'm a trained historian and I just got interested in him and his era. He was a southerner from Tennessee. I wanted to explore the impact of a southern bishop on an ethnic midwest diocese like Chicago. He's a friend I can visit with on my day off. I can go over to the archives and trash around for hours. I can forget my problems there. When I discover that a year's supply of toilet paper for the grammar school has gone out the back door, I can forget about it for a while at the archives. The cardinal [Joseph L. Bernardin] gave me carte blanche, maybe more than he realized. I'm into some wonderful stuff!

The people at the archives are very good to me. I may write a book about Stritch someday, but, right now, it's been a marvelous opportunity for me to meet some interesting people. That was a great era for the Chicago Church. I've been interviewing people who knew him and they are all extraordinary people. During a trip to Ireland, I even searched out some of Stritch's family. When I got near his ancestral home, someone met me and said: "Ah, you're the priest from Rome to investigate his cause for canonization." By the time I got to his village, the people were saying: "Ah, we hear that thousands visit his grave each year and that there have been miracles!" Can you believe it? Is this a great church or isn't it! (Laughs.)

Not long ago, I visited with Bill Quinn [Monsignor William J. Quinn, now pastor emeritus of St. Eulalia, Maywood, Illinois]. An incredible man! He knows the Church but he's still excited about it. Bill was involved with the YCS [Young Christian Students] and YCW [Young Christian Workers] movements. Those were the basic Christian communities of years ago, much like the small Christian communities we're hearing about today. They make as much good sense today as they did years ago.

Men like Bill Quinn never stopped reading. He was ordained in 1941, but his mind remains as active as it ever was. Guys like him can talk about theology or poetry, and they can filter their priestly experience through what they've read.

I'm involved in at least five projects now and they all excite me. But I'm afraid that my ordination classmates aren't reading. Maybe it's the malaise that they find themselves in. Maybe they don't see reading as liberating. I love it. I recall an old story about Reynie Hillenbrand when he was rector of the major seminary. He used to tell his ordination classes: "When you leave here to begin your priesthood, your pastors can keep you from doing a lot of things, but they can't keep you from thinking." And that's what keeps me sane and excited.

You know, for the past six years while I've been pastor here, I've put a poem in the parish bulletin every week. A good poem. Gerard Manley Hopkins, Thomas Merton, Yeats, and other Irish poets. No doggeral. Good stuff. I do occasional poems of my own. You can't write *down* to your people; you've got to write *up*.

You know, we've got to stop approaching our theology as if it were botany. We can't just synthesize it. We've got to nourish our people, help them to internalize their learning.

I've heard other priests say that all that reading gets you away from your people. That's b.s. If priests don't read, you'll generally find that, at forty, their interests become a boat or a car.

Every year my priesthood gets more exciting. I'm getting more done and meeting more people. I was ordained in 1977 but I lived here at St. Malachy's as early as 1971 when I was both a lay person and a seminarian. After I was ordained, I was assigned to George Kane's parish in Schaumberg. He was an extraordinary mentor. He taught me that being a priest was nothing more than helping people to make sense out of their lives.

All these readings, all this research, all this travel have caused me to think of the Church as a whole nation. Not long ago, while in London, I con-celebrated Mass at St. Paul's, a wonderful experience. Who knows, I could die an Anglican vicar in one of those little English villages!

I remain close to a few priest friends but my support system is largely lay people. In fact, my best friends are lay people. One is a former classmate and the other is a family that has virtually adopted me. Lay people won't let me get away with anything. Without them, I'd be drinking my brains out. But my friend Mary told me to take a hard look at my drinking. Now I've stopped. I'm getting up early in the morning and going to the lakefront and running. Now, thanks to those honest lay people, I'm back in suits that fit. If I were drinking, all my projects would come crashing down. I just couldn't do what I do if I drank. There was drink in my family. No one admitted it so the problem continued. We all became adult children of alcoholics.

Who would I ordain? I don't think I'd ordain anyone who doesn't read the *New York Times* or who hasn't written a sonnet. You know, there's an incredible presence of provincialism in the seminaries and the priesthood. We're encouraging a pale mentality. If priests are going to survive, they can't be narrow. They can't go on talking in the same way. But, sadly, that's what we're doing.

If Chicago is going to have only four hundred active priests by the year 2000, then we've got to talk about ordaining four hundred married men and four hundred women. We've got to talk about ordaining people from the community, or at least validating their natural leadership. When I'm not here, Josephine and Clara [pastoral associates] can run the place. They do a wonderful job.

We simply cannot continue to do things the way we've been doing them. Now we're trying to put those electro-pads or paddles or whatever they call them on a dead Church. I believe that something or someone will come along and force a change. The parish priests are becoming less and less tolerant of the Church putting words in the mouth of the risen Christ.

I'm reading *Desegregating the Sanctuaries* these days. It's about black priests in the American church. The bishops were afraid to deal with the situation of accepting black men into the seminaries, so they ran. They did nothing. As recently as 1945, Cardinal Stritch was writing to bishops, urging them to take Afro-American candidates for priesthood. Chicago ordained its first black priest in 1949, not a great record. St. Malachy's was black for twenty years before we got our first black priest. We've virtually lost the black community.

Now, look at this country. Look at the new nationalities and races. They are going to require new responses, new thinking. So with the Church. We can no longer think of an exclusively male clergy anymore. It just won't wash.

Our scriptural theology is so much better than our canons and rules. Two thousand men tied to the pope aren't going to make any difference. Dorothy Day says more by her life than all of these. We can't go among the poor and holler at them with picket signs and protests about abortion. I'm beginning to wonder myself about our teaching on abortion. You know, we seem to have decided that the definition of death is the cessation of all brain activity. Do you think that life begins when brain activity begins? I don't know. I only know that we can't bring the poor and the homeless into our shelter to feed them and then yell at them for fifteen minutes about abortion.

As for St. Malachy's, I can only tell you that the people of my parish aren't going to be reading pastorals. They are people of deep expression; they're big-shouldered and gregarious, with all sorts of vulnerabilities. But they are lovers of people. They see Christianity through a telescope, not a rearview mirror.

I want to stay in urban work, Afro-American or Hispanic. I've been in it most of my priestly life. I was here as a seminarian and later as an associate pastor. I became attached to the faith and the spontaneity of black people. Just the way Afro-Americans deal with life is real. Besides, I've just got to talk with city people. They're real.

The Church has never been as well-ordered as we thought it was. It's always been sloppy. It's fruitless to tighten it up. I don't think that we're going to be a Eucharist-less people. That would rival the days of Diocletian. This is a country where Catholics take their faith seriously. There are lots of historical conclusions from the risen Christ that are really just cultural constructs of the era. They can be changed. Josephine, our pastoral associate, could lead the people of St. Malachy's.

I'm afraid that the Church is simply trying to keep the institution going. I'm afraid that we're not trying to be salt and life to our people. I'm afraid that we're pointing toward exclusivity.

Yes, I've heard that this area is going to be yuppified or gentrified or whatever it's called. The developers are creeping up Washington Boulevard, building their townhouses. You saw the ones over on Taylor Street, the old Italian neighborhood. They're going for over $200,000. St. Malachy's is a poor ghetto now, but it's probably the most valuable land in Chicago. It was once a bon ton Irish parish, all white, and it could be that way again. I've heard that the developers are getting options to build a sports facility but that they'll retain the property option even if they don't build a new stadium. It's painful to see that the real estate consultant the developers are using is the same one the chancery uses. It gives a very wrong impression. The poor black community will be driven out.

Well, we've tried. I've worked with the local ministers and we're trying to salvage something for our people, but it's hard. If only those developers would permit some stores and restaurants around the new stadium so that it would provide jobs for our people and a chance for them to get into business. But you've seen the proposed design in the paper. It's a bunker with a parking lot. The developer gets it all—the tickets, the food, the souvenirs, everything! Sure, they're offering jobs, menial ones. But the Afro-American gets to own nothing.

We fought the lottery for much the same reasons. They were exploiting the poor, urging them to take chances on a raffle in which their odds of winning were nineteen million to one. They'd never put up billboards urging people to buy lottery tickets in the fancy suburbs. I asked our people to put their losing lottery tickets in the collection basket and then I made a stink in the press. At least we got the lottery billboards down.

If we're driven out, I'm going to try to persuade them to build a dozen six-unit apartments for our people, right near the church. The presence of black culture in America is one of its greatest gifts. It's as rich as the Irish tradition which brought laughter and music to the community. Black people are so realistic. You can't fool them. When you don't make sense they know it. They are a prophetic people. I can't imagine a genuinely Catholic parish without them.

I don't think that the chancery will close us down. They've cut our allotment by over $100,000, but we're hanging in there. I'm trying hard to keep a good grammar school. I'm told that, if you've got a good elementary school, they won't close you down. Brigid has been principal for over ten years and does a wonderful job. We did have to let some weak people go, but now our faculty is better than ever.

We do things differently. We don't look too closely at parish boundaries. We've got kids from nineteen parishes, I think. When we need a new teacher, we advertise in the *Chicago Tribune*, not the Catholic paper. We get far more and far better applicants and we don't look for those silly requirements that the Catholic School Board wants. We look for people with imagination and life. We insist that they be Catholics but we also want people who can write a poem. Heck, we just hired a kindergarten teacher who is in her seventies! She's marvelous.

Yes, we've got a parish staff of characters. Brother Bill and Brother Jim are the only two members of their religious order. They're social workers. They wander all over the place helping people, negotiating with the gangs and trying to settle family quarrels. You have to admire them. They face bullets. Then, there's Sister Maud. She's a Mercy, up in her seventies. She wanders around this neighborhood, fearless. She visits the sick; makes friends for us. When she wants a ride, she just waves down a police car. She's asked me to come with her on a home visit and, when I ask if she met the person somewhere in the parish, Maud says: "Oh, yes, I met her at a bus stop." And we've got Mother Teresa's nuns here. They run a soup kitchen and a shelter. Ultraconservative! They don't even come to our liturgies very often; some Opus Dei type says Mass for them, but they do feed the needy. And Old St. Patrick's sends us at least sixty-five volunteers to tutor our kids so that they'll get into a good school. They also help us with fund-raising events. And, we've got kids from Loyola Academy up in Wilmette. They come here during the summers; live here for a week or two and help to fix the place up. The Jesuits are good to me. They help fill in when I'm away for a Sunday.

We do O.K. We have a drop-in center in the projects and across the street we have a trailer where we distribute clothes. We often have more clothes than we need. People are generous.

Our people are wonderful. We have about three hundred families, but all kinds of others come in. Our children's choir is very good. It's directed by a Baptist woman. Our kids sing at other parishes and really get the crowds moving.

We don't ask a lot of questions around here. Questions make for tensions. When we tried to run a dance some time ago, the police were all over the place. They told me that gang leaders were in the crowd and all I could say was, "Well, are they behaving?" The police didn't like it and told me that I might need them some day. It took a while to convince them that we can't run dances to keep kids out of trouble and then give them a hard time.

Our people worship with their hearts more than their heads. I just can't take the grid of canon law and lay it over the parish or a parishioner. It just doesn't fit. That's why, when I get marriage cases, I prefer to take them to my own matrimonial tribunal and give them what I call the Afro-American privilege. Our European rules just don't make sense to them.

This is a church to come home to. It's a symbol in this neighborhood. When someone dies, their families see this church as a symbol and they come here. Few men live to be fifty-five and I've buried dozens of shooting victims. We don't ask a lot of questions. Some aren't Catholics; they have only a thin link with any church. There's a stereotype about black people. It says that they're all Baptists. Actually, 60 percent of the people we meet have no religious affiliation. But they come here in need and we bury them.

All we ask of our people is that they leave their sins at the door and come in.

· 36 ·

J. Timothy Power: The All-American Parish

About two hundred people gathered at the Pax Christi Community in Eden Prairie, Minnesota, to hold up the parents of a baby boy who died before he ever had a chance to ride a bike or make his First Communion. After the Gospel, Father Tim Power left the pulpit and stood before the boy's young parents to deliver his homily. He spoke to them as if they were the only people in the church. "At times of death," he said later, "you just try to do whatever you can do. It's no time to ask questions."

Tim Power understands the effectiveness of priestly salt. The congregation sat quietly while an enormously gifted pastor spoke to the huddled parents, attempting to explore the mystery of awful pain and its kinship with eternal joy.

The Pax Christi Community may be the best one-priest parish in America. Clearly, it is a template for what will become the paradigm of the majority of American Churches in the near future. Currently, there are 19,620 Catholic parishes in the U.S. The average parish has 2,300 parishioners, 1,300 of whom attend Mass in a given week. (Attendance varies; close to 60 percent in some rural areas, just under 25 percent in big cities.) Eighteen percent of parishes have fewer than 500 Catholics within their boundaries, but 15 percent have more than 5,000. Thirty-nine percent have from 1,500 to 5,000 Catholics and the bigger parishes may be getting even bigger. When Tim Power was first interviewed in December of 1988, Pax Christi had 2500 units. Two years later, it had 3,100.

The single presbyter is already commonplace. An estimated 1,900 parishes are now "priestless" in that they do not have a full time resident priest. Presently, there are some 3,400 one-priest parishes and that number increases daily. In Cincinnati, for example, projections indicate that the archdiocese will have just under 200 priests to serve 247 parishes by the year 2000. It means that parishes under 700 units will be either closed or priestless and those under 4,000 units will be one-priest parishes.

Tim Power was forty years old and had been ordained fifteen years when he became the founding pastor of Pax Christi. Eden Prairie is a high I.Q., upscale community of 16,000 people, about fifteen miles from Minneapolis. Family income is about $40,000 per year.

By 1981, the suburb's Catholics had already been organized for two years. They wanted a parish of their own. The archdiocese said they would oblige, provided that the people could sign up 350 families. Early Masses were in a hotel ballroom, a Lutheran church, a public school, and a warehouse. The parish community grew so rapidly that the church was finished barely eight years when an additional 22,000 square feet had to be added.

Power's pastoral style worked with his community. According to his parishioners, he has always been a sustaining presence rather than a benevolent dictator.

There is no parish school and none is planned. Some parish children attend one of the dozen Catholic schools in the area, but the majority are in local public schools. Pax Christi has an elaborate religious education structure coordinated by one full-time and five part-time educators who work with 350 trained volunteers to educate 1,100 students. Nearly 1,700, or more accurately 1,100 individuals when those who do double duty are considered, are involved in some phase of Pax Christi's mission.

Pax Christi understands the basic marketing principle that when the customer is served, the business succeeds. The phone is answered. Phone calls are returned. The office is open six days a week and the people who answer the phone can make decisions.

Pax Christi is a parish that recognizes change. "People change and needs change," its information packet proclaims. "So what was spirituality once is spirituality no more. What generally goes under the name of spirituality is merely the record of past methods."

We put our mission statement and our annual goal statement on the wall. We want people to see them. Our goal statement for 1990, for example, is to open ourselves to deeper intimacy with God, which opens us to deeper intimacy with others.

This space is used for worship but we also use it for religious education and concerts. All of the altar furniture and much of the worship-space seating is movable. We can assemble to worship or we can use the space for concerts, workshops, fairs, and other presentations. We place the Blessed Sacrament in the Thomas Merton Chapel. We project our prayers and songs on the wall. We've got a full-blown projection room. It keeps the people's heads up. The baptistry is huge. We put it there in the front of the church and gave it a womb shape in order to recall our entry into the believing community through baptism. Moving water is rich in symbolism and the pascal candle we keep nearby heightens that awareness. And there's the reconciliation room. It provides continuing healing, so we keep it near the baptistry.

It's a far cry from the horse-and-Bible days. We went against some traditional liturgical principles but we wanted this place to look like a living room. We used wood, moving water, stone, growing plants, and quality art work. We wanted the characteristics of what we see, hear, touch, and taste to influence our immersion into the presence of God. We wanted space for meeting and greeting. So we put in benches and trees to facilitate conversations before and after all celebrations. Then, we have the Dorothy Day social space immediately adjacent so that we would emphasize our dual spiritual and social nature.

The altar furniture is simple and solid. The altar emphasizes family meals as well as the pascal meal. The pulpit gives prominence to the Word, and the presider's chair indicates a focal point for ministry. We put the altar with seating on three sides. It encourages community as we look at each other's faces. We didn't put in kneelers because we wanted to emphasize the shared prayer rather than private prayer at our liturgical celebrations.

Sometimes, I think we may be creating a monster. Sometimes I wonder if it's all going to collapse. We have just over 3,100 families. We are considering satellite chapels to handle the overflow. There are a number of Protestant churches in the area for sale. We tried to make the exterior blend with the environment. We built here on Purgatory Creek. Yes, we can bottle and sell purgatory water! (Laughs.)

Anyway, I'm the lone priest here, although I get help on Sundays. Because I'm the only priest, we're becoming declericalized. That's going to happen elsewhere in the Church. Now, we are being forced to turn to the people. I think that we will soon be switching roles. For the next few centuries or so, we could be moving away from a clergy-dominated Church to a laity-dominated Church. It's ironic. I talk to my Protestant minister friends and they seem to be having an opposite problem. With so many ministers available, their congregations are insisting on hiring only ordained ministers.

Priesthood as we know it is going down. The day of the priest as the answer person is over. We priests are being invited to be more collegial. We are now more than a faith community. Our bishop [John R. Roach, archbishop of St. Paul-Minneapolis] allows a great variety of church to happen. Pax Christi shouldn't be viewed as the norm in this archdiocese; nor should a conservative Church be seen as the norm.

We will be ten years old in May, 1991. At some point in all of this, I stopped worrying about what "they" would do. I started to worry about what I could do. "They" could stop us here. That would hurt us but it wouldn't destroy us. Legal structures sometimes make us do what we don't want to do. But I've had support. I've also found that if you do your job well, you will accumulate too many tasks and things. Maybe we should divest every seven years.

I like what I'm doing. I like the challenge. I wanted a parish that was just far enough away from Vatican II to appreciate the longer tradition. A lot of our people don't even remember Vatican II and the emphasis on the longer traditions lets us be creative. I was also helped by being a founding pastor. I didn't inherit any baggage. We can take Gospel values and make sure that they meet the needs of the people.

I just had my yearly job review by the people. That's not an official procedure in the archdiocese. Some years ago, we sent a copy of the annual review of the pastor to the chancery and they didn't know where to file it. In any case, one member of the review committee came to me to present the findings. It's a real healthy system. They are nudging me to take more time off. I need to consider how much more power I can give away to others. I need to pick up a few courses on managing as this place grows. We're now well beyond the entrepreneurial stage. I'm discovering that large fundamentalist churches have already experienced some of the same problems and have found ways to solve them. We can learn from them.

The presence of a priest is most important these days, not his administrative skills. I walk the aisles before and after each Mass. It's a great time to hug kids. I leave all the details to others. In this parish, we have fifty people trained to visit the sick. So what am I needed for? I'm needed to be visible and to preside in the larger assemblies. I'm needed to be available at the time of death. We have twenty to twenty-five funerals a year and I must be there for the families. When there's a funeral, all other activities are rescheduled. I preside at the funeral liturgy but we have laity trained to do the wake and graveside services. I'm also there to preside at a memorial Mass we have every three months for anyone who has had a loss. They bring pictures of the deceased and put them on the wall. We get about 150 people each time. But, again, I do mostly Eucharist with our people.

We now have four staff who report to me: two men and two women. They are in charge of administration, praying, learning, and caring. When questions arise, I refer the questioners to one of these people. They assign the tasks to others. Of course, there's overlapping. Many of our staff have double titles. The titles are very important, however, especially for people like us who are breaking new ground. The structure remains a one-presbyter model and the staff is always urging me not to overdo or I'll burn out.

We do have an awful lot of marriages. We often have weekday weddings or evening weddings to accommodate the larger numbers. There are a lot of young people. After a while, you develop an approach to handling the many questions that come with marriage. I see each couple twice. I do a faith assessment. If I don't know the couple well, I try to put some flesh and bones into the evaluation. I ask them to tell me about their relationship with God, about how they and God get along. Sometimes, we agree that they shouldn't be married, or at least not married here. Other staff people take over the marriage preparation and I see the couple a second time to decide how we're going to pray together. We have about 120 to 130 weddings a year. It's a problem for me. Some couples come in two years in advance and want to pick a date. It's happened that I've lost my annual vacation because of weddings. So now, I have to block off vacation time two years in advance, even if I don't know where I'm going. We're politely firm on saying no to home weddings or weddings in some grove. If some want to get married in a woodland setting, we have an outdoor worship space here, right on the property.

We get our share of annulment petitions. I still fill them out. I've got it down to a system and I can generally complete one in about twenty minutes. I still submit them, partly in the hope that they'll get so many that the whole system will eventually topple.

We are serious about social concerns and healing ministries. The names of our various meeting rooms are chosen for a purpose. The Anne Frank Library is obvious; the Bill W. Lounge honors the cofounder of Alcoholics Anonymous and is where our twelve-step support groups meet. There are rooms commemorating Martin Luther King, Jr., Archbishop Oscar Romero, St. Vincent de Paul, Sojourner Truth [former slave], Chief Joseph [Native-American leader] and the American Martyrs. We want these dedications to speak to the people and to prompt action. Presently, for example, a small group of our people are experimenting with Eucharist-less Sundays, just as their fellow Christians in Latin America must do because of the desperate shortage of priests. In Latin America, half the population never receives the Eucharist and, for most of the others, it's three or four times each year. Some of our people are trying that. They'll report back on their feelings of hunger, or anger or pain and indifference.

We subscribe to twenty-eight homily services. I know that's an awful lot. It averages only about $10 per Sunday. But I try never to forget that priestly presence. Most of the people will see me only on Sunday. I've got to do a good job for them. I spend about two hours each week just getting images; then I start the real work of preparing the homily. We also subscribe to about twenty-five magazines, as well as *The Christian Science Monitor* and *The Tablet* [a highly-regarded Catholic newspaper out of London]. Of course, I can't go through them all. There's a lot of waste, but the materials are all passed on to the staff.

When you share ministry and power, things begin to happen. There are over eighty telephone numbers in our information bulletin. People can call any one of them for specific needs. I have a fifty-five to sixty hour a week commitment. I'm off duty from Sunday afternoon until Tuesday morning. And, if I show up on Monday, my day off, the staff will throw me out. Since we had no formal church in the early days, the custom of daily Mass never took hold. If I'm not available for daily liturgy, the people conduct a Eucharistic service. The parishioners respect the power of ordination but they understand the rights and obligations conferred on them by baptism. We have fifteen couples on our baptism team. They meet weekly with parents and godparents. Twenty couples are involved in marriage preparation, and we train our parents to prepare their children for first Penance and first Eucharist.

We have a fund that provides an endowment for a visiting staff member. Recently, it was a female Episcopal minister and, just before that, a Dominican priest. He was the one who told us that we weren't dealing justly with our kids. As a result, we set up a task force to examine how well we were passing on the Christian tradition. We ended up shifting the Confirmation program, establishing peer ministries and opening up our lector and commentator ministry to teenagers.

Our collections aren't spectacular. We take in about $16,000 a week. Our people give about 1 or 2 percent of their income. We're still trying to teach our people that money is not a dirty word. We're a large staff—eleven full-time and twenty-two part-time. Five of our people are completing graduate studies in theology at St. Thomas and St. Catherine colleges. There are fourteen resigned priests in the parish, seven of them active. If the pope ever changed the rules, we'd have a surplus of clergy!

The bigger we get the tougher it is to get volunteers, but with more people retiring at sixty-five, there are more available to volunteer. They do wonderful work. We're still trying to train people to do things I can't do because of the size of the parish. You know, it's easier to be one priest in a large parish than it is to be one priest in four small parishes. Those priests have to drive twenty-five miles between masses. It's got to be hard.

We've got to be able to convey to people that we priests can't always be there. Not long ago, a young husband asked me to be on hand for the birth of their child. The doctor had informed them that the baby might die soon after delivery. There wasn't any way I could be there, so I told the father that he was entitled to baptize the child. Well, the baby did die, but the father is still grateful that he had a chance to baptize his son. We've got to convince people that, as Christians, they can do these things.

I live a few miles away. I share the house with three lay people who work in non-parish jobs. I pray with them at the start of each day. They are very healing and helpful. They won't let me take my work home. And I've got a good network of friends. Most of my social relationships are lay people. I'm in a support group of ten priests. We meet monthly for an overnight. It's been going on for thirteen years. It's really clicked. We share supper together, really undress emotionally. It helps a great deal.

I try to strike a balance between being a priest and a shaman. People seem to want a shaman. I'm reminded of the kid who saw me at Mass and said that he was going to do that some day. I'm kind of a zoo keeper, showing off all the species and all the needs. I'm here to create an environment, to whip people into shape, as it were, and to see them thrive. I'm part magician. A magician is one who can see the illusion. Priests understand illusion. It's all a kind of prayer and zoo keeping, and finding out who the other magicians are.

I think that we're going to have to go through some confusion until we find out what the Church is. We're going to have language problems and a lot of things will get out of proportion. The sooner we can have the debate of authority versus Eucharist, the sooner things are going to be settled. If changes aren't made, priesthood as we know it will disappear, and perhaps that's good. Then, something can grow in its place. The debate is no longer over celibacy. That is no longer an issue in so many places. The debate is really about selective celibacy.

Anyway, I just try to ask people where God is in their lives. There's some messiness here. We make mistakes. At Pax Christi, we've had to let some ministries die. We even had a "funeral" for one recently and laid it to rest.

The diocese gives me as much latitude as it can. I don't get a lot of hassle. I feel supported. I do wish that bishops would sit down once in a while with people and listen, especially with those involved in second marriages. They would understand the sincerity of these people and sense their pain.

On the back of the parish's information brochure, we have a saying that is adapted from the book called *The Song of the Bird*. It fairly well describes the direction of this community and my priestly life. We "cut the coat to fit the person; we don't cut the person to fit the coat." It is no spirituality if it doesn't perform its function for you. A blanket is no blanket if it does not keep you warm.

Gary Reller: More Than Just a Union

"Priests are the most powerless people in the world," the elderly nun said. She had been teaching at a major seminary for years. She loved the clergy but was not blind to its weaknesses. When her bishop heard the remark, he bristled, but was at a loss to define what power diocesan clergy had over their lives.

In 1948 priest-sociologist Joseph H. Fichter, S.J., published the first of a projected four studies on the ministry of the Catholic priest. Titled *The Dynamics of a City Church*, it described the manner in which the parish clergy performed their sacramental, liturgical, and instructional functions. Conservative Catholics were shocked by the book. The remaining three studies were suppressed.

Fichter continued his research, however, sending questionnaires to priests over the years (in spite of objections from some bishops that he failed to communicate with them for prior authorization). His book, *Religion as an Occupation* (1961) spelled out the difference between the functionary and the professional. Another study, *America's Forgotten Priests* (1968), which focused on the associate pastors, touched so many episcopal nerve endings that it was roundly condemned by the then apostolic delegate, Egidio Vagnozzi. (The Vatican doesn't do studies. As recently as the 1990 Synod on the Priesthood, Bishop Donald Wuerl of Pittsburgh was chided for even meeting with a group of resigned priests.)

Fichter's studies showed clear evidence of growing clergy unrest. But the bishops ignored the warning signs, preferring instead to do their own study. The United States Catholic Conference (USCC), administrative arm of the National Conference of Catholic Bishops, funded an expensive study conducted by the National Opinion Research Center (NORC). The NORC study confirmed Fichter's findings. In his words, both studies confirmed "dissatisfaction with seminary training, poor communication with bishops and chancery officials, problems of assignment, promotion and retirement, the imperative need for clergy senates, personnel committees, grievance procedures and due process." But the answers of their own report were largely unused. (The bishops continue to fund studies and to functionally ignore them. One of the most recent, *The Catholic Priest in the U.S.*, an exhaustive study that concludes that the declining number of priests will neither bottom out nor reverse itself, was met by tempered criticism by the bishops. One bishop said, without any research, that the downward trend would turn around; another chided the study makers for their lack of faith in the Holy Spirit.)

But the founders of the National Federation of Priests' Councils used the valuable data for initiative, inspiration, and influence. Its first president, Patrick J. O'Malley of Chicago, Illinois, wrote that the NFPC could not "sit back awaiting some mandate from on high." He urged the founding members to begin to plan ahead, reminding them that even the most progressive dioceses often ignored their own research.

To understand the depth of the problem, one would have to revert to the 1960s when, following the assassinations of Martin Luther King, Jr. and Robert Kennedy, the civil rights movement reached top speed. At this time, the founding priests of the NFPC were having difficulty getting the use of a church hall to hold their meetings. Earlier, John Hill, now a resigned priest from Los Angeles, had done a mailing to all the clergy, attempting to organize a union, and had received only two dozen replies. It was a time when, in some dioceses, priests could visit their parents in distant cities only with permission of the ordinary; had to observe an evening curfew, and were expected to walk the pastor's dog.

The NFPC changed much of that. Organized in May, 1968, it has addressed virtually every issue touching on the lives of priests and has had significant impact on their working conditions. It has insisted on more thoughtful planning studies than the counting of new telephone installations to dictate Church growth. While bishops are part of a medieval authority structure, the vast majority are caring, sensitive men. They read the NFPC material and did what they could to implement the findings.

Union organizers, observing the fact that the NFPC had addressed thirty-three to thirty-five disparate social issues in the past twenty years, would fault them for their lack of focus. But they are believing priests. They often put aside their personal concerns to address issues such as racism, unemployment, arms and violence, prisons, energy, women, AIDS, the mentally ill, etc. They might have fared better if they had stuck to bread-and-butter issues but their very callings dictated a different path.

First seen as a kind of clerical teamster's union, the NFPC got a mixed reception from the bishops. According to Father Francis F. Brown of Steubenville, author of *Priests in Council*, a history of the NFPC, the bishops gave the group a cold reception. Cardinal Lawrence Shehan of Baltimore called them "selfish." Incredibly, Cardinal James F. McIntyre of Los Angeles called the NFPC an "intrusion of democracy." Cardinal Patrick O'Boyle of Washington, D.C., forbade any representative from his diocese to attend the early conventions. Even Cardinal Richard Cushing of Boston suggested that priests (and nuns) who got involved with such groups had no true vocation. The defenders of *Rerum Novarum* were reacting like American moguls. But, over the years, the movement gradually gravitated toward the center where they met with bishops who had undergone a change of heart.

Priests enjoy few benefits for their efforts. A sampling of twenty dioceses reveals that the average compensation package of a priest ordained twenty-five years is only $12,837, exclusive of board and room. Some dioceses are as low as $6,300 per year, with no Social Security contribution or pension. Pensions over $10,000 are extremely rare. Most are in the $8,000 range and considerably lower if the priest continues to live in the rectory. (Relatively affluent New York, for example, awards a $9,000 pension at age seventy-five, an age few clergy achieve. Gallup, New Mexico, offers $4,800 at that age, well below the poverty line. For most, the car allowance is woefully short of their costs even for strictly parish work; dental and optical insurance are rare. Priests must often rely on the contributed services of their professional parishioners; vesture in pension plans is often given only after twenty-five years of service. Psychological services are provided only through the kindness of the bishop and only at the risk of raising suspicions that affect the remainder of a priest's life.

Roy Larsen, former religion editor of the *Chicago Sun-Times*, observed that the NFPC may have hurt itself by attempting to be as deadly serious as the bishops. Now, he observes, the priests have outgrown that syndrome, which continues to hobble the bishops. What might have been a subconscious struggle for power is now gone. NFPC members now look for justice. Now, too, the vast majority of the bishops view NFPC representatives as colleagues. The theme of their 1990 conference was personal spirituality in times of transition. During their April, 1991 meeting the NFPC called for discussion and consideration of the ordination of women.

Helena isn't a big diocese. We have fifty-six parishes; I think only five of them have more than one priest. The median age of our priests is around fifty-six. The bishop [Eldon F. Curtiss] is around fifty-eight. He succeeded Ray Hunthausen [Raymond G. Hunthausen, now archbishop of Seattle]. Hunthausen was a native of the area; Curtis is from Oregon. He sees himself as a liberal, but the priests view him as a conservative. He's done a good job.

We've got to come to a new awakening of the needs of priests in terms of their health and wellness, and their retirement. We need to show a real concern for their living situation, and we've got to build some flexibility into the system.

There has also been a lot of concern in recent years about alcoholism and sexual issues. It is a genuine concern, not just a cover-up, and not just a scandal that has to be addressed. The issues are alcoholism and sex and we've got to deal with them.

I'm a native of Oregon, Montana, and Alaska—mostly Montana. My dad was in the sawmill business in Oregon. When it began to wane, we moved to Alaska and then Montana. Dad's been dead for twenty years now. He was a cradle Catholic but Mom was a convert from Oklahoma. She's still alive.

In Oregon, we belonged to a small, two-priest parish, twelve miles from our home. It was run by Benedictine monks from Mt. Angel. My first Catholic school was in Bozeman, Montana. I attended through first year high-school. Then, there were five high schools in four years, from a hundred coed students in Bozeman to a thousand all-boys in Portland. In Portland, I was impressed with a Jesuit education; it was a turning point for me in terms of a quality education.

I entered Carroll College in Helena, Montana, and took the preseminary program. Carroll is small, maybe eleven hundred students. There were sixty of us in the seminary program. We lived in a separate dorm and were required to major in philosophy. It was a great experience. We mixed with other students. I value it over my major seminary experience at St. Thomas in Denver. I was ordained in 1971.

I enjoyed parish work. My last parish before taking this job was in Kalispell, Montana, at Risen Christ parish, about 250 families in a pocket of growth in Montana. It was a new parish. I was alone but had some women religious on the staff. Montana isn't growing much. The population is still less than 800,000. About 131,000 Catholics.

I was involved in the NFPC back in Helena. I was on the board for three years and got this job as executive director for two years. I like this job, partly because I know when it's ending. There are a Marianist brother and a religious sister working with me. We have thirty priests on the executive board, one from each ecclesial province. They're all elected. Just a little over half of the dioceses in the United States belong to the NFPC, about 90 out of 175. Some bishops have invited us in, but the priests' councils in the dioceses chose not to affiliate. Now, with the new code of canon law, the presbyteral senates have become presbyteral councils under the bishop. It could change the makeup of NFPC.

This organization has a reputation of being a bit to the left and, through the seventies, it was. We passed a lot of flashy resolutions, but we also did a lot of hard work and didn't get much credit. Now, it's changed. We've matured; we now have a healthy respect for the bishops.

The federation began with a union look. We were talking about education for priests, retirement norms, and other benefits. We're still dealing both with the concerns *of* priests and concerns *for* priests. We're still concerned about priestless parishes. Parishes without ordained priests may be a necessity now, but they don't seem to be the long term solution. And a people without Eucharist is not a substitute.

We're still looking at a health insurance plan. It used to cost $800 to insure a priest; now it could cost $5,000. We've got to pool to reduce costs.

Recently, we did a survey of salary and benefits paid to priests in all the dioceses in the U.S. Jack Frerker of Belleville, Illinois, gathered data on salaries, benefits, and retirements. We think it will help in some decision making. We've learned that retiring priests are receiving only 80 percent of the income they received while they were active. Yet, to survive, they need about 120 percent. Many received no Social Security benefits; if they had it at all, they had to pay their own.

Priests have workaholic personalities. It's part of them, and a lot of it is guilt. Many have a low self-concept and a strange relationship with their bishop who controls 100 percent of their lives. Bishops can dictate your salary, parish, work—your whole life. You literally can't function without them. They can even control your future after retirement. That's beginning to change. There's more autonomy. Some priests are even deciding where they are living. Presently, most priests aren't permitted to function unless they live in a rectory. It leaves them without a haven.

Priesthood can be tiring and frustrating, especially when one has to respond to and defend legitimate pastoral decisions. Those decisions are not appreciated, only defended. Priests are often treated as if they had no sense. The simplest decisions are made for them. So they lose their self-esteem. You can't spend your life defending. It's true that some priests will just tell you to "play the party line." But that leads to just giving up. A lot of priests have done that and I'm concerned. We can't just give up.

The federation was founded in Chicago. We were sort of a loose-knit group of priests, trying to form a federation that would help us respond to Vatican II. We thought we could develop a common voice for priests. Of course, some priests didn't like it. We're still trying to live down a bit of our history. We were talking about married priests, women priests, and the like. We don't do that so much anymore. We used to be able to send in resolutions and bring them to the floor. There were sometimes twenty or thirty resolutions, some of them voted on at the eleventh hour. Naturally, some of it drew the attention of the press and we came out looking like a radical group.

Recently, we abolished the resolution process. Now, each council can bring out resolutions. They can work on priestless liturgies, presbyteral senates, ministry to AIDS victims, ministry to gays and lesbians, whatever. Sometimes, we have workshops going on the road. The process is better now. Now, it's tempered and we don't get the attention of the press. Some say that we sold out to the National Conference of Catholic Bishops (NCCB). Now, we live on dues paid by the dioceses or councils or associations. We don't take individual memberships. But now we're more acceptable to more priests. We just got a nice grant, for example, to study Eucharist-less liturgies. We'll be able to make a contribution to that topic. It's far better than the resolution process when we often had to vote on a resolution at 11:00 o'clock that was brought to the floor at 9:30.

Celibacy is an issue, but it's not the only issue. We need to build respect for priesthood, respect for ministry. Ordaining married men would also serve to create a new pool. As our numbers go down while the Catholic population goes up, we are more and more necessary. At the recent Synod on the Priesthood in Rome [October, 1990], the delegates were told that they couldn't talk about certain subjects, but they did anyway. The Church does a wonderful job at intimidation, but that's on the decline.

I don't see any influx into the priesthood under the present discipline. The real stress will come when we reach a certain age, when we're at a point in our lives when we're no longer buying into guilt.

Yes, I've heard that the priesthood is being filled up with gay priests. I don't know whether it's true or not. I suppose that, as long as the gay population in the priesthood is no higher than the percentage of the gay population at large, it would be acceptable. But I've heard that the percentage among priests is higher. However, I'm awfully naïve about such things.

I've been going to conventions for the last ten years. Each year, I hear more talk of departures from the priesthood. I get to talk to the guys who are left behind. "So-and-so's my friend, and he's gone after thirty years," they'll say. Then, they will ask: "What about me?" They want to know how they'll do the work with fewer people and what their lives will be like.

The little issues are still alive and taking unnecessary time by the bishops. When I presided, I used to receive the Eucharist after the people did, for example. Sometimes, good order dictated this. And, after all, I was the host and the host should insure that all are fed at the table. That bothered some people. It led to some conflict. It should not have even been an issue.

I'm rather pessimistic about the future. The Church just isn't going to become what it thought it was going to become. We're not unlike Israel, which thought it would become a peaceful and prosperous nation in twenty or thirty years. Now, they recognize that it will take several generations. It will be the same with the Church.

· 38 ·

Peter Simon: HIV Positive

After a series of long-distance calls, we met at a bus stop in a large city. I wasn't certain that he would show up. He could have had second thoughts.

The bus stop seemed like an odd place to meet. However, I think he was wary of meeting me in his parish and risking introductions.

Peter Simon arrived as promised and we went to a decently clean coffee shop in a tired old neighborhood. It was well after the breakfast hour. We had the place to ourselves.

Not a great many priests have AIDS, but the percentage is generally considered to be significantly higher than the population at large. One treatment center said that it had treated about twenty priests with AIDS in an eighteen-month period but didn't say if they were all from one diocese. At the medical center where Peter Simon is receiving treatment, there are five priests in treatment.

Priests with AIDS are hard to locate and few will talk, even if promised anonymity. Secrecy remains the order of the day. Sometimes, silence is the price of getting financial help from the diocese. AIDS is an expensive illness.

When a priest dies of AIDS, it is rarely mentioned. Obituaries vary. Some read, "after a long illness." Others say nothing or simply lie, generally identifying the cause of death as cancer. However, attending physicians no longer want to be identified with such deceits. They can get into trouble, even risk malpractice claims.

One diocese that lost two priests to AIDS simply did not report their deaths or even attend their funerals. When asked, they responded: "These men were not active in the diocese at the time." Their deaths were handled the way clerical suicides were once handled. In another diocese, however, when a resigned priest died of AIDS, an auxiliary bishop and virtually the priest's entire ordination class took part in a touching Eucharistic liturgy. Earlier, the archbishop himself had visited the man in the hospital, although he had been an inactive priest for over a decade. Charity varies with the theology and/or the ambition of the bishop.

Peter Simon wrote to a friend of mine and, almost parenthetically, mentioned his condition. My friend responded, asking permission to inform me. Simon responded and agreed to be interviewed on the condition that he have anonymity. Thus, many details have been changed.

The coffee shop wasn't far from Peter Simon's parish. He had been stationed there for just over a year. When diagnosed as HIV positive, his bishop had hastily, but not punitively, arranged to assign him to St. Esau's. His bishop has been very kind and understanding, frequently asking about his condition, emotionally and spiritually, as well as physically.

Peter Simon has been a diocesan priest for over twenty years. He looks his age but is measurably better looking and trimmer than many of his priestly colleagues who never recovered from the seminary dining rooms. He is well-groomed, carefully but not expensively dressed. He speaks quietly, smiles a lot, is witty and articulate—like most priests. Overall, his dress, speech, or other mannerisms do not reflect the wearisome "swish" stereotype. Yet he looks identifiably gay.

Simon has a low-key pastoral style that makes most priests so well-liked. He appears to echo the sentiments of those he meets. During our interview, a young black man, who had once sung in the parish choir, happened by. "Good morning, Father," he said with obvious pleasure. "It's so good to see you again!" Simon answered easily: "It's good to see you, too, Warren. How are you?" "I'm fine, praise God," the young man said, "and you, Father?" Simon answered: "I'm fine, too, praise God. Come over to the church soon. We'd love to have you." It was the small change of good ministry.

No one seems to know the precise percentage of priests with some homosexual orientation. If there is a gay underworld among the Catholic clergy it is terribly elusive. Older priests tend to think the percentage among the younger clergy is high; referring to themselves, younger priests give a lower figure and counter by suggesting that the older clergy have drowned their instincts in alcohol. Younger clergy will protest that the older men are latent homosexuals but that the tendency has been buried so deep it is functionally inactive. Such suppression, they claim, leads to the unusual number of mean-spirited, rigid pastors.

Others will point to bishops whom they claim have submerged such tendencies under layers of power and watered silk but who surrounded themselves with good-looking clergy. When Father Richard McBrien, chairman of the theology department at the University of Notre Dame, asked in a 1987 article in *Commonweal*: "Do homosexual bishops give preference, consciously or not to gay candidates for choice pastorate?" he rattled both higher and lower clergy. Conversely, an editor of an influential Catholic paper said that he gets a significant number of calls from lower clergy who want to "out" their bishop. The callers allege that they were once the bishop's lovers and were now being passed over for appointments. "I can't bring myself to print such stuff," the editor said. "I can't even be certain that it's true."

Homosexual priests will say that at least half of the priesthood is gay. Bishops and seminary rectors tend to be defensive, either denying the presence of any active homosexual in the clerical population or stating that the percentage of homosexual clergy does not exceed that of the population at large, about 10 percent. (Yet, one seminary professor at a large diocesan seminary stated that an entire floor in his theologate was occupied by gay seminarians.) A. W. Richard Sipe's study states that 20 percent of priests have some homosexual orientation, twice the presumed rate in the general population. Further, Sipe states that half of the homosexual priests are sexually active—twice the rate of heterosexual priests. Sipe cites Katie Leishman's article in *Atlantic Monthly* which estimates that at least one-third of priests under forty-five are homosexuals and that most are sexually active. The task force on gay/lesbian issues in San Francisco states that the gay priest population is 30 percent.

An NBC report on celibacy and the clergy out of Chicago stated that "anywhere from 23 percent to 58 percent" of the Catholic clergy have a homosexual orientation. A newly ordained priest from a large, multi-diocesan seminary believes that at least half his classmates were gay, and a gay Catholic layman, who frequents gay bars in his city stated, "I just can't go into a gay bar without meeting at least one priest." He added that most of the priests he meets are from religious orders. "I'm told that the diocese punishes its diocesan priests if they're seen in a gay bar," he said. "That's terribly ironic since some of the ones meting out the punishments are gay themselves." (One priest who has monitored the complicated heterosexual versus homosexual guessing game said that the percentage of homosexual clergy is about the same in religious orders as it is among the diocesan priests.) Sipe's estimate is that by the year 2010, if the present trend continues, the majority of the clergy will be homosexual.

Denial and secrecy are still the commonplace defenses to most sexual problems among priests, especially for homosexual priests. Secrecy remains an integral part of virtually all intimate relationships among the clergy. Separating the healthy confidences from the unhealthy ones can be extraordinarily difficult.

However, it appears to be changing slowly. There is more discussion of sexual issues in most seminaries than in the past. A few dioceses are inviting ordained priests back to the seminary for weekend seminars, generally masked under lofty expressions of celibacy but often dealing with basic sexual issues. The discussions appear to have some benefit for the younger clergy. However, priests over fifty-five appear to be extremely reluctant to discuss such issues, even with classmates they have known for decades—and most priests are over fifty-five.

Sexual issues among clergy get terribly complicated. Some priests make clear distinctions between homosexual versus gay priests. The former suggests an orientation; the latter suggests a life-style. The homosexual priest remains as celibate as his efforts will allow; the gay priest gives vent to his homosexual leanings, sometimes proclaiming that "celibacy applies only to heterosexual priests." Some gay priests neatly divide their priestly and sexual lives, giving credence to the "closet" syndrome. Others apply for one-priest parishes, often in poor neighborhoods, where they can be effective pastors and yet pursue a gay life-style away from the gaze of their fellow priests. (One prominent priest-writer terms them "lavender rectories.")

Opinions vary regarding the pastoral impact of homosexual versus heterosexual priests. Some priests believe that the sexual orientation affects the way in which a pastor serves his congregation. "His sexual orientation defines just how a pastor will view his mission and the priorities of the parish," one pastor observed. Perhaps so, but other priests said that they lived with fellow priests for years without even being aware that they were homosexually inclined. Again, it gets terribly complicated.

It would appear that, in a hostile theological environment, homosexually inclined priests develop other problems. Over 50 percent of clergy treated for alcoholism have some homosexual concerns, according to one study. Others informally report that the sexual orientation issue hobbles priestly effectiveness, i.e., efforts to come to terms with their own sexuality drain pastoral energies.

In any case, as one priest observed: "Now that it's out, we can't seem to stop talking about it."

T he bishop has been good to me. He let me come here to this parish where the pastor is a very decent fellow. I really don't know if many other priests know about my condition. The bishop moved me here without consulting the Priests' Personnel Board. I assume that he had to tell them something. I don't know. I can only tell you that my contacts with my fellow priests have lessened a great deal since I learned that I was HIV positive. Maybe the word is out. Maybe they're afraid of getting AIDS!

(Laughs.) Maybe they just don't want to be associated with a gay priest. On the other hand, I haven't been too involved with a lot of them in recent years anyway.

I've been doing a lot of drug and alcohol rehabilitation work. In fact, I was seriously considering leaving the active ministry to do this work full time when I was diagnosed. I prayed about this for a couple of years. I asked God to do something that would make me stay. Well, I have my answer now!

During my twenty years in the priesthood, I've been in eight parishes. Only one of them—the one I'm in now—was free of drugs and alcohol. It's so pervasive. The clergy are an enabling group. In one parish, I turned in my own pastor because he had a serious drinking problem, and, you know, they reacted as if I had done something wrong! They were angry. I was told to tell the parishioners that Father had gone out West to do further studies. Such hypocrisy! Such a cover-up! Such a shame!

Matt Fox [controversial Dominican priest-teacher and author] has written that the Church is a dysfunctional family, and he's so right. The problem isn't celibacy. It's one of intimacy. Look at ____ ____. (a well-known priest). He's still on drugs and alcohol and nothing is done.

You know, we should replace our clergy meeting structure with Alcoholics Anonymous spirituality. We'd be much better off.

We grow more dysfunctional. The church is running scared. It gives carte blanche to the black and Latino priests. They're terribly afraid of losing them. As a consequence, the problems of addiction are only growing worse, especially among the minorities, and there are all kinds of cases of priests absconding with parish funds.

My own life-style could have been anything I wanted it to be. I guess it was, in a way. Now, however, they just tell you that they love you and leave you alone. We're so isolated. What we need is some closeness, some companionship, some intimacy. But you don't get it and you end up misbehaving and pilfering.

That terrible problem with *Humanae Vitae* [Paul VI's encyclical on birth control] is still residually corrosive. Many men have mellowed since that time, but many left, and most of the others are still hurting. That encyclical had a great impact on the laity, but it had an impact on the clergy, too. Priests who dissented are still being treated badly. It destroyed their morale.

In my diocese, there is a noticeable absence of fraternity. In my seminary class, there wasn't much fraternity to begin with. Now, after twenty years, we've met as a group only three times. And individually there isn't much contact. Perhaps I'm part of the reason. Priests tend to stay away from bad-news priests like me.

Clergy relationships are pretty thin in this diocese. We had Vince Dwyer come here, you know, the man who specializes in priestly relationships, prayer groups, and all that. Well, he was good but his program wasn't successful here. We're a diocese of loners.

We tried some sort of sexual adjustment workshop. That didn't work, either. The diocese could deal with obscenities and orgies but not with two adults who love one another. They could crush Dignity [a group of lesbian/ gay lay Catholics] but not pornography. They couldn't distinguish having sex from making love. They can tolerate two priests who are male lovers but none that are in love with a female.

Now, since Dignity was banned, we're dealing with warring factions. There are still five hundred guys going to Dignity liturgies under another name. They're among the finest liturgies in town. Gays know how to pray. And about 20 percent of them are resigned priests and another 20 percent are guys going into the seminary. It's crazy!

Maybe it's just my own projection, but the source of all my pain in the Church has been the clergy. When I was associated with Dignity, I felt a real sense of community, much more so than with my fellow priests. I like to socialize. Dignity was a great outreach. Now, the bishop has closed it down. At least, he won't let them pray together in the churches. So, I've lost something very important. We didn't get together for sex, you know. We gathered to worship God and to discuss those things that touched our hearts. I've witnessed much more sex in rectories than I did in Dignity and even in gay bars. I've had much more serious discussions with gays than I've had with clergy. All the clergy want to talk about is sports! Now, the Gay A.A. (Alcoholics Anonymous) has become an important source for me.

My involvement with Dignity, the Gay A.A., and with people with drug and alcohol problems were all kind of an avocation until recently. The work led me to PWA (Persons with AIDS) and that has become my priestly work. Now, PWA meets in my parish. It's been turned into a kind of religious inquiry service. People are actually joining up! It's wonderful! The Church can deal with dying people. It's the living they can't deal with. Hell, they're all recovering Catholics! They're returning to the Church!

When I was in the seminary and during my years as a young priest, we dealt with sex by drinking. I never drank until I became a priest. Now, when I return to the seminary where I studied, I'd swear that 90 percent of the seminarians are gay. It makes sense. Hell, the vocation directors are gay! My seminary took candidates from a number of dioceses. Maybe that's why many were gay. It is easier to hide the obvious away from home. It's all out in the open now. Good Lord, just go out there and look at a procession. It's a gay parade. It's anything goes now. You should hear the conversations! Well, maybe they're dealing with it better.

Five of my best friends have left the priesthood. They are all gay. There was another one. He died of cancer.

I've been in drug and alcohol counseling for ten years now, I guess. I'm good at it. But this diocese hasn't been one where people can grow. I'm good at working with the terminally ill, too, but the bishop kept putting me into parish work.

I began drinking as a young priest and, about ten years ago, I had become a full-blown alcoholic. I went over to Washington and into St. Luke's, that clinic run by Michael Peterson, the priest-psychiatrist who worked with alcoholics, addicts, and pedophiles in the priesthood. I was there a long time. After I left St. Luke's, I spent some time with my family down South. I thought about entering a religious order. I even went to their headquarters for a period of discernment but I soon discovered that the novice master was an alcoholic and that my spiritual advisor tried to put a move on me. Hell, their vocation director died of AIDS! I didn't need that.

Look, I'm not anxious to out anyone, but Michael Peterson used to say that most clergy are sexually dysfunctional [Peterson died of AIDS in Washington, D.C.]. Just look at the homophobic ones. Well over half of them are homosexual!

I'll never forget one seminary rector who stated that, in all his years as rector, he had never encountered a gay seminarian. The man died of AIDS! The denial is awful.

Not long after I was ordained, I found myself growing increasingly confused by what I was seeing in the priesthood. I lived for three years with a man who was a child molester, for example, and the diocese was covering for him. In those days, they handled all the sexual-offender cases in a legal way, not in a moral or pastoral way. They're still doing it. It's still denial and threats.

Not long ago, I talked with a sexual-offender counselor and she told me some crazy stories about how my diocese reacts to these cases.

Anyway, I went to a chancery official and told him that I wanted to find a rectory that was sober, sane, and spiritual. He said, "Peter, you're not going to find that in this diocese. What you're talking about is an ideal."

John McNeill [former Jesuit; acknowledged homosexual] says that clergy are ego-dystonic, that is, with abnormal egos. Some suffer from a lack of any sexual or intimate life. When I was in treatment, I recall one priest who said that he had one sexual experience in his thirty years in the priesthood. He said it was the greatest night of his life! (Laughs.)

Priests are often very passive. Others are all mixed up. And they act out. They never actualize their potential.

I still meet priests in gay bars. I don't go to these bars for sex, but I do go for companionship. We can talk about serious things in these bars. We can hold deep theological discussions. In rectories, you never hear such discussions. In a gay bar, a priest will tell you that he's had only one sexual experience in a lifetime. At best, he could only give a vague idea what sexual intimacy—or any intimacy—was all about. And that's what leads to crazy conduct.

I'm thinking of one man who has carried on a twelve-year gay relationship with two married men. Now, he's dumped them both, telling them that they're getting in the way of his career. See, it's that kind of craziness. But it leads right up to the bishops. Did you see that situation in _____? The state wanted to pass an amendment that would outlaw housing and job discrimination against gays. The bishops came out against it. But when the gays threatened to out the gay bishops and priests, the Church backed down. It's crazy!

I've gotten more isolated from my fellow priests, I guess. I really have no solid clergy friends. All they want to do is go places now. I need to talk. I avoid the annual clergy retreat now. I just don't want to be bothered. I make mine at a retreat house run by nuns. They're wonderful, much more compassionate, much more nurturing. It's a climate conducive to health.

The pastor where I am now is wonderful. A fine man. He seems to understand. We may be one of the best parishes in the diocese for liturgies, and the church is filled with gays on Sunday. We even have members of a transvestite group! They come to church in coats and ties and then go off to their cross-dressing club. We also have a traditional Mass on Sunday. It attracts a lot of real conservatives and a lot of gays who like the pre-Vatican II liturgies. A lot of the conservatives are terribly homophobic but I also think they are closet gays. It makes for some powerful contradictions.

Years ago, I used to be a hot number, I guess. I was really out of control. I sure got lots of invitations. I was offered promotions in exchange for sexual favors. I turned them down. I'm just not built that way. Yet, I've seen wonderful men who are not gay but who support an adult approach to the issue being turned down for promotion. So, we end up with homophobic priests buying vacation homes together so that they can have trysts in their little chalets. Some get to be bishops. It's crazy!

It's not really a gay-straight issue. It's an intimacy issue. I'm thinking of a priest in _____. He was walking out of his parish and the pastor, who is now a bishop, didn't even say "good bye." That man would have stayed if he felt some caring. We're now in a catch-22 situation: celibacy but no intimacy. The isolation only grows.

You saw that piece in the *National Catholic Reporter* about the gaying of the clergy in Philadelphia. Well, it's even more so here. Sure, our gay bars have their clergy nights, too, and chancery officials show up. Some priests can emotionally separate their priestly life and their gay life. No guilt, no nothing. Just two lives.

I've got friends in Washington, D.C. I did some studies there and recovered from my alcoholism there. They're gay. They run a very discreet gay dating service. It's expensive. They get a lot of clergy business. What does that tell you? And down South two others run a gay resort. Very nice. Very discreet. Why, they get so many priests that they actually schedule liturgies.

Oh, I'm very serene now. I've never felt better. I'm more enthused, more involved, less selfish. I don't know what the future will bring. Perhaps the bishop is being nice to me because he thinks I'm going to die soon. But I'm not! The doctor has me on some new medication. I feel great.

I've got to leave now. I hear confessions at noon. I've become a good confessor, I think. It has something to do with accepting myself as I am.

What would I say to the Church? I'd tell them to grow up. I guess I'd tell them not to be afraid of the devil within them. It could become an angel.

· 39 ·

Daedalus Stephens:
Disillusioned Idealist

Daedalus Stephens (pseudonym) left the active ministry only four years after his ordination. After training periods that can stretch as long as twelve years, nearly 25 percent of the average ordination class leave the ministry within the first ten years of their ordination. If other professions had as high an attrition rate, there would be great alarm. One source, a seminary president, confided that the cost of an education at a major seminary can range between $8,000 and $37,000 per year. With an attrition rate of 93 percent from high-school seminary through ordination and nearly 40 percent after ordination through Silver Anniversary, the costs are staggering. Daedalus Stephens paid some of his own seminary expenses. Still, the direct cost of supplying his two years of college and four years of major seminary education were at least $100,000. His diocese got a four-year return on its investment—a rather cold but necessary way of looking at a vocation. (Dental school dropout rate is around 7 percent. Once dentists are in practice, the dropout rate is under 5 percent. Professions with dropout rates as high as the priesthood would first face loss of accreditation of their schools and, later, the ultimate loss of the profession.)

Bishops are generally talented and thoughtful people. They commissioned studies on the priesthood as early as 1965. The statistics are clear enough. Entries continue to be low; attrition rates at the first levels remain high; resignations have slowed but continue. In addition, the priesthood has been studied by experts from a psychological, spiritual, theological, historical, liturgical—even an ecumenical—perspective. "The data is there," one observer said. "Even the solutions are there, but the bishops cannot accept the solutions. They are caught with rules that simply no longer work."

Daedalus Stephens was student body president at his Catholic high school. He enrolled in a state college where he completed two years as a business major before entering the diocesan college seminary. After two years, he left. "I left because I had to," he said. "I returned two years later because I had to." In the interim, he completed his college degree and earned an M.A. at a Catholic university. He was ordained after four years at the major seminary during which he taught at a nearby Catholic high school. After three years in a parish, he asked for a leave of absence. Within that year, he found a job with a promising future, met a young, Catholic woman, and applied for laicization. The dispensation process is not yet complete but Daedalus and Molly are now married. "I'd really like to get an annulment," Daedalus said. "I honestly don't believe that the sacrament took."

("I'm probably being too careful," he added, "but I'd just as soon this interview be anonymous. I don't think my employers would mind; they're well aware of my background; in part, they hired me because of it. But it would just cause some needless explanations.")

O ne prominent priest in this diocese said recently that he doesn't think there has been a worse time for priests or the priesthood. I guess I'd agree.

The yuppies are my generation. They're not going to church. But they're doing good things. I talk with them a lot. They really feel that they don't need the Church—and they're right! When they go to church, what they often hear is not credible. The young people don't really give a damn about Hunthausen [Archbishop Raymond Hunthausen of Seattle]. They see that case of his with the Vatican as a pure power struggle. They don't even know all the details of the case, only that it smells. But when you ask them about church, they'll point to the Hunthausen case and say: "See? That's why we don't go to church."

In my parish, we had kids in second grade who no longer go to church. My generation at least went to church through high school. This generation won't. I was in a great parish with a great pastor, but we were getting only 30 percent at Mass on Sunday. I think the world has gotten so incredibly secular that there's no need for an institutional Church. People only seem to need us at those big moments—hatched, matched, and dispatched—or maybe, First Communion and Confirmation, too. I'm beginning to think that there should be some minimum requirement about Mass, some deeper commitment.

I remember when the bishop addressed the priests' senate. He said: "We cannot assume that the values that traditionally have given meaning and credibility to our ministry and life-style are still operative; indeed they are questioned and sometimes ridiculed." He was right on target.

Not many years ago, the proudest parents on the block had three sons and two daughters. One was a priest, one a doctor, one a lawyer, and the two girls were teachers in Catholic grammar school. Something like that. Today, those parental aspirations may remain, but the inherent occupational value has disintegrated. Today, we're told that all priests have psychosexual problems. All lawyers, especially those who enter politics, are crooks. All doctors are in it for the money. All teachers lack the good old dedication for Catholic education.

Thirty years ago, priests were supported by full churches and requests for their blessing. As the only ones who could "do it" they were valuable. Now, the Church has become a voluntary society. People choose to attend on their own timetable, their own terms. It's gotten so that Sunday Mass attendance is no longer a valid criterion for evaluating religious faith. And ministry just isn't valued in the same way, either.

At Vatican II, the priests were the ones who asked to come off the pedestals and gain feet of clay. So now that our feet are dirty, how do we clean our shoes? Priests have to find new ways to hear and to invite means of support and affirmation. Priests' ego needs must be met where the Church is, not where it was. I think that a priest's own value will come from intimate friends and nourishing prayer. The value of priesthood will come from *who* priests are, not *what* they are. The credibility of the Church will come when we get honest with the world.

Honest, there are days when I felt like a well-paid prostitute. People came only when they needed me. They'll tell you that they haven't been inside a church since their Confirmation twelve years ago. Now, they want to get married. Again, I had to ask, "What does it mean to be Catholic?" People came to my parish for a funeral; cried their eyes out during my homily; then I never saw them again. Or some young person will say, "I'm getting married in this church because of my mother." No other reason! I was asked to witness something that they didn't even believe in. Shouldn't we have some minimum standards, or was I just mayonnaise to spread over some event?

All that sounds like I'm trying to make the Church a club. It's not that. It's just that I have to ask how important it is to be in church. How important is it for the *priest* to be in church? Would people miss us if we weren't there? Gosh, in some neighborhoods, belonging to a church is like belonging to the local lyric opera.

I had a friendly encounter with the bishop when he came to confirm. I call Confirmation the sacrament of exodus. I asked him how he could go around, confirming all those kids, when he knew that it would be the last time they would be in church until they came to get married or buried. You know, even for my brothers, the Church is a nonissue.

There were ten in my class. One guy lasted less than a year. He went ape after ordination. Got a woman pregnant and rumors had it that he was involved with others. I was the second to leave. We never got together since the day we were ordained. Oh, a few of us would go out from time to time. But the class never met to do a reunion. There was one guy that I never saw again.

A few of the guys have had a tough time. They weren't well received. One guy has had three liturgy committees quit on him. I can't really blame them. Hell, one Sunday morning, he rang the church bell ninety-six times!

Again, I was in a very good parish with a great pastor and another associate. But the three of us had radically different views of priesthood. Harry (the pastor) is a low-key natural leader. He's a down-to-earth beer belly who prays and reads a lot and tries to keep the belly off by jogging. Some years before I came to the parish, I think he was involved with a woman. She was a good person and Harry fell hard. It wasn't one of those grubby affairs. It was based on real caring. Anyway, they mutually decided that his priesthood was more important. It must have been a tough decision; I don't know if he ever recovered. Something went out of him.

The associate was a nice guy; he was ordained four years ahead of me. But I just couldn't warm up to him. He tried. He'd come to my room and say that we ought to be talking more, sharing things. Tom said that he couldn't wait to be a priest. I guess I never felt that way. I was ordained only one day and I was mad at the church.

I'm afraid we didn't have any real community life. We each had our own phone, which was very necessary, but it meant that we could stay in our room and take and make calls.

Harry says that priests still give witness. I don't know if we do. I loved doing liturgies. I loved giving homilies. I loved standing outside the church and greeting the people. Sometimes, people would say to me: "You're not like a priest." Now, that's a shitty compliment! Many of them saw a priest as one who couldn't or wouldn't have relations with women or else one that could and was up to no good.

For me priesthood was a good day but a lonely night. I had a spiritual director. I met with him often. He used to tell me that I would work as hard as I could and stay out as long as I could, doing things just so I wouldn't have to face myself and my priesthood. I thought that by keeping busy I could crowd out my problems, but it only made them worse. In a way, my outside work did energize me for work in the parish. I came back, filled with ideas. So, there I was. I loved everything I was doing but I was burning out.

As lonely as I may have been, I found myself looking for time alone. I needed time to prepare. Getting ready for a good homily was like preparing for a prize fight. I needed time. Yet, after Mass on Sunday, after I had busted my ass on a homily, the people would come out and say: "How are ya, Father? Whaddya think of those Giants?"

I used to like to greet and seat people before Mass, especially the little old ladies. But, when I did, I'd grab a missalette for them and a host would fall out. Their children would come to church because their parents forced them. They'd go to Communion and then leave the host in the missalette. It was part superstition, part fear, part hostility—I don't know. A lot of Old-Country stuff. A lot of ignorance still out there.

I really don't think we can marry people anymore unless we're reasonably sure that there's a connection. I'm not even sure we can bury them. Before I left, I was doing non-Eucharistic funerals. I didn't want to embarrass anyone, so we'd have a regular liturgy and I'd just skip over most of the Canon. I mean some of these families hadn't been near a church in so long that it would be foolish to call them to Eucharist.

I found that, when I asked people how they expressed their faith and how they planned to get from where they were to where they wanted to be, that they started thanking me. I really felt that we had to challenge them more, but we've gotten too timid.

We've lost a thousand people in my parish in three years. Most were move-aways or deaths. It's a first generation parish. Those old people came for the morning Mass, but their children won't.

I think that through it all my morale was good but my concerns were many. Not long before I left, I met with a dozen priests, guys ordained from three months to thirty-four years. We talked about morale. There wasn't the usual cluck of clerical gatherings. We talked seriously. The conversation left me hope-filled. We talked about the studio weddings we were asked to do, the giving of First Communion at funerals, and Confirmation as a sacrament of exodus. We asked each other whether or not people who no longer value organized religion could value us.

I recall an article in *U.S. Catholic* in which the writer suggested that priests should sit in church one day a week, all day, in prayer. That would be ministerial suicide. It would trivialize the ministry.

My friend, Sue, said that the Church can't have any real significance until it gets honest about celibacy, women, and the pill. Yet, even if we could resolve these issues, priestly morale and the need for prayer would remain a problem. I found the day-to-day living of celibacy very frustrating. A lot of forced hypocrisy. My sister would come to town to visit. We're very close. We both love folk music. I'd take her over to Sycamore Street to one of those trendy folk places—and I'd have to worry about someone seeing us. I told myself that I didn't give a damn, but it bothered me. I was bothered, too, by the fact that gay priests could meet anywhere—even live together in rectories or at summer homes they bought together—and nothing was said. Celibacy is only for heteros! It bothered me when I met a young woman in the parking lot at the parish. I was wearing an old state-college sweatshirt from a state where skiing is a big sport. She said that we'd have to go skiing someday. I told her that I was a priest, and she just shrugged, like "so what?" She either didn't value celibacy or didn't understand it. And I got even angrier when the priests were all called together to discuss celibacy and the diocese had a lawyer speak to us. Over half of us were really wrestling with the problem and they had a lawyer talk to us!

I can see a scenario when I could say that what I've been saying won't be accepted anymore. I did not leave the active priesthood for a specific reason. It's a whole medley of things, from a dedicated pope who took a bullet but who is destructive of all those things I've hinted at.

Priesthood is in a precariously fragile position. Morale and credibility have never been worse. Yet, to focus only on problems and not on strategies can become a self-fulfilling prophecy of self-destruction. This should be a time to bond, not to bomb. It's time to stop the bitching and start the building. The gains of the past must be celebrated and shared. Otherwise, we'll return to those closed windows.

I'm sounding conservative! Me, a flaming liberal! It's just that I have found parishes where priests minister to people out of love, not jargon. They don't talk about Church; they are Church. I think there is still hope.

No, I'd never go back. It's over for me. I'm at peace.

· 40 ·

Theodore C. Stone: The Faith of the People

Ted Stone is in his sixties; he was ordained nearly forty years ago. He still whistles. He looks younger than most of his classmates. He's a small man with a bouncy walk and boundless energy. He has a salesman's hope and an altar boy's smile. Like most priests, he can talk with the best of them. Just meeting him makes you feel good.

Ted Stone reads the Scriptures and then tries to live them. His copy of the Documents of Vatican II is literally worn out from reading and underlining. According to one close observer, Ted Stone did more for CCD and liturgy education than anyone in the archdiocese of Chicago. He left active ministry in 1970; applied to return in 1984, and was accepted in 1991. Presently, he is an associate pastor at Our Lady Mother of the Church in Chicago. He lives in nearby Park Ridge with his daughter, Beth, and his son, Tim.

This used to be the cook's room. Now, it's my office. The cook is over at St. Ferdinand's. We just didn't need a cook anymore. The young priests were raised on junk food, I guess. No more sit-down meals. I miss that. No time for informal dialogue. I guess that it's partly the shortage of priests. Only two here, and now myself. I come for breakfast here, however, and we have a dialogue. You just can't say everything at meetings. A lot of small but important stuff gets missed.

I love my home. It's home for Beth and Tim. It's over a hundred years old and I worked on every board in it. If the cardinal asked me to move into a rectory, I'd have to talk to him about it.

You know, a person can't go through a lifetime closing doors. After a while, you can't relate. And that's what can happen in a rectory.

A group of priests can decide to live together as a family. My class owns a home together up in Cedar Lake. It was a large class—fifty of us for Chicago alone. Four are dead now and ten have resigned. Most of the rest share this house. We try to gather there on Wednesdays, although I've only been able to get up there about every six weeks. It's got four bedrooms for those who want to stay over and it can accommodate fifteen or twenty if we have a gathering. Larry Hanley's at St. Peter's in Antioch, not far from Cedar Lake. He looks after it. As a matter of fact, when I got my rescript, Larry said: "Congratulations, Ted. Now that you're back, start paying your dues!" (Laughs.)

I think I'm the first priest who got permission to leave, permission to marry, had children, lost my wife, and returned. Oh, there are some married priests who are in active practice. You've read about those in Eastern Europe who got married after ordination and some who were married when ordained. But that was all sub rosa, outside Vatican jurisdiction. I was told of a Latin American bishop who informed the pope that he had four priests who were doing great work in his diocese and that all four were married and had families. The pope just shrugged.

Cardinal Bernardin [archbishop of Chicago] is a process man. It took six and a half years for him to get this rescript. But he never lost hope. He spent at least twenty minutes alone with John Paul II and they talked about nothing else. The pope agreed that I should be reinstated. The cardinal told Cardinal Ratzinger [Joseph Ratzinger, prefect of the Congregation for Doctrine of the Faith] both before and after. And Ratzinger told him after the audience that cardinals enjoy a special relationship with the Holy Father and that he only had to put it in writing. Bernardin went back to his room and wrote a letter immediately. Oh sure, I know that Cardinal Bernardin could have just come home and reinstated me without any more paperwork. After all, the pope had given permission. But the cardinal is always trying to establish precedents, always trying to make changes. He has always seen me as one of his priests. He was ordained in 1952, too, so he has adopted our class as his.

In July 1990, I wrote a letter to Ray Goedert [vicar for priests]. He's a classmate. I suggested to him that maybe what the pope meant was simply to take me back and assign me, just as one would with a newly-ordained. That would have been fine with me. I know that Bernardin had written a very strong letter. But those delays were testing my patience. I'm just in awe of the Cardinal; after all those rebuffs, he still had hope. It gave me hope. During these years away from active ministry, I found that I could do less than a lay person. Oh, I guess I could have been a lector or commentator, or even distributed Communion, but I didn't want to do anything that would make waves. So, on Sundays, I used to stand in the foyer greeting people before and after Mass. I've been a pastoral associate here since 1984. When I arrived,

I preached at all the Masses and told them that I was a resigned priest and a widower with two children, and that I had applied to return to full ministry. I asked for their prayers. All through these years of waiting, I never met anyone who wasn't overjoyed. Maybe there were some, but I never met them.

I was beginning to lose some hope. In October 1990, the *National Catholic Reporter* carried an article that said that optional celibacy and married priests, including resigned married priests, had already been dealt with in a definitive way and would not be open to discussion during the Synod on the Priesthood. I thought that such a statement would cut off my chances. But, instead, not long after, I met Bernardin at a retreat. He pulled me aside and told me that he had called someone at the Congregation for Doctrine of the Faith and had been informed that the approval had gone through. But he told me to say nothing until the official rescript arrived. Oh, I wanted so much to celebrate at Christmas! I kept saying to myself, "It's going to come soon." And finally, on January 7, 1991, it arrived. All in Latin! *Reintegratio cum nulla preconditione.* My Latin is terribly rusty. But it means "reinstated without any conditions." It means that I don't have to return to the seminary for retraining. I've been going back there for years anyway, doing my retreat days and all that. My spiritual director is there and I have been getting lessons on now to celebrate liturgy. It means that I could be a pastor someday. I'd love to have a parish. I think that I have a gift for bringing disparate groups together. I think that I could do a good job in a troubled parish.

Being a single parent hasn't been an obstacle to my pastoral work. I'm just ten minutes away. I'm here by 9:30 in the morning and I stay until 3:30. Then, I go home; have a few hours with the children, and can be back here by 6:30 for evening meetings. I've already told Joe [Joseph F. Ognibene, pastor and classmate] that he could put the call-forwarding line in my house, now that I can take calls. I haven't been able to do that—even bring Communion to shut-ins—all these years. Oh, I've helped a few people when they were dying, but now I can be there for them, and it won't interfere with my home life. Beth is away at college now and Tim can take care of himself, in spite of his developmental disability.

I'm a Chicagoan. Spent twelve years in the seminary system. I got interested very early in teaching religion to teenagers, especially the "publics" as we used to call public school kids. I was at St. Tarcisius Parish. We soon had a program there that brought in 90 percent of the kids in the neighborhood, many of them not even Catholics. Cardinal Stritch established the Confraternity of Christian Doctrine program in 1940 and put John Gleason [Chicago priest] as its first director. In the forties and fifties, these programs worked exceptionally well. Joe Richards and Doc Farrell [Chicago priests] were especially effective in black ministry. Sometimes, 150 were baptized in a single ceremony. This was the era of "released time." We even had days of recollection for public school kids. There were problems but, with 25,000 students in the program, it was a great success.

I joined the CCD program in 1957. Cardinal Cody [archbishop of Chicago, 1965-82] made me director in 1966. My job was to develop parish high-school religion programs. The winds of biblical and liturgical change were blowing at that time. In 1958, Johannes Hofinger, a Jesuit, from the East Asian Pastoral Institute, came to the Chicago CCD office and spoke of kerygmatic renewal in religious education. It was sweeping the world. It was like rediscovering the fundamentals.

The kerygmatic approach wasn't like the Baltimore Catechism. It went to the heart of the Christian message. It was Christ-centered around the pascal mystery of involvement in the dying and rising of Jesus. I got caught up in it.

In 1960, Cardinal Meyer [Albert Meyer, archbishop of Chicago, 1958-65] sent me to Germany to work with catechetical leaders. This was the period of John XXIII, just before Vatican II, when there was a dramatic revitalization of catechetics. In that year, too, Jim McCarthy [Chicago priest] and I began to develop catechetical faith communities, small groups of catechists who met regularly to grow together in their faith. These small groups led to a major change in the CCD structure. It was during that time that Jim McCarthy also developed the SPRED (Special Religious Education Division) for the mentally handicapped. It was a vibrant period. Gerry Weber and Jim Kilgallon developed their manuals and text books for elementary schools; Mark Link, another Jesuit, did the same for high schools. Dan Cantwell and Dan Lupton introduced catechists and others to the treasures of the Bible, and Jim Hill and I collaborated in writing an adult catechism that reflected the renewal in catechetics.

In 1964, Alphonse Nebreda, a Jesuit, and I founded the Institute of Pastoral Studies at Loyola University of Chicago, with Mike Gannon, another Jesuit. I was also vice president of the National Liturgy Conference. Oh, I was doing an awful lot of things! With Peter Foote, Walt Imbiorski, and John Hill, I edited commentaries on the Documents of Vatican II to keep catechists and other ministerial leaders abreast of developments. To implement the changes introduced by Vatican II, we set up fifty-two liturgy training programs around the diocese. There were 445 parishes back then and 431 of them sent parishioners. We had 11,000 people at the weekly sessions!

But I was over my head. Too much work. I was burning out and filling up with anger. I had moved the office over to Fry Street and was hiring lots of lay people. By 1967, we had thirty full-time people who worked with thousands of volunteers. Our texts were selling all over the country. I never took royalties from any of these sales. I simply thought that the profits would go to support the program. Instead, not long after Cardinal Cody came I discovered that the CCD monies were being siphoned off to aid Catholic schools. Soon, our budget was cut and we had to start letting people go. I tried to place these well-educated people in other dioceses. When Cody learned that our best people were going elsewhere, he blew up. He brought me in and yelled at me: "I'm the bishop here!" He was angry because it didn't look good, sending these people to other dioceses. He would have preferred to simply let them go, but I couldn't do that in conscience.

I wrote to bishops and priests and told them of the cutbacks. I asked for money. We got some contributions but certainly not enough—nowhere near what we were earning on our books. The pastors must have thought that I had flipped. In retrospect, I should have confronted the issues, but in those days I knew nothing of confrontation. I watched helplessly as the programs were cut back.

I went off and made a retreat, but was still terribly angry. Bishop Buswell [Charles A. Buswell, retired bishop of Pueblo, Colorado] offered to take me but I refused. Looking back, I think there was a lot of self-deception on my part. It was an era of getting into relationships and, while I wasn't involved with anyone, the times had an impact on me. I just walked away.

I went to see the cardinal. I guess I was hoping that he'd say something to cure the anger or the pain. I told him that I wanted to apply for laicization. He said only one thing: "Now, Ted, don't organize against the Church." I still feel sorrow for the man. He never really knew me.

Although it was a time of relationships, I knew nothing of them. In fact, I had problems with relationships. I was sending people away to work elsewhere and I didn't even know if they cared for me. I didn't even ask. Judy O'Sheil was working there in those days. She was enormously talented in music. Her "Peace" song is still being sung today, especially at those Teen Encounters Christ functions. But, like the others, I tried to send her away.

I ran away. I felt a need to get away from Chicago where I was too well known. I didn't want to give scandal. I went to Washington, D.C., linked up with John Mulholland, and began a six-month job search. I even investigated the Peace Corps. Then, Vail Scott from Chicago met me in D.C. and told me that there was an ideal job for me at the Department of Mental Health back home. They were forming a new region and they needed someone for organization. I was interviewed and offered a job by Dr. Patrick Staunton. But I had just done a film on the new rite of Christian Burial for the funeral directors. I had a little money, so I took my mother on a trip to California. I was still running.

In California, I talked with Monsignor John Scanlon, an old friend, and, while with him, I asked myself: "What am I running away from?" Later during that trip, my closest friend, John Grathwahl [Lansing priest] met me at Vail, Colorado, and we talked. Dave Myron at the Peace Corps contacted me out there and offered to put me in charge of job training for the Far East. But Pat Staunton called too. So, I stopped running. I changed my ticket and went back to Chicago and the Department of Mental Health.

The job started in February 1970. In April, Judy called just to say hello. I asked her out to dinner. Eight months later, we were married. It was that fast!

I worked with the Department of Mental Health until 1983. I worked with some wonderful people but I also got a whole new perspective on bureaucracy. We have such wonderful freedom in the Church! In the Mental Health Department, I often felt that the only purpose was to preserve people's jobs. Certainly, that was far more important than the people we were supposed to be helping. But I never had the guts to quit. We had two children. I learned something about how people must work at less than satisfying jobs when they have children.

Judy died in 1981, when Beth was nine and Tim was seven. Then, I couldn't have quit even if I wanted to. In 1983, there was a reorganization and my job was eliminated.

The next eighteen months were important for me. I grew close to a group of resigned priests known as the Upper Room. They used to gather and pray together. Carole and Marty Hegarty gave me a Liturgy of the Hours and I began praying the Hours again. In time, I thought about working in a parish.

I spent six months visiting all the priests I knew—old guys, young guys, pastors, and associates. It was an interesting journey. They were all wonderfully positive. I visited Gene Lyons, an older priest. I was worried about the older men. He met with his class and they were unanimous in their approval of my return to some kind of pastoral work. One priest said simply: "Hell, Ted, why don't you come back to full ministry?"

I made an appointment to see the cardinal. He must have heard the gossip because he already knew what I was going to ask. But I had been told that he likes people to have their homework done, so I went with Plan A and Plan B—full priestly ministry or working in a parish. I tried to read from my notes. He listened. You know the way he looks right at you? Well, I couldn't read the notes, I was so nervous. He interrupted me and said simply: "I'm not interested in Plan B. The Vatican would look very favorably on your return." I could hardly believe it!

I was so happy that, when I left the chancery office and met a priest friend just outside on Superior Street, I blurted it out. We started dancing in the street! By that evening, I had told a few others. I finally got a call from Jim Roache, the cardinal's vicar. He told me that I'd better keep it under my hat. So I had to keep quiet.

I went home and wrote my life story for the pope. I thought that the process would be very fast. But it turned out to be very slow.

I came to Our Lady Mother of the Church in December 1984. I started the RCIA (Rite of Christian Initiation for Adults) right away and began working on social concerns and the ministry to the elderly. The people were magnificent, very accepting. I was able to live each day to the fullest, even while waiting.

My case went to the Congregation on the Doctrine of the Faith. That was unusual. Another man who returned after leaving, getting married, adopting a child, getting a divorce, and entering an A.A. program was returned to ministry through the Congregation on Religious. I had permission to leave and to marry. I had done it by the book. So, I ended up in Ratzinger's congregation. I think that they viewed my resignation as something based on faith or doctrine or philosophy—something like that. I just don't know. Anyway, it went to the Doctrine of the Faith. And I think that slowed it down.

The first refusal came with the explanation that the Church never ordains men who have minor children. I was baffled by that explanation since I was already ordained. Besides, there was no definition of what constituted a minor child. Cardinal Bernardin tried to get an answer to that one. They answered that the minority age should be established by local custom. I think the cardinal was trying to set a precedent.

It stayed that way for over six years. The cardinal asked at least four times. There was a lot of correspondence. Finally, it came.

The cardinal invited me to his home the Saturday morning after the rescript came. We concelebrated with Ray Goedert and Joe Ognibene. Beth came in from Oberlin where she's studying music. She played her violin during the Mass. Tim said that he almost cried and Beth described it all as a sign of hope for the Church.

The past six years have been good ones. They were years of real formation in ministry. I learned to take people as they are. I learned that we priests don't have all the truth. I've learned that Rome does need some restructuring but that we must have hope that it will. I've found Jesus in parts of people—an elderly woman's smile, the helping hands of someone guiding a spouse into church, that sort of thing. I visit a man who is caring for his terribly sick wife and he shares a joke with me. I find Jesus in his laughter even as he has to care for a bedridden wife. I witness their pain and I hear their hope. I see their faith and I witness the hope of the cardinal. I share that hope. I have great faith in that prayer in the Canon: "Look not upon our sins but on the faith of your Church." It will all work out.

They'll announce my return to full ministry in next week's bulletin. I won't be there. I'm giving a retreat. But the following week, I'll preach at all the Masses and I'll preside at the 12:00. I'm looking for a simple crystal bowl for the hosts. I want all the Eucharist in one bowl from which we will all share—and I want everyone to see the Bread of Christ. I hope you'll come.

POSTSCRIPT: After the interview, we went to a local restaurant for lunch. An elderly parishioner was also waiting to be seated. "Good morning, Ted," she started to say. She stopped, smiled, and whispered: "Good morning, Father."

· 41 ·

Mel Swift: Sex Offender

Mel Swift (a pseudonym) is a convicted pedophile. In the strict, clinical sense, a pedophile is one who is attracted to prepubescents. However, the word is also used to describe those who are preoccupied with adolescents. According to psychotherapist A. W. Richard Sipe, author of *A Secret World: Sexuality and the Search for Celibacy*, a landmark study of celibacy published in late 1990, 2 percent of priests are pedophiles in the clinical sense and another 4 percent are preoccupied with adolescents. (Sipe points out that not all 6 percent act out their inclinations.)

Mel Swift is attracted to adolescents. One can only guess, but he could also be a homosexual, a trait he would then share with at least 20 percent of priests whom Sipe's twenty-five-year study reveals have some homosexual orientation. Sipe's figure is low compared with current estimates of the number of gay clergy. Some sources claim that the number of homosexual clergy might be as high as 75 percent in certain dioceses. This is a doubtful figure, but 30 percent would not be an imprudent estimate. Critics of Sipe and his research suggest that he is a resigned priest with an ax to grind and that his research figures have been garnered from interviews with troubled priests whom he encountered in therapy.

If Swift is a homosexual, however, it may not be linked to his pedophilia. The percentage of homosexual pedophiles is actually lower than heterosexual pedophiles.

Pedophilia has been variously described as "a problematic link between celibacy and priesthood" and "the second largest single expense in any diocese." It is not confined to Roman Catholic clergy. Many active pedophiles are married. Some are physicians, lawyers, teachers, clergy of other denominations, etc. However, the higher incidence of pedophilia among priests appears to be tied closely to the lowered morale of priests who must wrestle daily with the various emotional stages of celibate adjustment.

Priests share the anger of the laity over the painful issue of pedophilia. "These men ought to be counseled out of the priesthood as fast and firmly as possible," one angry pastor said. He cited one pedophile who had cost his diocese over $200,000, mostly in psychiatric fees. "We're closing schools while spending money on a man who is a full-time patient," he said. "He isn't going to get better and his problem is only aggravated by his priesthood."

The American Church's response to what appears to be a growing problem has been less than exemplary. In spite of some statements and administrative gestures, one diocese after another appears to have continued to place the avoidance of scandal before the welfare of the victims. One source holds that there has even been pressure from the Vatican to develop uniform, national guidelines for responding to the problem, but several bishops have denied this. Although one lawyer, who specializes in sexual abuse cases, stated that he was presently involved in fifty cases in nine states and was aware of specific cases in forty-three states, the American bishops have yet to formulate a public national policy. Meanwhile, the cost to the American church in legal fees, out of court settlements, counseling fees for the victims and their families, as well as the priests, have been estimated at between $100 million and $300 million.

The Church of Canada was rocked by a scandal in its St. Johns, Newfoundland, diocese that resulted in the public resignation of the archbishop. A special, five-member commission appointed in 1989 to investigate a scandal that had been growing for at least a decade delivered a devastating indictment of an archbishop and a church that had stonewalled charges of many cases of pedophilia by five diocesan priests and at least ten religious brothers and laymen. The archbishop thwarted efforts to show a compassionate face toward the victims. In the process, he caused enormous damage, rendering his sixty diocesan priests objects of ridicule and suspicion.

With rare exceptions, the discredited archbishop's conduct echoed that of his fellow bishops. Although they have met several times in closed sessions to address the problem, no uniform policy guidelines have been adopted. A few American dioceses have publicly published guidelines. The majority have not.

In mid-1990, the special commission in Newfoundland closed its seven-hundred-page report with fifty-five guidelines for dealing with pedophilia cases. No American diocese has adopted them. Incredibly, a number of dioceses still refuse to recognize that the problem even exists while others still see it as primarily a legal problem. Some bishops place their own local authority over the need for national guidelines and, according to one observer, "the other bishops are not anxious to adopt guidelines that some of their members won't follow."

Perhaps more than any other single issue, the pedophilia problem describes a church more interested in preserving structures than in helping victims. Tom Fox, editor of the *National Catholic Reporter*, which has published an award-winning investigative series on the problem, states that "the image offered is that of an institution focused on itself and not on its pastoral mission, an organization that has purchased a legal system at the cost of timeless truths and values."

No one can estimate the impact of the growing scandal on priestly vocations or the effect that the dangerous lack of accountability may have on the faithful. Ironically, the pedophile issue may provide the means by which the laity attain shared power within the church. In Canada, an angry laity confronted Newfoundland's Alphonsus Penney and demanded action. Archbishop Penney ordered the investigation and resigned when confronted by the consequences of his own actions. In announcing his resignation, he stated abjectly: "We are a sinful church. We are naked. Our anger, our anguish, our shame and our vulnerability are clear to the whole world."

Mel Swift is a fictional name. He has no diocese or city. Other details were altered to mask his shame and his anger—and that of his victims. Yet, he is in every diocese. His file is still marked "sub secreto." Swift's case could not be covered up. The victim and his family retained an attorney, reported the case to juvenile authorities and the local state's attorney *before* informing the chancery office. Most cases are not prosecuted. Only the victims are punished.

I don't know. Sometimes I think life isn't worth living anymore.

I put a check in the basket last Sunday. The pastor knows me. I spent six years in the seminary with him in this diocese. I thought if he saw my name and realized I was living in his parish, he'd give me a call. But I never heard from him. Maybe he never noticed.

I've been out of prison for a year now, but I've only been working four months. Every time I filled out a job application and told the truth about my conviction, I was out on the street in a matter of minutes. This time I lied and, so far, no one has suspected anything. They like me. I'm a good worker, but the long hours are very hard on me. It's over the counter sales and the place is open from nine to nine. If I want to earn any money, I've got to be there most of the time. It's sixty hours a week. I'm sixty-two years old. I don't know if I can do it much longer.

When I got out of prison, there were a lot of people in my hometown who were willing to help me. But the bishop used his influence with the probation people to get me out of the area. I guess he thought I had caused him enough trouble. My probation officer told me that I had to come here where I know only a few priests and a woman who is married to one of my best friends from prison.

I wanted to go back to school. I'm pretty good at interior design. But my probation officer told me that he'd have to notify the security people at the school I wanted to attend and I couldn't face that.

You know, I'm a pretty good writer. All those parish bulletins and lots of articles in the diocesan paper. I wrote out every homily, not like some of those guys who were still sobering up from the night before when they got into the pulpit.

I wrote a lot in prison. I could have been the editor of the prison paper, but the other prisoners had the position sewn up. Besides, in prison sex offenders are the lowest form of life. The best jobs go to the prisoners who have done violent crimes. They've got status. Even the guards respect them. I wrote for these guys, but they treated me like scum. I could write for a paper now, but who would hire me?

I was sentenced to eight years. After my arrest, the bishop bailed me out and I was sent to one of these places in the East for alcoholics and the drug addicted, along with people accused of sex offenses. It was the only place where I felt understood, the only place where I got any professional help. They gave me a complete physical and then they let me rest. Then, they listened to me and helped me to get back on my feet. They took the pressure off me. I wasn't angry anymore.

During the entire time in prison, I never saw anyone who could give me any professional help. Except for those three months at that hospital for troubled priests, the diocese never offered any, either.

I was exhausted. I worked very hard in my parish. The people liked me and I liked them. The bishop had me doing all kinds of other jobs—nothing official—but I'm very creative and he was forever calling me to help with church renovations. I loved the work—really put myself into it. But I was always tired.

I never had time to sit around with my fellow priests. I found a lot of them boring anyway. I barely had time for my family. My mother still lived in town but my sister was 120 miles away and my brothers are both with the federal government in Washington, D.C. I didn't get to see any of them much. I wish I had now. During my time in prison, my mother and sister came every month. It was a five-hour drive. My mother is in her eighties now. She was at my ordination in her new hat; now she had to hand her pocket-book to a dumb bastard of a guard so he could go through it before she visited her son, the priest. It hurt to see that. She's been so faithful.

My trial was all over the papers. It isn't a big diocese and my parish was in a small town with only three other parishes. My lawyer really didn't work for me; he worked for the bishop. In the end, he represented the diocese's interests.

The judge was a Catholic and we thought that would help. But it didn't. It may have made it worse. On the day I was sentenced, the diocese had asked at least a dozen priests to be in the courtroom. I guess they thought it would soften up the judge. It didn't. I got more time than most sex offenders.

I'll never forget looking around after the sentence before I was taken away. All those priests were leaving the courtroom. Not one came up to me to say anything. Maybe they couldn't, but I never felt so alone.

The young man's family sued. It was a big settlement, out of court. Of course, I wasn't there and wasn't told the terms. I guess I cost the church some money! I guess such payouts turn the church into crooked book-keepers. There wasn't any malpractice insurance anymore, at least not for sex offenders. So, the diocese had to bury the payout somewhere in its finances. It means that some accountant has to cheat; it means that an accounting firm has to lie. It means that they have to lie about your whereabouts. "On leave," they generally say.

Prison was hell. In prison, sex offenders are the lowest form of life. Guards steer a wide path of violent prisoners, but they love to beat up on a sex offender. Their superiors won't ever discipline them. They leave you alone after a while, but the verbal abuse is always there. You're called every filthy name they can think of.

For the first eighteen months, I was in a maximum security prison. There, the gangs ran the place. At one level, it looked like the guards were in charge. But underneath, it was the gangs. They controlled the quality of your life. I was a little white man in a prison filled with young black men. I wasn't prejudiced before then, but I am now.

My only defense was my ability to talk. Still, life there was awful. The noise in the tiers was unbelievable. I never got a full night's sleep. I yearned for someone with whom I could carry on a conversation.

The Church has lost the prisons. The chaplain works for the state. He isn't going to challenge the system. Besides, the whole chaplain system has been taken over by the Fundamentalists. One day, one of those fundies came up to me in the rec room and asked if I wanted to learn about Jesus. I couldn't stop myself. I just blurted out that I was a priest and that I already knew about Jesus. He left me in a second!

During my time in prison, I was still officially considered a priest. The bishop didn't boot me out until I got out of prison. I never quite understood that. But I wasn't allowed to say Mass because it required wine, and alcohol wasn't allowed inside the prison. The fact that the chaplain was permitted to bring it in for his Mass didn't quite register on those bureaucratic minds. The chaplain didn't push the issue. He didn't want a sex offender saying Mass. I couldn't even be a sacristan. A long-term prisoner had that job.

I served forty-eight months—just half my sentence. The last thirty months were at a minimum security prison out in the country. Here, each prisoner had his own small room. You could actually lock it. They didn't have a prisoner count every few hours. We only had to report in every two hours. Life got a little easier.

I tried to take some courses—computers and design—that sort of thing. But prisons don't cater to people who studied in Rome and who can speak four languages. Besides, the teachers were local types—very limited, very bigoted. They had great fun with their sex offender priest. They would start the class; gives us something to do and then play cards with their cronies on the staff and among the prisoners. I only learned as much as the slowest learners.

A few of my priest friends came to see me. One man came almost every month, even though it took him most of his day off. It meant a great deal to me. The prison authorities tried to stop the visits, saying that I was having too many. But I threatened to take the matter to court. They just didn't like priests.

After I got out, some people said they had written me, but I never got the letters. They told me that they sent them to the chancery office. Maybe the chancery just threw them away. After all, I didn't exist.

My probation officer here in the city helped me find a garden apartment. That's a fancy word for a basement apartment. Now, I'd like to move closer to my job because I can't drive. Can't get a license. It takes me ninety minutes to get to work on three buses.

The bishop came to see me in my apartment. I hadn't seen him since my arrest nearly six years ago. He said that he didn't want to assign this job to anyone else, and then he said: "I'm going to read this document to you and, when I have finished, you will no longer be a priest." I guess he meant that I could no longer function. I don't know. I was too stunned.

He read it and I was out. I wasn't even asked to sign it. I guess I could have asked for a canonical trial or whatever it's called. But that's not how you think in such circumstances. I had $2,400 in unpaid medical bills and I thought that the bishop was going to help me with them, so I just went along.

He was polite. When he finished, he got up, put on his coat and left. I've never heard from him since. I called about the medical bills, but he wouldn't take my calls. Now, the personnel office for the diocese won't take my calls, either. Now I know what he meant by no longer being a priest.

They told us not to pay Social Security in our diocese. Some of the priests just ignored the bishop and paid their own, as if they were self-employed. They're retired now and drawing Social Security. I shouldn't have obeyed. I could look forward to a better income. Now, I've got to work forty quarters—ten years—before I'm fully qualified. I'm not even sure I'll live that long.

The Church is still not handling the sex-offender issue in any other way but as a legal matter. It's still protecting itself, not helping the offender or the so-called victims. The boy I was accused of abusing was practically a grown man, for God's sake. Oh, I could tell you a lot of stories.

In a few months, I'll be off parole. It will be easier. It means that I can look for a better job. I've lost touch with most of my fellow priests now. Perhaps that's good, but I wish I could talk to some of them, perhaps even confront them. Then the anger wouldn't burn so much.

Oh, I don't know. I get so depressed. I really don't know if I can go on. It could have been so different.

· 42 ·

James E. Wilbur: Once a Priest

Jim Wilbur spent twenty-six years as a seminarian and priest before resigning from the active ministry. He is one of over 17,000 resigned priests in the U.S. According to CORPUS, a group of resigned priests "united for service," over half of this number would willingly return to active service if the Church would permit married priests and introduce the ordination of women. The majority of resigned priests ("ex-priest" is a misnomer) are involved in the work of the Church as teachers, social workers, directors of shelters, nursing homes, government programs, etc. The difference is that only a handful are employed by the institutional Church.

In common with most resigned priests, Jim remains a faithful Catholic. With his wife Joan, he is active at Sheil Center, the Catholic community of Northwestern University. His involvement with the Church both at work and in the community rivals that of active priests. He speaks from the same depth of conviction as any caring pastor. If he appears angry, it is an anger fueled by caring, not indifference.

Wilbur represents a treasury of talent that the institutional church cannot officially draw upon. With a mind that matches his 6'6" frame, he is a thesaurus of information that only over forty years of unwavering interest could acquire. When his active priest classmates gather for their annual anniversary Mass, Jim Wilbur plans the liturgy. They know who can do it best. When he gathers for retreats or days of recollection with a group of resigned priests, Jim supplies every detail of the liturgies. Jim's fellow priests know what they have.

Jim Wilbur is a priest forever.

I went to the cardinal's mansion to tell him I was leaving. We talked past each other for about twenty minutes. Then, he walked me to the door and said: "Tell your dear mother that I will pray for her."

It was easier to get dispensed in those days. I left in 1970, Paul VI's time. I went to the chancellor and he said: "Sure, Jim, just write something up." I had written seventeen pages. I didn't have to. It was intended as a first draft. There were typos and other errors, but the chancellor just said: "Oh, don't bother rewriting. We'll send it just the way it is." The petition was approved just like that.

When the papers came back, I went to St. Clement's to sign them. The man in charge of that sort of thing was living there. We had been in the seminary together. He was a chancery official and he's a bishop now. He left Joan on a chair in the lobby and took me into an office where I signed the papers. I didn't get any copies. It was all very formal.

"John, you know this is a fiction," I said to him. "I could sign loads of papers and I'd still be a priest." He answered: "I know, Jim, but we have to do this or all the guys would leave tomorrow."

I was ordained in 1956 after five years at Quigley and seven at St. Mary of the Lake. Not long after I left, I married Joan. Before that, I had gone to work at J. S. Paluch and Company. They're a family company that dates to 1913. We've been called the General Motors of the missalette field. I guess we are. We've got about 60 percent of the market.

Monsignor John O'Connell coined the term "missalette." Sometime in the mid-1950s, he began passing out a single sheet at Mass, mostly to aid the singers. It grew to six pages when more hymns were added and became a full-sized monthly missalette in 1965. I'm editor-in-chief of Paluch's liturgical publications. I worked for them one day a week even while I was in the active priesthood.

In those early days, we had to be very careful. Cardinal Cody would insist that we send someone to his office with the page proofs each week before he would give his imprimatur. Once, he fought us very hard on a single line that was taken verbatim from the Sacramentary! He didn't know much about liturgy.

For the most part the missalette was well received. I recall only one priest who saw himself as the great liturgist. He always gave us a hard time, but he was a total turd.

Lately, some pedants are insisting that the missalette is a distraction, that it takes people away from the music or the listening to the Word. They've got to be elitists who must celebrate Eucharist in small groups, not in a big church with kids crying and buses going by.

I've always been interested in liturgy. In the seminary, every class had one or two liturgists. Gerry Siwek and I got involved in liturgy and spent much of our spare time reading and researching. At St. Mary's, there were two schools—philosophy and theology. The rules were strict and there were loads of them. Philosophers could read *The New World* [diocesan newspaper] and *America*, not much else. Theology students, however, could read *Liturgical Arts* and *Commonweal*. A great deal of reading time depended on the use of the gym. If the philosophy students were using the gym, the theology students were free to walk the grounds or go to the library. The library had great stuff. Here, I could read *Orate Fratres* [once popular liturgical magazine] and books such as Gueranger's *Liturgical Year*.

I still love the liturgy. I guess I am still very much a priest. Even a few bishops call me for information on rulings of all kinds. Most probably don't know that I'm a resigned priest.

When I think about my years in ministry, I had bad luck in my pastors. I spent six years with a Prussian general, five with a janitor, and one with a man who read his breviary and the *Chicago Tribune*. A couple of bad assignments in a row like that can do a lot of damage.

In those days, a curate had little freedom and less to say about the parish. After the last Mass on Sunday, the pastor and the senior associates were gone. The young priest had to be there for Sunday baptisms and had to take the phone. Some young men were badly hurt when they witnessed the realities of rectory life. One guy asked to be transferred when he found his pastor in bed with the housekeeper. He ended up in a second parish with a pastor who brought Communion to sick women and went to bed with them. When he told the chancellor, he was instantly informed that there was no truth in such talk. So, he left. He was pretty bitter.

Too often, the living situation for many priests was destructive. It was emotionally and physically exhausting. But it wasn't just that. I may still be too close to it, but I found that I couldn't follow the Church's teaching on birth control even before *Humanae Vitae* was issued in 1968. Everyone's expectation was that some change was coming. Then Paul VI went against the advice of his own commission. I couldn't teach that. I couldn't handle that in the confession box. Today, the parish clergy have totally tuned out Roman talk on sexuality. I don't know how they handle it in the box.

There is a great difference between Roman and Anglo-Saxon law. Until about fifteen years ago, if a man was going to leave, he did so out of respect for the law. If he could no longer observe celibacy, he acknowledged this and resigned. That's the Anglo-Saxon view of law. Now, however, it seems that we have drifted into a view of priestly discipline that is drawn from old Roman law. Celibacy is seen as an ideal to be achieved. You sort of work toward it and hope you'll achieve it before you die. As a result, there are terrible abuses and no social or legal balances within the system. Unfaithfulness is tolerated.

Then, there was the low morale. In the 1950s and 1960s, priests were kept on a string. There was a terrible abuse of authority. Some men still have so much ambition that they run over others to further their careers. Today, rectories have changed, but men still don't comprehend how to make community. Now, many live alone or at least are living their own lives. They give their parish about twenty to twenty-five hours a week. Some don't even live in the rectory. You can't even get them to come to a chicken dinner at the parish.

One gay pastor lives with his lover. He goes there every night. Others spend a great deal of their time on their own, away from their parishes. They're more concerned with their private condos or vacation homes.

I asked Pedro Rodriquez [Chicago pastor] about the morale problem recently. He said that he wasn't certain what proportion is low morale and what proportion is simply fatigue. Priests are weary of going to nonproductive meetings in which they hear nothing or are told that nothing can be done. The meetings just produce a group groan.

Oh, it's still challenging. The Church is still in revolution. By 1991, we'll have a new lectionary with a new reading structure and readings for anointing, penitential rites, and feasts of the saints. By 1992, there'll be a new sacramentary. There's an effort to get these translations into much better English, not words that sound as if they had been translated from Latin. You know, the Italian church has created a cycle of three years of prayers. All original, not just translated from Latin. We must do that. And we need to come up with more eucharistic prayers, not ones based on Latin, but originating in English. Just look at the Maronite Rite. There can't be more than 20,000 of them in this country and yet they have about 138 eucharistic prayers! Here we are, saddled with three or four, none with any mention of the Holy Spirit being called down upon the gifts.

But more needs to happen. There is an evident lack of reading and study among so many priests. They don't even read Scripture! They don't know how to pray. Look at John Krump [close friend of Wilbur's; chaplain at Northwestern University until his death in August 1990.] John did wonderful liturgies but you also felt that he was praying, not just mouthing written words. He would spend eleven hours preparing a single homily. I've heard homilies in which the pastor spent time asking the people to pray for his favorite football team. Just awful! Others are just word machines. And I've suffered through some awful "pop" liturgies.

Oh, I guess I'd take a job at the chancery office if the cardinal asked me. But they're not going to be hiring resigned priests who are married. There have been a few. One married priest was head of Catholic Charities in his diocese until he died and another is presently heading the Catholic Charities office in his diocese. There are two working in liturgy training programs, but for the most part, our education and talents go unused.

I was very much involved in CORPUS in its early days. In a sense, it was founded out of my living room. When it started, CORPUS was fighting for a nonsacramental ministry for resigned priests. At the start, there were five of us, gathering in each other's basements. Over the years, it has grown an awful lot, with chapters all over the country. After a while, it seemed to me that we were losing our focus. As our mailing list grew, our issues became more diffuse. We were all over the place—everything from banning the bomb to not putting diapers down the toilet. That was like waving a red flag in the face of the bishops.

I understand that CORPUS has narrowed its focus again, but I haven't been involved since 1982. I'm not confident that the church will ever use us. Did you hear Cardinal Lucas Moreira Neves, the recording secretary of the Synod [The bishops' Synod on the Priesthood, held at the Vatican in October 1990.] He said that the synod should not spend time discussing the celibacy requirement, the ordination of women, and assigning ministerial tasks to laicized priests. That doesn't give much hope.

There is so much that needs changing. You can feel it in our office when the calls come in. The culture and manners of the Hispanic clergy, for example, are such a contrast to the Anglo clergy. The Hispanics are low-key, polite, warm, and friendly. The Anglos are authoritative, brusque, hurried.

The collar is still a symbol of power, control, and authority. Look at that English cardinal, the one before Hume. He was asked by Malcolm Muggeridge to summarize the Church in one word. He answered "authority." Not love. Authority!

I see so many parishes being destroyed by incompetents or by angry or just lazy men. I knew of one pastor who was so lazy that he wouldn't even issue marriage certificates! It was a postage stamp-sized parish and, after he left, the new priest learned the names of everyone in the parish and turned it around.

I witness a ridiculous spending of funds on irrelevance while our schools and salary scales grow more inadequate. One bishop's study showed that the average wage of a church employee was $22,258. Nationally, that was 17.5 percent below the median for comparable positions. Twenty percent of married employees have no fringe benefits and 40 percent had to rely on outside employment to survive. That's disgraceful.

I've been thinking a lot about the words "magisterium" and "ministerium" lately. Magisterium has it root in "magnus," which means great or powerful. It suggests a dictator, a chief, president, leader, or teacher. Ministerium comes from a root word that means small. It suggests service, effort, endeavor, and assistance. It echoes John 3:30, "He must increase; I must decrease." But there is nothing of ministerium in our present Church structure. Instead, we have Roman contortions in defense of their own silliness, legislation that makes catechists out of theologians, unreasonable attention being give to right-wing groups such as Opus Dei and Communione e Liberazione, and bishops being appointed solely on the basis of their loyalty.

As a practical matter, there is a complete rejection of respect for the individual conscience and an incredible strangling of national bishops' conferences. We are sinking into a "Johntocracy."

I've been reading David Tracy [priest-theologian at the University of Chicago]. He uses the word "crisis" in its Greek sense—that is a sorting out, a use of judgment or discretion. Tracy says that we can no longer assume the cultural superiority of Western theology and that a Eurocentric theology simply cannot survive. There are now more Catholics in the southern hemisphere than in the northern hemisphere. As a result, there is a great cultural shift under way. Tracy says that much dialogue is needed. Instead, we continue to get a monologue.

At the recent National Conference of Catholic Bishops meeting, the bishops were given reports that informed them that the average Catholic parishioner was forty-seven years old while the average American was twenty-two. They heard other reports on the graying and the gaying of the clergy. But, sadly, we continue to witness politics over gospel, prudence over everything else, "for the good of the church and the faith."